KU-147-692

THE BOOK

VW Polo

Cigarette lighter fitted 4/4/02 : See Page 9·1

Service and Repair Manual

A K Legg LAE MIMI

(813-208-6Y8)

Models covered

All VW Polo Hatchback, Saloon/Classic and Coupé models,
including special and limited edition versions
1043 cc, 1093 cc & 1272 cc

Covers most mechanical features of Vans
Does not cover revised Polo range introduced November 1990

ABCDE
FGHIJ
KLMNO
PQRST
3

Printed by **J H Haynes & Co Ltd, Sparkford, Nr Yeovil, Somerset BA22 7JJ, England**

Haynes Publishing
Sparkford, Nr Yeovil, Somerset BA22 7JJ, England

Haynes North America, Inc
861 Lawrence Drive, Newbury Park, California 91320, USA

Editions Haynes S.A.
Tour Aurore - La Défense 2, 18 Place des Reflets,
92975 PARIS LA DEFENSE Cedex, France

Haynes Publishing Nordiska AB
Box 1504, 751 45 UPPSALA, Sweden

Contents

LIVING WITH YOUR VW POLO

VW Part Numbers

In-line fuel filter — 251. 201. 511G — Filter Fuel.

Rear Hub bearing Seal — 357. 501. 641. B.

Outer CV Joint boot kit — W871. 498. 203 A. [0400301 Repair Kit]

Front Brake Caliper Screw (Bolt) — Nº147153 approx 60p+Vat > 71p. (Feb2902)

Rear Exhaust. (VW)(Leistritz). Nº 867253609AJ. £36 + Vat on 13/7/02

Rear Exhaust rubber ring — Nº 1912 53147 A. £1.20+Vat — — —

Brake bleed nipple (Front) — Nº 357615273 £3.50 +Vat on 21/01/03

(too big) (Rear) Nº 3A0GN475 £0.84+VAT — — (Wrong)

Rear — Nº 113611475 £3.50+Vat on 13/02/03

Air Filter Element : 052. 129. 620 KH1 AG201

Oil Filter (Same as Audi 80) A. 056. 115. 561G 10. E02 Filter Oil

Sump Plug Copper Ring AN. 013. 849. 2 12/04 Seal.

Contents

Introduction to the VW Polo and Classic

The VW Polo was introduced in December 1981 as a hatchback, although its shape is more like an estate car. In March 1982 the Polo Classic was introduced which is the saloon car version, and then in 1983 the Polo Coupé was introduced. The engine is available in 1043cc, 1093cc and 1272cc sizes and additionally the 1093cc engine is available as an economy version designated the Formel E.

The overhead camshaft engine is mounted transversely at the front of the car with the gearbox mounted on the left-hand end of the engine. The final drive is located at the rear of the gearbox and driveshafts transmit the drive to the roadwheels. The VW Polo and Classic are well engineered cars returning excellent fuel consumption figures.

Information on later models can be found in the Supplement at the end of this manual.

Volkswagen Polo

Acknowledgements

Thanks are due to Champion Spark Plug who supplied the illustrations showing spark plug conditions. Sykes-Pickavant Limited provided some of the workshop tools. Special thanks are due to all those people at Sparkford who helped in the production of this manual.

We take great pride in the accuracy of information given in this manual, but vehicle manufacturers make alterations and design changes during the production run of a particular vehicle of which they do not inform us. No liability can be accepted by the authors or publishers for loss, damage or injury caused by errors in, or omissions from, the information given.

Volkswagen Polo Classic

Working on your car can be dangerous. This page shows just some of the potential risks and hazards, with the aim of creating a safety-conscious attitude.

General hazards

Scalding

• Don't remove the radiator or expansion tank cap while the engine is hot.
• Engine oil, automatic transmission fluid or power steering fluid may also be dangerously hot if the engine has recently been running.

Burning

• Beware of burns from the exhaust system and from any part of the engine. Brake discs and drums can also be extremely hot immediately after use.

Crushing

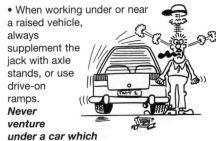

• When working under or near a raised vehicle, always supplement the jack with axle stands, or use drive-on ramps. *Never venture under a car which is only supported by a jack.*
• Take care if loosening or tightening high-torque nuts when the vehicle is on stands. Initial loosening and final tightening should be done with the wheels on the ground.

Fire

• Fuel is highly flammable; fuel vapour is explosive.
• Don't let fuel spill onto a hot engine.
• Do not smoke or allow naked lights (including pilot lights) anywhere near a vehicle being worked on. Also beware of creating sparks (electrically or by use of tools).
• Fuel vapour is heavier than air, so don't work on the fuel system with the vehicle over an inspection pit.
• Another cause of fire is an electrical overload or short-circuit. Take care when repairing or modifying the vehicle wiring.
• Keep a fire extinguisher handy, of a type suitable for use on fuel and electrical fires.

Electric shock

• Ignition HT voltage can be dangerous, especially to people with heart problems or a pacemaker. Don't work on or near the ignition system with the engine running or the ignition switched on.

• Mains voltage is also dangerous. Make sure that any mains-operated equipment is correctly earthed. Mains power points should be protected by a residual current device (RCD) circuit breaker.

Fume or gas intoxication

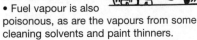

• Exhaust fumes are poisonous; they often contain carbon monoxide, which is rapidly fatal if inhaled. Never run the engine in a confined space such as a garage with the doors shut.
• Fuel vapour is also poisonous, as are the vapours from some cleaning solvents and paint thinners.

Poisonous or irritant substances

• Avoid skin contact with battery acid and with any fuel, fluid or lubricant, especially antifreeze, brake hydraulic fluid and Diesel fuel. Don't syphon them by mouth. If such a substance is swallowed or gets into the eyes, seek medical advice.
• Prolonged contact with used engine oil can cause skin cancer. Wear gloves or use a barrier cream if necessary. Change out of oil-soaked clothes and do not keep oily rags in your pocket.
• Air conditioning refrigerant forms a poisonous gas if exposed to a naked flame (including a cigarette). It can also cause skin burns on contact.

Asbestos

• Asbestos dust can cause cancer if inhaled or swallowed. Asbestos may be found in gaskets and in brake and clutch linings. When dealing with such components it is safest to assume that they contain asbestos.

Special hazards

Hydrofluoric acid

• This extremely corrosive acid is formed when certain types of synthetic rubber, found in some O-rings, oil seals, fuel hoses etc, are exposed to temperatures above 400°C. The rubber changes into a charred or sticky substance containing the acid. *Once formed, the acid remains dangerous for years. If it gets onto the skin, it may be necessary to amputate the limb concerned.*
• When dealing with a vehicle which has suffered a fire, or with components salvaged from such a vehicle, wear protective gloves and discard them after use.

The battery

• Batteries contain sulphuric acid, which attacks clothing, eyes and skin. Take care when topping-up or carrying the battery.
• The hydrogen gas given off by the battery is highly explosive. Never cause a spark or allow a naked light nearby. Be careful when connecting and disconnecting battery chargers or jump leads.

Air bags

• Air bags can cause injury if they go off accidentally. Take care when removing the steering wheel and/or facia. Special storage instructions may apply.

Diesel injection equipment

• Diesel injection pumps supply fuel at very high pressure. Take care when working on the fuel injectors and fuel pipes.

⚠ *Warning: Never expose the hands, face or any other part of the body to injector spray; the fuel can penetrate the skin with potentially fatal results.*

Remember...

DO

• Do use eye protection when using power tools, and when working under the vehicle.

• Do wear gloves or use barrier cream to protect your hands when necessary.

• Do get someone to check periodically that all is well when working alone on the vehicle.

• Do keep loose clothing and long hair well out of the way of moving mechanical parts.

• Do remove rings, wristwatch etc, before working on the vehicle – especially the electrical system.

• Do ensure that any lifting or jacking equipment has a safe working load rating adequate for the job.

DON'T

• Don't attempt to lift a heavy component which may be beyond your capability – get assistance.

• Don't rush to finish a job, or take unverified short cuts.

• Don't use ill-fitting tools which may slip and cause injury.

• Don't leave tools or parts lying around where someone can trip over them. Mop up oil and fuel spills at once.

• Don't allow children or pets to play in or near a vehicle being worked on.

For information applicable to later models, see Supplement at end of manual

Dimensions

Overall length:	
Without headlight washer	143.9 in (3655 mm)
With headlight washer	144.5 in (3670 mm)
Overall width	62.2 in (1580 mm)
Overall height (unladen)	53.3 in (1355 mm)
Ground clearance	4.2 in (106 mm)
Wheelbase	91.9 in (2335 mm)
Track:	
Front	51.4 in (1306 mm)
Rear	52.4 in (1332 mm)
Turning circle	32.8 ft (10 m)

Weights

Gross vehicle weight	2492 lb (1130 kg)
Unladen weight:	
1.05 litre models	1543 lb (700 kg)
1.1 litre models	1566 lb (710 kg)
1.3 litre models	1588 lb (720 kg)
Maximum roof rack load	110 lb (50 kg)
Maximum trailer weight:	
Unbraked (1.05 litre models)	838 lb (380 kg)
Unbraked (1.1 and 1.3 litre models)	860 lb (390 kg)
Braked (1.05 litre models)	1323 lb (600 kg)
Braked (1.1 and 1.3 litre models)	1433 lb (650 kg)

Capacities

Engine oil:	
With filter	5.3 pt (3.0 litre)
Without filter	4.4 pt (2.5 litre)
Difference between minimum and maximum marks	1.8 pt (1.0 litre)
Cooling system (including heater):	
With internal expansion tank	7.9 pt (4.5 litre)
With external expansion tank	11.4 pt (6.5 litre)
Fuel tank	8.0 gal (36.0 litre)
Manual gearbox	3.9 pt (2.2 litre)

Jump starting

When jump-starting a car using a booster battery, observe the following precautions:

✔ Before connecting the booster battery, make sure that the ignition is switched off.

✔ Ensure that all electrical equipment (lights, heater, wipers, etc) is switched off.

✔ Make sure that the booster battery is the same voltage as the discharged one in the vehicle.

✔ If the battery is being jump-started from the battery in another vehicle, the two vehcles MUST NOT TOUCH each other.

✔ Make sure that the transmission is in neutral (or PARK, in the case of automatic transmission).

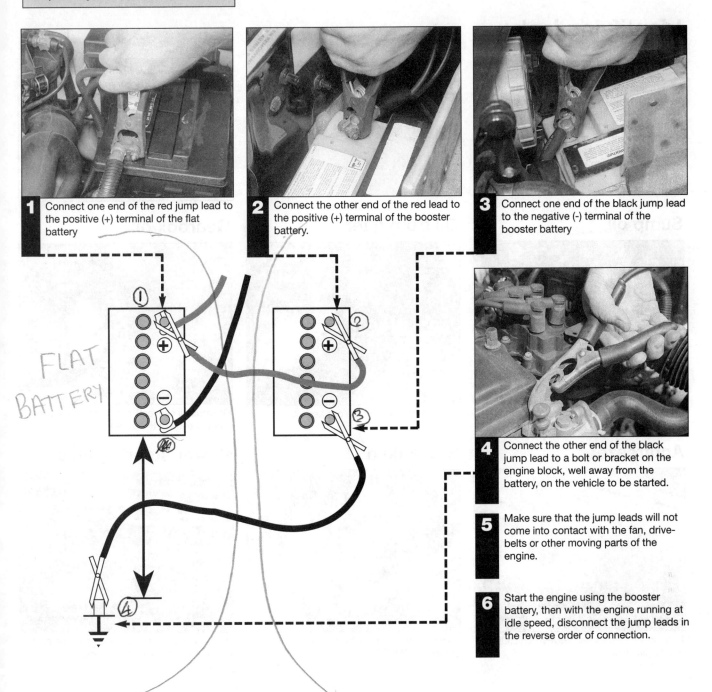

1 Connect one end of the red jump lead to the positive (+) terminal of the flat battery

2 Connect the other end of the red lead to the positive (+) terminal of the booster battery.

3 Connect one end of the black jump lead to the negative (-) terminal of the booster battery

4 Connect the other end of the black jump lead to a bolt or bracket on the engine block, well away from the battery, on the vehicle to be started.

5 Make sure that the jump leads will not come into contact with the fan, drive-belts or other moving parts of the engine.

6 Start the engine using the booster battery, then with the engine running at idle speed, disconnect the jump leads in the reverse order of connection.

Identifying leaks

Puddles on the garage floor or drive, or obvious wetness under the bonnet or underneath the car, suggest a leak that needs investigating. It can sometimes be difficult to decide where the leak is coming from, especially if the engine bay is very dirty already. Leaking oil or fluid can also be blown rearwards by the passage of air under the car, giving a false impression of where the problem lies.

 Warning: Most automotive oils and fluids are poisonous. Wash them off skin, and change out of contaminated clothing, without delay.

 HAYNES HiNT *The smell of a fluid leaking from the car may provide a clue to what's leaking. Some fluids are distinctively coloured. It may help to clean the car carefully and to park it over some clean paper overnight as an aid to locating the source of the leak.*

Remember that some leaks may only occur while the engine is running.

Sump oil

Engine oil may leak from the drain plug...

Oil from filter

...or from the base of the oil filter.

Gearbox oil

Gearbox oil can leak from the seals at the inboard ends of the driveshafts.

Antifreeze

Leaking antifreeze often leaves a crystalline deposit like this.

Brake fluid

A leak occurring at a wheel is almost certainly brake fluid.

Power steering fluid

Power steering fluid may leak from the pipe connectors on the steering rack.

Jacking and towing

The jack supplied with the car tool kit should only be used for changing roadwheels (photos). When using a trolley jack, position it only beneath the sill panels where indicated by the arrow shape, and preferably use a block of wood between the jack and the body. Always support the car with axle stands before working beneath it.

Towing eyes are provided beneath the front and rear bumpers on the right-hand side (photos). When being towed, the ignition key should be inserted and turned to position 2 so that the direction indicators, the horn, and if required the windscreen wipers can be used. To prevent any overheating of the ignition coil, disconnect the LT lead from the negative terminal on the coil. Note that the brake servo is inoperative with the engine stopped, so more pedal pressure will be required.

Spare wheel location

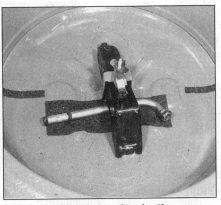

The tool kit is located under the spare wheel

Jacking point indicated by arrow shape

Front towing eye

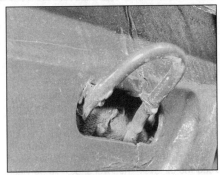

Rear towing eye

Maintenance is essential in the interests of safety, performance and economy. Over the years the need for periodic lubrication - oiling, greasing, and so on - has been greatly reduced if not totally eliminated. This has unfortunately tended to lead some owners to think that because no such action is required, components either no longer exist, or will last for ever. This is certainly not the case; it is essential to carry out regular visual examination as comprehensively as possible in order to spot any possible defects at an early stage before they develop into major expensive repairs.

On vehicles covering less than 10 000 miles (15 000 km) a year, the 10 000-mile maintenance tasks should be carried out once a year.

Vehicles used under adverse conditions (eg extremes of climate, full-time towing, predominantly short journeys) may benefit from more frequent maintenance than that specified here. The same applies to older and high-mileage examples.

Every 250 miles (400 km) or weekly
- [ ] Check the engine oil level and top up if necessary
- [ ] Check the coolant level and top up if necessary
- [ ] Top up windscreen/rear window washer reservoirs, adding a screen wash
- [ ] Check operation of all lights, wipers, horn, etc
- [ ] Check the tyre pressures and adjust if necessary

Every 5000 miles (7500 km)
Note: *Frequent oil and filter changes are good for the engine. We recommend changing the oil at the mileage specified here, or at least twice a year if the mileage covered is less.*
- [ ] Change engine oil and renew oil filter

Every 10 000 miles (15 000 km)
- [ ] Check and if necessary adjust the clutch
- [ ] Check for oil, fuel and coolant leaks
- [ ] Check antifreeze concentration and adjust if necessary
- [ ] Check valve clearances and adjust if necessary
- [ ] Check condition of alternator drivebelt and adjust tension if necessary
- [ ] Renew the spark plugs
- [ ] Renew the contact points and adjust dwell angle
- [ ] Adjust ignition timing
- [ ] Check exhaust system for leaks and damage
- [ ] Adjust the slow running
- [ ] Check gearbox oil level and top up if necessary
- [ ] Check for oil leaks
- [ ] Check the driveshaft CV joint boots for damage
- [ ] Check the brake lines, hoses and unions for leaks and damage

- [ ] Check the disc pads and rear brake shoe linings for wear
- [ ] Check the brake fluid level and top up if necessary
- [ ] Check the battery electrolyte level and top up with distilled water if necessary
- [ ] Check headlight beam alignment and adjust if necessary
- [ ] Check steering gear bellows for leaks and damage
- [ ] Check steering tie-rod ends for wear and condition of boots
- [ ] Check tread depth and condition of tyres
- [ ] Lubricate all hinges and catches
- [ ] Check the underbody for corrosion and damage and reseal as necessary

Every 20 000 miles (30 000 km)
- [ ] Renew the air cleaner element
- [ ] Renew the fuel filter
- [ ] Inspect crankcase ventilation components and clean or renew as necessary

Every 40 000 miles (60 000 km)
- [ ] Renew timing belt

Every two years (regardless of mileage)
- [ ] Renew coolant
- [ ] Renew the brake fluid, and check the condition of the visible rubber components of the braking system

Maintenance procedures

1 Engine

1 Check the engine oil level as follows.
2 The car must be parked on level ground, and the engine must have been stopped for a few minutes to allow the oil to return to the sump.
3 Open the bonnet. Withdraw the dipstick and wipe it on a clean rag. Re-insert the dipstick, making sure it is fully home, then withdraw it and read the oil level. The level should lie between the MAX and MIN marks (or within the hatched area) near the bottom of the dipstick (photos).

1.3A Checking engine oil level

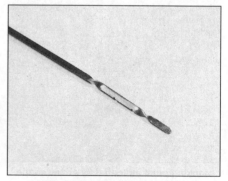
1.3B Oil level dipstick markings

1.4 Topping up engine oil level

4 If the oil level is approaching the minimum mark, top up via the oil filler cap on the camshaft cover, using oil of the correct quality and viscosity (see Recommended lubricants and fluids). To raise the level from MIN to MAX, approximately 1 litre (1.8 pints) of oil will be needed (photo). Allow time for the oil to flow down to the sump before rechecking the level.

5 When the level is correct, refit the dipstick (and the oil filler cap, if removed) and close the bonnet.

6 All engines use some oil, but heavy oil consumption will be due to leakage or to mechanical wear. See Chapter 1, Section 46.

7 Change the engine oil and renew the oil filter as follows.

8 Bring the engine to operating temperature. Park the car on level ground and stop the engine. Open the bonnet and remove the oil filler cap.

9 Wipe clean the area around the sump drain plug. Place a drain pan of adequate capacity below the plug. Unscrew and remove the drain plug. Do not lose the plug washer. Hot oil will flow out of the drain plug hole - take care to avoid scalding.

10 Allow the oil to drain for at least 15 minutes. Renew the oil filter in the meantime (Chapter 1, Section 20).

11 Refit the sump drain plug, using a new washer if necessary. Tighten the plug to the specified torque.

12 Pour the specified quantity of fresh engine oil into the filler orifice. Refit the oil filler cap.

13 Run the engine. When it is started, the oil pressure warning light will stay on for longer than usual while the filter fills with oil. Do not rev the engine during this period.

14 Allow the engine to run for a couple of minutes, at the same time checking the oil filter for leaks.

15 Stop the engine, wait a few minutes and check the oil level. Top up if necessary

16 Dispose of the old oil safely and in a non-polluting fashion.

17 Make a general inspection of the engine for evidence of oil or coolant leaks and correct as necessary.

18 Check the valve clearances on rocker finger engines. See Chapter 1, Section 41.

19 Inspect the hoses and oil separator of the crankcase ventilation system. Clean or renew as necessary. See Chapter 1, Section 21.

20 Although not specified by the makers, it is recommended that the timing belt be renewed as a precautionary measure. If the belt slips or breaks in service, considerable damage may be caused. See Chapter 1, Sections 12 and 40.

2 Cooling system

1 Check the coolant level as follows.

2 Open the bonnet. With the engine cold, the coolant level visible in the expansion tank must be between the MIN and MAX lines. (On early models without a separate expansion tank it is necessary to remove the radiator filler cap to check the level. This must only be done with the system cold.)

3 If topping up is necessary, slacken the expansion tank or radiator filler cap and allow any pressure to escape.

Remove the cap and add coolant to bring the level to the MAX mark.

Caution: Risk of scalding if the system is hot.

4 Normally, losses from the system should be negligible. Regular need for topping-up can only be due to leakage or persistent overheating, either of which must be corrected.

5 Do not use plain water for topping-up, except in an emergency, as this will dilute the original coolant further than intended. Make good such dilution as soon as possible by draining some coolant and refitting with neat antifreeze.

6 Check the concentration of the antifreeze mixture using a proprietary antifreeze tester. The tester works in a similar way to a battery hydrometer. Make good any dilution as just described.

7 Inspect the cooling system hoses and hose clips; renew any which are in poor condition. Also inspect the radiator fins, and clear out any debris using a soft brush or a jet of compressed air.

8 Although not specified by the makers, it is recommended that the coolant be renewed. At the same time the system should be flushed. See Chapter 2, Sections 2 to 5.

3 Fuel and exhaust systems

1 Check the condition and security of the exhaust system. See Chapter 3, Section 17.

2 Check the carburettor slow running adjustment. See Chapter 3, Section 13, and (when applicable) Section 4 in Chapter 12.

3 Inspect the fuel tank, fuel pipes and hoses for leakage or damage. Repair or renew as necessary, taking appropriate precautions.

4 Renew the air cleaner element. See Chapter 3, Section 2.

5 Renew the in-line fuel filter. See Chapter 3, Section 4.

4 Ignition system

1 Renew the spark plugs. See Chapter 4, Section 8. (The spark plugs specified in Chapter 12 are supposedly long-life types, which need only be renewed every 20 000 miles. If this interval is adopted, the plugs should be inspected and gapped every 10 000 miles.)

2 Renew the contact breaker points on models so equipped. Adjust the dwell angle and check the timing. See Chapter 4, Sections 2, 3 and 6. There is no need for regular checking of ignition timing on models with electronic ignition.

3 Periodically clean and inspect the HT leads, distributor cap and rotor arm. Renew components which are cracked, burnt or otherwise in poor condition.

5 Clutch

1 Check the clutch adjustment and correct if necessary. See Chapter 5, Section 2. This is not necessary on models with a self-adjusting clutch (see Section 6 of Chapter 12).

6 Manual gearbox

1 No maintenance is specified by the makers apart from a periodic inspection for oil leaks from the gearbox, and subsequent rectification. The prudent owner may consider the following additional tasks worthwhile.

2 Check the gearbox oil level as follows. Park the car on level ground. Open the bonnet and locate the oil filler/level plug (on the left-hand side of the gearbox (photo).

6.2 Gearbox filler plug location

6.5 Using a key to remove the gearbox drain plug

3 Wipe clean around the plug, then unscrew and remove it. The oil level should be up to the bottom of the plug hole. Top up if necessary with the specified oil. Allow any excess to flow out of the hole, then refit the plug and tighten it.
4 Frequent need for topping-up can only be due to a leak, which must be rectified.
5 Change the oil if wished every 50 000 miles or so (photo).

7 Driveshafts

1 Inspect the CV joint bolts for leakage and damage. Renew as necessary (Chapter 7, Section 3).

8 Braking system

1 Check the brake fluid level (the prudent owner will check more often than specified) (photo). See Chapter 8, Section 2.

9.4 Checking alternator drivebelt tension

8.1 Checking brake fluid level

9 Electrical system

1 Top up the windscreen and rear window washer reservoirs. Use clean water and a proprietary screen wash additive (photos). In freezing conditions use an additive with antifreeze properties, or add up to 10% methylated spirit to the water, to prevent freezing. Do not use cooling system antifreeze.
2 Check the operation of all the lights, wipers,

9.1A Topping up windscreen washer fluid

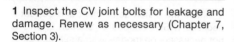

10.1A Checking tyre pressures

horn, etc. Repair or renew as necessary.
3 Carry out the battery maintenance operations described in Chapter 9, Section 3.
4 Check the condition and tension of the alternator drivebelt (photo). See Chapter 9, Section 7, or Section 9 in Chapter 12.
5 Have the headlamp beam alignment checked. See Chapter 9, Section 26.

10 Suspension and steering

1 Check tyre pressures and make a quick inspection of the visible tread and sidewalls (photos). See Chapter 10, Section 22.
2 Regularly carry out the checks described in Chapter 10, Section 2.

11 Bodywork and fittings

1 For maintenance information, refer to Chapter 11, Sections 2, 3 and 6.
2 On models with a sliding roof, periodically clean the guide rails and spray them with a silicone lubricant.

9.1B Rear window washer fluid container

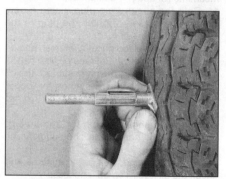

10.1B Checking tyre tread depth

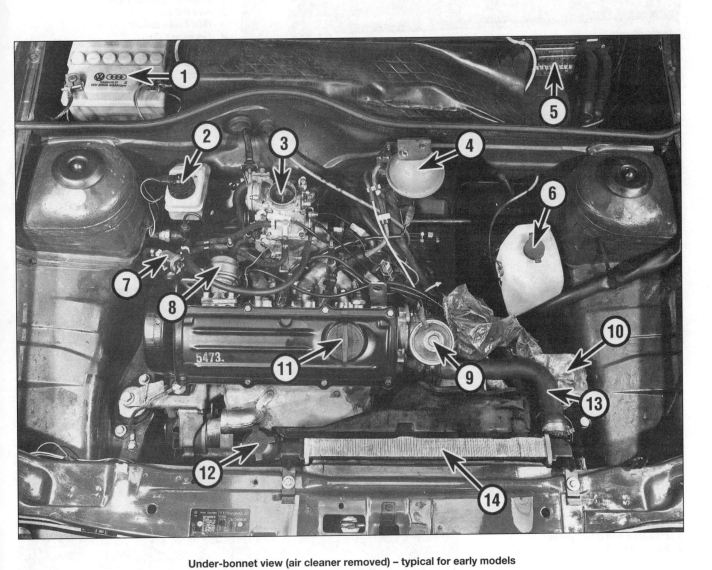

Under-bonnet view (air cleaner removed) – typical for early models

1 Battery
2 Brake hydraulic fluid reservoir
3 Carburettor
4 Vacuum reservoir (1.05 litre models only)
5 Fusebox
6 Windscreen washer reservoir
7 Fuel filter
8 Fuel pump
9 Distributor
10 Coil
11 Oil filler cap
12 Radiator filler cap
13 Top hose
14 Radiator

View of front underside of car

1   Lower suspension arm
2   Anti-roll bar
3   Disc brake caliper
4   Driveshaft (RH)
5   Front towing eye
6   Oil filter
7   Sump
8   Exhaust downpipe
9   Gearchange assembly
10 Gearbox
11 Driveshaft (LH)

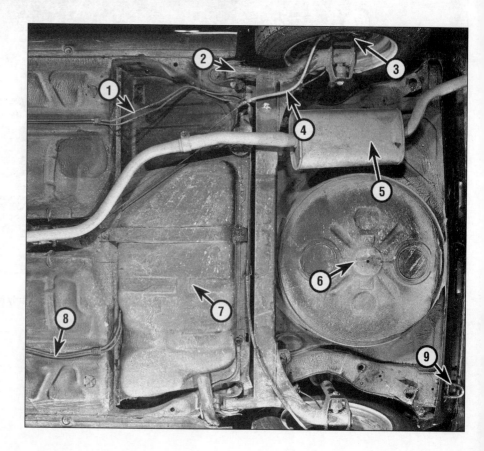

View of rear underside of car

1   Brake hydraulic pipes
2   Rear axle
3   Rear brake drum
4   Handbrake cable
5   Exhaust rear silencer
6   Spare wheel well
7   Fuel tank
8   Fuel feed and return pipes
9   Rear towing eye

Tyre condition and pressure

It is very important that tyres are in good condition, and at the correct pressure - having a tyre failure at any speed is highly dangerous. Tyre wear is influenced by driving style - harsh braking and acceleration, or fast cornering, will all produce more rapid tyre wear. As a general rule, the front tyres wear out faster than the rears. Interchanging the tyres from front to rear ("rotating" the tyres) may result in more even wear. However, if this is completely effective, you may have the expense of replacing all four tyres at once! Remove any nails or stones embedded in the tread before they penetrate the tyre to cause deflation. If removal of a nail does reveal that

the tyre has been punctured, refit the nail so that its point of penetration is marked. Then immediately change the wheel, and have the tyre repaired by a tyre dealer.

Regularly check the tyres for damage in the form of cuts or bulges, especially in the sidewalls. Periodically remove the wheels, and clean any dirt or mud from the inside and outside surfaces. Examine the wheel rims for signs of rusting, corrosion or other damage. Light alloy wheels are easily damaged by "kerbing" whilst parking; steel wheels may also become dented or buckled. A new wheel is very often the only way to overcome severe damage.

New tyres should be balanced when they are fitted, but it may become necessary to re-balance them as they wear, or if the balance weights fitted to the wheel rim should fall off. Unbalanced tyres will wear more quickly, as will the steering and suspension components. Wheel imbalance is normally signified by vibration, particularly at a certain speed (typically around 50 mph). If this vibration is felt only through the steering, then it is likely that just the front wheels need balancing. If, however, the vibration is felt through the whole car, the rear wheels could be out of balance. Wheel balancing should be carried out by a tyre dealer or garage.

1 Tread Depth - visual check
The original tyres have tread wear safety bands (B), which will appear when the tread depth reaches approximately 1.6 mm. The band positions are indicated by a triangular mark on the tyre sidewall (A).

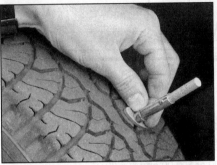

2 Tread Depth - manual check
Alternatively, tread wear can be monitored with a simple, inexpensive device known as a tread depth indicator gauge.

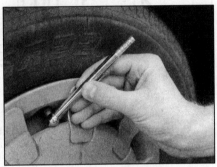

3 Tyre Pressure Check
Check the tyre pressures regularly with the tyres cold. Do not adjust the tyre pressures immediately after the vehicle has been used, or an inaccurate setting will result.

Tyre tread wear patterns

Shoulder Wear
Underinflation (wear on both sides)
Under-inflation will cause overheating of the tyre, because the tyre will flex too much, and the tread will not sit correctly on the road surface. This will cause a loss of grip and excessive wear, not to mention the danger of sudden tyre failure due to heat build-up.
Check and adjust pressures
Incorrect wheel camber (wear on one side)
Repair or renew suspension parts
Hard cornering
Reduce speed!

Centre Wear
Overinflation
Over-inflation will cause rapid wear of the centre part of the tyre tread, coupled with reduced grip, harsher ride, and the danger of shock damage occurring in the tyre casing.
Check and adjust pressures

If you sometimes have to inflate your car's tyres to the higher pressures specified for maximum load or sustained high speed, don't forget to reduce the pressures to normal afterwards.

Uneven Wear
Front tyres may wear unevenly as a result of wheel misalignment. Most tyre dealers and garages can check and adjust the wheel alignment (or "tracking") for a modest charge.
Incorrect camber or castor
Repair or renew suspension parts
Malfunctioning suspension
Repair or renew suspension parts
Unbalanced wheel
Balance tyres
Incorrect toe setting
Adjust front wheel alignment
Note: *The feathered edge of the tread which typifies toe wear is best checked by feel.*

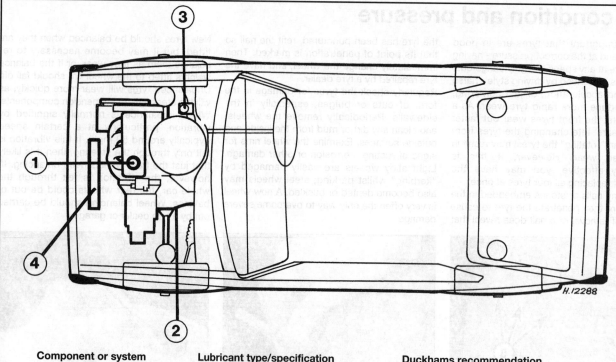

Component or system	Lubricant type/specification	Duckhams recommendation
Engine (1)	Multigrade engine oil, viscosity range SAE 15W/40 to 20W/50, to VW 501 01, 500 00 or 500 00 **and** 505 00	Duckhams QXR, QS, Hypergrade Plus or Hypergrade
Gearbox (2)	Gear oil, viscosity SAE 80 to API-GL 4	Duckhams Hypoid 80W/90
Brake hydraulic system (3)	Hydraulic fluid to FMVSS 116 DOT 4	Duckhams Universal Brake and Clutch Fluid
Cooling system (4)	Ethylene glycol based antifreeze with corrosion inhibitors	Duckhams Antifreeze and Summer Coolant

Choosing your engine oil

Oils perform vital tasks in all engines. The higher the engine's performance, the greater the demand on lubricants to minimise wear as well as optimise power and economy. Duckhams tailors lubricants to the highest technical standards, meeting and exceeding the demands of all modern engines.

HOW ENGINE OIL WORKS

• Beating friction

Without oil, the surfaces inside your engine which rub together will heat, fuse and quickly cause engine seizure. Oil, and its special additives, forms a molecular barrier between moving parts, to stop wear and minimise heat build-up.

• Cooling hot spots

Oil cools parts that the engine's water-based coolant cannot reach, bathing the combustion chamber and pistons, where temperatures may exceed 1000°C. The oil assists in

transferring the heat to the engine cooling system. Heat in the oil is also lost by air flow over the sump, and via any auxiliary oil cooler.

• Cleaning the inner engine

Oil washes away combustion by-products (mainly carbon) on pistons and cylinders, transporting them to the oil filter, and holding the smallest particles in suspension until they are flushed out by an oil change. Duckhams oils undergo extensive tests in the laboratory, and on the road.

OIL CARE
FOLLOW THE CODE
OIL BANK LINE
0800 66 33 66

Note: It is antisocial and illegal to dump oil down the drain. To find the location of your local oil recycling bank, call this number free.

Chapter 1 Engine

For modifications, and information applicable to later models, see Supplement at end of manual

Contents

1

Degrees of difficulty

Easy, suitable for novice with little experience 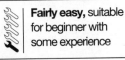	Fairly easy, suitable for beginner with some experience 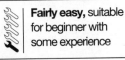	Fairly difficult, suitable for competent DIY mechanic 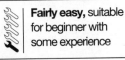	Difficult, suitable for experienced DIY mechanic 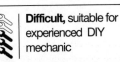	Very difficult, suitable for expert DIY or professional

Specifications

Type .... Four cylinder in-line, overhead camshaft, transverse mounting

Engine code letters
GL .... 1.05 litre → *HZ. See page 12.2*
HB .... 1.1 litre
HH .... 1.3 litre

General

	GL	HB	HH
Bore	75 mm (2.953 in)	69.5 mm (2.736 in)	75 mm (2.953 in)
Stroke	59 mm (2.323 in)	72 mm (2.835 in)	72 mm (2.835 in)
Capacity	1043 cc	1093 cc	1272 cc
Output	29 kW (40 bhp) at 5300 rpm	37 kW (50 bhp) at 5800 rpm (standard) at 5600 rpm (Formel E)	44 kW (60 bhp) at 5600 rpm
Torque (max)	74 Nm at 2700 rpm	77 Nm at 3500 rpm (standard), 82 Nm at 3300 rpm (Formel E)	95 Nm at 3400 rpm
Compression ratio	9.3 to 1	8.0 to 1 (standard) 9.7 to 1 (Formel E)	8.2 to 1
Compression pressures	8 to 11.5 bar (116 to 166 lbf/in²)	6 to 10 bar (87 to 145 lbf/in²) to 799 999 6 to 11 bar (87 to 110 lbf/in²) from 800 000	6 to 10 bar (87 to 145 lbf/in²)
Firing order	1-3-4-2 (No 1 at timing belt end)		

Crankshaft

Main journal diameter(standard)	53.96 to 53.97mm(2.124 to 2.125in)
Undersizes	-0.25 mm (0.01 in), -0.5 mm (0.02 in), -0.75 mm (0.03 in)
Crankpin journal diameter (standard)	41.96 to 41.97 mm (1.651 to 1.652 in)
Undersizes	-0.25 mm (0.01 in), -0.5 mm (0.02 in), -0.75 mm (0.03 in)
Endfloat	0.07 to 0.20 mm (0.003 to 0.008 in)
Main bearing running clearance	0.03 to 0.17 mm (0.001 to 0.007 in)
Crankpin running clearance	0.02 to 0.095 mm (0.008 to 0.004 in)

Connecting rods

Endfloat on crankpin	0.05 to 0.40 mm (0.002 to 0.016 in)

Pistons

	GL and HH	HB
Diameter:		
Standard	74.98 mm (2.952 in)	69.48 mm (2.735 in)
Oversizes	+0.25 m m (0.010 in), +0.50 m m (0.020 in), + 1.00 mm (0.040 in)	
Clearance in cylinder bores (new)	0.03 mm (0.001 in)	

Piston rings

End gap (15.0mm/0.6in from bottom of cylinder):	
Compression rings	0.30 to 0.45 mm (0.012 to 0.018 in)
Oil scraper ring	0.25 to 0.40 mm (0.010 to 0.016 in)
Clearance in groove	0.02 to 0.15 mm (0.0008 to 0.006 in)

Gudgeon pins

Length:	
GL and HB from 800 000	54mm (2.126in)
HH and HB to 799 999	58 mm (2.284 in)

Cylinder head

Distortion (max)	0.1 mm (0.004 in)
Minimum dimension for machining	119.3 mm (4.697 in)

Camshaft

Run-out (max)	0.02 mm (0.0008 in)
Endfloat	0.15 mm (0.006 in)

Valves

Head diameter:	
Inlet	34.0 mm (1.339 in)
Exhaust	29.1 mm (1.106in)
Stem diameter:	
Inlet	7.97 mm (0.314 in)
Exhaust	7.95 mm (0.313 in)
Valve length:	
Inlet - GL	110.5 mm (4.350 in)
Inlet - HB, HH	104.0 mm (4.094 in)
Exhaust - GL	110.5 mm (4.350 in)
Exhaust - HB, HH	104.0 mm (4.094 in)
Seat angle	45°
Seat width	2.0 mm (0.079 in)
Valve rock in guide (max):	
Inlet	1.0 mm (0.040 in)
Exhaust	1.3 mm (0.051 in)

Valve clearances

Cold engine:	
Inlet	0.10mm (0.004in)
Exhaust	0.20 mm (0.008 in)
Warm engine:	
Inlet	0.15 mm (0.006 in)
Exhaust	0.25 mm (0.010 in)

Valve timing (at 1 mm/0.04 in valve lift with zero valve clearance)

	GL 799 999	HB to 800 000	HB from	HH
Inlet opens	9° ATDC	2° BTDC	3° BTDC	3° BTDC
Inlet closes	13° ABDC	38° ABDC	28° ABDC	46° ABDC
Exhaust opens	15° BBDC	41° BBDC	31° BBDC	47° BBDC
Exhaust closes	11° BTDC	3° BTDC	3° BTDC	TDC

Lubrication system

Oil pressure at 2000 rpm and temperature of 80°C (176°F) . . . . 2.0 bar (29.0lbf/in²)
Oil pressure switch:
    Off pressure(0.3 bar switch) . . . . 0.15 to 0.45 bar (2.2 to 6.51bf/in²)
    On pressure (1.8 bar switch) . . . . 1.6 to 2.0 bar (23.2 to 29.0 lbf/in²)
Oil pump:
    Type . . . . Bi-rotor, driven from front of crankshaft
Oil filter type . . . . Champion C101
Oil type/specification . . . . Multigrade engine oil, viscosity range SAE 15W/40 to 20W/50,
to VW 501 01, 500 00 or 500 00 **and** 505 00

Torque wrench settings

	lbf ft	Nm
Cylinder head bolts (engine cold):		
1st stage	30	40
2nd stage	44	60
3rd stage	Additional 1/2 turn in one or two movements	
Main bearing cap bolts	48	65
Connecting rod nuts (threads oiled):		
1st stage	22	30
2nd stage	Additional 1/4 turn in one movement	
Valve cover	7	10
Camshaft sprocket	59	80
Sump	15	20
Oil drain plug	22	30
Oil pressure switch	18	25
Crankshaft sprocket	59	80
Drivebelt pulley	15	20
Engine and gearbox mountings:		
M10 bolts	33	45
M8 bolts	18	25

1 General description

The engine is of four cylinders, in-line, overhead camshaft type mounted transversely at the front of the car, with the gearbox on the left-hand side. The top of the engine is inclined slightly forwards.

The crankshaft is of five bearing type, and the centre main bearing incorporates thrust washers to control crankshaft endfloat.

The camshaft is driven by a toothed timing belt from a sprocket on the front of the crankshaft, and the timing belt also drives the water pump. The valves are operated by followers which pivot on adjustable ball head studs. The cylinder block is of cast iron and the cylinder head of light alloy.

The bi-rotor oil pump is located on the front of the cylinder block and driven by the crankshaft.

A positive crankcase ventilation system is incorporated.

2 Major operations possible with the engine in the car

The following operations can be carried out without having to remove the engine from the car:

(a) Removal and servicing of the cylinder head, camshaft, and timing belt.
(b) Removal of the flywheel and clutch after removing the gearbox.
(c) Renewal of the crankshaft front and rear oil seals.
(d) Removal of the sump.
(e) Removal of the oil pump.
(f) Removal of the piston/connecting rod assemblies.
(g) Renewal of the engine mountings.

3 Major operations only possible after removal of the engine from the car

The following operations can only be carried out after removal of the engine from the car:
(a) Renewal of the crankshaft main bearings.
(b) Removal of the crankshaft.

4 Method of engine removal

The engine and gearbox must be lifted from the engine compartment as a complete unit, then separated on the bench.

5 Engine - removal

1 Remove the bonnet as described in Chapter 11.
2 Disconnect the battery negative lead.
3 Remove the air cleaner as described in Chapter 3.
4 Remove the radiator as described in Chapter 2.
5 Loosen the clip and disconnect the top hose from the thermostat housing.
6 Place a suitable container beneath the engine then unscrew the sump drain plug and drain the oil (photo). When completed, clean the drain plug and washer and tighten it into the sump.

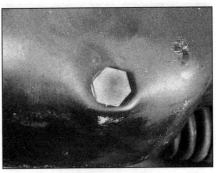

5.6 Sump drain plug

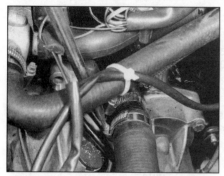

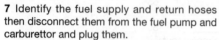

5.8 Removing the bottom hose from the rear engine coolant pipe

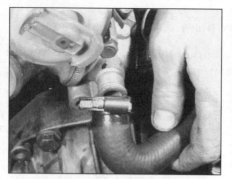

5.10A Disconnect the heater hoses from the thermostat housing . . .

5.10B . . . and coolant pipe

7 Identify the fuel supply and return hoses then disconnect them from the fuel pump and carburettor and plug them.

8 Loosen the clip and disconnect the bottom hose from the coolant pipe at the rear of the engine (photo).

9 Disconnect the accelerator and choke cables from the carburettor with reference to Chapter 3.

10 Disconnect the heater hoses from the thermostat housing and rear coolant pipe (photos).

11 Disconnect the following wiring after identifying each lead for location:

(a) *Oil pressure switch (rear of the cylinder head) (photo).*
(b) *Temperature sender unit (thermostat housing).*
(c) *Cut-off solenoid valve and automatic choke (carburettor).*
(d) *Inlet manifold pre-heating element and*

thermo-switch (beneath inlet manifold and in coolant hose) - on 1.05 litre models only.
(e) *Distributor HT and LT leads.*
(f) *Starter.*
(g) *Reversing light switch (gearbox).*
(h) *Gearchange and fuel consumption indicator (gearbox and sender in distributor vacuum line) Formel E models only.*
(l) *Ignition retard switch (carburettor) - 1.05 litre models only.*
(j) *Alternator.*

12 Disconnect and unclip the vacuum hoses from the distributor and inlet manifold as necessary.

13 Disconnect the clutch cable with reference to Chapter 5.

14 On 1.1 and 1.3 litre engines unbolt the exhaust connecting pipe from the bottom of the inlet manifold and remove the gasket.

15 Disconnect the exhaust downpipe from the exhaust manifold with reference to Chapter 3.

16 Disconnect the speedometer cable from the gearbox and place it on one side.

17 Apply the handbrake then jack up the front of the car and support it on axle stands.

18 Unbolt the front exhaust mounting and lower the exhaust to the floor.

19 If still attached, disconnect the main starter wire from under the car.

20 Unbolt the driveshafts from the drive flanges with reference to Chapter 7 and tie them to one side with wire.

21 Remove the screw from the shift rod coupling and ease the coupling from the rod. The screw threads are coated with a liquid locking agent, and if difficulty is experienced it may be necessary to heat up the coupling with a blowlamp, *however take the necessary fire precautions.*

22 Unscrew the nuts and bolts and remove the rear mounting bracket from the gearbox and mounting.

23 Attach a suitable hoist to the engine lifting hooks and take the weight of the engine and gearbox assembly.

24 Unscrew the mounting bolts from the brackets. also unscrew the bolt securing the earth strap to the right-hand side of the engine compartment (photos).

25 Raise the engine and gearbox assembly from the engine compartment while turning it as necessary to clear the internally mounted components. Make sure that all wires, cables and hoses have been disconnected (photo).

26 Lower the assembly onto a workbench or large piece of wood placed on the floor.

5.11A Oil pressure switch

5.11B Double oil pressure switch fitted to some models

5.24A Front engine mounting

5.24B Removing the engine earth strap

5.25 Removing the engine

6.4 Separating the engine and gearbox

8.1A Crankcase ventilation oil separator and hose

8.1B Removing an engine mounting

6 Engine - separation from gearbox

1 Remove the starter with reference to Chapter 9.
2 Unbolt and remove the cover plate from the clutch housing.
3 Unscrew and remove the engine to gearbox bolts.
4 Withdraw the gearbox from the engine keeping it in a horizontal position until clear of the clutch (photo). If it is seized on the locating dowels use a lever to free it.

7 Engine dismantling - general

1 If possible mount the engine on a proper stand for the dismantling procedure, but failing this support it in an upright position with blocks of wood.
2 Cleanliness is most important, and if the engine is dirty, it should be cleaned with paraffin or a water-soluble degreasant before dismantling.
3 Avoid working with the engine on a concrete floor, as grit presents a real source of trouble.
4 As parts are removed, clean them in a paraffin bath. However, do not immerse parts

with internal oilways in paraffin as it is difficult to remove, usually requiring a high pressure hose. Clean oilways with nylon pipe cleaners.
5 It is advisable to have suitable containers to hold small items according to their use, as this will help when reassembling the engine and also prevent possible losses.
6 Always obtain complete sets of gaskets when the engine is being dismantled.

HAYNES HiNT *Retain the old gaskets with a view to using them as a pattern to make a replacement if a new one is not available.*

7 When possible, refit nuts, bolts, and washers in their location after being removed, as this helps to protect the threads and will also be helpful when reassembling the engine.
8 Retain unserviceable components in order to compare them with the new parts supplied.

8 Ancillary components - removal

With the engine removed from the car and separated from the gearbox, the externally mounted ancillary components should now be removed before dismantling begins. The removal sequence need not necessarily follow the order given:

8.1C Rear engine mounting location

Alternator and drivebelt (Chapter 9)
Inlet manifold and carburettor (Chapter 3)
Exhaust manifold (Chapter 3)
Distributor (Chapter 4)
Fuel pump (Chapter 3)
Thermostat (Chapter 2)
Clutch (Chapter 5)
Crankcase ventilation hose (Section 21 of this Chapter) (photo)
Distributor cap and spark plugs (Chapter 4)
Oil filter (Section 20 of this Chapter)
Engine mountings (photos)
Dipstick
Oil pressure switch
Water temperature switch (Chapter 2)
Alternator mounting bracket and engine earth lead (photo)
Engine rear coolant pipe (photos)

8.1D Removing the alternator mounting bracket

8.1E Unscrew the nuts . . .

8.1F . . . and remove the engine rear coolant pipe

1

9.1A Unscrew the nuts and bolts . . .

9.1B . . . and remove the valve cover . . .

9.1C . . . and gasket

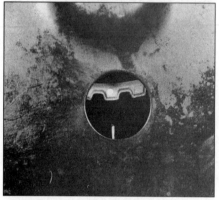

9.2A TDC mark on the camshaft sprocket, and pointer

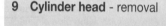

9 Cylinder head - removal

If the engine is still in the car, first carry out the following operations:
(a) Disconnect the battery negative lead.
(b) Remove the air cleaner and fuel pump with its driveshaft (Chapter 3).
(c) Drain the cooling system and remove the top hose and thermostat (Chapter 2).
(d) Remove the distributor and spark plugs (Chapter 4).
(e) Remove the inlet and exhaust manifolds (Chapter 3) although if necessary this can be carried out with the cylinder head on the bench.

(f)   Disconnect the wiring from the coolant temperature sender and oil pressure switch.

1 Unscrew the nuts and bolts from the valve cover and remove the cover together with the gasket and reinforcement strips (photos).
2 Turn the engine until the indentation in the camshaft sprocket appears in the TDC hole in the timing cover, and the notch in the crankshaft pulley is aligned with the TDC pointer on the front of the oil pump (photos). Now turn the crankshaft one quarter of a turn anti-clockwise so that neither of the pistons is at TDC.
3 Unbolt and remove the timing cover noting that the dipstick tube and earth lead are fitted to the upper bolts. Pull the dipstick tube from the cylinder block (photos).

9.2B Crankshaft pulley notch aligned with the TDC pointer

9.3A Timing cover bolt retaining the dipstick tube

9.3B Timing cover side bolt

9.3C Removing the dipstick tube

9.3D Timing cover side bolt and earth lead

9.3E Removing the timing cover

9.4 Showing timing cover plate upper bolt

9.5 A water pump retaining bolt

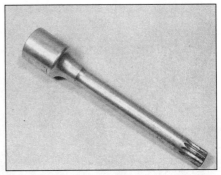

9.7A Special splined socket for unscrewing the cylinder head bolts

9.7B Engine lifting hook location

9.8 Removing the cylinder head

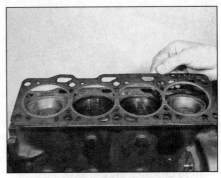

9.9 Removing the cylinder head gasket

1

4 Using a socket through the hole in the camshaft sprocket, unscrew the timing cover plate upper retaining bolt (photo).

5 Loosen the water pump retaining bolts, then turn the pump body clockwise to release the tension from the timing belt (photo). Remove the timing belt from the camshaft sprocket.

6 Remove the bolts and withdraw the timing cover plate followed by the water pump if required.

7 Using a splined socket, unscrew the cylinder head bolts half a turn at a time in the reverse order to that shown in Fig. 1.4. Note the location of the engine lifting hooks (photos).

8 Lift the cylinder head from the block (photo). If it is stuck, tap it free with a wooden mallet. Do not however insert a lever, as damage will occur to the joint faces.

9 Remove the gasket from the cylinder block (photo).

10 Camshaft - removal

If the engine is still in the car, first carry out the following operations:

(a) *Disconnect the battery negative lead.*
(b) *Remove the air cleaner and fuel pump (Chapter 3).*

(c) *Remove the distributor and spark plugs (Chapter 4).*

If the cylinder head is still fitted to the engine first carry out the procedure described in paragraphs 1 to 4 inclusive.

1 Unscrew the nuts and bolts from the valve cover and remove the cover together with the gasket and reinforcement strips.

2 Turn the engine until the indentation in the camshaft sprocket appears in the TDC hole in the timing cover, and the notch in the crankshaft pulley is aligned with the TDC pointer on the front of the oil pump. Now turn the crankshaft one quarter of a turn anticlockwise so that neither of the pistons is at TDC.

3 Unbolt and remove the timing cover noting

10.5 Removing the oil spray tube

that the dipstick tube and earth lead are fitted to the upper bolts.

4 Loosen the water pump retaining bolts, then turn the pump body clockwise to release the tension from the timing belt. Remove the timing belt from the camshaft sprocket.

5 Prise the oil spray tube from the top of the cylinder head (photo).

6 Note how the cam follower clips are fitted then prise them from the ball studs (photo).

7 Identify each cam follower for location then remove each one by levering with a screwdriver, but make sure that the peak of the relevant cam is pointing away from the follower first by turning the camshaft as necessary (photo).

8 Unscrew the camshaft sprocket bolt and

10.6 Removing a cam follower clip

10.7 Removing a cam follower

10.8 Unscrew the bolt . . .

10.9 . . . and remove the camshaft sprocket

10.10 Checking the camshaft endfloat

10.11 Removing the distributor flange

10.12 Removing the camshaft

remove the spacer (photo). The sprocket can be held stationary using a metal bar with two bolts, with one bolt inserted in a hole and the other bolt resting on the outer rim of the sprocket.

9 Tap the sprocket from the camshaft with a wooden mallet and prise out the Woodruff key (photo).

10 Using feeler blades check the camshaft endfloat by inserting the blade between the end of the camshaft and the distributor flanges (photo). If it is more than the amount given in the Specifications the components will have to be checked for wear and renewed as necessary.

11 Using an Allen key unscrew the bolts and remove the distributor flange (photo). Remove the gasket.

12 Carefully slide the camshaft from the cylinder head taking care not to damage the three bearing surfaces as the lobes of the cams pass through them (photo).

13 Prise the camshaft oil seal from the cylinder head (photo).

11 Cylinder head - dismantling

1 Remove the camshaft as described in Section 10.

2 Using a valve spring compressor, compress each valve spring in turn until the split collets can be removed. Release the

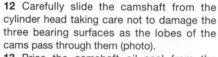

HAYNES HINT
If the retainers are difficult to remove do not continue to tighten the compressor, but gently tap the top of the tool with a hammer. Always make sure that the compressor is held firmly over the retainer.

compressor and remove the retainers and springs (photos).

3 Remove each valve from the cylinder head keeping them identified for location.

4 Prise the valve seals from the valve guides and remove the lower spring seats (photo).

5 Do not remove the cam follower ball studs unless they are unserviceable, as they are likely to be seized in the head.

10.13 Removing the camshaft oil seal

11.2A Compressing the valve spring to remove the split collets

11.2B Removing the valve springs and retainers

11.4 Removing the valve spring lower seats

12.3 Releasing the timing belt from the camshaft sprocket

12.6A Removing the crankshaft sprocket bolt

12 Timing belt and sprockets - removal

If the engine is still in the car, first carry out the following operations:
(a) Disconnect the battery negative lead.
(b) Remove the air cleaner (Chapter 3).
(c) Remove the alternator drivebelt (Chapter 9).

1 Turn the engine until the indentation in the camshaft sprocket appears in the TDC hole in the timing cover, and the notch in the crankshaft pulley is aligned with the TDC pointer on the front of the oil pump.
2 Unbolt and remove the timing cover noting that the dipstick tube and earth lead are fitted to the upper bolts.
3 Loosen the water pump retaining bolts, then turn the pump body clockwise to release the tension from the timing belt. Remove the timing belt from the camshaft sprocket (photo).
4 Using an Allen key unbolt the pulley from the crankshaft sprocket, then remove the timing belt.
5 To remove the camshaft sprocket unscrew the bolt and remove the spacer. Then tap off the sprocket and remove the Woodruff key. Do not turn the camshaft. The sprocket can be held stationary using a metal bar with two bolts, with one bolt inserted through a sprocket hole and the other bolt resting on the outer rim.

6 To remove the crankshaft sprocket unscrew the bolt and lever the sprocket from the crankshaft. Do not turn the crankshaft, otherwise the pistons may touch the valve heads. Hold the crankshaft stationary with a lever inserted in the starter ring gear (remove the starter as applicable). Remove the Woodruff key. Note that if the engine is in the car, the access hole in the right-hand engine compartment panel may be used. Cut a hole if one is not already there (photo).

13 Flywheel - removal

1 Remove the clutch as described in Chapter 5.
2 Hold the flywheel stationary with a lever or angle iron (photo) engaged with the starter ring gear.
3 Unscrew the bolts and lift the flywheel from the crankshaft (photo).
4 Remove the engine plate from the cylinder block (photo).

14 Crankshaft front oil seal - renewal

1 Remove the crankshaft sprocket with reference to Section 12.
2 If available use VW tool 2085 to remove the

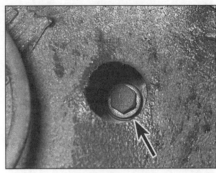

12.6B Showing access hole for crankshaft sprocket bolt

oil seal from the oil pump. Alternatively drill two diagonally opposite holes in the oil seal, insert two self-tapping screws, and pull out the seal with grips.
3 Clean the recess in the oil pump.
4 Smear a little engine oil on the lip and outer edge of the new oil seal, then fit it with tool 10-203 or by tapping it in with a suitable metal tube.
5 Refit the crankshaft sprocket with reference to Section 40.

15 Crankshaft rear oil seal - renewal

1 Remove the flywheel as described in Section 13.

13.2 One method of holding the flywheel stationary

13.3 Removing the flywheel

13.4 Removing the engine plate

15.4 The crankshaft rear oil seal and housing

15.7A Removing the crankshaft rear oil seal housing . . .

15.7B . . . and gasket

Method 1

2 Drill two diagonally opposite holes in the oil seal, insert two self-tapping screws, and pull out the seal with grips.
3 Clean the recess in the housing.
4 Smear a little engine oil on the lip and outer edge of the new oil seal then tap it into the housing using a suitable metal tube (photo).
5 Refit the flywheel as described in Section 36.

Method 2

6 Remove the sump as described in Section 16.
7 Unscrew the bolts and withdraw the housing from the dowels on the cylinder block. Remove the gasket (photo).
8 Support the housing and drive out the oil seal (photo).

9 Clean the recess in the housing.
10 Smear a little engine oil on the lip and outer edge of the new oil seal then tap it into the housing using a block of wood (photo).
11 Clean the mating faces then refit the housing together with a new gasket and tighten the bolts evenly in diagonal sequence to the specified torque.
12 Refit the sump and flywheel as described in Sections 35 and 36 respectively.

16 Sump - removal

If the engine is still in the car, first carry out the following operations:

(a) Jack up the front of the car and support it on axle stands. Apply the handbrake.
(b) Disconnect the right-hand side driveshaft (Chapter 7) and the exhaust system (Chapter 3).
(c) Unclip the alternator wire from the sump (photo).
(d) Drain the engine oil into a suitable container. Clean the drain plug and washer and refit it, tightening it to the specified torque.

1 Unscrew the bolts and withdraw the sump from the cylinder block (photo). If it is stuck, lever it away or cut through the gasket with a knife.
2 Scrape the gasket from the sump and cylinder block.

17 Oil pump - removal

1 Remove the timing belt and crankshaft sprocket as described in Section 12.
2 Remove the sump as described in Section 16.
3 Unbolt and remove the pick-up tube and strainer from the oil pump and cylinder block. Remove the flange gasket (photos).
4 Unscrew the bolts and withdraw the oil pump from the dowels on the front of the cylinder block. Note that the timing pointed bracket is located on the two upper central

15.8 Removing the crankshaft rear oil seal

15.10 Installing the new crankshaft rear oil seal

16.0 Showing the alternator wire clip on the sump

16.1 Removing the sump

17.3A Remove the stay bolts . . .

17.3B . . . and flange bolts . . .

17.3C . . . and remove the oil pump pick-up tube and strainer

17.4A Removing the oil pump . . .

bolts, and the timing belt guard on the two left-hand side bolts. Remove the gasket (photos).

18 Pistons and connecting rods - removal

1 Remove the cylinder head as described in Section 9.
2 Remove the sump as described in Section 16.
3 Unbolt and remove the pick-up tube and strainer from the oil pump and cylinder block. Remove the flange gasket.
4 Using a feeler gauge check that the connecting rod endfloat on each crankpin is within the limits given in the Specifications (photo). If not the components must be checked for wear and renewed as necessary.
5 Check the big-end caps and connecting rods for identification marks, and if necessary use a centre punch to mark them for location and position. Note that the cut-outs in the connecting rods and caps face the timing belt end of the engine. The arrows on the piston crowns also face the timing belt end of the engine (photo).
6 Turn the crankshaft so that No 1 crankpin is at its lowest point.
7 Unscrew the big-end nuts and tap free the cap together with its bearing shell (photo).
8 Using the handle of a hammer tap the piston and connecting rod from the bore and withdraw it from the top of the cylinder block (photo).
9 Loosely refit the cap to the connecting rod (photo).
10 Repeat the procedure given in paragraphs 7 to 9 on No 4 piston and connecting rod, then turn the crankshaft through half a turn and repeat the procedure on No 2 and 3 pistons.

19 Crankshaft and main bearings - removal

1 Disconnect the connecting rods from the crankshaft with reference to Section 18, however it is not essential to remove the

17.4B . . . and gasket

18.4 Checking the connecting rod endfloat

18.5 Piston crown showing arrow which faces the timing belt end of the engine

18.7 Removing a big-end cap

18.8 Removing a piston

18.9 Big-end bearing components

19.3 Checking the crankshaft endfloat

19.4 Crankshaft main bearing cap numbering

19.6 Removing the crankshaft

pistons or therefore to remove the cylinder head.

2 Remove the oil pump as described in Section 17, and the rear oil seal housing as described in Section 15.

3 Using a feeler gauge check that the crankshaft endfloat is within the limits given in the Specifications (photo). Insert the feeler gauge between the centre crankshaft web and the thrust washers. This will indicate whether new thrust washers are required or not.

4 Check that the main bearing caps are identified for location and position - there should be a cast number in the crankcase ventilation pipe/water coolant pipe side of the caps, numbered from the timing belt end of the engine (photo).

5 Unscrew the bolts and tap the main bearing caps free. Keep the bearing shells and thrust washers identified for position.

6 Lift the crankshaft from the crankcase and remove the remaining bearing shells and thrust washers but keep them identified for position (photo).

20 Oil filter - renewal

1 The oil filter should be renewed at the 5000 mile (7500 km) service. First place a suitable container beneath the oil filter. For better access either jack up the front of the car or position it on car ramps.

2 Using a strap wrench unscrew the filter from the cylinder block, and discard it (photo).

3 Wipe clean the sealing face on the block.

4 Smear a little engine oil on the sealing ring of the new filter then fit it to the block and tighten it by hand only (photo).

5 Wipe clean the filter and check it for leaks after starting the engine.

21 Crankcase ventilation system - description

The crankcase ventilation system is of the positive type and consists of an oil separator on the rear (water coolant pipe side) of the cylinder block, connected to the air cleaner by a rubber hose. Vacuum from the air cleaner provides a partial vacuum in the crankcase, and the piston blow-by gases are drawn through the oil separator and into the engine combustion chambers.

Periodically the hose should be examined for security and condition. Cleaning will not normally be necessary except when the engine is well worn. The oil separator should also be cleaned or renewed if it is clogged. Blockages in the system can cause oil leaks or contamination of the air cleaner.

22 Examination and renovation - general

With the engine completely stripped, clean all the components and examine them for wear. Each part should be checked, and where necessary renewed or renovated as described in the following Sections. Renew main and big-end shell bearings as a matter of course, unless you know that they have had little wear and are in perfect condition.

23 Oil pump - examination and renovation

The manufacturers do not supply any clearances for checking the wear of the oil pump gears, so it must be assumed to be in good order provided that the oil pressure is as given in the Specifications. This of course can only be checked with the engine assembled and, as a pressure gauge will not be available to the home mechanic, the work should be entrusted to a VW garage.

However a visual examination of the oil pump can be made if required as follows.

1 Using an Allen key unscrew the relief valve plug and extract the spring and plunger (photos).

2 Using an impact screwdriver remove the

20.2 Removing the oil filter

20.4 Tighten the oil filter by hand only

23.1A Unscrew the relief valve plug . . .

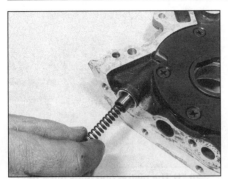

23.1B . . . and remove the spring and plunger

23.2A Use an impact screwdriver to remove the screws . . .

23.2B . . . then remove the oil pump cover . . .

cross-head screws and withdraw the cover from the pump (photos).

3 Remove the rotors noting that the indentation on the outer rotor faces the cover (photos).

4 Clean the components in paraffin and wipe dry, then examine them for wear and damage. If evident, renew the oil pump complete, but if in good order reassemble the pump in reverse order and tighten the screws and plug.

24 Crankshaft and bearings - examination and renovation

1 Examine the bearing surfaces of the crankshaft for scratches or scoring and, using a micrometer, check each journal and crankpin for ovality. Where the surfaces are worn or the ovality exceeds 0.03 mm (0.001 in) the crankshaft will have to be reground and undersize bearings fitted. An accurate check of the bearing running clearances can be made using perfect circle plastic such as Plastigage - the plastic strip is placed across the crankpin or journal and the bearing cap tightened to the specified torque. On the removal of the cap the width of the flattened plastic is measured with the gauge supplied (photos).

2 Crankshaft regrinding should be carried out by an engineering works who will supply the matching undersize main and big-end shell bearings.

3 If the crankshaft endfloat is more than the maximum specified amount, new thrust

washers should be fitted to the centre main bearing - these are usually supplied together with the main and big-end bearings on a reground crankshaft.

25 Cylinder block - examination and renovation

1 The cylinder bores must be examined for taper, ovality, scoring, and scratches. Start by examining the top of the bores; if these are worn, a slight ridge will be found which marks the top of the piston ring travel. If the wear is excessive, the engine will have had a high oil consumption rate accompanied by blue smoke from the exhaust.

2 If available, use an inside dial gauge to measure the bore diameter just below the

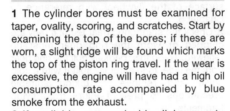

23.3A . . . and rotors

ridge and compare it with the diameter at the bottom of the bore, which is not subject to wear. If the difference is more than 0.006 in (0.152 mm), the cylinders will normally require reboring with new oversize pistons fitted.

3 Provided the cylinder bore wear does not exceed 0.008 in (0.203 mm), however, special oil control rings and pistons can be fitted to restore compression and stop the engine burning oil.

4 If new pistons are being fitted to old bores, it is essential to roughen the bore walls slightly with fine glasspaper to enable the new piston rings to bed properly.

5 Thoroughly examine the crankcase and cylinder block for cracks and damage and use a piece of wire to probe all oilways and waterways to ensure they are unobstructed.

6 Check the core plugs for leaks and security (photo).

23.3B The outer rotor indentation should face the cover

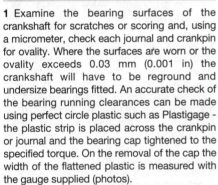

24.1A Plastigage strip for checking bearing running clearances

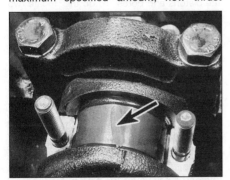

24.1B Checking the Plastigage strip with the gauge

25.6 Showing core plugs in the cylinder block

1

26.6 Checking the piston ring gaps

26.7A Checking the piston ring groove clearance

26.7B The piston ring gaps must be spaced at 120° intervals

26 Pistons and connecting rods - examination and renovation

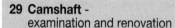

1 Examine the pistons for ovality, scoring and scratches. Check the connecting rods for wear and damage.
2 To remove the pistons from the connecting rods first mark the two components in relation to each other - the indentation on the bearing end of the connecting rod faces the same way as the arrow on the piston crown.
3 Prise out the circlips then dip the piston in boiling water, press out the gudgeon pin, and separate the piston from the connecting rod.
4 Assemble the pistons in reverse order.
5 If new rings are to be fitted to the original pistons, expand the old rings over the top of the pistons using two or three old feeler blades to prevent the rings dropping into empty grooves.
6 Before fitting the new rings insert each of them into the cylinder bore approximately 15.0 mm (0.6 in) from the bottom and check that the end gaps are as given in the Specifications (photo).
7 When fitting the rings to the pistons make sure that the TOP markings face towards the piston crown, and arrange the end gaps at

120° intervals. Using a feeler gauge check that the clearance of each ring in its groove is within the limits given in Specifications (photo).

27 Flywheel - examination and renovation

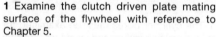

1 Examine the clutch driven plate mating surface of the flywheel with reference to Chapter 5.
2 Check the starter ring gear teeth; if they are chipped or worn the ring gear must be renewed. To do this, partially drill the ring gear from the side, then carefully split it with a cold chisel and remove it, taking suitable precautions to prevent injury from flying fragments.
3 Heat the new ring to 392°F (200°C) in an electric oven, then quickly fit it to the flywheel. Allow the ring to cool naturally without quenching.

28 Timing belt and sprockets - examination and renovation

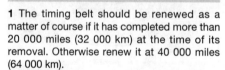

1 The timing belt should be renewed as a matter of course if it has completed more than 20 000 miles (32 000 km) at the time of its removal. Otherwise renew it at 40 000 miles (64 000 km).
2 The camshaft and crankshaft sprockets do not normally require renewal as wear takes place very slowly.

29 Camshaft - examination and renovation

1 Examine the camshaft bearing surfaces, cam lobes, and followers for wear. If excessive renew the shaft and followers.
2 Check the camshaft run-out by turning it between fixed centres with a dial gauge on the centre journal. If the run-out exceeds the amount given in Specifications, renew the shaft.

30 Cylinder head - decarbonising, valve grinding and renovation

1 Decarbonising will normally only be required at comparatively high mileages. However if performance has deteriorated even though engine adjustments are correct, decarbonising may be required, although this may be attributable to worn pistons and rings.
2 With the cylinder head removed, use a scraper to remove the carbon. Remove all traces of gasket then wash the cylinder head thoroughly in paraffin and wipe dry.
3 Use a straight edge and feeler blade to check that the cylinder head surface is not distorted. If it is, it must be resurfaced by a suitably equipped engineering works.
4 If the engine is still in the car, clean the piston crowns and cylinder bore upper edges, but make sure that no carbon drops between the pistons and bores. To do this, locate two of the pistons at the top of their bores and seal off the remaining bores with paper and masking tape. To prevent carbon build-up, polish the piston crown with metal polish, but remove all traces of the polish afterwards.
5 Examine the heads of the valves for pitting and burning, especially the exhaust valve heads. Renew any valve which is badly burnt. Examine

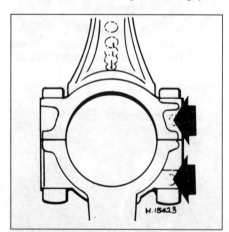

Fig. 1.1 The indentations on the big-end bearings (arrowed) must face the same way as the arrow on the piston crown (Sec 26)

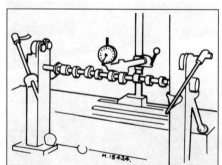

Fig. 1.2 Checking the camshaft run-out (Sec 29)

> **HAYNES HiNT** *Press a little grease between the two pistons and their bores to collect any carbon dust; this can be wiped away when the piston is lowered.*

32.2A Fitting the centre main bearing shell

32.2B Oiling the main bearing shells

32.3 Thrust washer location on the centre main bearing

the valve seats at the same time. If the pitting is very slight, it can be removed by grinding the valve heads and seats together with coarse, then fine, grinding paste. Note that the exhaust valves should not be recut, therefore they should be renewed if the sealing face is excessively grooved as a result of regrinding.

6 Where excessive pining has occurred, the valve seats must be recut or renewed by a suitably equipped engineering works.

7 Valve grinding is carried out as follows. Place the cylinder head upside down on a bench with a block of wood at each end.

8 Smear a trace of coarse carborundum paste on the seat face and press a suction grinding tool onto the valve head. With a semi-rotary action, grind the valve head to its seat, lifting the valve occasionally to redistribute the grinding paste. When a dull matt even surface is produced on both the valve seat and the valve, wipe off the paste and repeat the process with fine carborundum paste as before. A light spring placed under the valve head will greatly ease this operation. When a smooth unbroken ring of light grey matt finish is produced on both the valve and seat, the grinding operation is complete.

9 Scrape away all carbon from the valve head and stem, and clean away all traces of grinding compound. Clean the valves and seats with a paraffin soaked rag, then wipe with a clean rag.

10 If the valve guides are worn, indicated by a side-to-side motion of the valve, new guides

must be fitted. This work is best carried out by a VW garage as it involves the use of a special reamer.

11 If possible compare the length of the valve springs with new ones, and renew them as a set if any are shorter.

31 Engine reassembly - general

1 To ensure maximum life with minimum trouble from a rebuilt engine, not only must everything be correctly assembled, but it must also be spotlessly clean. All oilways must be clear, and locking washers and spring washers must be fitted where indicated. Oil all bearings and other working surfaces thoroughly with engine oil during assembly.

2 Before assembly begins, renew any bolts or studs with damaged threads.

3 Gather together a torque wrench, oil can, clean rag, and a set of engine gaskets and oil seals, together with a new oil filter.

32 Crankshaft and main bearings - refitting

1 Clean the backs of the bearing shells and the bearing recesses in the cylinder block and main bearing caps.

2 Press the main bearing shells into the cylinder block and caps and oil them liberally (photos).

3 Using a little grease, stick the thrust washers to each robe of the centre main bearings with their oilways facing away from the bearings in the block and cap (photo).

4 Lower the crankshaft into position, then fit the main bearing caps in their previously noted positions (photo). Note that the bearing shell lugs are adjacent to each other.

5 Insert the bolts and tighten them evenly to the specified torque (photo). Check that the crankshaft rotates freely then check that the endfloat is within the limits given in the Specifications by inserting a feeler gauge between the centre crankshaft web and the thrust washers.

6 Refit the rear oil seal bearing (Section 15) and oil pump (Section 34), and reconnect the connecting rods (Section 33).

33 Pistons and connecting rods - refitting

1 Clean the backs of the bearing shells and the recesses in the connecting rods and big-end caps.

2 Press the big-end bearing shells into the connecting rods and caps in their correct positions and oil them liberally (photos).

32.4 Fitting the centre main bearing cap

32.5 Tightening the main bearing bolts

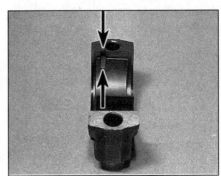
33.2A Fitting a big-end bearing shell

33.2B Showing correct location of tabs on big-end bearings

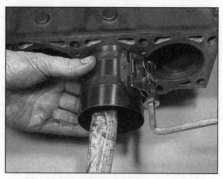

33.3 Using a ring compressor when installing the pistons

33.4 Tightening the big-end bearing nuts

3 Fit a ring compressor to No 1 piston then insert the piston and connecting rod into No 1 cylinder (photo). With No 1 crankpin at its lowest point, drive the piston carefully into the cylinder with the wooden handle of a hammer, and at the same time guide the connecting rod into the crankpin. Make sure that the arrow on the piston crown faces the timing belt end of the engine.

4 Fit the big-end bearing cap in its previously noted position then fit the nuts and tighten them evenly to the specified torque (photo).

5 Check that the crankshaft turns freely and use a feeler gauge to check that the

connecting rod endfloat is within the limits given in the Specifications.

6 Repeat the procedure given in paragraphs 3 to 5 for No 4 piston and connecting rod, then turn the crankshaft through half a turn and repeat the procedure for No 2 and 3 pistons.

7 Refit the oil pump pick-up tube and strainer (Section 34), sump (Section 35), and cylinder head (Section 39).

34 Oil pump - refitting

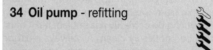

1 Renew the oil seal in the oil pump housing with reference to Section 14 (photos).

2 Locate a new gasket on the dowels on the front of the cylinder block.

3 Locate the oil pump on the block making sure that the inner rotor engages the flats on the crankshaft. Do not damage the oil seal.

4 Insert bolts together with the timing pointer bracket and timing belt guard, and tighten them evenly to the specified torque (photo).

5 Locate a new gasket on the flange face then fit the pick-up tube and strainer, insert the bolts, and tighten them to the specified torque.

6 Refit the sump (Section 35), and timing belt and sprocket (Section 40).

34.1A Prising out the oil pump oil seal

34.1B Fitting the new oil seal to the oil pump

34.4 Fitted location of the oil pump

35 Sump - refitting

1 If applicable (ie engine has been dismantled), refit the crankshaft rear oil seal and housing with reference to Section 15.

2 Clean the mating faces of the sump and cylinder block.

3 Locate the new gasket either on the sump or block, then fit the sump, insert the bolts and tighten them evenly in diagonal sequence to the specified torque (photo). If required, the two bolts at the flywheel end of the sump can be replaced by socket head bolts to facilitate their removal with the engine in the car.

4 If the engine is in the car refill the engine with oil, fasten the alternator wire to the sump clip, and lower the car to the ground.

36 Flywheel - refitting

1 Locate the engine plate on the dowels on the cylinder block.

2 Clean the mating faces of the flywheel and crankshaft, then locate the flywheel in position. Note that the bolt holes only align in one position as they are offset.

3 Apply liquid locking fluid to the threads of the bolts, then insert them and tighten them in

35.3 Fitting the sump gasket

36.3A Applying liquid locking fluid to the flywheel bolts

36.3B Tightening the flywheel bolts

37.3 Fit the plastic sleeve on the valve stem . . .

diagonal sequence to the specified torque while holding the flywheel stationary (photos).
4 Refit the clutch as described in Chapter 5.

37 Cylinder head - reassembly

1 Fit the valves in their correct locations in the cylinder head.
2 Working on each valve at a time first locate the valve spring lower seat in position.
3 Before fitting the valve seal, locate the special plastic sleeve provided in the gasket set over the valve stem in order to prevent damage to the seal (photo).
4 Slide the new seal over the valve stem and press it firmly onto the guide using a metal tube (photo). Remove the plastic sleeve.
5 Fit the spring and retainer over the valve stem, then compress the spring with the compressor and insert the split collets. Release the compressor and remove it.
6 Repeat the procedure given in paragraphs 2 to 5 on the remaining valves. Tap the end of each valve stem with a non-metallic mallet to settle the collets.
7 Refit the camshaft as described in Section 38.

38 Camshaft - refitting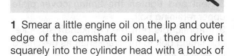

1 Smear a little engine oil on the lip and outer edge of the camshaft oil seal, then drive it squarely into the cylinder head with a block of wood.
2 Oil the camshaft bearing surfaces then slide the camshaft into position taking care not to damage the oil seal (photo).
3 Fit the distributor flange together with a new gasket, and tighten the socket head bolts.
4 Using a feeler gauge check that the camshaft endfloat is as specified.
5 Fit the Woodruff key then fit the sprocket to the camshaft followed by the spacer and bolt. Tighten the bolt while holding the sprocket stationary with a metal bar and two bolts (photo).
6 Fit the cam followers by turning the camshaft so that the relevant cam lobe peak is pointing away from the valve, then tap the follower between the valve stem and cam, and onto the ball stud.
7 Slide the cam follower clips into the grooves on the ball studs and locate the upper ends on the cam followers.
8 Adjust the valve clearances as described in Section 41.
9 Turn the camshaft so that the indentation in

the sprocket is pointing downwards and in line with the pointer on the timing cover plate (photo).
10 Turn the crankshaft a quarter of a turn clockwise so that the notch in the crankshaft pulley is aligned with the **TDC** pointer on the front of the oil pump.
11 Fit the timing belt to the camshaft sprocket and water pump.
12 Using a screwdriver in the water pump, turn the pump anti-clockwise and tension the timing belt until it can just be turned through 90° with the thumb and forefinger midway between the camshaft sprocket and water pump.
13 Tighten the water pump bolts when the belt tension is correct, and check the timing marks are still aligned.

1

37.4 . . . then fit the new oil seal

38.2 Oiling the camshaft bearing surfaces

38.5 Method of tightening the camshaft sprocket bolt

38.9 Showing TDC pointer and indentation on camshaft sprocket

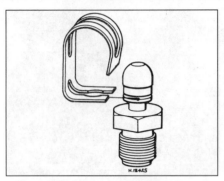

Fig. 1.3 Showing cam follower clip and groove in ball stud (Sec 38)

39.2 Correct fitting of the cylinder head gasket

39.4 Tightening the cylinder head bolts

14 Fit the dipstick tube to the cylinder block.

15 Fit the timing cover, insert the bolts with the earth lead and dipstick tube bracket, and tighten the bolts.

16 Press the oil spray tube into the top of the cylinder head.

17 Refit the valve cover with a new gasket, locate the reinforcement strips, and tighten the nuts and bolts.

18 If the engine is in the car reverse the preliminary procedures given in Section 10.

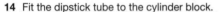

39 Cylinder head - refitting

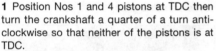

1 Position Nos 1 and 4 pistons at TDC then turn the crankshaft a quarter of a turn anti-clockwise so that neither of the pistons is at TDC.

2 Make sure that the faces of the cylinder head and block are perfectly clean then locate the new gasket on the block making sure that all oil and water holes are visible - the gasket part number should be uppermost (photo).

3 Lower the cylinder head onto the gasket, then insert the bolts together with the engine lifting hooks.

4 Using a splined socket tighten the bolts in the stages given in the Specifications, using the sequence shown in Fig. 1.4 (photo).

5 Refit the water pump if applicable (Chapter 2).

6 Fit the timing cover plate and insert the water pump bolts loosely.

7 If required refit the camshaft with reference to Section 38.

8 Refit and tighten the timing cover plate upper retaining bolt.

9 If applicable refit the crankshaft sprocket and timing belt to the crankshaft as described in Section 40 (photo).

10 Turn the camshaft so that the indentation in the sprocket is aligned with the pointer on the timing cover plate.

11 Turn the crankshaft a quarter of a turn clockwise so that the notch in the crankshaft pulley (temporarily refit it if necessary) is aligned with the **TDC** pointer on the front of the oil pump.

12 Fit the timing belt to the camshaft sprocket and water pump.

13 Using a screwdriver in the water pump, turn the pump anti-clockwise and tension the timing belt until it can just be turned through 90° with the thumb and forefinger midway between the camshaft sprocket and water pump (photo).

14 Tighten the water pump bolts when the tension is correct, and check that the timing marks are still aligned.

15 Fit the dipstick tube to the cylinder block.

16 Fit the timing cover, insert the bolts with the earth lead and dipstick tube bracket, and tighten the bolts.

17 Refit the valve cover with a new gasket, locate the reinforcement strips, and tighten

the nuts and bolts.

18 If the engine is in the car reverse the preliminary procedures given in Section 9.

40 Timing belt and sprockets - refitting

1 Fit the Woodruff key in the crankshaft and tap the sprocket into position.

2 Insert the bolt and tighten it to the specified torque while holding the crankshaft stationary with a lever in the starter ring gear.

3 Fit the Woodruff key to the camshaft then fit the sprocket followed by the spacer and bolt. Tighten the bolt while holding the sprocket stationary with a metal bar and two bolts.

4 Locate the timing belt on the crankshaft sprocket then fit the pulley, insert the bolts, and tighten them with an Allen key.

5 Turn the camshaft so that the indentation in the sprocket is aligned with the pointer on the timing cover plate. Check that the notch in the crankshaft pulley is aligned with the TDC pointer on the front of the oil pump.

6 Fit the timing belt to the camshaft sprocket and water pump.

7 Using a screwdriver in the water pump, turn the pump anti-clockwise and tension the timing belt until it can just be turned through 90° with the thumb and forefinger midway between the camshaft sprocket and water pump.

39.9 Fitting the crankshaft sprocket and timing belt

39.13 Tightening the timing belt

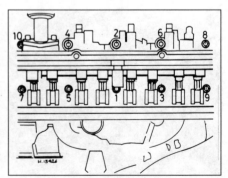

Fig. 1.4 Cylinder head bolt tightening sequence (Sec 39)

41.2 Adjusting the valve clearances

8 Tighten the water pump bolts when the tension is correct, and check that the timing marks are still aligned.

9 Fit the timing cover, insert the bolts with the earth lead and dipstick tube bracket, and tighten the bolts.

10 If the engine is in the car, reverse the preliminary procedures given in Section 12.

41 Valve clearances - adjustments

After overhauling the cylinder head the valve clearances should be adjusted on the bench, then again after the engine has completed 600 miles (1000 km).

1 With the valve cover removed turn the engine or camshaft (ie if head removed) until both cam peaks for No 1 cylinder are pointing upwards, at equal (but opposite) angles to the valve stems. In this position, both inlet and exhaust valve clearances can be checked.

2 Insert a feeler blade of the correct thickness (see Specifications) between the cam and cam follower. If the blade is not a firm sliding

fit turn the adjustable ball stud as necessary using an Allen key (photo). The valves from the timing belt end of the engine are in the following order: Inlet - Exhaust - Inlet - Exhaust - Inlet - Exhaust - Inlet - Exhaust.

3 Repeat the procedure given in paragraphs 1 and 2 for the remaining valves. If the engine is rotated in its normal direction, adjust the valves of No 3 cylinder followed by No 4 cylinder and No 2 cylinder.

4 Refit the valve cover together with a new gasket.

42 Ancillary components - refitting

Refer to Section 8 and refit the listed components with reference to the Chapters or Sections as applicable.

43 Engine - refitting to gearbox

Reverse the procedure given in Section 6.

44 Engine - refitting

Reverse the removal procedure given in Section 5 but note the following additional points:

(a) *When lowering the assembly into the engine compartment connect the right-hand driveshaft to the drive flange first.*

(b) *Assemble the engine mountings loosely initially and tighten them only after the*

assembly is central without straining the mountings.

(c) *Adjust the clutch cable as described in Chapter 5.*

(d) *On 1.05 litre models the white vacuum pipe must be fitted to the bottom (retard) connection on the distributor, and the black pipe to the top (advance) connection.*

(e) *Adjust the accelerator and choke cables as described in Chapter 3.*

(f) *Refill the engine with oil and water.*

45 Engine - adjustment after major overhaul

1 With the engine refitted to the car, make a final check to ensure that everything has been reconnected and that no rags or tools have been left in the engine compartment.

2 If new pistons or crankshaft bearings have been fitted, turn the carburettor engine speed screw in about half a turn to compensate for the initial tightness of the new components.

3 Fully pull out the choke and start the engine. This may take a little longer than usual as the fuel pump and carburettor float chamber may be empty.

4 As soon as the engine starts, push in the choke to the detent. Check that the oil pressure light goes out.

5 Check the oil filter, fuel hoses, and water hoses for leaks.

6 Run the engine to normal operating temperature, then adjust the slow running as described in Chapter 3.

7 If new pistons or crankshaft bearings have been fitted, the engine must be run-in for the first 500 miles (800 km). Do not operate the engine at full throttle or allow the engine to labour in any gear.

1

Fault Finding overleaf

Fault finding - engine

Engine fails to start

☐ Discharged battery
☐ Loose battery connection
☐ Loose or broken ignition leads
☐ Moisture on spark plugs, distributor cap, or HT leads
☐ Incorrect spark plug gap or contact points dwell angle
☐ Cracked distributor cap or rotor
☐ Dirt or water in carburettor
☐ Empty fuel tank
☐ Faulty fuel pump
☐ Faulty starter motor
☐ Low cylinder compression

Engine misfires

☐ Spark plug gap or contact points dwell angle incorrect
☐ Faulty coil or condenser
☐ Dirt or water in carburettor
☐ Burnt out valve
☐ Leaking cylinder head gasket
☐ Distributor cap cracked
☐ Incorrect valve clearances
☐ Uneven cylinder compressions

Engine idles erratically

☐ Inlet manifoid air leak
☐ Cylinder head gasket leaking
☐ Worn camshaft lobes
☐ Faulty fuel pump
☐ Incorrect valve clearances
☐ Carburettor slow running adjustment incorrect
☐ Uneven cylinder compressions

Engine stalls

☐ Carburettor adjustment incorrect
☐ Inlet manifold air leak
☐ Ignition timing incorrect

Excessive oil consumption

☐ Worn pistons and cylinder bores
☐ Valve guides and valve stem seals worn
☐ Oil leak from oil seal

Engine backfires

☐ Carburettor adjustment incorrect
☐ Ignition timing incorrect
☐ Incorrect valve clearances
☐ Inlet manifold air leak
☐ Sticking valve

Chapter 2 Cooling system

Contents

Degrees of difficulty

Easy, suitable for novice with little experience	**Fairly easy,** suitable for beginner with some experience	**Fairly difficult,** suitable for competent DIY mechanic	**Difficult,** suitable for experienced DIY mechanic	**Very difficult,** suitable for expert DIY or professional

Specifications

System type .... Pressurised with pump driven by timing belt, front mounted radiator with internal or external expansion tank, electric cooling fan

Radiator cap pressure .... 17.4 to 21.8lbf/in² (1.2 to 1.5 bar)

Thermostat
Opening temperature .... 92°C (197°F)
Fully open temperature .... 108°C (226°F)
Minimum stroke .... 7.0 mm (0.28 in)

Cooling fan thermo-switch
Switch-on temperature .... 93° to 98°C (199° to 208°F)
Switch-off temperature .... 88° to 93°C (190° to 199°F)

[handwritten: VW Part 323959481A 95-84° approx £15. Halfords XEFS 29. £9.99]

System capacity (including heater)
With internal expansion tank .... 7.9 pt (4.5 litre)
With external expansion tank .... 11.4 pt (6.5 litre)

Antifreeze

Concentration	Protection down to
40%	- 25°C (- 13°F)
50%	- 35°C (- 31°F)
Type/specification	Ethylene glycol based antifreeze with corrosion inhibitors

Torque wrench settings	lbf ft	Nm
Temperature sender unit	7	10
Water pump	7	10
Cooling fan thermo-switch	18	25
Cooling fan bracket	7	10
Thermostat cover	15	20

1 General description

The cooling system is of pressurised type and includes a front mounted radiator, water pump driven by the timing belt, and a thermostatically operated electric cooling fan. Circulation through the radiator is controlled by a thermostat located in a housing on the left-hand end of the cylinder head below the distributor. The radiator is of aluminium construction with side tanks, incorporating crossflow circulation, and according to the model the expansion tank may be located internally in the radiator side tank or externally in the engine compartment. No drain plugs are provided.

The system functions as follows. Cold water from the bottom of the radiator circulates through the bottom hose to the water pump via the coolant pipe located at the rear of the engine. The pump impeller forces the water around the cylinder block and head passages. After cooling the cylinder bores, combustion surfaces, and valve seats, the water reaches the cylinder head outlet and is diverted through hoses to the inlet manifold and then to the coolant pipe when the thermostat is closed. A further hose from the cylinder head outlet allows water to circulate through the heater matrix in the passenger compartment and back to the coolant pipe. Initially the circulation is through the engine and heater, but when the coolant reaches the predetermined temperature (see Specifications), the thermostat opens and the water then circulates through the top hose to the top of the radiator. As the water passes through the radiator tubes, it is cooled by the inrush of air when the car is in forward motion,

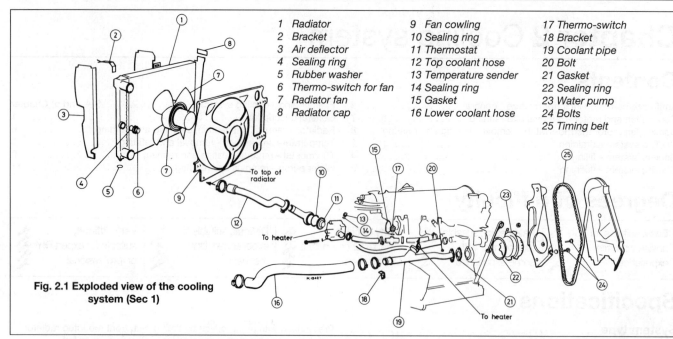

1 Radiator
2 Bracket
3 Air deflector
4 Sealing ring
5 Rubber washer
6 Thermo-switch for fan
7 Radiator fan
8 Radiator cap
9 Fan cowling
10 Sealing ring
11 Thermostat
12 Top coolant hose
13 Temperature sender
14 Sealing ring
15 Gasket
16 Lower coolant hose
17 Thermo-switch
18 Bracket
19 Coolant pipe
20 Bolt
21 Gasket
22 Sealing ring
23 Water pump
24 Bolts
25 Timing belt

Fig. 2.1 Exploded view of the cooling system (Sec 1)

supplemented by the action of the electric cooling fan when necessary. Having reached the bottom of the radiator, the water is cooled and the cycle is repeated.

The electric cooling fan is controlled by a thermo-switch located in the left-hand side of the radiator.

2 Cooling system - draining

1 It is preferable to drain the cooling system when the engine has cooled. If this is not possible, place a cloth over the radiator or expansion tank filler cap and turn it slowly in an anti-clockwise direction until the pressure starts to escape.
2 When all the pressure has escaped, remove the filler cap.
3 Set the heater controls to maximum heat, then place a suitable container beneath the left-hand side of the radiator.
4 Loosen the clip and ease the bottom hose away from the radiator outlet. Drain the coolant into the container.

3 Cooling system - flushing

1 After some time the radiator and engine waterways may become restricted or even blocked with scale or sediment which can reduce the efficiency of the cooling system. When this occurs, the coolant will appear rusty and dark in colour and the system should then be flushed. In severe cases, reverse flushing may be required, although if a reputable antifreeze/corrosion inhibitor has

been in constant use this is unlikely.
2 With the coolant drained, disconnect the top hose from the radiator. Insert a garden hose and allow the water to circulate through the radiator until it runs clear from the bottom outlet.
3 If, after a reasonable period the water still does not run clear, the radiator can be flushed with a good proprietary cleaning agent.
4 Disconnect the heater hose from the cylinder head outlet and insert a garden hose in the heater hose. With the heater controls set at maximum heat, allow water to circulate through the heater and out through the bottom hose until it runs clear.
5 In severe cases of contamination the system should be reverse flushed. To do this, remove the radiator, invert it and insert a garden hose in the outlet. Continue flushing until clear water runs from the inlet.
6 The engine should also be reverse flushed. To do this, disconnect the heater hose from the cylinder head outlet and insert a garden hose in the outlet. Continue flushing until clear water runs from the bottom hose.

4 Cooling system - filling

1 Reconnect all the hoses and check that the heater controls are set to maximum heat.
2 Remove the rubber strip and plastic cover from the plenum chamber behind the engine compartment, then loosen the bleeder screw on the heater temperature control valve (photo).
3 Pour the recommended coolant into the radiator or expansion tank (as applicable) until it reaches the maximum mark (photo). While doing this watch the heater bleeder, and tighten the screw when bubble-free water comes out.
4 Refit the plastic cover and rubber strip to the plenum chamber.
5 Refit and tighten the filler cap then run the engine at a fast idling speed for approximately 10 seconds.
6 Stop the engine and top-up the coolant

4.2 Bleeder screw location for the cooling system

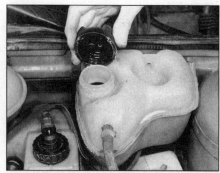

4.3 Filling the cooling system

Fig. 2.2 Coolant level marks on radiator with internal expansion tank (top) and external expansion tank (bottom) (Sec 4)

level as necessary to the maximum mark. Refit the filler cap.

7 After running the engine to normal operating temperature (ie until the electric cooling fan operates), the coolant level should be rechecked with the engine cold.

5 Antifreeze/corrosion inhibitor mixture - general

1 The manufacturers install G11 antifreeze/corrosion inhibitor mixture in the cooling system when the car is new. Every 10 000 miles (15 000 km) or 12 months the concentration of the coolant should be checked by a VW garage and if necessary topped up with fresh mixture.

2 The mixture must remain in the cooling

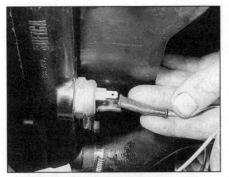

6.3A Disconnect the wiring from the thermoswitch . . .

system at all times as it prevents the formation of scale and also provides a higher boiling point than plain water - this maintains the efficiency of the coolant particularly when the engine is operating at full load.

3 The concentration of the mixture can be calculated according to the lowest ambient temperature likely to be encountered as given in the Specifications. However it should never be less than 40%.

4 Before adding new mixture, check all hose connections for tightness.

6 Radiator - removal, inspection, cleaning and refitting

1 Disconnect the battery negative lead.

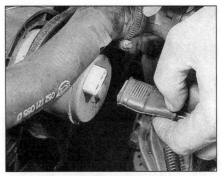

6.3B . . . and cooling fan motor

2 Drain the cooling system as described in Section 2.

3 Disconnect the wiring from the thermoswitch and cooling fan motor (photos).

4 Disconnect the top hose and expansion tank hose (if applicable) from the radiator (photo).

5 Remove the screw and washer, and withdraw the upper retaining clip from the right-hand side of the radiator (photos).

6 Move the top of the radiator rearwards and remove the air deflectors (2 screws) (photo).

7 Lift the radiator out of the lower mounting rubbers and withdraw it from the engine compartment taking care not to damage the matrix (photos).

8 Remove the screws and withdraw the cowling and fan from the radiator.

9 It is not possible to repair this radiator without special equipment, although minor

2

6.4 Disconnecting the top hose

6.5A Remove the screw . . .

6.5B . . . and lift out the radiator retaining clip

6.6 Removing the radiator air deflectors

6.7A Removing the radiator

6.7B Showing the radiator lower mounting stubs

7.4 Cooling fan and mounting nuts

8.3 Cooling fan motor thermo-switch

9.2A Unscrew the socket head bolts . . .

leaks may be cured using a suitable sealant with the radiator *in situ*.

10 Clean the radiator matrix of flies and small leaves with a soft brush or by hosing, then reverse flush the radiator as described in Section 3. Renew the hoses and clips if they are damaged or deteriorated.

11 Refitting is a reversal of removal, but if necessary renew the radiator lower mounting rubbers. Fill the cooling system as described in Section 4.

7 Cooling fan and motor - removal and refitting

1 Disconnect the battery negative lead.

2 Disconnect the wiring from the cooling fan motor.

3 Remove the four screws and lift the cowling together with the cooling fan and motor from the radiator.

4 Remove the nuts and withdraw the cooling fan and motor from the cowling (photo).

5 If necessary the fan can be separated from the motor by prising off the clamp washer. On AEG motors drive out the roll pin, and on Bosch motors remove the shakeproof washer. Assemble the components in reverse order using a new clamp washer.

6 Refitting is a reversal of removal.

9.2B . . . and remove the thermostat cover

8 Cooling fan motor thermo-switch - removal, testing and refitting

1 Disconnect the battery negative lead.

2 Drain the cooling system as described in Section 2.

3 Unscrew the thermo-switch from the left-hand side of the radiator and remove the sealing ring (photo).

4 To test the thermo-switch suspend it with a piece of string so that its element is immersed in a container of water. Connect the thermoswitch in series with a 12 volt test lamp and battery. Gradually heat the water and note the temperature with a thermometer. The test lamp should light up at the specified switch-on temperature and go out at the specified switch-off temperature. If not, renew the thermo-switch.

5 Refitting is a reversal of removal, but fit a new sealing ring and tighten the thermo-switch to the specified torque. Fill the cooling system as described in Section 4.

9 Thermostat - removal, testing and refitting

1 The thermostat is located in the outlet housing on the left-hand end of the cylinder

9.3 Removing the thermostat cover sealing ring

head. To remove it, first drain the cooling system as described in Section 2.

2 Unscrew the bolts and remove the thermostat cover (photos). Place the cover with top hose still attached to one side.

3 Remove the sealing ring (photo).

4 Extract the thermostat from the outlet housing.

5 To test whether the unit is serviceable, suspend it with a piece of string in a container of water. Gradually heat the water and note the temperature at which the thermostat starts to open. Continue heating the water to the specified fully open temperature then check that the thermostat has opened by at least the minimum amount given in the Specifications. Remove the thermostat from the water and check that it is fully closed when cold.

6 Renew the thermostat if it fails to operate correctly.

7 Clean the thermostat seating and the mating faces of the outlet housing and cover.

8 Refitting is a reversal of removal, but fit a new sealing ring and tighten the cover bolts to the specified torque - the breather hole in the thermostat should face upwards. Fill the cooling system as described in Section 4.

10 Temperature sender unit - removal and refitting

1 It is not necessary to drain the cooling system if some form of plug such as an old sender unit or rubber plug is available. First release any pressure in the system by unscrewing the pressure cap - *if the system is still hot, observe the precaution in Section 2.* With all pressure released, tighten the cap again.

2 Locate the sender unit on the cylinder head outlet housing, then disconnect the wiring lead (photo).

3 Unscrew and remove the temperature sender unit and plug the aperture.

4 Refitting is a reversal of removal, but tighten the sender unit to the specified torque. Check and if necessary top-up the cooling system with reference to Section 4.

10.2 Temperature sender unit location

11.6A Removing the water pump

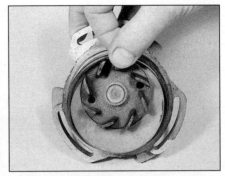

11.6B Removing the water pump sealing ring

11 Water pump - removal and refitting

1 Drain the cooling system as described in Section 2.

2 Remove the air cleaner and air ducting as described in Chapter 3, and disconnect the battery negative lead.

3 Unbolt and remove the timing belt cover.

4 Turn the engine with a spanner on the crankshaft pulley bolt until the timing cover plate upper retaining bolt is visible through the camshaft sprocket hole. Unscrew and remove the bolt.

5 Align the timing marks and release the timing belt from the water pump and camshaft sprocket with reference to Chapter 1.

6 Remove the bolts and withdraw the timing cover plate followed by the water pump. Remove the sealing ring (photos).

7 It is not possible to repair the water pump, and if faulty it must be renewed. Clean the mating faces of the water pump and cylinder block.

8 Refitting is a reversal of removal, but fit a new sealing ring and refer to Chapter 1 when fitting and tensioning the timing belt. Fill the cooling system as described in Section 4.

Fault finding - cooling system

Overheating

☐ Low coolant level
☐ Faulty pressure cap
☐ Thermostat sticking shut
☐ Open circuit thermo-switch
☐ Faulty cooling fan motor
☐ Clogged radiator matrix
☐ Retarded ignition timing

Slow warm-up

☐ Thermostat sticking open
☐ Incorrect thermostat

Coolant loss

☐ Damaged or deteriorated hose, or loose clip
☐ Leaking water pump
☐ Leaking cylinder head outlet or coolant pipe gasket
☐ Leaking cylinder head gasket
☐ Leaking radiator

Notes

Chapter 3 Fuel and exhaust systems

For modifications, and information applicable to later models, see Supplement at end of manual

Contents

Degrees of difficulty

Easy, suitable for novice with little experience	Fairly easy, suitable for beginner with some experience	Fairly difficult, suitable for competent DIY mechanic	Difficult, suitable for experienced DIY mechanic	Very difficult, suitable for expert DIY or professional

Specifications

Air cleaner .... Automatic load and temperature sensitive control, with renewable paper element.

Element type:
1.05 .... Champion W101
1.1 .... Champion W101
1.3 (up to Aug. 1983) .... Champion W101
1.3 (from Aug. 1983) .... Champion W102

Fuel filter
All models .... Champion L104

Fuel pump
Type .... Mechanical, diaphragm operated by plunger from the camshaft
Pressure at engine speed of 1000 rpm with return line clamped ..... 0.20 to 0.25 bar (2.9 to 3.6 lbf/in²)

Carburettor

	1.05 litre (29 kW)	1.1 litre (37 kW) up to HB 799 999	1.1 litre Formel E (37 kW) from HB 800 000	1.3 litre (44 kW)
Type	Solex downdraught with manual choke			
Code	31PIC-7	31PIC-7	31PIC-7	34PIC-6
Venturi	23	25.5	23	24.5
Main jet	X117.5	X132.5	X115	X120
Air correction jet with emulsion tube	125Z	105V	120Z	85Z
Idling fuel jet	40	40.5	40	52.5
Idling air jet	100	90	100	130
Auxiliary fuel/air jet (in float chamber)	-	-	35/130	35/15° (from 1/82 only)
Auxiliary fuel jet	30	30	-	40 (to 12/81 only)
Auxiliary air jet	130	100	-	100 (to 12/81 only)
Enrichment (primary/secondary)	60/60	100/-	60/60	95/95
Injection capacity (cm³/stroke)	0.9 ± 0.15	0.9 ± 0.15	0.9 ± 0.15	0.7 ± 0.15
Float needle valve	1.5	1.5	1.5	1.5
Float needle valve washer thickness (mm)	2.0	2.0	2.0	0.5
Fast idling speed (rpm)	2400 + 100	2400 ± 100	2500 ± 100	2600+100
Choke valve gap (mm)	1.8 ± 0.2	2.0 ± 0.2	2.2 ± 0.2	2.0 ± 0.2
Throttle valve gap smooth running detent (mm)	2.5 ± 0.3	4.0 ± 0.3	2.5 ± 0.3	4.5 ± 0.5
Idling speed (rpm)	950 ± 50	950 ± 50	950 ± 50	950 ± 50
CO content %	1.0 ± 0.5	1.0 ± 0.5	1.0 ± 0.5	1.0 ± 0.5

3

Fuel tank capacity	8 Imp gal (36 litre)	

Fuel octane rating (minimum)

Formel E models	98 RON (4 star)	
Except Formel E models	91 RON (2 star)	

Torque wrench settings

	lbf ft	Nm
Fuel pump	15	20
Fuel tank	18	25
Carburettor	18	25
Inlet manifold	18	25
Exhaust heater pipe to inlet manifold	18	25
Intermediate flange nuts	7	10
Inlet manifold cover	7	10
Inlet manifold pre-heater	7	10
Exhaust manifold	18	25
Hot air shroud	7	10
Downpipe clamp	15	20
Downpipe flange	22	30
Exhaust heater pipe support	15	20
Intermediate exhaust clamps	18	25

1 General description

The fuel system consists of a rear mounted fuel tank, a camshaft operated fuel pump and a Solex PIC downdraught carburettor incorporating a manual choke with automatic override.

The air cleaner is of automatic air temperature control type and incorporates a disposable paper element.

The exhaust system on the 1.05 litre engine is in two sections - the downpipe and front section, and the silencer and tailpipe. On 1.1 and 1.3 litre models the exhaust system is in four sections - the twin downpipe section, intermediate flexible pipe, front silencer and pipe, and the rear silencer and tailpipe. Additionally on 1.1 and 1.3 litre models a flexible and rigid pipe connect the downpipe to the exhaust heated inlet manifold.

On 1.05 litre models the inlet manifold is heated by an electric preheater unit.

2 Air cleaner element and body - removal and refitting

1 The air cleaner element should be renewed every 20 000 miles (30 000 km). To do this prise back the clips and lift off the cover, then lift out the element (photos).
2 Wipe down the inside of the air cleaner with a cloth. Also clean the inside of the cover.
3 Fit the new element and locate the cover on the air cleaner body with the slotted tab over the tab on the intake. Refit the clips.
4 To remove the body first remove the element.
5 Disconnect the hot air hose from the exhaust manifold shroud (photo).
6 Unscrew the retaining nuts then lift the unit from the carburettor and disconnect the vacuum and crankcase ventilation hoses (photos).

2.1A Removing the air cleaner cover

2.1B Removing the air cleaner element

2.5 Hot air hose connected to the exhaust manifold shroud

2.6A Air cleaner retaining nuts

2.6B Air temperature sensor vacuum connections

3.1A Air cleaner vacuum unit

3.1B Removing the air temperature control unit

3.5 Upper view of the air temperature sensor

7 If necessary unclip and remove the air temperature control vacuum unit and intake pipe.

8 Refitting is a reversal of removal, but make sure that the rubber seal is correctly located on the carburettor.

3 Air cleaner air temperature control - checking

1 Unclip and remove the vacuum unit and intake pipe but leave the vacuum pipe connected (photos).

2 Suspend a thermometer in the flow of air through the inlet duct then start the engine. Between -20°C (-4°F) and +20°C (68°F) the control flap in the unit should be a maximum of 2/3rds open to admit hot air from the exhaust manifold (if a sheet metal type air cleaner is fitted it must not be more than 1/2 open). Above 20°C (68°F) the control flap must close the hot air supply.

3 The control flap movement can be checked by sucking on the vacuum inlet.

4 With the engine running and inlet air temperature above 20°C (68°F), disconnect the vacuum hose from the vacuum unit. The control flap should fully open within a maximum of 20 seconds.

5 If the control unit does not operate

correctly, renew it together with the temperature sensor (photo).

6 Refit the vacuum unit and intake pipe.

4 Fuel pump and filter - testing, removal and refitting

1 The fuel pump is located on the right-hand side of the engine by the air cleaner. To test it accurately, connect a pressure gauge in the outlet pipe and check that the pressure is as given in the Specifications with the engine running at the specified speed.

2 Alternatively a less accurate method is to disconnect the supply pipe from the carburettor (air cleaner removed) and also disconnect the LT lead from the coil positive terminal. Spin the engine on the starter while holding a wad of rag near the fuel pipe. Well defined spurts of fuel should be ejected from the pipe if the fuel pump is operating correctly, provided there is fuel in the fuel tank. Before obtaining a replacement pump it is worthwhile removing the pump cover (1 screw) where this is possible, to clean out any sediment; also check the in-line filter for blockage (photo).

3 The in-line filter should be renewed every 20 000 miles (30 000km). To do this, remove the clips and extract the filter (photo). If necessary renew the crimped type clips with

screw type ones. Fit the new filter in a horizontal position with its arrow facing the flow of fuel towards the fuel pump and make sure that it is firmly held by the plastic support clip.

4 To remove the fuel pump first remove the air cleaner as described in Section 2.

5 Identify the hoses for position, then disconnect them from the pump (photo).

6 Using an Allen key, unscrew the retaining bolts, then withdraw the pump from the cylinder head and remove the sealing ring. Note the earth lead location (photos).

7 Clean the mating faces of the pump and cylinder head.

8 Refitting is a reversal of removal, but renew the sealing ring and tighten both to the specified torque. When refitting the cover

3

4.2 Removing the fuel pump cover – not possible on all fuel pumps

4.3 The in-line fuel filter

4.5 Disconnecting the fuel pump hoses

4.6A Unscrew the bolts . . .

4.6B . . . and withdraw the fuel pump

4.6C Showing the fuel pump sealing ring

4.8 Alignment indentations on the fuel pump cover

Fig. 3.1 Fuel tank components (Sec 5)

1 Small breather line
2 Gravity valve (not all countries)
3 Rubber housing
4 Retaining ring
5 Cap
6 Washer
7 Large breather line
8 Fuel tank
9 Fuel gauge sender
10 Drain hose
11 Sealing ring
12 Return line (blue)
13 Transparent suction line
14 Security strap

make sure that the alignment indentations are correctly engaged (photo). Renew crimped type clips with screw type ones.

5 Fuel tank - removal, servicing and refitting

For safety reasons the fuel tank must always be removed in a well ventilated area, never over a pit.

1 Disconnect the battery negative lead.
2 Siphon or pump all the fuel from the fuel tank (there is no drain plug) (photo).
3 Lift the rear seat cushion, remove the cover plate, and disconnect the wiring from the gauge sender unit.
4 Jack up the rear of the car and support on axle stands. Chock the front wheels and remove the right-hand side rear wheel.
5 Disconnect the breather hoses from the filler neck.
6 Remove the filler neck rubber tube together with the drain hose.
7 Disconnect the fuel hoses at the front of the fuel tank.
8 Support the fuel tank with a trolley jack and length of wood, then unscrew the retaining nuts and bolts, detach the strips, and lower the tank to the ground (photo).
9 If the tank is contaminated with sediment or water, remove the gauge sender unit as described in Section 6 and swill the tank out

5.2 Fuel tank filler cap

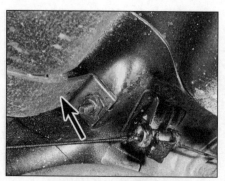

5.8 Fuel tank retaining strap

5.10 Fuel tank vent hose

6.2 Disconnecting the wiring from the fuel tank sender unit

7.3A Accelerator cable and quadrant

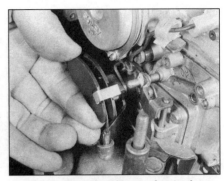

7.3B Disconnecting the accelerator inner cable

with clean fuel. If the tank is damaged or leaks, it should be repaired professionally or alternatively renewed. *Do not under any circumstances solder or weld a fuel tank.*

10 Refitting is a reversal of removal, but the bottom surface of a new tank should first be given a coat of underseal. Make sure that the rubber packing strips are fitted to the retaining straps. Refit the hoses free of any kinks - note that the blue hose goes to the upper connection. Check that the vent (drain) hose is clipped securely to the tank flange (photo).

6 Fuel gauge sender unit - removal and refitting

For safety reasons the fuel gauge sender unit must always be removed in a well ventilated area, never over a pit.

1 Disconnect the battery negative lead.
2 Lift the rear seat cushion, remove the cover plate, and disconnect the wiring from the gauge sender unit (photo).
3 Using two crossed screwdrivers turn the sender unit anti-clockwise and withdraw it from the fuel tank. Remove the gasket.
4 Refitting is a reversal of removal, but always fit a new gasket. Note that when correctly fitted the wiring points towards the breather connection. The new gasket should be coated with graphite powder.

7 Accelerator cable - removal, refitting and adjustment

1 Disconnect the battery negative lead.
2 Remove the air cleaner as described in Section 2.
3 Prise the clip from the throttle lever quadrant, then open the throttle by hand and disconnect the inner cable (photos).
4 Release the cable grommet from the support bracket (photos).
5 Working inside the car remove the lower facia panel then unclip the inner cable from the accelerator pedal (photo).
6 Withdraw the complete cable into the engine compartment together with the rubber grommets.
7 Refitting is a reversal of removal, but make sure that it is free of any kinks and correctly aligned. Finally adjust it as follows before refitting the air cleaner.
8 Position a piece of wood 5.0mm (0.2in) thick between the accelerator pedal arm and the floor, and have an assistant keep the pedal fully depressed.
9 Pull the outer cable so that the throttle is fully open, and insert the spring clip in the groove next to the support bracket grommet washer (photo).
10 Remove the piece of wood and refit the air cleaner.

7.4A Showing the accelerator cable support bracket

8 Choke cable - removal, refitting and adjustment

1 Disconnect the battery negative lead.
2 Remove the air cleaner as described in Section 2.
3 Using a screwdriver loosen the inner and outer cable clamps and disconnect the cable from the carburettor (photo).
4 Working inside the car remove the lower facia panel.
5 Pull out the clip and remove the choke knob.
6 Unscrew the ring and withdraw the cable from the facia.

7.4B Removing the accelerator outer cable

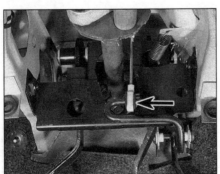

7.5 Inner cable connection to the accelerator pedal

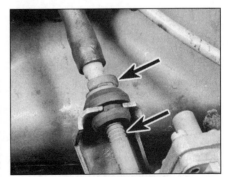

7.9 Showing accelerator cable clip and adjustment grooves

8.3 Removing the choke cable

9.2 Showing accelerator pedal and pivot

10.1A View of throttle lever end of carburettor

10.1B View of float chamber end of the carburettor

10.1C View of choke vacuum control end the carburettor

7 Disconnect the wiring and withdraw the complete cable from inside the car.

8 Refitting is a reversal of removal, but make sure that the cable is correctly aligned, and that the grommets are firmly fitted in the bulkhead. Finally adjust it as follows before refitting the air cleaner.

9 Locate the outer cable in the clamp so that its end protrudes approximately 12.0 mm (0.47 in). Tighten the clamp with the outer cable in this position.

10 Push the choke knob fully in then pull it out 3.0 mm (0.12 in) - switch on the ignition and check that the warning lamp is not lit.

11 Insert the inner cable into the choke lever clamp and fully open the choke lever by hand. Tighten the inner cable clamp screw in this position.

12 Refit the air cleaner.

9 Accelerator pedal - removal and refitting

1 Remove the lower facia panel.

2 Disconnect the accelerator cable from the pedal (photo).

3 Prise out the clip and remove the pivot pin.

4 Remove the accelerator pedal. If necessary press out the pivot pin bushes.

5 Refitting is a reversal of removal, but lubricate the bushes with a little grease. Check the cable adjustment with reference to Section 7.

10 Carburettor - general description

The Solex PIC carburettor is of downdraught type incorporating a manual choke with automatic override control. The cut-off solenoid is activated by the ignition switch and cuts the supply of mixture to the idling system when the ignition is switched off, thereby preventing running on (dieselling).

The accelerator pump is of the diaphragm type. When starting from cold, the manual choke valve provides fuel enrichment. A bi-metallic coil is heated by the ignition and gradually opens the choke valve to prevent over-enrichment. Additionally a vacuum

operated device opens the choke valve when the engine is accelerated or is running at high speed (photos).

Certain models are provided with part throttle channel heating in the carburettor for improved cold running, and on some later models the system is controlled by a thermo-switch in contact with the fuel in the float chamber.

11 Carburettor - removal and refitting

1 Disconnect the battery negative lead.

2 Remove the air cleaner as described in Section 2 (photo).

3 Identify the fuel feed and return hoses then disconnect them (photo).

4 Disconnect the accelerator and choke cables with reference to Sections 7 and 8.

5 Disconnect the carburettor earth lead from the fuel pump retaining bolt earth terminal.

6 Disconnect the wiring from the cut-off solenoid, choke control, and throttle valve switch (photo).

7 Disconnect the vacuum hose.

8 Remove the nuts from under the inlet manifold and withdraw the carburettor upwards. Remove the gasket and do not lose the insulator washers (photos).

9 Clean the mating faces of the carburettor and inlet manifold.

10 Refitting in a reversal of removal, but

11.2 View of carburettor with air cleaner removed

11.3 Disconnecting the fuel hoses

11.6 Cut-off solenoid and wiring

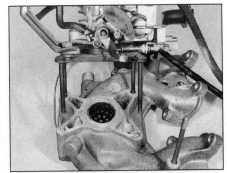

11.8A Removing the carburettor

11.8B Lower view of the carburettor and gasket

always fit a new gasket and tighten the nuts evenly to the specified torque. Adjust the accelerator and choke cables with reference to Section 7 and 8. Adjust the slow running as described in Section 13.

12 Carburettor - dismantling, reassembly and adjustment

1 With the carburettor removed from the engine clean the external surfaces with paraffin and wipe dry.
2 Remove the screws from the cover noting the location of the earth lead (photo).
3 Lift off the cover and remove the gasket (photo).

12.2 Showing carburettor cover and screws

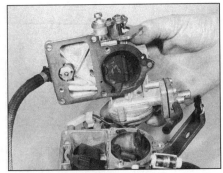

12.3 Removing the carburettor cover

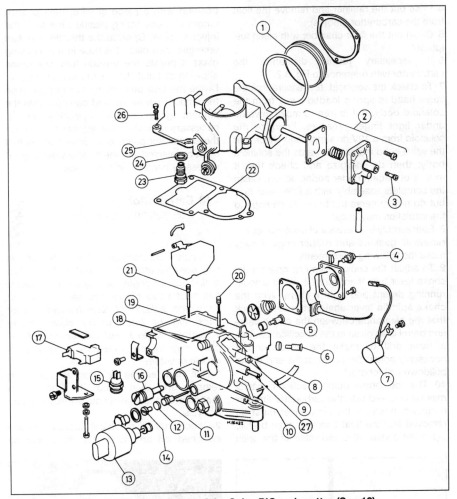

Fig. 3.2 Exploded view of the Solex PIC carburettor (Sec 12)

1 Choke cover
2 Pulldown device
3 Adjustment screw (choke valve gap)
4 Adjustment screw (injection capacity)
5 Auxiliary fuel jet (except 052 129 017 B/D)
6 Pilot jet
7 Bypass passage heater
8 Limiting screw
9 Tamper-proof cap
10 Connector for distributor advance unit
11 CO adjusting screw
12 Tamper-proof cap
13 Bypass air cut-off valve
14 Main jet
15 Thermoswitch
16 Idle adjustment screw
17 Throttle valve switch
18 Detent roller
19 Injection pipe
20 Air correction jet with emulsion tube
21 Auxiliary fuel/air jet
22 Gasket
23 Float needle valve
24 Washer
25 Eccentric pin
26 Screws
27 Temperature regulator connection (air cleaner)

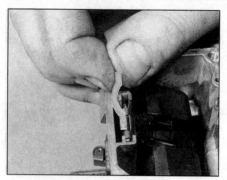

12.4A Prise out the retainer . . .

12.4B . . . and remove the float

12.5 View of carburettor with cover removed

4 Prise out the retainer and remove the float from the carburettor (photos).

5 Clean out the float chamber with clean fuel (photo).

6 If necessary further dismantle the carburettor with reference to Fig. 3.2.

7 To check the solenoid, first ensure that the valve head is spring-loaded away from the solenoid body, but is free to move inwards under light finger pressure. Energize the solenoid from a 12V dc supply and check that the valve head is drawn towards the solenoid body; then de-energize and check that it moves out again under spring action. Clean the complete assembly with a little clean fuel, but do not immerse the body, as damage to the insulation may occur.

8 Reassembly is a reversal of dismantling, but renew all gaskets and rubber rings. Finally make the following adjustments.

9 To adjust the choke valve gap operate the choke lever fully then return it to the smooth running detent and hold it there. With the choke spindle lever against the cam check that the clearance between the choke valve and barrel is as given in the Specification. Use a twist drill to make the check and if necessary adjust the screw at the end of the pulldown unit (photos).

10 The accelerator pump injection capacity may be checked with the carburettor fitted or removed, however the air cleaner must be removed and the float chamber must be full. Open the choke valve and retain in the open

position with a piece of wire, then push a length of close fitting plastic tube over the injection pipe. Operate the throttle until fuel emerges then place the tube in a measuring glass. Operate the throttle fully five times allowing at least three seconds per stroke. Divide the final quantity by five to determine the amount per stroke and compare with the amount given in the Specifications. If necessary reposition the adjusting screw on the accelerator pump lever. Note that the fuel must be injected into the throttle valve gap - if necessary bend the injection pipe.

13 Carburettor - slow running adjustment

Accurate adjustment of the carburettor is only possible after adjustment of the ignition timing, dwell angle, and spark plug gaps. Incorrect valve clearances can also effect carburettor adjustment. Note that tamperproof caps may be fitted to the slow running adjustment screws and the removal of the caps may be prohibited by legislation in certain countries.

1 Run the engine to normal operating temperature then stop it. Connect a tachometer and if available an exhaust gas analyser.

2 Check that all electrical accessories are switched off and note that slow running

adjustments should not be made while the radiator cooling fan is running.

3 Disconnect the crankcase ventilation hose from the air cleaner body and plug the air cleaner outlet.

4 Start the engine and let it idle. Check that the engine speed and CO content are as given in the Specification. If not, turn the two screws located above the cut-off solenoid alternately as necessary (photo). Screw A is turned clockwise to reduce the idle speed; screw B is turned clockwise to weaken the mixture and thus reduce CO content.

5 If an exhaust gas analyser is not immediately available, an approximate mixture setting can be made by turning the mixture screw to give the highest engine speed.

6 Reconnect the crankcase ventilation hose. If this results in an increase in the CO content, the engine oil is diluted with fuel and should be renewed. Alternatively, if an oil change is not due, a long fast drive will reduce the amount of fuel in the oil.

7 Stop the engine and remove the tachometer and exhaust gas analyser.

8 To adjust the fast idle speed first check that the engine is still at normal operating temperature. Remove the air cleaner.

9 With the engine stopped, pull the choke control knob fully out then push it in to the smooth running detent.

10 Retain the choke valve in its open position using an elastic band.

12.9A Checking the choke valve gap with a twist drill

12.9B Adjusting screw location for choke valve gap

13.4 Idle speed (A) and mixture (B) adjusting screw locations

14.2 Exhaust connecting pipe for heating the inlet manifold on 1.1 and 1.3 litre engines

14.4A Unscrew the bolts . . .

14.4B . . . and remove the heater element from the inlet manifold

14.4C Removing the sealing ring from the heater element

14.5A Location of thermo-switch for controlling the inlet manifold heater element

14.5B Inlet manifold preheater thermo-switch and housing

11 Connect a tachometer then start the engine and check that the fast idling speed is as given in the Specification. If not turn the adjustment screw on the side of the choke lever cam. Note that this screw may also have a tamperproof cap.

12 Stop the engine, disconnect the tachometer and elastic band, and refit the air cleaner. Push the choke control knob fully in.

14 Inlet manifold preheating - description and testing

1 On 1.05 litre engines the inlet manifold is heated by water from the cooling system and by a heater element located in the bottom of the manifold beneath the carburettor.

2 On 1.1 and 1.3 litre engines the inlet manifold is heated by exhaust gas channelled from the exhaust downpipe by a connecting pipe (photo).

3 The heater element fitted to 1.05 litre engines can be checked by disconnecting the supply wire and connecting on ohmmeter between the wire and earth - 0.25 to 0.50 ohms should be recorded.

4 To remove the element disconnect the wire, then unscrew the bolt and withdraw the unit. Remove the sealing ring and gasket (photos). When refitting always renew the sealing ring and gasket.

5 The heater element is controlled by a thermo-switch located in the coolant supply hose to the inlet manifold. To test the thermo-switch unscrew it from the housing and plug the hole. With an ohmmeter connected to the terminals gradually heat the base of the unit in hot water. Below approximately 65°C (149°F) there should be zero resistance (ie internal contacts closed), and above approximately 75°C (167°F) there should be maximum resistance (ie internal contacts open). If not, renew the thermoswitch (photos).

15 Inlet manifold - removal and refining

1 Remove the carburettor as described in Section 11.

2 On 1.05 litre models disconnect the preheater element wire, drain the cooling system (Chapter 2) and disconnect the coolant hoses from the manifold.

3 On 1.1 and 1.3 litre models unscrew the nuts and disconnect the exhaust connecting pipe. Remove the gasket.

4 Where applicable disconnect the vacuum hose(s) (photo).

5 Unscrew the nuts and bolts and withdraw the inlet manifold from the cylinder head (photos). Remove the gasket.

6 Clean the mating faces of the manifold and cylinder head. If necessary the endplate and

15.4 Disconnecting the vacuum reservoir hose from the inlet manifold

15.5A Unscrew the nuts and bolts . . .

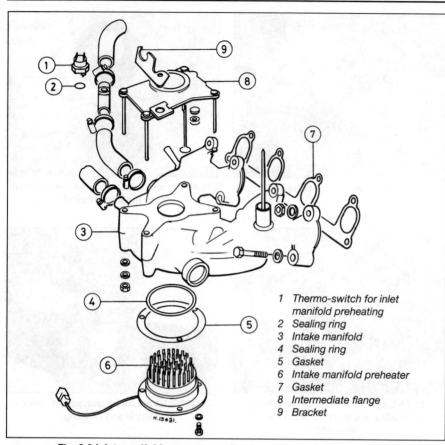

1 Thermo-switch for inlet manifold preheating
2 Sealing ring
3 Intake manifold
4 Sealing ring
5 Gasket
6 Intake manifold preheater
7 Gasket
8 Intermediate flange
9 Bracket

Fig. 3.3 Inlet manifold components fitted to 1.05 litre models (Sec t 5)

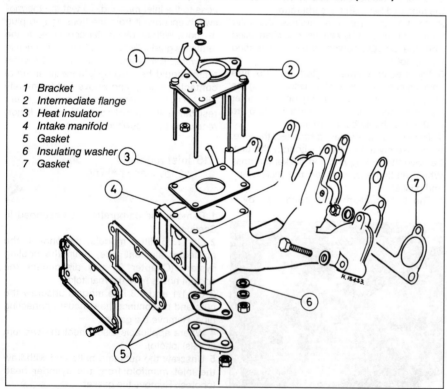

1 Bracket
2 Intermediate flange
3 Heat insulator
4 Intake manifold
5 Gasket
6 Insulating washer
7 Gasket

Fig. 3.4 Inlet manifold components fitted to 1.1 and 1.3 litre models (Sec 1 5)

15.5B . . . and withdraw the inlet manifold

15.5C Removing the inlet manifold gasket

gasket, heat deflector and insulator may be removed from the inlet manifold on 1.1 and 1.3 litre models.
7 Refitting is a reversal of removal, but always fit new gaskets and tighten nuts and bolts evenly to the specified torque.

16 Exhaust manifold - removal and refitting

1 Disconnect the flexible hose from the hot air shroud on the exhaust manifold.
2 Unscrew the three nuts and remove the hot air shroud and outlet tube (photos).
3 On 1.05 litre models unscrew the bolts and

16.2A Unscrew the nuts. . .

16.2B . . . and remove the hot air shroud and outlet tube

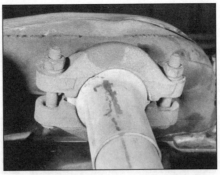

16.3 Exhaust downpipe clamp on 1.05 litre models

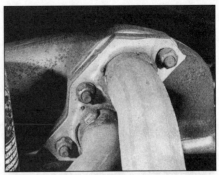

16.4 Exhaust downpipes on 1.1 and 1.3 litre models

remove the clamp securing the downpipe to the manifold (photo).

4 On 1.1 and 1.3 litre models unscrew the nuts and detach the twin downpipe from the manifold (photo). Remove the gasket.

5 Unscrew the nuts and withdraw the exhaust manifold from the cylinder head. Remove the gaskets (photos).

6 Clean the mating faces of the manifold and cylinder head, also the downpipe faces.

7 Refitting is a reversal of removal, but always fit new gaskets and tighten nuts and bolts evenly to the specified torque. On 1.05 litre models smear a little exhaust jointing paste on the downpipe flange before fitting it to the manifold.

17 Exhaust system - checking, removal and refitting

1 The exhaust system should be examined for leaks, damage, and security every 10 000 miles (15 000 km). To do this, apply the handbrake and allow the engine to idle. Check the full length of the exhaust system for leaks from each side of the car in turn, while an assistant temporarily places a wad of cloth over the tailpipe. If a leak is evident, stop the engine and use a proprietary repair

kit to seal it. If the leak is excessive, or damage repair is not possible, renew the section. Check the rubber mountings for deterioration, and renew them if necessary.

2 To remove the exhaust system jack up the front and rear of the car and support it on axle stands. Alternatively locate the front wheels on car ramps and jack up the rear, supporting it on axle stands.

3 Unscrew the clamp bolts or flange nuts securing the downpipe(s) to the manifold.

4 On 1.1 and 1.3 litre models loosen the clip and disconnect the flexible hose from the downpipe (photo).

16.5A Removing the exhaust manifold

16.5B Showing the exhaust manifold gaskets

17.4 Flexible pipe fitted to the front of the exhaust pipe on 1.1 and 1.3 litre models

1 Warm air shroud
2 Gasket
3 Exhaust manifold
4 Clamp
5 Connecting pipe
6 Flexible pipe
7 Front exhaust pipe
8 Flexible pipe
9 Support loop
10 Front silencer
11 Main silencer
12 Rubber mounting

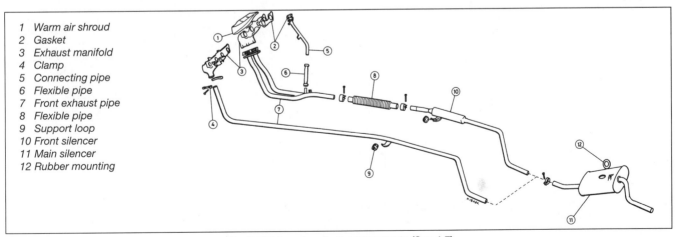

Fig. 3.5 Exhaust system components (Sec 1 7)

17.5 Detaching the exhaust from the front mounting strap

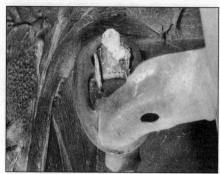

17.6A An exhaust mounting rubber

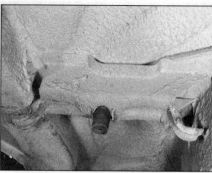

17.6B Exhaust rear mounting bracket

5 Unbolt the front of the system from the mounting strap (photo).
6 Release the mounting rubbers from the hooks and lower the exhaust system to the ground (photos).
7 If necessary remove the relevant section by releasing the clamps. Tap around the joint

with a hammer and twist the two sections from each other. If difficulty is experienced, heat the joint with a blow lamp to assist removal.
8 Refitting is a reversal of removal, but fit new gaskets as applicable and assemble the complete system loosely in position before

finally tightening the clamps and mounting bolt. On 1.05 litre models smear a little exhaust jointing paste on the downpipe flange before fitting it to the manifold. Finally run the engine and check for leaks as described in paragraph 1.

Fault finding - fuel and exhaust systems

Excessive fuel consumption
- [ ] Air cleaner element choked
- [ ] Leak in fuel tank, carburettor or fuel lines
- [ ] Mixture adjustment incorrect
- [ ] Valve clearances incorrect
- [ ] Worn carburettor
- [ ] Needle valve sticking open

Insufficient fuel supply or weak mixture
- [ ] Faulty fuel pump
- [ ] Leak in fuel lines
- [ ] Leaking inlet manifold gasket
- [ ] Leaking carburettor gasket
- [ ] Mixture adjustment incorrect

Chapter 4 Ignition system

For modifications, and information applicable to later models, see Supplement at end of manual

Contents

Degrees of difficulty

| Easy, suitable for novice with little experience | Fairly easy, suitable for beginner with some experience | Fairly difficult, suitable for competent DIY mechanic | Difficult, suitable for experienced DIY mechanic | Very difficult, suitable for expert DIY or professional |

Specifications

System type .... 12 volt battery, coil, and distributor with contact breaker points

Coil
Primary winding resistance .... 1.7 to 2.1 ohm
Secondary winding resistance .... 7000 to 12 000 ohm

Distributor
Rotor rotation .... Anti-clockwise (viewed from flywheel end)
Rotor cut-out speed (if applicable) .... 6300 to 6700 rpm
Dwell angle:
  Setting .... 47° ± 3° (53% ± 3%)
  Wear limit .... 42° to 58° (47% to 64%)
Contact breaker gap (for initial setting) .... 0.4 mm (0.016 in)
Centrifugal advance:
  1.05 litre .... Begins 1500 to 1700 rpm, 27° to 31° at 4000 rpm
  1.1 litre (standard) .... Begins 1050 to 1450 rpm, 26° to 30° at 4400 rpm
  1.1 litre (economy) .... Begins 1200 to 1450 rpm, 20° to 24° at 5300 rpm
  1.3 litre .... Begins 1050 to 1450 rpm, 26° to 30° at 4400 rpm
Firing order .... 1-3-4-2 (No 1 at timing belt end)

Ignition timing (at idling speed)
1.05 litre (vacuum hoses connected) .... 5° ± 1° BTDC
1.1 litre (vacuum hose disconnected) .... 10° ± 1° BTDC
1.3 litre (vacuum hose disconnected) .... 5° ± 1° BTDC

Spark plugs
Type .... Champion N7YCC or N7YC
Electrode gap:
  N7YCC spark plugs .... 0.8 mm (0.032 in)
  N7YC spark plugs .... 0.7 mm (0.028 in)

HT leads
Up to 1984 .... Champion LS-08 set
1984 on .... Champion LS-08 set plus adaptor kit A

Torque wrench settings

	lbf ft	Nm
Spark plugs	16	20
Distributor clamp bolt	7	10

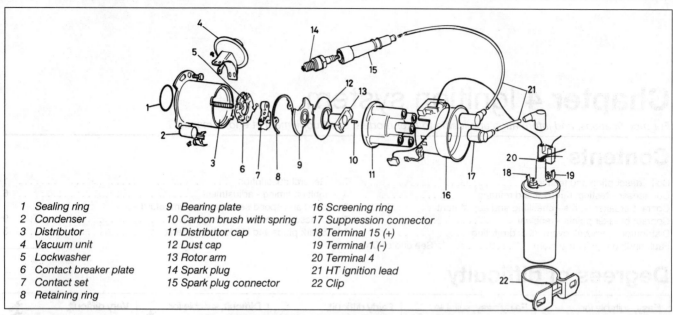

1 Sealing ring
2 Condenser
3 Distributor
4 Vacuum unit
5 Lockwasher
6 Contact breaker plate
7 Contact set
8 Retaining ring
9 Bearing plate
10 Carbon brush with spring
11 Distributor cap
12 Dust cap
13 Rotor arm
14 Spark plug
15 Spark plug connector
16 Screening ring
17 Suppression connector
18 Terminal 15 (+)
19 Terminal 1 (-)
20 Terminal 4
21 HT ignition lead
22 Clip

Fig. 4.1 Exploded view of ignition components (Sec 1)

1 General description

A conventional ignition system is fitted consisting of the battery, coil, distributor, and spark plugs. The distributor is mounted on the left-hand end of the cylinder head and is driven directly from the camshaft.

In order that the engine can run correctly, it is necessary for an electrical spark to ignite the fuel/air mixture in the combustion chamber at exactly the right moment in relation to engine speed and load. The ignition system is based on feeding low tension voltage from the battery to the coil, where it is converted to high tension voltage. The high tension voltage is powerful enough to jump the spark plug gap in the cylinders many times a second under high compression, providing that the system is in good condition and that all adjustments are correct.

The ignition system is divided into two circuits, the low tension circuit and the high tension circuit. The low tension (sometimes known as the primary) circuit consists of the battery, lead to the ignition switch, lead from the ignition switch to the low tension or primary coil windings (terminal +), and the lead from the low tension coil windings (coil terminal-) to the contact breaker points and condenser in the distributor. The high tension circuit consists of the high tension or secondary coil windings, the heavy ignition lead from the coil to the distributor cap, the rotor arm, and the spark plug leads and spark plugs.

The system functions in the following manner. Low tension voltage is changed in the coil into high tension voltage by the opening and closing of the contact breaker points in the low tension circuit. High tension voltage is then fed via the carbon brush in the centre of the distributor cap to the rotor arm of the distributor, and each time it comes in line with one of the four metal segments in the cap, which are connected to the spark plug leads, the opening and closing of the contact breaker points causes the high tension voltage to build up, jump the gap from the rotor arm to the appropriate metal segment, and so via the spark plug lead to the spark plug, where it finally jumps the spark plug gap before going to earth. The ignition is advanced and retarded automatically, to ensure that the spark occurs at just the right instant for the particular load at the prevailing engine speed.

The ignition advance is controlled both mechanically and by a vacuum operated system. The mechanical governor mechanism comprises two weights, which move out from the distributor shaft as the engine speed rises due to centrifugal force. As they move outwards they rotate the cam relative to the distributor shaft, and so advance the spark. The weights are held in position by two light springs and it is the tension of the springs which is largely responsible for correct spark advancement.

The vacuum control consists of a diaphragm, one side of which is connected via a small bore tube to the carburettor, and the other side to the contact breaker plate. Depression in the inlet manifold and carburettor, which varies with engine speed and throttle opening, causes the diaphragm to move, so moving the contact breaker plate, and advancing or retarding the spark. 1.05 litre engines are also equipped with a load and speed sensitive vacuum retard system.

The ignition system incorporates a sensitive wire which is in circuit all the time that the engine is running. When the starter is operated, the resistance is bypassed to provide increased voltage at the spark plugs.

2 Contact breaker points - checking and adjustment

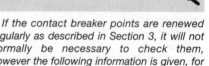

If the contact breaker points are renewed regularly as described in Section 3, it will not normally be necessary to check them, however the following information is given, for in the event of breakdown, starting difficulties or power loss.

1 Remove the polythene cover then prise the two clips from the distributor cap (photo). Where an interference screen is fitted, disconnect the earth cable and low tension lead if applicable. Remove the cap from the distributor.

2.1 The distributor, showing cap retaining clips

2.2 Removing the dust cover

2.5A Checking the contact points gap with a feeler gauge

2.5B Adjusting the contact points gap (bearing plate removed for clarity)

2 Pull off the rotor arm and remove the dust cover (photo).
3 Using a screwdriver open the points and check the condition of the faces. If they are pitted and discoloured, remove them as described in Section 3 and dress them using emery tape or a grindstone making sure that the surfaces are flat and parallel with each other. If the points are worn excessively, renew them. If the points are in good condition, check their adjustment as follows.

Adjustment

4 Turn the engine with a spanner on the crankshaft pulley bolt until the moving contact point is fully open with the contact heel on the peak of one of the cam lobes.
5 Using a feeler blade check that the gap between the two points is as given in the Specifications. If not, loosen the fixed contact screw and reposition the fixed contact until the feeler blade is a firm sliding fit between the two points. In order to make a fine adjustment slightly loosen the screw then position the screwdriver in the fixed contact notch and the two pips on the contact plate. With the gap adjusted tighten the screw (photos).
6 Using a dwell meter check that the dwell angle of the contact points is as given in the Specifications while spinning the engine on the starter. If not, re-adjust the points gap as necessary - reduce the gap in order to

increase the dwell angle, or increase the gap in order to reduce the dwell angle.
7 Clean the dust cover and rotor arm then refit them. Do not remove any metal from the rotor arm segment.
8 Wipe clean the distributor cap and make sure that the carbon brush moves freely against the tension of the spring. Clean the metal segments in the distributor cap, but do not scrape away any metal otherwise the HT spark at the spark plugs will be reduced. Also clean the HT leads and coil tower.
9 Refit the distributor cap and interference screen where applicable. Refit the polythene cover.
10 Start the engine and check that the dwell angle is as given in the Specifications both at idling and higher engine speeds. A decrease in dwell angle at high engine speeds indicates a weak spring on the moving contact point.
11 After making an adjustment to the contact points the ignition timing should be checked and adjusted as described in Section 6.

3 Contact breaker points - renewal

1 The contact breaker points should be renewed at the 10 000 mile (15 000 km) service.

2 Remove the polythene cover then prise the two clips from the distributor cap. Where an interference screen is fitted, disconnect the earth cable and low tension lead if applicable. Remove the cap from the distributor.
3 Pull off the rotor arm and remove the dust cover.
4 Remove the screws and withdraw the bearing plate (photos).
5 Disconnect the moving contact low tension lead from the terminal then remove the retaining screw and withdraw the contact breaker set from the distributor (photos).
6 Wipe clean the contact breaker plate in the distributor and make sure that the contact surfaces of the new contact breaker set are clean. Lubricate the arm surface and moving contact pivot with a little multi-purpose grease. Use only a small amount, otherwise the contact points may become contaminated.
7 Fit the contact set on the baseplate and refit the retaining screw. Connect the low tension lead to the terminal.
8 Refit the bearing plate and tighten the screws.
9 Adjust the contact breaker points as described in Section 2, paragraphs 4 to 11 inclusive.

4

2.5C Showing the two pips and notch for inserting a screwdriver when adjusting the contact points gap (bearing plate removed for clarity)

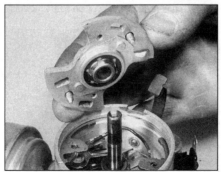

3.4 Removing the bearing plate (late models)

3.5 Showing the contact points fitted to the distributor

4.5 Condenser location

4 Condenser - testing, removal and refitting

1 The condenser is fitted in parallel with the contact points and its purpose is to reduce arcing between the points and also to accelerate the collapse of the coil low tension magnetic field. A faulty condenser can cause the complete failure of the ignition system, as the points will be prevented from interrupting the low tension circuit.
2 To test the condenser, remove the distributor cap, rotor arm and dust cover and rotate the engine until the contact points are closed. Switch on the ignition and separate the points - if this is accompanied by a strong blue flash the condenser is faulty (a weak white spark is normal).
3 A further test can be made for short circuiting by removing the condenser and connect a test lamp and leads to the supply lead and body (ie connect the condenser in series with a 12 volt supply). If the test lamp lights, the condenser is faulty.
4 If the correct operation of the condenser is in doubt, substitute a new unit and check whether the fault persists.
5 To remove the condenser remove the polythene cover from the distributor then unscrew the condenser retaining screw and disconnect the low tension supply lead (at the coil on some models) (photo).
6 Withdraw the condenser sufficient to disconnect the moving contact supply lead

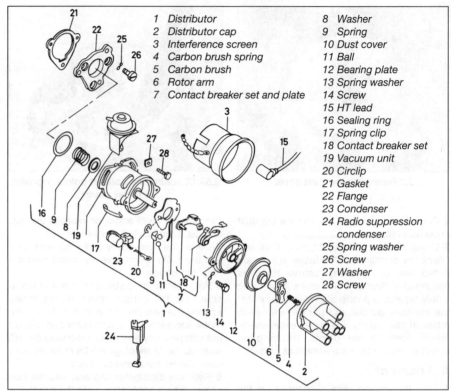

1 Distributor
2 Distributor cap
3 Interference screen
4 Carbon brush spring
5 Carbon brush
6 Rotor arm
7 Contact breaker set and plate
8 Washer
9 Spring
10 Dust cover
11 Ball
12 Bearing plate
13 Spring washer
14 Screw
15 HT lead
16 Sealing ring
17 Spring clip
18 Contact breaker set
19 Vacuum unit
20 Circlip
21 Gasket
22 Flange
23 Condenser
24 Radio suppression condenser
25 Spring washer
26 Screw
27 Washer
28 Screw

Fig. 4.2 Exploded view of alternative distributor (Sec 5)

then withdraw the condenser. If the moving contact supply lead has insufficient length it will be necessary to remove the distributor cap, rotor arm, dust cover and bearing plate first.
7 Refitting is a reversal of removal.

5 Distributor - removal, overhaul and refitting

1 Disconnect the battery negative lead.
2 Remove the polythene cover then prise the two clips from the distributor cap. Where an interference screen is fitted disconnect the earth cable.
3 Remove the distributor cap and disconnect the low tension lead (at the coil on some models).

4 Disconnect the vacuum hose(s) - where two are fitted, identify them for position (photo).
5 The distributor driveshaft is located in the end of the camshaft by an off centre key, and therefore the procedure in this paragraph is only strictly necessary for checking purposes such as when fitting a new distributor. Turn the engine so that the rotor arm points to the No 1 cylinder TDC groove on the distributor arm (lift the dust cover first) (photo). The mark on the crankshaft pulley should be aligned with the TDC pointer with No 1 piston (timing belt end) at TDC compression.
6 Mark the distributor flange and cylinder head in relation to each other.
7 Unscrew the bolts and withdraw the distributor (photos). Remove the sealing ring and gasket as applicable.

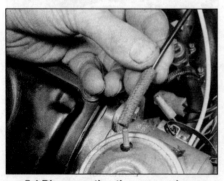
5.4 Disconnecting the vacuum hose

5.5 Showing the rotor arm aligned with the No 1 cylinder TDC groove on the distributor rim

5.7A Unscrew the retaining bolts . . .

5.7B . . . and remove the distributor

5.9A Correct fitted position of the bearing plate retaining ring

5.9B Removing the bearing plate retaining ring

8 Remove the contact points and condenser with reference to Sections 3 and 4.

9 If applicable mark the position of the bearing plate retaining ring then remove it (photos).

10 Extract the circlip securing the vacuum unit arm to the contact breaker plate.

11 Remove the retaining screws then unhook the arm and withdraw the vacuum unit.

12 Remove the side screws noting the location of the earth lead terminal, then remove the contact breaker plate by turning it anti-clockwise to align the lugs with the cut-outs if applicable.

13 Wipe clean all the electrical components and clean the distributor body assembly with paraffin then wipe dry.

14 Check all components for wear and damage referring to Sections 2 and 4 for the contact breaker points, distributor cap, rotor and condenser.

15 Reassembly and refitting is a reversal of removal and dismantling, but lubricate the centrifugal mechanism and contact breaker plate with a little multi-purpose grease (photo). Adjust the contact breaker points as described in Section 2 and the ignition timing as described in Section 6. Always renew the sealing ring and gasket.

6 Ignition timing - adjustment

Accurate ignition timing is only possible using a stroboscopic timing light or by using a special instrument connected to the flywheel TDC sender unit through the aperture in the top of the gearbox bellhousing. The latter will not normally be available to the home mechanic. For initial setting-up purposes, the test bulb method can be used, but this must always be followed by the stroboscopic timing light method.

Test bulb method (initial setting-up)

1 Remove No 1 spark plug (timing belt end) with reference to Section 8 and place a finger or thumb over the aperture.

2 Turn the engine in the normal running direction (clockwise viewed from the crankshaft pulley end) until pressure is felt in No 1 cylinder indicating that the piston is commencing its compression stroke. Use a spanner on the crankshaft pulley bolt, or engage top gear and pull the car forwards.

3 Continue turning the engine until the line on the crankshaft pulley is aligned with the first pointer projecting out of the timing cover. Do not align the mark with the second pointer which is at top dead centre (TDC).

4 Remove the distributor cap and check that the rotor arm is pointing towards the No 1 HT lead location in the cap.

5 Connect a 12 volt test bulb between the distributor (or coil-) LT terminal and a suitable earthing point.

6 Loosen the distributor retaining bolts sufficient to turn the distributor.

7 Switch on the ignition. If the bulb is already lit turn the distributor slightly anti-clockwise until the bulb goes out.

8 Turn the distributor clockwise until the bulb just lights up, indicating that the points have just opened. Tighten the bolts.

9 Switch off the ignition and remove the test bulb.

10 Refit the distributor cap and No 1 spark plug. Once the engine has been started, check the timing stroboscopically as follows:

5.15 Align the rotor arm with the No 1 cylinder TDC groove on the rim before refitting the distributor

Stroboscopic timing light method

11 On 1.1 and 1.3 litre engines disconnect and plug the distributor vacuum advance hose.

12 Wipe clean the timing mark on the crankshaft pulley and if necessary highlight it with chalk or white paint.

13 Connect the timing light to the engine in accordance with the manufacturer's instructions.

14 Start the engine and run it at idling speed. To ensure that the engine speed variation is minimal, it should be at normal operating temperature.

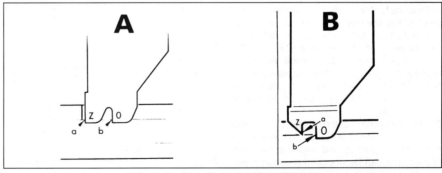

Fig. 4.3 Ignition timing pointers (Sec 6)

A *1.1 litre engines*
B *1.05 and 1.3 litre engines*

a = Z reference edge for timing degrees BTDC

b = O reference edge for No 1 cylinder TDC

7.1 The coil

8.2 Removing a spark plug

It's often difficult to insert spark plugs into their holes without cross-threading them. To avoid this possibility, fit a short piece of rubber hose over the end of the spark plug. The flexible hose acts as a universal joint, to help align the plug with the plug hole. Should the plug begin to cross-thread, the hose will slip on the spark plug, preventing thread damage.

15 Point the timing light at the timing mark and the left-hand pointer, they should appear to be stationary and aligned. If they are not aligned loosen the retaining bolts and turn the distributor clockwise to advance and anti-clockwise to retard the ignition timing. Tighten the bolts when the setting is correct.

16 Gradually increase the engine speed while still pointing the timing light at the timing marks. The mark on the crankshaft pulley should appear to move anti-clockwise proving that the centrifugal weights are operating correctly. If not, the centrifugal mechanism is faulty and the distributor should be renewed.

17 Accurate checking of the vacuum advance (and retard where fitted) requires the use of a vacuum pump and gauge. However, providing that the diaphragm unit is serviceable, the vacuum hose(s) firmly fitted, and the internal mechanism not seized, the system should work correctly.

18 Switch off the engine, remove the timing light and refit the vacuum hose where applicable.

7 Coil - description and testing

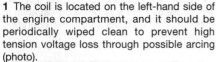

1 The coil is located on the left-hand side of the engine compartment, and it should be periodically wiped clean to prevent high tension voltage loss through possible arcing (photo).

2 To ensure the correct HT polarity at the spark plugs, the coil LT leads must always be connected correctly. The ignition lead from the fusebox must be connected to the positive (+) terminal 15, and the distributor lead (usually green) must be connected to the negative (-) terminal 1. Incorrect connections can cause bad starting, misfiring, and short spark plug life.

3 Complete testing of the coil requires special equipment, however if an ohmmeter is available the primary and secondary winding resistances can be checked and compared with those given in the Specifications. During testing the LT and HT wires must be disconnected from the coil. To test the primary winding, connect the ohmmeter

between the two LT terminals. To test the secondary winding, connect the ohmmeter between the negative (-) terminal 1 and the HT terminal.

8 Spark plugs and HT leads - general

1 The correct functioning of the spark plugs is vital for the correct running and efficiency of the engine. It is essential that the plugs fitted are appropriate for the engine, and the suitable type is specified at the beginning of this chapter. If this type is used and the engine is in good condition, the spark plugs should not need attention between scheduled replacement intervals. Spark plug cleaning is rarely necessary and should not be attempted unless specialised equipment is available as damage can easily be caused to the firing ends.

2 To remove the spark plugs first remove the air cleaner as described in Chapter 3, then disconnect the HT leads after noting their positions. Always pull on the end fittings otherwise the leads may be damaged internally. Unscrew and remove the spark plugs using a proper plug spanner (photo).

3 The condition of the spark plugs will also tell much about the overall condition of the engine. If the insulator nose of the spark plug is clean and white, with no deposits, this is

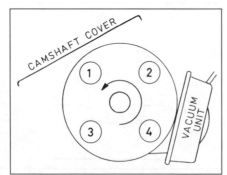

Fig. 4.4 Showing HT lead positions in distributor cap (Sec 8)

Vacuum unit position may vary

indicative of a weak mixture, or too hot a plug. (A hot plug transfers heat away from the electrode slowly - a cold plug transfers it away quickly.)

4 If the tip and insulator nose is covered with hard black-looking deposits, then this is indicative that the mixture is too rich. Should the plug be black and oily, then it is likely that the engine is fairly worn, as well as the mixture being too rich.

5 If the insulator nose is covered with light tan to greyish brown deposits, then the mixture is correct and it is likely that the engine is in good condition.

6 The spark plug gap is of considerable importance, as, if it is too large or too small. the size of the spark and its efficiency will be seriously impaired. The spark plug gap should be set to the figure given in the Specifications at the beginning of this Chapter.

7 To set it, measure the gap with a feeler gauge, and then bend open, or close, the outer plug electrode until the correct gap is achieved. The centre electrode should never be bent as this may crack the insulation and cause plug failure, if nothing worse.

8 Always tighten the spark plugs to the specified torque.

9 Periodically the spark plug leads should be wiped clean and checked for security to the spark plugs.

9 Load and speed sensitive vacuum retard - description and checking

1 1.05 litre engines are equipped with a load and speed sensitive vacuum retard system which prevents engine pinking (spontaneous combustion as opposed to controlled combustion). The system operates at engine speeds below 3600 rpm with the carburettor

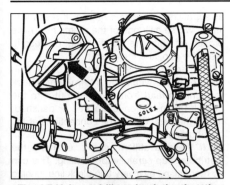

Fig. 4.5 Using a drill to check the throttle valve switch operation (Sec 9)

9.2A The vacuum retard system throttle valve switch fitted to the carburettor on 1.05 litre engines

9.2B The vacuum retard system vacuum reservoir located on the bulkhead on 1.05 litre engines

throttle valve opened more than 30°, and under these conditions the ignition timing is retarded by 6°.

2 The speed sensitive switch is located behind the facia panel and the throttle valve switch is located on the carburettor. With both switches closed, vacuum passes from the spherical reservoir on the bulkhead, through the solenoid valve to the retard side of the vacuum unit. With both switches open, the retard side of the vacuum unit is ventilated to atmosphere and no ignition retard occurs (photos).

3 A check valve is fitted into the vacuum line to the reservoir. Note that the white side of the valve must be towards the reservoir.

4 To check the system first remove the air cleaner and plug the intake temperature control vacuum hose.

5 Connect a stroboscopic timing light to the engine. Start the engine and note the ignition timing at idling speed.

6 Manually close the throttle valve switch (ie with the engine still at idling speed), and check that the ignition is retarded by 6°.

7 To check the engine speed switch, connect a 12 volt test lamp between the battery positive terminal and each of the terminals on the throttle valve switch in turn. With the ignition on (engine stopped) disconnect the lead from the terminal on which the test lamp lights up this is the lead to the speed switch. With the test lamp lead connected to the lead, start the engine and slowly increase its speed - at 3600 + 100 rpm the test lamp should go out. If not, the speed switch is defective and should be renewed.

8 To check the throttle valve switch connect the test lamp between the free terminal and a suitable earth point with the engine stopped. Insert a 10.5 mm drill between the throttle valve lever and the full throttle stop in order to open the throttle valve by approximately 25°. Switch on the ignition and check that the test lamp remains off. Repeat the test using a 9.0 mm drill and the test lamp should now light up as the throttle valve is approximately 35° open.

9 Adjustment of the throttle valve switch is only possible with the carburettor removed. With the carburettor inverted, insert a 4.0 mm

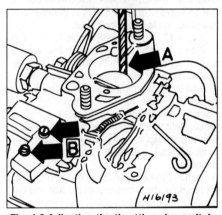

Fig. 4.6 Adjusting the throttle valve switch (Sec 9)

A Drill   B Adjusting screws

drill between the throttle valve and the carburettor barrel wall. Loosen the screws and adjust the switch so that the points just close. Tighten the screws and check that the switch operates at the correct throttle valve opening, then refit the carburettor.

Fault finding - ignition system

By far the majority of breakdown and running troubles are caused by faults in the ignition system, either in the low tension or high tension circuit. There are two main symptoms indicating ignition faults. Either the engine will not start or fire, or the engine is difficult to start and misfires. If it is a regular misfire, ie the engine is only running on two or three cylinders, the fault is almost sure to be in the secondary, or high tension, circuit. If the misfiring is intermittent the fault could be in either the high or low tension circuits. If the car stops suddenly, or will not start at all, it is likely that the fault is in the low tension circuit. Loss of power and overheating, apart from faulty carburation settings, are normally due to faults in the distributor or incorrect ignition timing.

Engine fails to start

1 If the engine fails to start and the car was running normally when it was last used, first check there is fuel in the petrol tank. If the engine turns over normally on the starter motor and the battery is evidently well charged, then the fault may be in either the high or low tension circuits. First check the HT circuit. If the battery is known to be fully charged, the ignition light comes on, and the starter motor fails to turn the engine, check the tightness of the leads on the battery terminals and the security of the earth lead to its connection to the body. It is quite common for the leads to have worked loose, even if they look and feel secure. If one of the battery terminal posts gets very hot when trying to

work the starter motor, this is a sure indication of a faulty connection to that terminal.

2 One of the most common reasons for bad starting is wet or damp spark plug leads and distributor. Remove the distributor cap. If condensation is visible internally dry the cap with a rag and wipe over the leads. Refit the cap.

3 If the engine still fails to start, check that current is reaching the plugs, by disconnecting each plug lead in turn at the spark plug end, and holding the end of the cable about 136 inch (5mm) away from the cylinder head. Spin the engine on the starter motor.

4 Sparking between the end of the cable and the head should be fairly strong with a regular blue spark. (Hold the lead with rubber to avoid electric shocks.) If current is reaching the plugs, then remove them and clean and regap them. The engine should now start.

5 If there is no spark at the plug leads, take off the HT lead from the centre of the distributor cap and hold it to the block as before. Spin the engine on the starter once more. A rapid succession of blue sparks between the end of the lead and the block indicate that the coil is in order and that the distributor cap is cracked, the rotor arm faulty or the carbon brush in the top of the distributor cap is not making good contact with the rotor arm. Or possibly the points are in bad condition; clean and reset them.

6 If there are no sparks from the end of the lead from the coil, check the connections at the coil end of the lead. If it is in order start checking the low tension circuit.

7 Use a 12 volt voltmeter, or a 12 volt bulb and two lengths of wire. With the ignition switch on and the points open test between the low tension wire to the coil (it is marked +) and earth. No reading indicates a break in the supply from the ignition switch. Check the connections at the switch to see if any are loose. Refit them and the engine should run. A reading shows a faulty coil or condenser or broken lead between the coil and the distributor.

8 Remove the condenser from the distributor and remove the distributor cap, rotor and dust cover. With the points open, test between the moving point and earth. if there now is a reading then the fault is in the condenser. Fit a new one and the fault is cleared.

9 With no reading from the moving point to earth, take a reading between earth and the negative (-) terminal of the coil. A reading here indicates a broken wire which must be renewed between the coil and distributor. No reading confirms that the coil has failed and must be renewed. For these tests it is sufficient to separate the contact breaker points with a piece of paper.

10 If the engine starts when the starter motor is operated, but stops as soon as the ignition key is returned to the normal running position, the resistive wire may have an open circuit. Connect a temporary lead between the coil positive (+) terminal and the battery positive (+) terminal. If the engine now runs correctly, renew the resistive wire. Note that the resistive wire must not be permanently bypassed, otherwise the coil will overheat and be irreparably damaged.

Engine misfires

11 If the engine misfires regularly, run it at a fast idling speed. Pull off each of the plug caps in turn and listen to the note of the engine. Hold the plug cap in a dry cloth or with a rubber glove as additional protection against a shock from the HT supply.

12 No difference in engine running will be noticed when the lead from the defective circuit is removed. Removing the lead from one of the good cylinders will accentuate the misfire.

13 Remove the plug lead from the end of the defective plug and hold it about 3/16 inch (5mm) away from the block. Restart the engine. If the sparking is fairly strong and regular, the fault must lie in the spark plug.

14 The plug may be loose, the insulation may be cracked, or the points may have burnt away, giving too wide a gap for the spark to jump. Worse still, one of the points may have broken off. Either renew the plug, or clean it, reset the gap, and then test it.

15 If there is no spark at the end of the plug lead, or if it is weak and intermittent, check the ignition lead from the distributor to the plug. If the insulation is cracked or perished, renew the lead. Check the connections at the distributor cap.

16 If there is still no spark, examine the distributor cap carefully for tracking. This can be recognised by a very thin black line running between two or more electrodes, or between an electrode and some other part of the distributor. These lines are paths which now conduct electricity across the cap, thus letting it run to earth. The only answer in this case is a new distributor cap.

17 Apart from the ignition timing being incorrect, other causes of misfiring have already been dealt with under the section dealing with the failure of the engine to start. To recap, these are that:

(a) *The coil may be faulty giving an intermittent misfire*
(b) *There may be a damaged wire or loose connection in the low tension circuit*
(c) *The condenser may be short circuiting*

18 If the ignition timing is too far retarded it should be noted that the engine will tend to overheat, and there will be a quite noticeable drop in power. If the engine is overheating and the power is down, and the ignition timing is correct, then the carburettor should be checked, as it is likely that this is where the fault lies.

Car Mechanics June 97 says : Push pedal up + down a few times.
Free play should be 15 mm (0.69")
Car Mechanics Nov 98 says "Clutch pedal should be level with brake". see below.

5•1

The max. height of the clutch and brake pedals is limited in each case by a mechanical stop. So there is no point in trying to adjust the clutch so that its pedal is the same height as the brake pedal. Adjust it to give 15mm free play at the pedal.

Chapter 5 Clutch

For modifications, and information applicable to later models, see Supplement at end of manual

Contents

Degrees of difficulty

Easy, suitable for novice with little experience		Fairly easy, suitable for beginner with some experience		Fairly difficult, suitable for competent DIY mechanic		Difficult, suitable for experienced DIY mechanic		Very difficult, suitable for expert DIY or professional	

Specifications

Clutch type	Single dry plate, diaphragm spring pressure plate, cable actuation
Free play at clutch pedal	15 to 20 mm (0.6 to 0.8 in)

Clutch disc

Diameter	180 mm (7.09 in)
Maximum run-out (2.5mm/0.1 in from outer edge)	0.4 mm (0.016 in)

Pressure plate

Maximum inward taper	0.3 mm (0.012 in)
Diaphragm spring finger scoring depth (maximum)	0.3 mm (0.012in)

Torque wrench settings

	lbf ft	Nm
Pressure plate	18	25
Flywheel	55	75
Guide sleeve	11	15

5

1 General description

The clutch is of single dry plate type with a diaphragm spring pressure plate, and actuation is by cable. The pressure plate assembly is bolted to the flywheel and transmits drive to the friction disc which is splined to the gearbox input shaft. Friction linings are riveted to each side of the disc and radial damper springs are incorporated in the hub in order to cushion rotational shocks.

When the clutch pedal is depressed, the cable pulls the arm on the release shaft, and the release bearing is pushed along the guide sleeve against the diaphragm spring fingers. Further movement causes the diaphragm spring to withdraw the pressure plate from the friction disc which also moves along the splined input shaft away from the flywheel. Drive then ceases to be transmitted to the gearbox.

Then the clutch pedal is released, the diaphragm spring forces the pressure plate back into contact with the friction disc which then moves along the input shaft into engagement with the flywheel. Drive is then transmitted directly through the clutch to the gearbox.

Wear of the friction disc linings causes the pressure plate to move closer to the flywheel and the cable free play to decrease. Cable adjustment must therefore be carried out as described in Section 2.

2 Clutch cable - adjustment
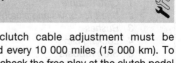

1 The clutch cable adjustment must be checked every 10 000 miles (15 000 km). To do this, check the free play at the clutch pedal by measuring the free distance it has to be moved in order to take up the slack in the cable. If the distance is not as given in the Specification adjust the cable as follows.

2.2 Clutch cable and release arm showing adjustment nut

3.2 Clutch cable support clip location

3.4 Pulling the clutch cable through the steering gear

2 Locate the release arm on the gearbox clutch housing then turn the adjusting nut and half-round seating until the adjustment is correct (photo). Depress the arm if necessary to enable the nut to be turned more easily, and if the nut is tight on its thread, hold the inner cable with a spanner.

3 Make sure that the adjusting nut is correctly seated in the release arm before finally checking the adjustment.

3 Clutch cable - renewal

1 Unscrew the clutch cable adjusting nut and slide the end fitting from the release arm on the gearbox clutch housing. Alternatively push

the release arm inwards and remove the end fitting.

2 Release the outer cable from the gearbox and support clip (photo).

3 Working inside the car reach up behind the facia and unhook the inner cable from the clutch pedal.

4 Pull the cable assembly through the bulkhead and withdraw it from the engine compartment. On left-hand drive models release the cable from the retaining clip. On right-hand drive models press the retaining sleeve downwards from the steering gear (photo).

5 Fit the new cable using a reversal of the removal procedure, but first lightly grease the inner cable by pulling it from the outer cable at each end. Finally adjust the cable as described in Section 2.

4 Clutch pedal - removal and refitting

1 Disconnect the clutch cable from the release arm on the gearbox clutch housing and from the top of the clutch pedal with reference to Section 3.

2 Prise the clip from the end of the pedal pivot shaft.

3 On left-hand drive models withdraw the pivot shaft sufficient to remove the clutch pedal from the bracket. On right-hand drive models the pivot shaft must first be withdrawn through the brake pedal.

4 Clean the pedal and pivot shaft and examine them for wear. If the bushes are worn they can be removed using a soft metal drift, and the new bushes installed using a vice to press then into position. Check the rubber foot pad and the stop rubber on the bracket, and renew them if necessary.

5 Refitting is a reversal of removal, but apply a little multi-purpose grease to the pivot shaft and bushes. Finally adjust the cable as described in Section 2.

5 Clutch - removal and refitting

1 Remove the gearbox as described in Chapter 6.

2 Mark the pressure plate cover and flywheel in relation to each other.

3 Using an Allen key unscrew the bolts securing the pressure plate cover to the flywheel in diagonal sequence one turn at a time (photo). If the key handle is pressed towards the centre of the flywheel it should be possible to loosen the bolts while holding the cover stationary by hand. If necessary hold the flywheel stationary using a screwdriver inserted in the starter ring gear teeth.

4 Withdraw the pressure plate assembly and the friction disc from the flywheel. Note that the friction disc hub extension containing the cushion springs faces the pressure plate.

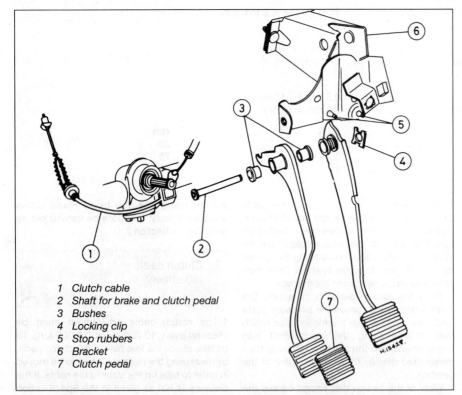

1 Clutch cable
2 Shaft for brake and clutch pedal
3 Bushes
4 Locking clip
5 Stop rubbers
6 Bracket
7 Clutch pedal

Fig. 5.1 Showing clutch cable and pedal components on right-hand drive models (Sec 4)

5.3 Removing the pressure plate bolts

5.7 Showing the friction disc and centralising tool

5.8 Fitting the pressure plate assembly

5 Check the clutch components as described in Section 6.

6 Before commencing the refitting procedure, a tool must be obtained for centralising the friction disc, otherwise difficulty will be experienced when refitting the gearbox. Unlike the normal arrangement, the gearbox input shaft does not enter a bush or bearing in the rear of the crankshaft. If, however, the friction disc is not centralised the gearbox dowels will not be aligned correctly.

TOOL TIP

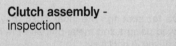

If a clutch centralising tool is not available a wooden mandrel may be made to these dimensions

A 18.24 mm
B 70.00 mm
C 20.00 mm
D 14.81 mm

7 Clean the friction faces of the flywheel and pressure plate, then fit the centralising tool to the crankshaft and locate the friction disc on it with the hub extension outwards (photo).

8 Fit the pressure plate assembly to the flywheel (in its original position if not renewed), then insert the bolts and tighten them evenly in diagonal sequence to the specified torque (photo).

9 Check the release bearing as described in Section 7 before refitting the gearbox as described in Chapter 6.

6 Clutch assembly - inspection

1 Examine the surfaces of the pressure plate and flywheel for signs of scoring. Light scoring is normal, but if excessive the pressure plate must be renewed and the flywheel either machined or renewed.

2 Check the pressure plate diaphragm spring fingers for wear caused by the release bearing. If the scoring exceeds the maximum depth given in the Specifications, renew the assembly.

3 Using a straight edge and feeler blade, check that the inward taper of the pressure plate does not exceed the maximum amount given in the Specifications (photo). Also check

for loose riveted joints and for any cracks in the pressure plate components.

4 Check the friction disc linings for wear and renew the disc if the linings are worn to within 1.0 mm (0.04in) of the rivets.

5 Check that the friction disc damper springs and all rivets are secure, and that the linings are not contaminated with oil. Temporarily fit the disc to the gearbox input shaft and check that the run-out does not exceed that given in the Specifications.

6 If the clutch components are contaminated with oil, the leak should be found and rectified. The procedure for renewing the crankshaft oil seal is described in Chapter 1, and the procedure for renewing the gearbox input shaft oil seal is described in Chapter 6.

7 Having checked the clutch disc and pressure plate, it is always worthwhile to check the release bearing with reference to Section 7.

7 Release bearing and shaft - removal, checking and refitting

1 With the gearbox removed, unhook the return spring from the release arm (photo).

2 Turn the release arm to move the release bearing up the guide sleeve, then disengage the two spring clips from the release fork and withdraw the bearing (photos).

5

6.3 Checking the pressure plate for taper

7.1 Clutch release arm return spring

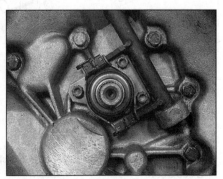

7.2A Showing the release bearing fitted to the arm

7.2B Release bearing showing retaining clips

7.5A Unscrew the splined bolts . . .

7.5B . . . and withdraw the guide sleeve

3 Note how the springs and clips are fitted then prise the clips from the release bearing.

4 Spin the bearing by hand and check it for roughness, then attempt to move the outer race laterally against the inner race. If any excessive roughness or wear is evident, renew the bearing. Do not wash the bearing in solvent if it is to be re-used.

5 Using a splined socket, unbolt and remove the guide sleeve from the clutch housing (photos).

6 Using a narrow drift, drive the release shaft outer bush from the clutch housing. Alternatively prise out the bush.

7 Pull the release shaft from the inner bearing then withdraw the shaft and arm from the housing (photo).

8 Check the bushes and bearing surfaces of the shaft for wear and also check the guide

7.7 Removing the release shaft

sleeve for scoring. The inner bush may be removed using a soft metal drift and the new bush driven in until flush.

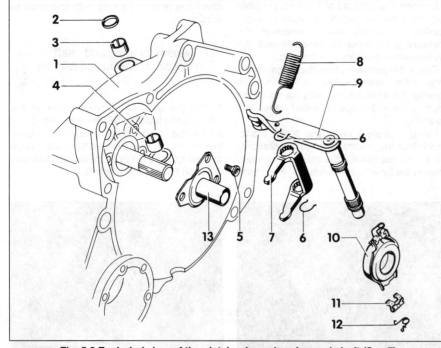

7.9 Showing the location tab on the release shaft outer bush

9 Refitting is a reversal of removal, but lubricate all bearing surfaces with a little high melting point grease. Make sure that the release shaft outer bush is correctly sealed with the tab located in the cut-out in the clutch housing (photo).

Fig. 5.2 Exploded view of the clutch release bearing and shaft (Sec 7)

1 Guide sleeve	4 Bush	7 Release bearing
2 Socket head bolt	5 Release shaft	8 Retaining clip
3 Release spring	6 Bush	9 Retaining spring

Fault diagnosis - clutch

Judder when taking up drive
☐ Loose engine/gearbox mountings
☐ Friction bearings worn or contaminated with oil
☐ Worn splines on gearbox input shaft and friction disc

Clutch fails to disengage
☐ Incorrect cable adjustment
☐ Friction disc sticking on input shaft splines (may be due to rust if car off
☐ road for long period)

Clutch slips
☐ Incorrect cable adjustment
☐ Friction bindings worn or contaminated with oil

Noise when depressing clutch pedal
☐ Worn release bearing
☐ Worn or broken pressure plate diaphragm spring fingers

Chapter 6 Manual gearbox and final drive

For modifications, and information applicable to later models, see Supplement at end of manual

Contents

Degrees of difficulty

Easy, suitable for novice with little experience 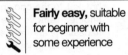	Fairly easy, suitable for beginner with some experience	Fairly difficult, suitable for competent DIY mechanic	Difficult, suitable for experienced DIY mechanic	Very difficult, suitable for expert DIY or professional

Specifications

Type . . . . Four forward speeds and reverse, synchromesh on all forward speeds, integral final drive

Code number 084

Code letters
1.05 litre engine . . . . GU
1.1 litre engine (standard) . . . . GW
1.1 litre engine (Formel E) . . . . QS (to 7.82)
3D (from 8.82)
1.3 litre engine . . . . GU

Ratios (teeth) . . . .

	GU	GW	QS	3D
1st	3.45:1 (38:11)	3.45:1 (38:11)	3.45:1 (38:11)	3.45:1 (38:11)
2nd	1.95:1 (41:21)	1.95:1 (41:21)	1.77:1 (39:22)	1.77:1 (39:22)
3rd	1.25:1 (60:48)	1.25:1 (60:48)	1.04:1 (55:53)	1.08:1 (56:52)
4th	0.89:1 (51:57)	0.89:1 (51:57)	0.80:1 (48:60)	0.80:1 (48:60)
Reverse	3.38:1 (44:13)	3.38:1 (44:13)	3.38:1 (44:13)	3.38:1 (44:13)
Final drive	4.27:1 (64:15)	4.57:1 (64:14)	4.06:1 (65:16)	4.06:1 (65:16)
Speedo drive	0.60:1 (12:20)	0.60:1 (12:20)	0.60:1 (12:20)	0.60:1 (12:20)

Oil capacity . . . . 3.9 pt (2.2 litre)

Oil type/specification . . . . Gear oil, viscosity SAE 80 to API-GL 4

Torque wrench settings	lbf ft	Nm
Gearbox to engine	41	55
Gearshift lever lower housing	11	15
Gearshift lever stop plate	7	10
Shift and clamp bolt	15	20
Shift rod coupling screw	15	20
Bearing cover	18	25
Reverse relay bolt	26	35
Filler and drain plugs	18	25
Reversing light switch	22	30
Clutch housing to gearbox housing	18	25

6

2.8 Coolant pipe support bracket location

2.10 Clutch housing cover plate

2.11A Reversing light switch location

1 General description

The manual gearbox incorporates four forward speeds and one reverse speed, with synchromesh engagement on all forward gears. Gearshift is by means of a floor mounted lever which pivots in a ball socket, and a shift rod and coupling connected to the gearbox selector rods.

The final drive (differential) is located within the gearbox housings, and the helical gear on the unit is driven by a gear on the end of the output shaft.

Drain and filler plugs are provided, and a

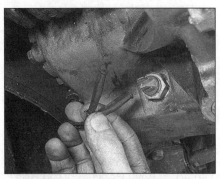

2.11B Disconnecting the reversing light switch wiring

2.11C Gearchange/consumption indicator switch location

magnetic swarf collector is located in the bottom of the gearbox.

When overhauling the gearbox, due consideration should be given to the costs involved, since it is often more economical to obtain a service exchange or good secondhand gearbox rather than fit new parts to the existing gearbox.

2 Gearbox - removal and refitting

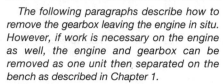

The following paragraphs describe how to remove the gearbox leaving the engine in situ. However, if work is necessary on the engine as well, the engine and gearbox can be removed as one unit then separated on the bench as described in Chapter 1.

1 The engine must be supported before the gearbox can be removed and it is recommended that a hoist is used or alternatively a lifting bar as shown in Fig. 6.1. As the gearbox is removed downwards, first position the car over an inspection pit or jack up the front of the car and support on axle stands. Apply the handbrake. Take the weight of the engine with the hoist or lifting bar.
2 Remove the air cleaner as described in Chapter 3.
3 Disconnect the battery earth lead.
4 Remove the windscreen washer bottle and place it to one side.

2.14A Engine rear mounting bracket

5 Disconnect the clutch cable from the gearbox with reference to Chapter 5.
6 Unscrew and remove the engine to gearbox bolts that can be reached from the top of the gearbox.
7 Remove the starter with reference to Chapter 9.
8 Loosen the clip securing the support bracket to the coolant pipe at the rear of the engine, remove the upper starter bolt if necessary, and move the bracket away from the gearbox (photo).
9 Remove the left-hand front engine mounting bracket by unscrewing the nuts securing it to the gearbox, removing the mounting bolt, and removing the bolt securing the earth strap.
10 Working beneath the car, unbolt and remove the cover plate from the clutch housing (photo).
11 Disconnect the wiring from the reversing light switch and gearchange/consumption indicator switch (photos).
12 Disconnect the inner ends of the driveshafts from the gearbox flanges with reference to Chapter 7 and tie them out of the way.
13 Unscrew the collar and disconnect the speedometer cable from the gearbox.
14 Unscrew and remove the remaining engine to gearbox bolts noting the location of the rear mounting bracket (photos).
15 Unscrew the rear mounting nut and remove the bracket, or leave the mounting on

2.14B Removing the rear mounting bracket bolts

2.15 Removing the rear engine mounting and bracket

2.16A Disconnecting the shift rod coupling

2.16B Removing the shift rod coupling

2.16C Shift rod adaptor and bush

the bracket and remove the mounting bolts (photo).

16 Remove the screw from the shaft rod coupling and ease the coupling from the rod. The screw threads are coated with a liquid locking agent and if difficulty is experienced it may be necessary to heat up the coupling with a blowlamp, however take the necessary fire precautions. If required, remove the coupling ball from the adaptor (photos).

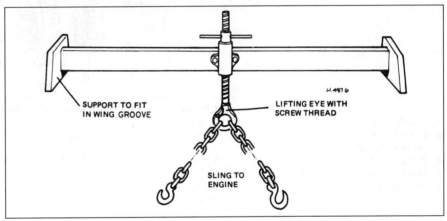

Fig. 6.1 Suggested engine lifting bar (Sec 2)

SUPPORT TO FIT IN WING GROOVE

LIFTING EYE WITH SCREW THREAD

SLING TO ENGINE

17 Support the gearbox on a trolley jack then withdraw it from the engine keeping it in a horizontal position until clear of the clutch. If necessary use a lever to free the gearbox from the locating dowels.

18 Lower the gearbox and remove it from under the car.

19 Refitting is a reversal of removal, but first smear a little molybdenum disulphide based grease on the splines of the input shaft, and make sure that the engine rear plate is correctly located on the dowels. Delay fully tightening the mounting nuts and bolts until the gearbox is in its normal position. Adjust the gearchange if necessary, as described in Section 11.

6

3 Gearbox overhaul - general

Overhauling a manual transmission unit is a difficult and involved job for the DIY home mechanic. In addition to dismantling and reassembling many small parts, clearances must be precisely measured and, if necessary, changed by selecting shims and spacers. Internal transmission components are also often difficult to obtain, and in many instances, are extremely expensive. Because of this, if the transmission develops a fault or becomes noisy, the best course of action is to have the unit overhauled by a specialist repairer, or to obtain an exchange reconditioned unit.

Nevertheless, it is not impossible for the more experienced mechanic to overhaul the transmission, provided the special tools are available, and that the job is done in a

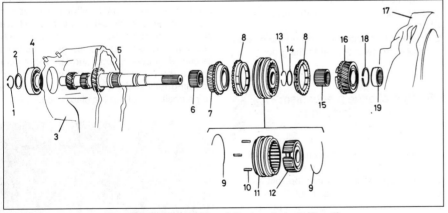

Fig. 6.2 Exploded view of the input shaft (Sec 3)

1 Circlip
2 Shim
3 Gearbox housing
4 Grooved ball bearing
5 Input shaft
6 Needle bearing for 3rd gear
7 3rd speed gear

8 Synchro rings for 3rd and 4th gears
9 Spring
10 Key
11 Sleeve
12 Synchro hub
13 Circlip

14 Thrust washer
15 Needle bearing for 4th gear
16 4th speed gear
17 Clutch housing
18 Circlip
19 Needle bearing

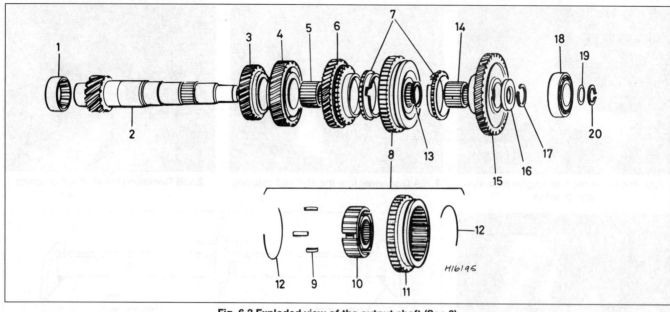

Fig. 6.3 Exploded view of the output shaft (Sec 3)

1 *Needle bearing*
2 *Output shaft*
3 *4th speed gear*
4 *3rd speed gear*
5 *Needle bearing for 2nd gear*
6 *2nd speed gear*

7 *Synchro ring for 1st and 2nd gears*
8 *Sleeve hub for 1st and 2nd gears*
9 *Key*
10 *Hub*
11 *Sleeve*
12 *Spring*
13 *Circlip*

14 *Needle bearing for 1st gear*
15 *1st speed gear*
16 *Thrust washer*
17 *Circlip*
18 *Grooved ball bearing*
19 *Shim*
20 *Circlip*

deliberate step-by-step manner so that nothing is overlooked.

The tools necessary for an overhaul may include internal and external circlip pliers, bearing pullers, a slide hammer, a set of pin punches, a dial test indicator, and possibly a hydraulic press. In addition, a large, sturdy workbench and a vice will be required.

During dismantling of the transmission, make careful notes of how each component is fitted, to make reassembly easier and accurate.

Before dismantling the transmission, it will help if you have some idea which area is malfunctioning. Certain problems can be closely related to specific areas in the gearbox, which can make component examination and replacement easier.

4 Drive flange oil seals - renewal

1 Jack up the front of the car and support on axle stands. Apply the handbrake.
2 Detach the inner ends of the driveshafts from the drive flanges with reference to Chapter 7 and tie the driveshafts to one side.
3 Unscrew the bolt from the centre of each drive flange using a bar and two temporarily inserted bolts to hold the flange stationary.
4 Place a container beneath the gearbox then

remove the drive flanges and lever out the old oil seals. Identify the flanges side for side.
5 Clean the recesses then drive in the new oil seals using a suitable length of metal tubing.
6 Smear a little grease on the lips of the oil seals, and insert the drive flanges.
7 Insert the bolts and tighten them to the specified torque using the bar and bolts to hold the flanges stationary.
8 Refit the driveshafts with reference to Chapter 7.
9 Check and if necessary top up the gearbox oil level then lower the car to the ground.

5 Gearchange mechanism - removal, refitting and adjustment

1 Jack up the front of the car and support on axle stands. Apply the handbrake.
2 With neutral selected mark the shift rod and coupling in relation to each other, then unscrew the coupling clamp and pull out the shift rod.
3 Working inside the car unscrew the gear knob and remove the gaiter.
4 Unscrew the nuts from the ball housing stop plate, and withdraw the complete gearchange mechanism upwards into the car (photo). Recover the spacers.
5 Dismantle the mechanism as necessary

and examine the components for wear and damage. Renew as necessary.
6 Lubricate the joints and bearing surfaces with high melting point grease then refit using a reversal of the removal procedure. If a new coupling has been fitted it will be necessary to adjust the coupling position - this is best carried out by a VW garage using tool 3069, but if necessary the following method can be used in an emergency. With the coupling disconnected and the gearbox in neutral have an assistant hold the gear lever in neutral position between 3rd and 4th gear positions (ie half way between front and rear movement and to the right). Engage the shift rod and coupling fully and with the gear lever in the same position, tighten the clamp bolt.

5.4 View of the gearchange mechanism housing

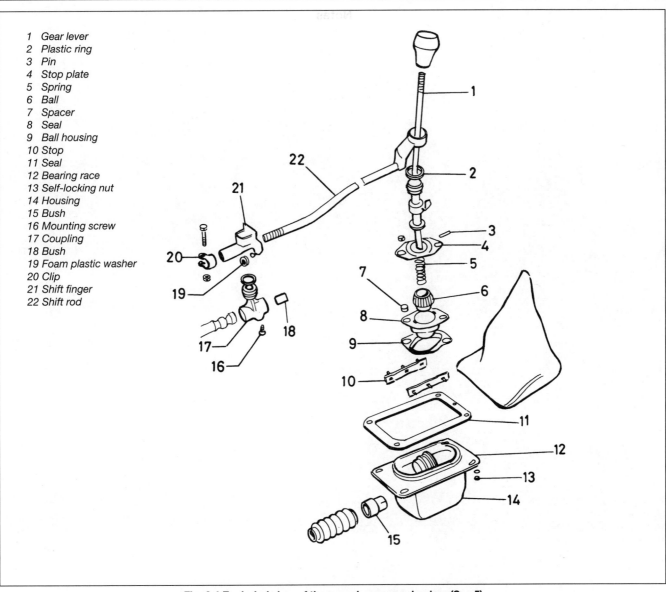

1 Gear lever
2 Plastic ring
3 Pin
4 Stop plate
5 Spring
6 Ball
7 Spacer
8 Seal
9 Ball housing
10 Stop
11 Seal
12 Bearing race
13 Self-locking nut
14 Housing
15 Bush
16 Mounting screw
17 Coupling
18 Bush
19 Foam plastic washer
20 Clip
21 Shift finger
22 Shift rod

Fig. 6.4 Exploded view of the gearchange mechanism (Sec 5)

6

Fault finding - manual gearbox and final drive

Ineffective synchromesh
☐ Worn synchro rings

Jumps out of gear
☐ Weak or broken detent spring
☐ Worn selector forks
☐ Worn gears and/or synchro sleeves

Noisy operation
☐ Worn bearings
☐ Worn gears

Difficult engagement of gears
☐ Worn selector components
☐ Clutch fault

Notes

Chapter 7 Driveshafts

Contents

Degrees of difficulty

Easy, suitable for novice with little experience	Fairly easy, suitable for beginner with some experience	Fairly difficult, suitable for competent DIY mechanic	Difficult, suitable for experienced DIY mechanic	Very difficult, suitable for expert DIY or professional

Specifications

Type .... Solid (left) and tubular (right) driveshafts with constant velocity joints at each end.

Outer CV joint diameter
All models except Coupé .... 75 mm (2.95 in)
Coupé .... 81 mm (3.19 in)

CV joint lubrication
Grease type .... VW G-6.2 grease

Torque wrench settings

	lbf ft	Nm
Driveshaft to flange	33	45
Driveshaft nut	155	210

1 General description

Drive from the differential unit to the roadwheels is provided by two driveshafts. Each driveshaft has a constant velocity joint (CVJ) at each end, the inner joint being flanged and secured to the final drive flange by bolts, and the outer joint being splined to the hub and secured with a nut.

The left-hand driveshaft is of solid construction and is shorter than the tubular right-hand driveshaft.

2 Driveshaft - removal and refitting

1 Remove the wheel trim from the relevant wheel.
2 With the handbrake applied, loosen the driveshaft nut. The nut is tightened to a high torque and a socket extension may be required.

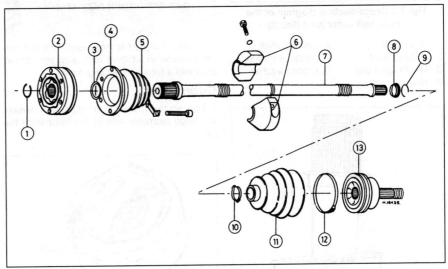

Fig. 7.1 Exploded view of the right-hand side driveshaft (Sec 1)

1 Circlip
2 Inner constant velocity joint
3 Dished washer
4 Protective cap
5 Joint boot
6 Balance weight
7 Shaft
8 Dished washer
9 Circlip
10 Clip
11 Joint boot
12 Hose clip
13 Outer constant velocity joint

2.5 Showing the driveshaft inner joint

2.6 Refitting the driveshaft to the final drive flange

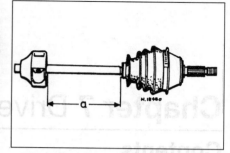

Fig. 7.2 Location of the balance weight on the right-hand side driveshaft (Sec 2)

Dimension a = 151.0 mm (5.95 in)

3 Jack up the front of the car and support it on axle stands. Remove the roadwheel.

4 Using a suitable splined key, unscrew and remove the bolts securing the inner CV joint to the final drive flange. Note the location of either spacer plates. Support the inner end of the driveshaft on an axle stand.

5 Remove the outer nut and washer, then turn the steering on full lock and tap the driveshaft from the splined hub using a soft

head mallet. When removing the right-hand side driveshaft it is advantageous to disconnect the anti-roll bar front mountings and the track control arm from the strut. Do not move the car on its wheels with either driveshaft removed, otherwise damage may occur to the wheel bearings (photo).

6 Refitting is a reversal of removal, but first clean the hub and driveshaft splines and the mating faces of the inner CV joint and final drive flange (photo). Smear· a little molybdenum based grease on the splines. Fit a new outer nut and tighten it to the specified torque with the car lowered to the ground. Tighten the inner bolts to the specified torque. On the right-hand side driveshaft make sure that the balance weight is located with its conical side facing the gearbox and the opposite side in the groove on the driveshaft. Where there is no groove, locate it on the point mark at the dimension shown in Fig. 7.2.

2 Using a soft faced mallet drive the outer joint from the driveshaft.

3 Extract the circlip from the driveshaft and remove the spacer (if fitted) and dished washer noting that the concave side faces the end of the driveshaft.

4 Slide the rubber boot and clips from the driveshaft.

5 Mark the hub in relation to the cage and joint housing.

6 Swivel the hub and cage and remove the balls one at a time.

7 Turn the cage until the rectangular apertures are aligned with the housing then withdraw the cage and hub.

8 Turn the hub and insert one of the segments into one of the rectangular apertures, then swivel the hub from the cage.

9 Note that the joint components including the balls form a matched set and must only be fitted to the correct side.

10 Clean the components in paraffin and examine them for wear and damage. Excessive wear will have been evident when driving the car especially when changing from acceleration to overrun. Renew the components as necessary.

11 Commence reassembly by inserting half the amount of special grease (ie 45g) into the joint housing.

12 Fit the hub to the cage by inserting one of the segments into the rectangular aperture.

13 With the rectangular apertures aligned with the housing, fit the hub and

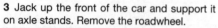

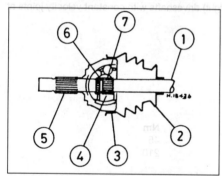

Fig. 7.3 Cross-section diagram of the driveshaft outer joint (Sec 3)

1 Driveshaft
2 Rubber boot
3 Worm drive clip
4 Bearing race
5 Splined shaft
6 Distance washer
7 Dished washer

3 Driveshaft - dismantling and reassembly

If either CV joint is worn excessively it can be renewed in kit form including the rubber boot and a tube of special grease.

Outer joint

1 Loosen the rubber boot clips and release the large diameter end of the boot from the joint.

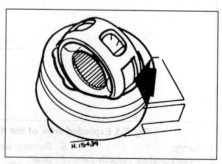

Fig. 7.5 Removing the cage and hub from the outer joint housing (Sec 3)

Arrow shows rectangular aperture

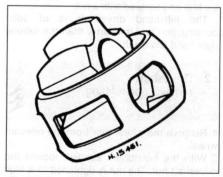

Fig. 7.6 Removing the outer joint hub from the cage (Sec 3)

Fig. 7.4 Showing correct fitting of the dished washer (Sec 3)

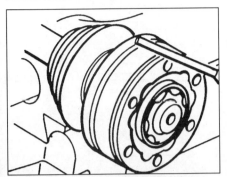

Fig. 7.7 Removing the plastic cap from the inner joint housing (Sec 3)

3.19 The retaining circlip on the driveshaft inner joint

3.25 Removing the joint hub and cage

3.27 Joint hub, cage and housing

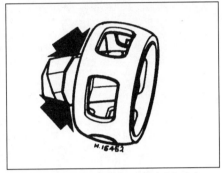

Fig. 7.8 Removing the inner joint hub from the cage (Sec 3)

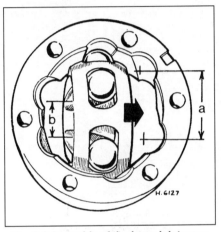

Fig. 7.9 Assembly of the inner joint cage end hub to the housing (Sec 3)

a must be aligned with b

cage to the housing in its original position.
14 Swivel the hub and cage and insert the balls from alternate sides.
15 Fit the rubber boot and clips on the driveshaft.
16 Fit the dished washer and spacer (if applicable) to the driveshaft and insert the circlip in the groove.
17 Locate the outer joint on the driveshaft and using a soft faced mallet, drive it fully into position until the circlip is engaged.
18 Insert the remaining grease in the joint then locate the boot and tighten the clips.

Inner joint

19 Extract the retaining circlip (photo).
20 Using a small drift drive the plastic cap from the joint housing. Loosen the clip and slide the rubber boot away from the joint.
21 Support the joint over the jaws of a vice and using a soft metal drift, drive out the driveshaft.
22 Remove the dished washer from the driveshaft noting that the concave side faces the end of the driveshaft.

23 Slide the rubber boot and clip from the driveshaft.
24 Mark the hub in relation to the cage and joint housing.
25 Turn the hub and cage 90° to the housing and press out the hub and cage (photo).
26 Extract the balls then turn the hub so that one of the track grooves is located on the rim of the cage, and withdraw the hub.
27 Note that the joint components including the balls form a matched set and must only be fitted to the correct side (photo).
28 Clean the components in paraffin and examine them for wear and damage. Excessive wear will have been evident when driving the car especially when changing from acceleration to overrun. Renew the components as necessary.
29 Commence reassembly by fitting the hub to the cage.
30 Insert the balls into position using the special grease to hold them in place.
31 Press the hub and cage into the housing making sure that the wide track spacing on the housing will be adjacent to the narrow

spacing on the hub (see Fig. 7.9) when fully assembled. Note also that the chamfer on the hub splines must face the large diameter side of the housing.
32 Swivel the cage ahead of the hub so that the balls enter their respective tracks then align the hub and cage with the housing.
33 Check that the hub can be moved freely through its operating arc.
34 Fit the rubber boot and clip to the driveshaft followed by the dished washer.
35 Mount the driveshaft in a vice then drive the joint onto the driveshaft using a suitable metal tube on the hub.
36 Fit the returning circlip in its groove.
37 Insert the remaining grease in the joint then tap the plastic cap into position.
38 With the rubber boot correctly located, tighten the clip.

Fault finding - driveshafts

Vibrations and noise on turns
☐ Worn driveshaft joints

Noise on taking up drive
☐ Worn driveshaft joints
☐ Worn drive flange and/or driveshaft splines
☐ Loose driveshaft bolts or nut

Notes

Chapter 8 Braking system

For modifications, and information applicable to later models, see Supplement at end of manual

Contents

Degrees of difficulty

Easy, suitable for novice with little experience 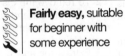	**Fairly easy,** suitable for beginner with some experience	**Fairly difficult,** suitable for competent DIY mechanic	**Difficult,** suitable for experienced DIY mechanic	**Very difficult,** suitable for expert DIY or professional

Specifications

System type . . . . Hydraulic, dual circuit split diagonally, with discs front and self-adjusting drums on rear, pressure regulator on rear brakes on some models. Cable operated handbrake on rear wheels

Front brakes
Disc thickness (new) . . . . 10.0 mm (0.394 in)
Disc thickness (minimum) 8.0mm (0.315in)
Maximum disc run-out . . . . 0.06 mm (0.002 in)
Disc pad thickness - new (including backplate) . . . . 15.0 mm (0.591 in)
Disc pad thickness - minimum (including backplate) . . . . 7.0 mm (0.28 in)

Rear brakes
Drum internal diameter (new) . . . . 180.0 mm (7.087 in)
Drum internal diameter (maximum) . . . . 181.0 mm (7.126 in)
Maximum drum run-out:
   Radial (at friction surface) . . . . 0.05 mm (0.002 in)
   Lateral (wheel contact surface) . . . . 0.2 mm (0.008 in)
Lining thickness:
   Minimum (including shoe) . . . . 5.00 mm (0.20 in)
   Minimum (excluding shoe) . . . . 2.5 mm (0.10 in)

General
Master cylinder type . . . . ATE (Teves) or FAG (Shafer)

Pressure regulator test pressures:

	Front	Rear
1st test	50 bar (725 lbf/in²)	27 to 31 bar (392 to 450 lbf/in²)
2nd test	100 bar (1450 lbf/in²)	59 to 54 bar (725 to 783 lbf/in²)

Brake fluid type/specification . . . . Hydraulic fluid to FMVSS 116 DOT 4

Torque wrench settings

	lbf ft	Nm
Caliper to wheel bearing housing	52	70
Splash plate to strut	7	10
Wheel bolts	81	110
Backplate to rear axle	44	60

8

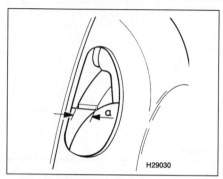

Fig. 8.1 Checking the disc pad wear through the front wheel (Sec 3)

a = 7 mm (0.28 in) minimum

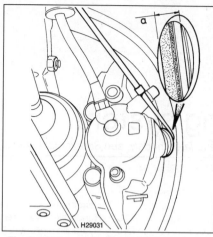

Fig. 8.2 Using a mirror to check the inner disc pad wear (Sec 3)

a = 7 mm (0.28 in) minimum

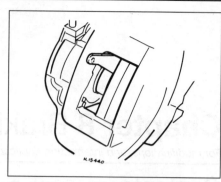

Fig. 8.3 Using a 20° angle gauge to set the caliper piston (Sec 3)

1 General description

The braking system is of hydraulic, dual circuit type with discs at the front and self-adjusting drum brakes at the rear. The hydraulic circuit is split diagonally so that with the failure of one circuit, one front and rear brake remain operative. A load sensitive pressure regulator is incorporated in the rear hydraulic circuits on some models to prevent the rear wheels locking in advance of the front wheels during heavy application of the brakes. The regulator proportions the hydraulic pressure between the front and rear brakes according to the load being carried

The handbrake operates on the rear wheels only and the lever incorporates a switch which illuminates a warning light on the instrument panel when the handbrake is applied. The same warning light is wired into the low hydraulic fluid switch circuit.

2 Routine maintenance

1 Every 10000 miles (15 000 km) the front disc pad linings and rear brake shoe linings should be checked for wear and renewed if necessary. At the same time check that the

hydraulic fluid in the master cylinder reservoir is between the minimum and maximum level marks. The reservoir is translucent and the check can be made without removing the filler cap. Note that the level will drop slightly as the front disc pad linings wear and it is not necessary to top up the level in this case. However if the level drops significantly the hydraulic circuit should be checked for leakage.

2 Every two years the hydraulic fluid must be renewed. At the same time check the operation of the low level warning switch as follows. Switch on the ignition and release the handbrake lever, then depress the float pin on the top of the fluid reservoir and check that the warning lamps light up on the instrument panel. Also at the same time check the condition of the hydraulic lines and hoses.

3 Disc pads -
inspection and renewal

1 The disc pad lining wear can be checked by viewing through a hole in the wheel rim and by using a mirror on the inside of the wheel. The use of a torch may also be necessary. if the

thickness of any disc pad is less than the minimum amount given in the Specification, renew the front pads as a set. Where the thickness is more than the minimum amount, 1mm (0.04in) of lining will last for approximately 1000 km (600 miles) under severe conditions and therefore due consideration must be made as to whether there is sufficient lining left before the next service.

2 To remove the disc pads first jack up the front of the car and support it on axle stands. Apply the handbrake and remove both front wheels.

3 Extract the spring clip from the inner ends of the retaining pins (photo).

4 Using a small punch drive out the retaining pins and remove the spreader spring (photos).

5 Using a pair of pliers, press each pad outwards from the brake disc in order to push the piston into the caliper and allow the pads to be removed .

6 Pull the inner pad from the caliper (photo). Mark it if it is to be refitted.

7 Press the caliper frame outwards to disengage the frame projection from the recess in the pad backing plate, then remove the outer pad (photos).

8 Brush the dust and dirt from the caliper, piston, disc and pads, *but do not inhale it as it is injurious to health.* Scrape any scale or rust from the disc and pad backing plates.

9 Using a piece of wood push the piston back into the caliper, but while doing this check the level of the fluid in the reservoir and if

3.3 Removing the disc pad retaining pin spring clip

3.4A Removing the retaining pins . . .

3.4B . . . and spreader spring

3.6 Removing the inner disc pad

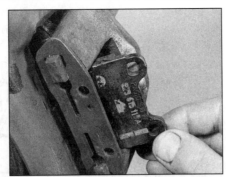

3.7A Removing the outer disc pad

3.7B Showing outer (left) and inner (right) disc pads

3.7C Showing frame projection for engagement with the outer disc pad

3.14 Correct installation of the disc pads

necessary draw off some with a pipette or release some from the caliper bleed screw. Tighten the screw immediately afterwards.

10 Check that the angle of the raised face of the piston is 20° to the upper inner face of the caliper. Make a gauge out of cardboard and if necessary turn the piston to its correct position.

11 Smear a little brake grease on the metal-to-metal contact surfaces of each pad backing plate.

12 Pull the caliper frame outwards, insert the outer pad and then press in the frame so that the projection engages the pad recess. Fit the inner pad.

13 Position the spreader spring on the pads then insert the retaining pins through the caliper and pad backing plates and tap them fully home.

14 Fit the spring clip to the inner ends of the retaining pins, turning the pins as necessary with a pair of pliers to align the holes (photo).

15 Repeat the procedure given in paragraphs 3 to 14 on the remaining front brake, then refit the wheels and lower the car to the ground.

16 Depress the footbrake pedal several times to set the pads, then check and if necessary top-up the level of fluid in the master cylinder reservoir.

4 Rear brake shoes - inspection and renewal

1 Jack up the rear of the car and support it on axle stands. Check the front wheels.

2 Working beneath the car remove the rubber plugs from the front of the backplates and check that the linings are not worn below the minimum thickness given in the Specifications. If necessary use a torch. Refit the plugs.

3 To remove the rear brake shoes, first remove the wheels.

4 Prise off the hub cap then extract the split pin and remove the locking ring.

5 Unscrew the hub nut and remove the thrust washer and outer wheel bearing.

6 Withdraw the brake drum. If difficulty is experienced, the brake shoes must be backed away from the drum first. To do this, insert a screwdriver through one of the bolt holes and push the automatic adjuster wedge upwards against the spring tension. This will release the shoes from the drum.

7 Brush the dust from the brake drum, brake shoes and backplate, but do not inhale it as it is injurious to health. Scrape any scale or rust from the drum. Note that the rear brake shoes should be renewed as a set of four.

8 Using a pair of pliers depress the steady spring cups, turn them through 90° and remove the cups, springs and pins (photo).

9 Note the location of the return springs and strut on the brake shoes, then lever the shoes from the bottom anchor. Unhook and remove the bottom return spring (photos).

10 Disengage the handbrake cable from the lever on the trailing brake shoe.

11 Release the brake shoes from the wheel

8

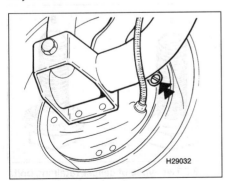

Fig. 8.4 Rear brake shoe lining inspection plug location (arrowed) (Sec 4)

4.8 Location of the rear brake shoe steady springs

4.9A Correct location of the rear brake components

4.9B Rear brake shoe bottom anchor

4.11 Showing the rear wheel cylinder and brake shoes

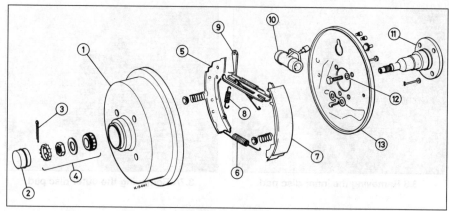

Fig. 8.5 Exploded view of the rear brake shoes and drum (Sec 4)

1 Brake drum	5 Upper return spring
2 Hub cap	assembly
3 Split pin	6 Lower return assembly
4 Bearing assembly	7 Brake shoe
	8 Spring for wedge

9 Wedge
10 Wheel (slave) cylinder
11 Stub axle
12 Lock washer
13 Backplate

cylinder, unhook the wedge spring and upper return spring and withdraw the shoes (photo).
12 Grip the strut in a vice and release the shoe, then remove the wedge and spring. The backplate and stub axle may be removed if necessary by unscrewing the four bolts after removing the wheel cylinder (Section 7). Note the location of the handbrake cable bracket. If the wheel cylinder is being left in position, retain the pistons with an elastic band, Check that there are no signs of fluid leakage and if

necessary repair or renew the wheel cylinder as described in Section 7.
13 Fit the new brake shoes using a reversal of the removal procedure, but note that the lug on the wedge faces the backplate. Check the brake drum for wear and damage as described in Section 8. Adjust the wheel bearings as described in Chapter 10. Finally, fully depress the brake pedal several times in order to set the shoes in their correct position.

5 Disc caliper - removal, inspection and refitting

1 Remove the disc pads as described in Section 3.

2 If available fit a hose clamp to the caliper flexible brake hose. Alternatively remove the fluid reservoir filler cap and tighten it down onto a piece of polythene sheet in order to reduce the loss of hydraulic fluid.
3 Loosen the brake hose union at the caliper.
4 Unscrew the two bolts securing the caliper to the wheel bearing housing, then unscrew the caliper from the hose.
5 Clean the external surfaces of the caliper with paraffin and wipe dry - plug the fluid inlet during this operation.
6 Remove the retaining spring then press the mounting frame from the cylinder and withdraw it from the floating frame.
7 Grip the floating frame in a vice, and using a soft metal drift, drive the cylinder from the frame.
8 Using air pressure from a foot pump in the fluid inlet, blow the piston from the cylinder, but take care not to drop the piston.
9 Prise the sealing ring from the cylinder bore and remove the piston dust cap and circlip.
10 Clean the components with methylated spirit and allow to dry. Inspect the surfaces of the piston, cylinder and frames for wear, damage and corrosion. If evident renew the

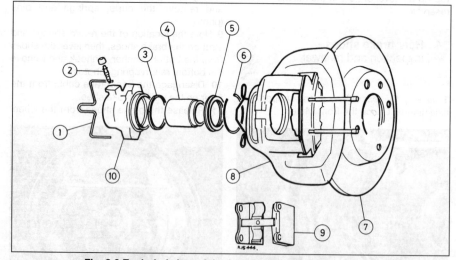

Fig. 8.6 Exploded view of the front brake disc caliper (Sec 5)

1 Locating spring	5 Dust cap	8 Caliper
2 Bleeder screw	6 Circlip	9 Brake pads
3 Sealing O-ring	7 Brake disc	10 Cylinder
4 Piston		

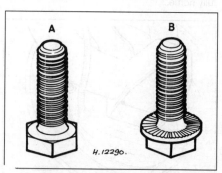

8.7 Two types of caliper retaining bolts (Sec 5)

a Early type   b Later ribbed type

Fig. 8.8 Showing chamfer modification required when fitting ribbed type bolts to early calipers (Sec 5)

caliper, but if the components are in good condition obtain a repair kit of seals.

11 Dip the new sealing ring in brake fluid and locate it in the cylinder bore groove using the fingers only to manipulate it.

12 Smear the piston with brake fluid, and press it into the cylinder then fit the dust cap and circlip.

13 Locate the cylinder in the floating frame and drive it fully home using a soft metal drift.

14 Fit the retaining spring then locate the mounting frame in the floating frame and press it onto the cylinder.

15 Refer to Section 3 and turn the piston so that its raised face is 20° to the upper inner face of the caliper.

16 Screw the caliper onto the brake hose so that when the caliper is in its fitted position the line on the hose is not twisted.

17 Fit the caliper to the wheel bearing housing then insert and tighten the bolts to the specified torque. Note that early models were fitted with standard bolts, however locking bolts incorporating ribbed shoulders were introduced on later models. If the ribbed type bolts are fitted to early models a 1 mm (0.04in) wide 45° chamfer must be made in the mounting frame holes (Fig. 8.8).

6.6 Brake disc retaining screw

18 Tighten the brake hose union.

19 Remove the hose clamp or polythene sheet.

20 Refit the disc pads as described in Section 3.

21 Top up the brake fluid reservoir and bleed the brakes as described in Section 12.

6 Brake disc - examination, removal and refitting

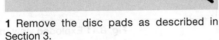

1 Remove the disc pads as described in Section 3.

2 Rotate the disc and examine it for deep scoring or grooving.

3 Using a dial gauge or metal block and feeler gauges, check that the disc run-out measured on the friction surface does not exceed the maximum amount given in the Specifications.

4 Using a micrometer check that the disc thickness is not less than the minimum amount given in the Specifications.

5 To remove the brake disc, remove the caliper as described in Section 5, but do not disconnect or loosen the brake hose. Locate the caliper on a stand to prevent straining the hose.

6 Remove the cross-head screw and withdraw the brake disc from the hub (photo).

7 If necessary the splash plate can be removed from the wheel bearing housing by unscrewing the three bolts.

8 Refitting is a reversal of removal, but make sure that the mating faces of the disc and hub are clean. Refer to Section 5 when refitting the caliper, and Section 3 when refitting the disc pads.

7 Rear wheel cylinder - removal, overhaul and refitting

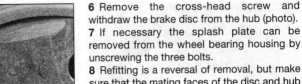

1 Remove the rear brake shoes as described in Section 4.

2 If available fit a hose clamp to the flexible brake hose. Alternatively remove the fluid reservoir filler cap and tighten it down onto a piece of polythene sheet in order to reduce the loss of hydraulic fluid.

3 Unscrew the hydraulic pipe union from the rear of the cylinder, and plug the end of the pipe (photo).

4 Remove the two screws and withdraw the wheel cylinder from the backplate.

5 Prise off the dust caps then remove the pistons keeping them identified for location. If necessary use air pressure from a foot pump in the fluid inlet.

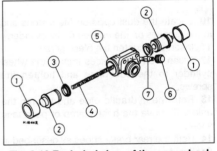

Fig. 8.10 Exploded view of the rear wheel cylinder (Sec 7)

1	Boot	5	Brake cylinder
2	Piston		housing
3	Cap	6	Dust cap
4	Spring	7	Bleed screw

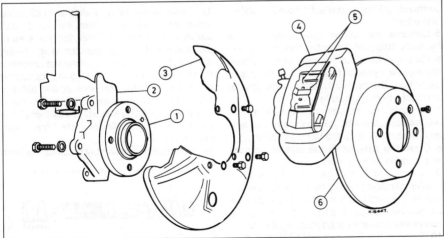

Fig. 8.9 Disc brake components (Sec 6)

1	Wheel hub	3	Splash plate	5	Brake pads
2	Wheel bearing housing	4	Brake caliper	6	Brake disc

7.3 Rear view of a rear wheel cylinder on the backplate

8

9.2 Brake master cylinder showing stop light and fluid level switch wiring

6 Remove the internal spring, and if necessary unscrew the bleed screw.

7 Clean all the components in methylated spirit and allow to dry. Examine the surfaces of the piston and cylinder bore for wear, scoring and corrosion. If evident, renew the complete wheel cylinder. If the components are in good condition, discard the seals and obtain a repair kit.

8 Dip the inner seals in clean brake fluid and fit them to the grooves on the pistons using the fingers only to manipulate them. Make sure that the larger diameter ends face the inner ends of the pistons.

9 Smear brake fluid on the pistons then insert the spring and press the pistons into the cylinder taking care not to damage the seal lips.

10 Locate the dust caps on the pistons and in the grooves on the outside of the cylinder.

11 Insert and tighten the bleed screw.

12 Clean the mating faces then fit the wheel cylinder to the backplate and tighten the screws.

13 Refit the hydraulic pipe and tighten the union. Remove the hose clamp or polythene sheet.

14 Refit the rear brake shoes as described in Section 4.

15 Top up the brake fluid reservoir and bleed the brakes as described in Section 12.

8 Brake drum - examination and renovation

1 Whenever the brake drums are removed, they should be checked for wear and damage. Light scoring of the friction surface is normal, but if excessive the drums must either be renewed as a pair or reground, provided that the maximum internal diameter given in the Specifications is not exceeded.

2 After a high mileage the drums may become warped and oval. The run-out can be checked with a dual gauge and if in excess of the maximum amounts given in the Specifications, the drums should be renewed as a pair.

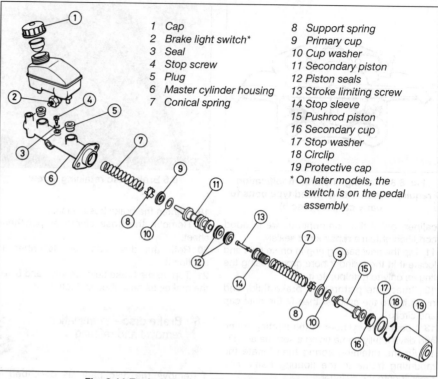

1	Cap
2	Brake light switch*
3	Seal
4	Stop screw
5	Plug
6	Master cylinder housing
7	Conical spring
8	Support spring
9	Primary cup
10	Cup washer
11	Secondary piston
12	Piston seals
13	Stroke limiting screw
14	Stop sleeve
15	Pushrod piston
16	Secondary cup
17	Stop washer
18	Circlip
19	Protective cap
*	On later models, the switch is on the pedal assembly

Fig. 8.11 Exploded view of the master cylinder (Sec 9)

9 Master cylinder - removal, overhaul and refitting

1 Disconnect the battery negative lead.

2 If fitted, disconnect the wiring from the stop-light and fluid level switches on the master cylinder and fluid reservoir filler cap (photo).

3 Remove the air cleaner as described in Chapter 3.

4 Place a suitable container beneath the master cylinder and place some cloth on the surrounding body to protect it from any spilled brake fluid.

5 Unscrew the unions and disconnect the hydraulic fluid pipes from the master cylinder.

6 Unscrew the mounting nuts and withdraw the master cylinder from the bulkhead and away from the pushrod. Remove the spacer and seal where applicable.

7 Remove the master cylinder from the engine compartment taking care not to spill any hydraulic fluid on the body paintwork.

8 Clean the exterior of the master cylinder with paraffin and wipe dry.

9 Note that it is only possible to overhaul master cylinders fitted to early models. On late models the circlip in the mouth of the cylinder cannot be removed and in this case the complete cylinder must be renewed if faulty.

10 Remove the filler cap and filter, and drain the fluid from the reservoir.

11 Unscrew and remove the stop light switch.

12 Pull the reservoir out of the rubber grommets, then prise the grommets from the cylinder.

13 Unscrew the stop screw and remove the washer from the top of the cylinder.

14 Remove the rubber boot from the end of the cylinder.

15 Push the primary piston in slightly, then extract the circlip from the mouth of the cylinder.

16 Extract all the components from the cylinder keeping them in their order of removal. If necessary tap the cylinder on a block of wood to remove the secondary piston.

17 Clean all the components in methylated spirit and examine them for wear and damage. In particular check the surfaces of the piston and cylinder bore for wear, scoring and corrosion. If evident, renew the complete master cylinder, but if in good condition discard all the inner components and obtain a repair kit which includes all the components and a special fitting sleeve. Check that all the parts in the cylinder are free and unobstructed.

18 Commence reassembly by smearing fresh

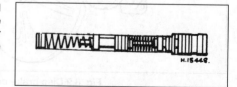

Fig. 8.12 Master cylinder repair kit in special fitting sleeve (Sec 9)

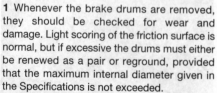

brake fluid on the cylinder bore then grip the cylinder in a vice.

19 Insert the fitting sleeve in the cylinder, then using a screwdriver, push the entire contents in the cylinder.

20 With the primary piston depressed, insert the stop screw together with a new washer and tighten it. Remove the fitting sleeve.

21 Fit the stop washer and circlip in the mouth of the cylinder then fit the rubber boot.

22 Dip the rubber grommets in brake fluid and press them into the cylinder, then press the reservoir into the grommets.

23 Insert and tighten the stop-light switch.

24 Fit the filter and filler cap.

25 Refitting is a reversal of the removal procedure, but fit a new mounting seal where applicable. Bleed the hydraulic system as described in Section 12.

10 Brake pressure regulator - general

1 A brake pressure regulator is fitted in the rear brake circuit of some models and its purpose is to prevent the rear wheels locking in advance of the first wheels during heavy application of the brakes. The regulator is also load sensitive in order to vary the pressure according to the load being carried.

2 The regulator is located on the under-body, in front of the left-hand rear wheel.

3 Checking of the regulator is best left to a VW garage as special pressure gauges and spring tensioning tools are required. Adjustment is made by varying the spring tension, but this must be carried out by the garage.

4 Removal and refitting are straight forward but after fitting, bleed the hydraulic system as described in Section 12, and have the regulator adjusted by a garage.

11 Hydraulic pipes and hoses - inspection and renewal

1 At the intervals given in Section 2 clean the rigid brake lines and flexible hoses and check

Fig. 8.13 Brake pressure regulator location (Sec 10)

them for damage, leakage, chafing and cracks. If the coating on the rigid pipes is damaged or if rusting is apparent they must be renewed. Check the retaining clips for security, and clean away any accumulations of dirt and debris.

2 To remove a rigid brake pipe, unscrew the union nuts at each end and where necessary remove the line from the clips. Refitting is a reversal of removal.

3 To remove a flexible brake hose, unscrew the union nut securing the rigid brake pipe to the end of the flexible hose and remove the spring clip and hose end fitting from the bracket (photo). Unscrew the remaining end from the component on rigid pipe according to position. Refitting is a reversal of removal.

4 Bleed the complete hydraulic system as described in Section 12 after fitting a rigid brake pipe or flexible brake hose.

12 Hydraulic system - bleeding

1 If any of the hydraulic components in the braking system have been removed or disconnected, or if the fluid level in the master cylinder has been allowed to fall appreciably, it is inevitable that air will have been introduced into the system. The removal of all this air from the hydraulic system is essential if the brakes are to function correctly, and the process of removing it is known as bleeding.

2 There are a number of one-man, do-it-yourself, brake bleeding kits currently available from motor accessory shops. It is recommended that one of these kits should be used wherever possible as they greatly simplify the bleeding operation and also reduce the risk of expelled air and fluid being drawn back into the system.

3 If one of these kits is not available then it will be necessary to gather together a clean jar and a suitable length of clear plastic tubing which is a tight fit over the bleed screw, and also to engage the help of an assistant.

4 Before commencing the bleeding operation, check that all rigid pipes and flexible hoses are in good condition and that all hydraulic unions are tight. Take great care

11.3 Brake hydraulic line connection

not to allow hydraulic fluid to come into contact with the vehicle paintwork, otherwise the finish will be seriously damaged. Wash off any spilled fluid immediately with cold water.

5 If hydraulic fluid has been lost from the master cylinder, due to a leak in the system, ensure that the cause is traced and rectified before proceeding further or a serious malfunction of the braking system may occur.

6 To bleed the system, clean the area around the bleed screw at the wheel cylinder to be bled. If the hydraulic system has only been partially disconnected and suitable precautions were taken to prevent further loss of fluid, it should only be necessary to bleed that part of the system. However, if the entire system is to be bled, start at the wheel furthest away from the master cylinder (ie right-hand rear wheel). *LEFT! See 10*

7 Remove the master cylinder filler cap and top up the reservoir. Periodically check the fluid level during the bleeding operation and top up as necessary.

8 If a one-man brake bleeding kit is being used, connect the outlet tube to the bleed screw and then open the screw half a turn. If possible position the unit so that it can be viewed from the car, then depress the brake pedal to the floor and slowly release it. The one-way valve in the kit will prevent dispelled air from returning to the system at the end of each stroke. Repeat this operation until clean hydraulic fluid, free from air bubbles, can be seen coming through the tube. Now tighten the bleed screw and remove the outlet tube.

9 If a one-man brake bleeding kit is not available, connect one end of the plastic tubing to the bleed screw and immerse the other end in the jar containing sufficient clean hydraulic fluid to keep the end of the tube submerged. Open the bleed screw half a turn and have your assistant depress the brake pedal to the floor and then slowly release it. Tighten the bleed screw at the end of each downstroke to prevent expelled air and fluid from being drawn back into the system. Repeat this operation until clean hydraulic fluid, free from air bubbles, can be seen coming through the tube. Now tighten the bleed screw and remove the plastic tube.

10 If the entire system is being bled, the procedures described above should now be repeated at each wheel, finishing at the wheel nearest to the master cylinder. The correct sequence is as follows:

Left-hand rear wheel ✓
Right-hand rear wheel
Left-hand front wheel
Right-hand front wheel

Do not forget to recheck the fluid level in the master cylinder at regular intervals and top up as necessary.

11 When completed, recheck the fluid level in the master cylinder, top up if necessary and refit the cap. Check the 'feel' of the brake pedal which should be firm and free from any 'sponginess' which would indicate air still present in the system.

8

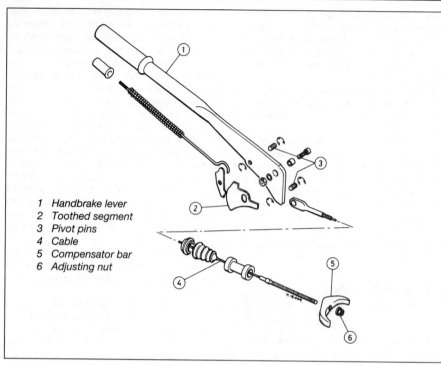

1 Handbrake lever
2 Toothed segment
3 Pivot pins
4 Cable
5 Compensator bar
6 Adjusting nut

Fig. 8.14 Exploded view of the handbrake lever (Sec 13)

12 Discard any expelled hydraulic fluid as it is likely to be contaminated with moisture, air and dirt which makes it unsuitable for further use.

10 Fully release the lever and check that both rear wheels rotate freely, then fully apply the lever and check that both rear wheels are locked.

11 Lower the car to the ground.

13 Handbrake lever - removal, refitting and adjustment

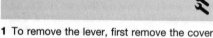

1 To remove the lever, first remove the cover if fitted and fully release the lever.

2 Extract one circlip from the cable pivot and push the pivot from the handbrake lever to release the cable.

3 Unscrew and remove the pivot bolt and withdraw the handbrake lever from the bracket.

4 If required remove the screw from the lever switch, disconnect the wiring, and remove the switch.

5 Extract the circlip and remove the pawl pivot, then remove the pawl and rod together with the spring and button.

6 Refitting is a reversal of removal, but smear a little molybdenum disulphide based grease on the pivoting surfaces. Finally adjust the handbrake as follows.

7 Chock the front wheels then jack up the rear of the car and support it on axle stands.

8 Fully release the handbrake then depress the brake pedal firmly once. Now pull the lever up to the second notch.

9 Check that it is just possible to turn each rear wheel by hand. If necessary adjust the handbrake by turning the nut on the rear of the compensator bar beneath the car.

14.4 Showing the handbrake cable compensator

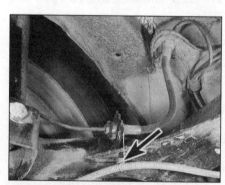

14.9 Mounting spring location for the left-hand side handbrake cable

14 Handbrake cables - removal and refitting

1 Chock the front wheels then jack up the rear of the car and support it on axle stands. Release the handbrake.

Front cable

2 If fitted, remove the cover from the lever.

3 Extract the circlip from the cable pivot and push the pivot from the lever.

4 Working beneath the car, unscrew and remove the adjusting nut from the rear of the compensator bar (photo). Remove the cable from the bar.

5 Release the rubber boot and withdraw the cable from under the car after removing the guides (photo).

6 Refitting is a reversal of removal, but adjust the handbrake as described in Section 13.

Rear cable

7 Remove the rear brake shoes as described in Section 4.

8 Working beneath the car, unscrew the adjusting nut from the rear of the compensator bar sufficient to detach the cable.

9 Remove the cross-head screw to release the right-hand side cable clip, and remove the tension spring from the left-hand side cable (photo).

10 Disconnect the cables from the brackets and pull them out from the backplates (photo).

14.5 Front handbrake cable and guide

14.10 Handbrake cable and bracket

11 Unscrew the nut and remove the cable guide wheel and plate.

12 Refitting is a reversal of removal, but lubricate the guide wheel with a little grease and adjust the handbrake as described in Section 13.

15 Footbrake pedal - removal and refitting

1 Working inside the car, remove the lower trim panel from around the steering column.

2 Prise the clip from the end of the pedal pivot shaft.

3 Unhook the return spring from the pedal.

4 Withdraw the pivot shaft sufficient to remove the pedal, at the same time pull the pushrod from the master cylinder.

5 Extract the clip, remove the pivot, and detach the pushrod from the pedal.

6 If necessary the pedal bracket can be removed after removing the clutch pedal and mounting nuts and bolts, the two nuts being the master cylinder mounting nuts.

7 Clean the pedal and pivot shaft and examine them for wear. If the bushes are worn, they can be removed using a soft metal drift, and the new bushes installed using a vice to press them into position. Check the rubber foot pad and the stop rubber on the bracket, and renew them if necessary.

8 Refitting is a reversal of removal, but apply a little multi-purpose grease to the pivot shaft and bushes. If the clutch pedal was removed, adjust the cable as described in Chapter 5. To adjust the footbrake pedal, fully depress and release the pedal, then check that there is between 2 and 4 mm (0.08 and 0.16in) free play measured at the foot pad. If necessary loosen the locknut and turn the master cylinder pushrod as required. Tighten the locknut after making the adjustment.

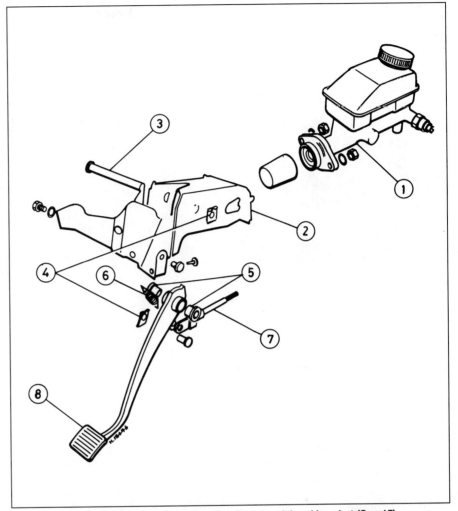

Fig. 8.15 Exploded view of the footbrake pedal and bracket (Sec 15)

1 Brake master cylinder assembly
2 Bracket
3 Pivot pin
4 Clip
5 Bush
6 Return spring
7 Adjusting pushrod
8 Brake pedal

Fault finding - braking system

Excessive pedal travel
- [ ] Brake fluid leak
- [ ] Air in hydraulic system
- [ ] Worn rear brake shoes

Brake judder
- [ ] Worn drums and/or discs
- [ ] Loose suspension anchor point
- [ ] Loose rear brake backplate

Brake pedal feels spongy
- [ ] Air in hydraulic system
- [ ] Faulty master cylinder seals

Uneven braking and pulling to one side
- [ ] Contaminated linings
- [ ] Seized wheel cylinder or caliper
- [ ] Incorrect and unequal tyre pressures
- [ ] Loose suspension anchor point
- [ ] Different lining material at each wheel

Excessive effort to stop car
- [ ] Seized wheel cylinders or calipers
- [ ] Incorrect lining material
- [ ] Contaminated linings
- [ ] New linings not yet bedded-in
- [ ] Excessively worn linings

8

Notes

Genuine new VW CigaretteLighter
fitted 4/4/02.
Fuse is 8A blade fuse in in-Line holder,
accessible by removing glove box.

Chapter 9 Electrical system

For modifications, and information applicable to later models, see Supplement at end of manual

Contents

Degrees of difficulty

Easy, suitable for novice with little experience	**Fairly easy**, suitable for beginner with some experience	**Fairly difficult**, suitable for competent DIY mechanic	**Difficult**, suitable for experienced DIY mechanic	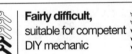 **Very difficult**, suitable for expert DIY or professional

Specifications

System type . . . . 12 volt, negative earth

Windscreen wiper blades . . . . Champion C41-01

Battery
Capacity . . . . 36 amp hr or 45 amp hr
Minimum voltage (under load) . . . . 9.6 volts at 110 amps

Alternator
Type . . . . Bosch or Motorola
Output at 3000 rpm (engine speed) . . . . 30 amps (45 amp model) 45 amps (65 amp model)
Regulator voltage . . . . 12.5 to 14.5 volts
Minimum brush length . . . . 5.0 mm (0.2 in)
Rotor winding resistance:
   45 amp . . . . 3.4 to 3.7 ohm
   65 amp . . . . 2.8 to 3.0 ohm

Starter motor
Minimum brush length 13.0mm (0.5in)
Commutator minimum diameter . . . . 33.5 mm (1.319 in)
Shaft endplay . . . . 0.05 to 0.30mm (0.002 to 0.012 in)
Commutator run-out . . . . 0.03 mm (0.001 in)

Fuses

Number	Component	Rating (amps)
1	Foglights	8
2	Rear foglight	8
3	Left side light and tail light, instrument panel lights	8
4	Right side light and tail light, number plate light, headlight washer	8
5	Left main beam	8
6	Right main beam, main beam warning light	8
7	Left dipped beam	8
8	Right dipped beam	8
9	Horn, idle cut-off solenoid, reversing light	8
10	Direction indicators	8
11	Interior light, ~~cigarette lighter~~, radio, clock	8
12	Hazard warning lights, stop-lights	8
13	Radiator cooling fan	16
14	Rear wiper, heater blower	16
15	Windscreen wipers, intermittent wiper unit	8
16	Heated rear window	16

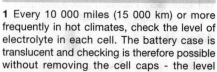

See note on previous page re cigarette lighter fuse

Bulbs

	Wattage
Headlamp:	
Standard	45/40
Halogen	60/55
Sidelamp	4
Tail lamp	10
Stop-light	21
Direction indicators	21
Foglamp	21
Reversing light	21
Stop/tail light (Classic)	21/5
Boot light (Classic)	5
Interior light	5
Number plate light	4

Torque wrench settings

	lbf ft	Nm
Starter	18	25
Wiper arm	3 to 4	4 to 6
Alternator bracket:		
Engine	33	45
Alternator	22	30

1 General description

The electrical system is of 12 volt negative earth type. The battery is charged by a belt-driven alternator which incorporates a voltage regulator. The starter motor is of pre-engaged

2.1 The battery is located on the bulkhead

type incorporating a solenoid which moves the drive pinion into engagement with the flywheel ring gear before the motor is energised.

Although repair procedures are given in this Chapter, it may well be more economical to renew worn components as complete units.

2 Battery - removal and refitting

1 The battery is located under the bonnet on the right-hand side of the bulkhead (photo).
2 Loosen the battery terminal clamp nuts and disconnect the negative lead followed by the positive lead.
3 Unscrew the bolt and remove the battery retaining clamp.
4 Lift the battery from its platform taking care not to spill any electrolyte on the bodywork.
5 Refitting is a reversal of removal, but make sure that the leads are fitted to their correct terminals, and do not overtighten the lead

clamp nuts or the battery retaining clamp bolt. Finally smear a little petroleum jelly on the terminals and clamps.

3 Battery - maintenance

1 Every 10 000 miles (15 000 km) or more frequently in hot climates, check the level of electrolyte in each cell. The battery case is translucent and checking is therefore possible without removing the cell caps - the level should be between the minimum and maximum lines.
2 If topping up is necessary the caps can be removed by piercing the notch with a screwdriver then turning the cap (with screwdriver still inserted) to the stop. The caps can then be unscrewed. Add distilled or deionized water to each cell as necessary then refit the caps.
3 At the same time wipe clean the battery case with a dry cloth. If there is any sign of

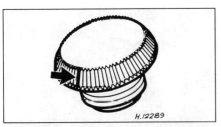

Fig. 9.1 Pierce the battery cap notch with a screwdriver when removing the caps (Sec 3)

corrosion on the terminals or lead clamps, disconnect the leads and clean them. Then refit them and smear the outer surfaces with petroleum jelly.

4 Similarly check the battery platform for corrosion and if necessary clean the deposits away. Then treat the affected metal with a proprietary antirust liquid and paint with the original colour.

5 If topping up the battery becomes excessive, check the casing for cracking. If evident it may be possible to repair it with a proprietary compound. Overcharging can also result in excessive topping up and in this case the voltage regulator should be checked.

6 If the battery condition is suspect, the specific gravity of the electrolyte in each cell should be checked using a hydrometer and compared with the following table:

	Ambient temperature above 25°C (77°F)	Ambient temperature below 25°C (77°F)
Fully charged	1.210 to 1.230	1.270 to 1.290
70% charged	1.170 to 1.190	1.230 to 1.250
Fully discharged	1.050 to 1.070	1.110 to 1.130

Note that the readings assume an electrolyte temperature of 15°C (60°F); for every 10°C (18°F) below 15°C (60°F) subtract 0.007, or above, add 0.007.

7 A variation of 0.040 or more between any cells indicates loss of electrolyte or deterioration of the internal plates.

8 A further test can be made using a battery heavy discharge meter. The battery should be discharged for a maximum of 15 seconds at a load of three times the ampere-hour capacity.

7.1 Checking the alternator drivebelt tension

Alternatively, connect a voltmeter across the battery terminals, and spin the engine on the starter with the coil low tension negative lead disconnected and the headlamps, heated rear window and heater blower switched on.

9 If the voltmeter reading remains above 9.6 volts, the battery condition is satisfactory. If the voltmeter reading drops below 9.6 volts and the battery has already been charged as described in Section 5, it is faulty and should be renewed.

4 Battery - electrolyte replenishment

1 If after fully charging the battery, one of the cells maintains a specific gravity which is 0.040 or more lower than the others, but the battery also maintains 9.6 volts during the heavy discharge test (Section 3), it is likely that electrolyte has been lost. In this case it will not suffice merely to refill with distilled water. Top up the cell with a mixture of 2 parts sulphuric acid to 5 parts distilled water.

2 When mixing the electrolyte, **never** add water to sulphuric acid, always pour the acid slowly onto the water in a glass container. If water is added to sulphuric acid, it will explode.

3 After topping up the cell with fresh electrolyte, recharge the battery and check the hydrometer readings again.

5 Battery - charging

1 In winter when a heavy demand is placed on the battery, such as when starting from cold and using more electrical equipment, the battery may occasionally require charging from an external source at a rate of 3 to 5 amps. Note that both battery terminal leads must be disconnected before charging and also the cell caps removed.

2 Continue to charge the battery until no further rise in specific gravity is noted over a three hour period.

3 Alternatively a trickle charger, charging at a rate of 1.5 amps, can be safely used overnight.

7.2 Loosening the adjusting link nut to adjust the alternator drivebelt tension

4 Special rapid boost charges are not recommended unless carried out by a qualified person using a thermostatic control, otherwise serious damage can occur to the battery plates through overheating.

5 While charging the battery, ensure that the temperature of the electrolyte never exceeds 40°C (104°F).

6 Alternator - maintenance and special precautions

1 At the 10 000 mile (15 000 km) service the alternator drivebelt should be checked for wear and damage and its tension adjusted as described in Section 7. At the same time check that the plug is pushed firmly into the terminals on the rear of the alternator.

2 Take extreme care when making electrical circuit connections on the car otherwise damage may occur to the alternator or other electrical components employing semi-conductors. Always make sure that the battery leads are correctly connected. Before using electric-arc welding equipment to repair any part of the car, disconnect the battery leads and alternator multi-plug. Never run the alternator with the multi-plug or a battery lead disconnected.

7 Alternator drivebelt - adjustment

1 The alternator drivebelt should be adjusted every 10 000 miles (15 000 km). To check its tension depress the belt firmly with a finger or thumb midway between the alternator and crankshaft pulleys. The belt should deflect approximately 5 mm (0.2 in) (photo).

2 If adjustment is necessary, loosen the nut on the adjusting link under the alternator. Also slacken the alternator pivot bolt and the link pivot bolt. Carefully lever the alternator away from the cylinder block until the belt is tensioned correctly, using a lever at the pulley end of the alternator (photo).

3 Hold the alternator in this position and tighten the nuts and bolts. Recheck the tension on completion.

8 Alternator - testing

Accurate testing of the alternator is only possible using specialised instruments and is therefore best left to a qualified electrician. If, however, the alternator is faulty the home mechanic should dismantle it with reference to Section 10 or 11 and check the condition of the brushes, soldered joints, etc. If the fault cannot be found, refit the alternator and have it checked professionally.

9

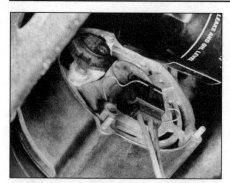

9.2 Showing multi-plug on the rear of the alternator

9.3 Loosening the alternator adjusting link inner bolt

9.5 Removing the alternator pivot bolt

9 Alternator - removal and refitting

1 Disconnect the battery negative lead.
2 Release the clip and pull the multi-plug from the rear of the alternator (photo).
3 Loosen the pivot and adjustment bolts then push the alternator in towards the engine and slip the drivebelt from the alternator and crankshaft pulleys (photo).
4 Remove the adjustment link nut and washer.
5 Support the alternator then remove the pivot bolt and withdraw the unit from the engine (photo).

6 Refitting is a reversal of removal, but before fully tightening the pivot and adjustment bolts, tension the drivebelt as described in Section 7.

10 Alternator (Bosch) - overhaul

1 Wipe clean the exterior surfaces of the alternator.
2 Remove the two screws and withdraw the voltage regulator and brush assembly from the rear of the alternator (photos).
3 Mark the housings and stator in relation to each other, then unscrew the through bolts and tap the drive end housing off.

4 Grip the pulley in a soft jawed vice and unscrew the nut. Tap the rotor shaft through the pulley and remove the spacers and fan noting the direction of rotation arrow on the front of the fan.
5 Using a three-arm puller press the rotor shaft out of the drive end housing. Note that the arms of the puller must be located on the bearing retainer, otherwise damage may occur to the retainer screws.
6 Remove the screws and the retainer and use a soft metal drift to drive out the bearing.
7 Using a puller, remove the bearing from the end of the rotor shaft.
8 If necessary the stator and diode plate can be removed from the end housing after removing the retaining screws.

1 Belt pulley
2 Fan
3 Spacer
4 Drive end housing
5 Bearing
6 Rotor
7 Bearing
8 Stator
9 Diode plate
10 Housing
11 Regulator
12 Regulator brushes

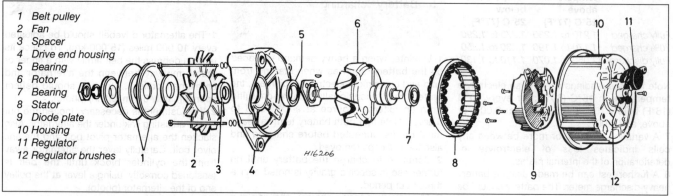

H16206

Fig. 9.2 Exploded view of the Bosch alternator (Sec 10)

10.2A Voltage regulator location

10.2B Removing the voltage regulator and brush assembly

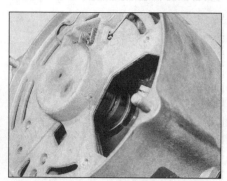

10.2C View of the slip rings with voltage regulator removed

10.10 Checking the length of the alternator brushes

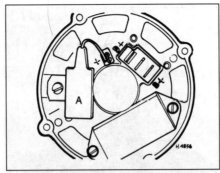

Fig. 9.3 Suppression condenser (A) on the rear of the alternator (Sec 10)

9 Clean all the components in paraffin or petrol and wipe them dry.

10 Check that the length of the carbon brushes is not less than the minimum amount given in the Specifications (photo). If necessary unsolder the leads and remove the old brushes then clean the housing, insert the new brushes, and solder the new leads into position.

11 The rotor bearings should be renewed as a matter of course.

12 To check the stator first identify the wire positions then unsolder them using long nose pliers to dissipate heat from the diode plate. Check the windings for short circuits by connecting an ohmmeter between each of the three wires (ie between wire 1 and 2, wire 1

and 3, and wire 2 and 3). Each reading should be between 0.18 and 0.20 ohm for the 45 amp alternator and between 0.10 and 0.11 ohm for the 65 amp alternator. Check the windings for insulation by connecting a 12 volt testlamp and leads between each of the wires and the stator ring. If the lamp illuminates, the windings are faulty.

13 Check the rotor windings for continuity by connecting an ohmmeter to the two slip rings. A reading of 3.4 to 3.7 ohm should be obtained for the 45 amp alternator, or 2.8 to 3.0 ohm for the 65 amp alternator. Check the windings for insulation by connecting a 12 volt testlamp and leads between each of the slip rings and the winding core. If the lamp illuminates, the windings are faulty.

14 The diodes can be checked by connecting an ohmmeter across them. The reading should be between 50 and 80 ohm in one direction and at or near infinity in the other direction (ie with lead positions reversed).

15 Clean the slip rings with fine glasspaper and wipe clean with a fuel moistened cloth.

16 Reassemble the alternator using a reversal of the dismantling procedure. When fitting the bearing to the rotor shaft, drive it on with a metal tube located on the inner race. If the diode plate has been renewed, a suppression condenser should be fitted to the rear of the alternator as shown in Fig. 9.3.

11 Alternator (Motorola) - overhaul

1 The procedure is similar to that described in Section 10, and the exploded diagrams of the 45 amp and 65 amp alternators are shown in Figs. 9.4 and 9.5. Identify the regulator wires for position before disconnecting them.

2 The 45 amp stator windings may be of two types, the early type can be recognised by having single wires soldered to the terminals whereas the later type has double wires on each terminal. The resistance of the early 45 amp windings should be between 0.27 and 0.3 ohm, the later 45 amp windings between

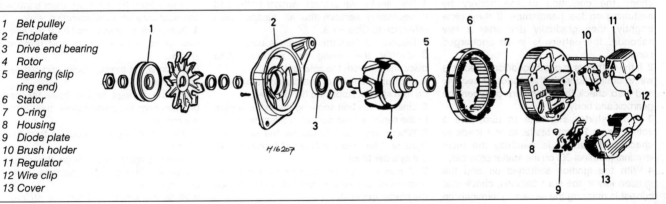

```
1  Belt pulley
2  Endplate
3  Drive end bearing
4  Rotor
5  Bearing (slip
   ring end)
6  Stator
7  O-ring
8  Housing
9  Diode plate
10 Brush holder
11 Regulator
12 Wire clip
13 Cover
```

Fig. 9.4 Exploded view of the Motorola 45 amp alternator (Sec 11)

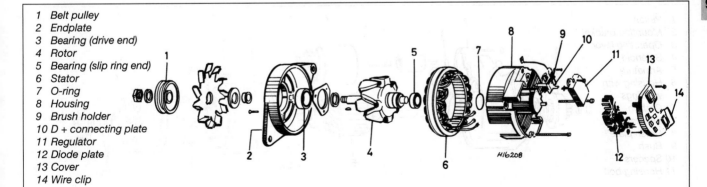

```
1  Belt pulley
2  Endplate
3  Bearing (drive end)
4  Rotor
5  Bearing (slip ring end)
6  Stator
7  O-ring
8  Housing
9  Brush holder
10 D + connecting plate
11 Regulator
12 Diode plate
13 Cover
14 Wire clip
```

Fig. 9.5 Exploded view of the Motorola 65 amp alternator (Sec 11)

Fig. 9.6 Showing the correct routing of the D+ wire on the 65 amp Motorola alternator (Sec 11)

13.7A Starter retaining bolts showing exhaust bracket location

13.7B Removing the starter motor

0.09 and 0.11 ohm, and the 65 amp windings between 0.13 and 0.15 ohm.

3 The resistance of the rotor windings should be between 3.8 and 4.2 ohm on both types of alternator, and the diode resistance between 50 and 80 ohm, the same as on the Bosch alternator.

4 On the 65 amp version the DT wire must be routed as shown in Fig. 9.6.

12 Starter motor - testing in the car

1 If the starter motor fails to operate, first check the condition of the battery by switching on the headlamps. If they glow brightly, then gradually dim after a few seconds, the battery is in an uncharged condition.

2 If the battery is in good condition, check the wiring connections on the starter for security and also check the earth wire between the gearbox and body.

3 If the starter still fails to turn, use a voltmeter or 12 volt testlamp and leads to check that current is reaching the main terminal (terminal 30) on the starter solenoid.

4 With the ignition switched on and the ignition key in the start position, check that current is reaching the remaining terminals on the solenoid. Also check that an audible click

is heard as the solenoid operates indicating that the internal contacts are closed and that current is available at the field windings terminal.

5 Failure to obtain current at terminal 50 indicates a faulty ignition switch.

6 If current at the correct voltage is available at the starter motor, yet it does not operate, the unit is faulty and should be removed for further investigation.

13 Starter motor - removal and refitting

1 Remove the windscreen washer bottle and if necessary remove the air cleaner with reference to Chapter 3.

2 Disconnect the battery negative lead.

3 Identify the wiring for position then disconnect it from the solenoid.

4 Jack up the front of the car and support it on axle stands. Apply the handbrake.

5 Unscrew the bolt securing the exhaust pipe to the support strap beneath the starter.

6 Where applicable unscrew the nuts and bolts and remove the support bracket from the cylinder block.

7 Unscrew and remove the retaining bolts, then unbolt the exhaust bracket and withdraw the starter (photos).

8 Refitting is a reversal of removal, but tighten

the bolts to the specified torque. Where a support bracket is fitted, do not fully tighten the nuts and bolts until the bracket is correctly located and free of any tension.

14 Starter motor - overhaul

1 Wipe clean the exterior surfaces of the starter motor.

2 Unscrew the terminal nut and disconnect the field windings lead from the solenoid.

3 Unscrew the bolts and withdraw the solenoid from the housing, then unhook the solenoid core from the operating lever.

4 Remove the screws and lift off the end cap, then prise out the circlip and remove the shims.

5 Unscrew the through bolts and remove the end cover.

6 Lift the springs and remove the carbon brushes from the brush holder, then withdraw the holder.

7 Remove the field coil housing from the end housing.

8 Using a metal tube drive the stop ring towards the pinion, then remove the circlip and stop ring.

9 Slide the armature from the pinion, and withdraw the pinion.

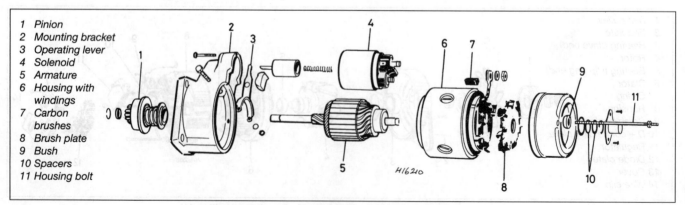

1 Pinion
2 Mounting bracket
3 Operating lever
4 Solenoid
5 Armature
6 Housing with windings
7 Carbon brushes
8 Brush plate
9 Bush
10 Spacers
11 Housing bolt

Fig. 9.7 Exploded view of the starter motor (Sec 14)

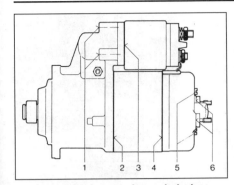

Fig. 9.8 Surfaces to be sealed when reassembling the starter motor (Sec 14)

1 *Solenoid securing screws*
2 *Stator/mounting surface*
3 *Solenoid joint*
4 *Starter/end cap joint*
5 *Through bolts*
6 *Shaft cover joint and screws*

10 Prise the rubber pad from the end housing.
11 Unscrew and remove the pivot bolt and withdraw the operating lever.
12 Clean all the components in paraffin and wipe dry. Check the pinion teeth for wear and pitting and check that the one-way clutch only allows the pinion to turn in one direction. Clean the commutator with a fuel moistened cloth and if necessary use fine glasspaper to remove any carbon deposits. If the commutator is worn excessively it can be machined provided that the diameter is not less than the amount given in the Specifications.
13 If the brushes are less than the minimum length given in the Specifications they must be renewed. To do this, crush the old brushes with a pair of pliers and clean the leads. Insert the leads into the new brushes and splay out the ends. Solder the wires in position but grip the wire next to the brush with long nosed pliers in order to prevent the solder penetrating the flexible section of the wire. File off any surplus solder.
14 Check the bush in the end cover and if necessary drive it out with a soft metal drift. Soak the end cover in hot oil for five minutes before driving the new bush into it.

15.1 Removing the plastic lid from the fuse box

15 Assemble the starter motor in reversal of the dismantling procedure but note that the unit must be sealed with suitable sealant on the surfaces shown in Fig. 9.8. Lubricate the pinion drive with a little molybdenum disulphide grease. Make sure that the stop ring is fitted from the inside of the circlip with the annular groove facing outwards, and also make sure that the stop ring turns freely on the shaft. Lubricate the solenoid and operating lever with a little molybdenum disulphide grease. When fitting the brush holder, the springs may be held in a raised position by using two lengths of bent wire.

15 Fuses - general
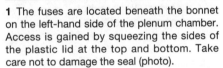

1 The fuses are located beneath the bonnet on the left-hand side of the plenum chamber. Access is gained by squeezing the sides of the plastic lid at the top and bottom. Take care not to damage the seal (photo).
2 The fuse circuits are given in the Specifications and the fuses are numbered in a clockwise sequence starting at the top left.
3 Blown fuses are easily recognised by the metal strip being burnt apart in the centre. Make sure that new fuses are firmly held between the terminals.
4 Always renew a fuse with one of identical

rating, and never renew it more than once without finding the source of the trouble (usually a short circuit).

16 Direction indicator and hazard flasher system - general

1 The flasher unit is located behind the glovebox. Remove trim as necessary for access.
2 Unplug the old flasher unit from its holder and plug in the new one. Do not drop it, it is fragile.
3 Should the flashers become faulty in operation, check the bulbs for security and make sure that the contact surfaces are not corroded. Check all the relevant wiring and terminals. If the flashers are still faulty and the relevant fuse has not blown, renew the flasher unit. If the fuse has blown, a short circuit may be the cause of the failure.

17 Ignition switch/steering column lock - removal and refitting

The procedure is described in Chapter 10 for the removal and refitting of the steering lock.

18 Combination switches - removal and refitting

1 Remove the steering wheel as described in Chapter 10.
2 Disconnect the battery negative lead.
3 Remove the screws and withdraw the steering column lower shroud.
4 Remove the three screws securing the combination switch (photo).
5 Disconnect the multi-plugs and withdraw the combination switch (photos).
6 If necessary the direction indicator switch

9

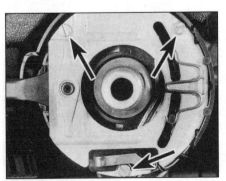

18.4 Combination switch screw locations

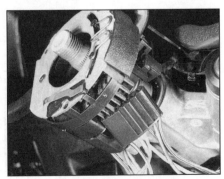

18.5A Disconnecting the multi-plugs from the combination switch

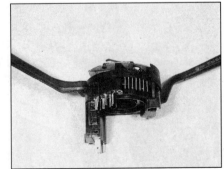

18.5B The combination switch

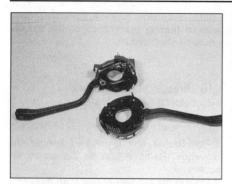

18.6 The direction indicator and windscreen wiper switches separated

19.2 Removing the foglight switch

19.3 Heated rear window switch with multi-plug removed

can be separated from the windscreen wiper switch (photo).

7 If the wiper switch is not fitted with an intermittent relay, this can be fitted with reference to the relevant wiring diagram. It will be necessary to remove the wedge from the switch.

8 Refitting is a reversal of removal, with reference to Chapter 10 when refitting the steering wheel.

19 Facia switches - removal and refitting

1 Disconnect the battery negative lead.
2 Remove the lower panel, reach up behind the switch and depress the spring clips in order to withdraw the switch (photo).

21.2 Courtesy light switch location

3 Disconnect the multi-plug and remove the switch (photo).
4 To refit the switch, simply reconnect the multi-plug and push the switch into the facia. Refit the lower panel.

20 Cigarette lighter - removal and refitting

1 Disconnect the battery negative lead.
2 Remove the lower facia panel then reach up and disconnect the wiring from the cigarette lighter.
3 Remove the retaining ring and withdraw the cigarette lighter from the facia.
4 Refitting is a reversal of removal.

21 Courtesy light switch - removal and refitting

1 Disconnect the battery negative lead.
2 Open the door and unscrew the cross-head screw from the switch (photo).
3 Withdraw the switch and disconnect the wiring. Tie a loose knot in the wire to prevent it dropping into the door pillar.
4 Check the switch seal for condition and renew it if necessary.
5 Refitting is a reversal of removal.

22 Speedometer cable - removal and refitting

1 Open the bonnet and then reach down behind the engine and unscrew the speedometer cable nut from the gearbox.
2 Withdraw the instrument panel sufficient to disconnect the cable with reference to Section 23 (photo).
3 Remove the air cleaner as described in Chapter 3.
4 Pull the speedometer cable through the bulkhead and withdraw it from the engine compartment.
5 Refitting is a reversal of removal. Make sure that the grommet is correctly fitted in the bulkhead and that there are no sharp bends in the cable. Do not grease the cable ends.

23 Instrument panel - removal and refitting

1 Disconnect the battery negative lead.
2 For better access remove the steering wheel as described in Chapter 10.
3 Unscrew the cross-head screws located above the instrument panel (photo). The lower edge of the surround is held by two spring clips; just pull it outwards to release them.

22.2 Showing the instrument panel end of the speedometer cable

23.3 Removing the instrument panel surround screws

23.4A Instrument panel retaining screw location

23.4B Disconnecting the multi-plug from the instrument panel

23.5A Front view of the instrument panel

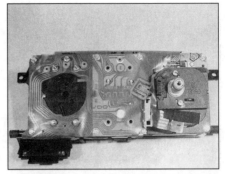

23.5B Rear view of the instrument panel

23.6 Instrument panel in fitted position

24.1 Voltage stabilizer location

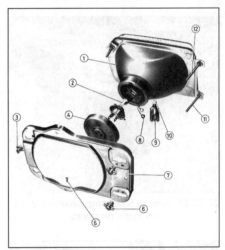

Fig. 9.9 Exploded view of the headlamp fitted to Polo Classic models (Sec 25)

1 Headlight unit
2 Halogen bulb
3 Plastic holder
4 Cap
5 Securing screw
6 Plastic holder
7 Support plate
8 Wire clip
9 Sidelight bulbholder
10 Sidelight bulb
11 Adjusting screw (vertical setting)
12 Adjusting screw (horizontal setting)

Unplug the switch multi-plugs and withdraw the instrument panel surround.
4 Unscrew the cross-head retaining screws and swivel the panel forwards sufficient to disconnect the speedometer cable and multi-plug (photos).
5 Withdraw the instrument panel from the facia (photos).
6 Refitting is a reversal of removal (photo).

24 Voltage stabiliser - testing and renewal

1 The voltage stabiliser is located on the rear of the instrument panel and its purpose is to provide constant voltage to the fuel and temperature gauges, and the temperature warning lamp (photo).
2 To check the voltage stabiliser remove the instrument panel as described in Section 23

then reconnect the multi-plugs. Connect a voltmeter between the + out terminal (+A) and the central earth terminal, then switch on the ignition. The voltage should be between 9.5 and 10.5 volts. If not, renew it as follows.
3 With the battery negative lead disconnected, unscrew the retaining screw and disconnect the pressed wires from the printed circuit.
4 Refitting is a reversal of removal.

25 Headlamp bulbs and headlamps - removal and refitting

1 To remove a headlamp bulb first open the bonnet and pull the connector from the rear of the headlamp (photo).
2 Prise off the rubber cap (photo).
3 On Polo and Polo Coupé models turn the retaining ring anti-clockwise and remove the

bulb (photos). On Polo Classic models squeeze the spring clips together and release it from the bulb, then remove the bulb.

25.1 Pull off the connector . . .

25.2 . . . prise off the rubber cap . . .

25.3A . . . remove the retaining ring . . .

25.3B . . . and remove the headlamp bulb

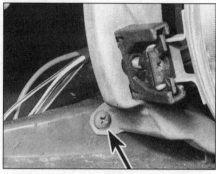

25.6A Headlamp carrier plate retaining screw

25.6B Showing the headlamp and carrier plate removed

25.6C Showing a headlamp beam adjuster with unit removed

26.5 Headlamp lower adjusting screw for vertical movement

4 Refitting is a reversal of removal, but make sure that the locating plug on the bulbholder engages the recess in the reflector.
5 To remove the headlamp unit, first remove the radiator grille as described in Chapter 11.
6 With the headlamp bulb removed, unscrew the screws securing the carrier plate to the front panel, and withdraw the unit (photos).
7 Refitting is a reversal of removal, but check and if necessary adjust the beam alignment as described in Section 26.

26 Headlamps - alignment

1 The headlamp beam alignment should be checked and if necessary adjusted every 10 000 miles (15 000 km).
2 It is recommended that the alignment is carried out by a VW garage using modern beam setting equipment. However in an emergency the following procedure will provide an acceptable light pattern.
3 Position the car on a level surface with tyres correctly inflated, approximately 10 metres (33 feet) in front of, and at right-angles to, a wall or garage door.
4 Draw a horizontal line on the wall or door at headlamp centre height. Draw a vertical line corresponding to the centre line of the car, then measure off a point either side of this, on

the horizontal line, corresponding with the headlamp centres.
5 Switch on the main beam and check that the areas of maximum illumination coincide with the headlamp centre marks on the wall. If not, turn the upper cross-head adjustment screw to adjust the beam laterally, and the lower screw to adjust the beam vertically (photo).

27 Lamp bulbs - renewal

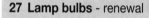

Note: *Lamp bulbs should always be renewed with ones of similar type and rating as listed in the Specifications.*

Sidelights

1 Open the bonnet and pull the connector from the sidelight bulbholder located beneath the headlamp bulb.
2 Turn the bulbholder anti-clockwise and remove it from the reflector (photo).
3 Depress and twist the bulb to remove it (photo).

Rear lights

4 Open the tailgate or bootlid as applicable and pull the connector from the bulbholder (photo).
5 Release the bulbholder from the lamp unit

27.2 Removing the sidelight bulbholder

27.3 Sidelight bulb and bulbholder

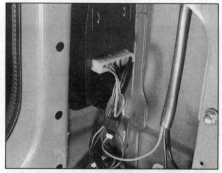

27.4 Showing rear light wiring connector

27.5 Depress the clips to remove the rear light bulbholder

27.6 Showing rear light bulbs in the bulbholder

27.7 Removing the front indicator lamp lens

by prising out or depressing the clips as applicable (photo).
6 Depress and twist the relevant bulb to remove it (photo).

Front indicator lights

7 Remove the cross-head screws and withdraw the lens (photo).
8 Depress and twist the bulb to remove it (photo).
9 If necessary the lamp unit can be withdrawn from the bumper and the wiring disconnected (photo).
10 When refitting the lens make sure that the gasket is correctly located.

Number plate light

11 Remove the cross-head screws and withdraw the lens and cover (photo).
12 Depress and twist the bulb to remove it.
13 When refitting the lens and cover make sure that the lug is correctly located.

Interior light

14 Using a screwdriver depress the spring clip then withdraw the light from the roof (photos).
15 Release the festoon type bulb from the spring terminals.
16 When fitting the new bulb make sure that the terminals are tensioned sufficient to retain

the bulb. The switch end of the light should be inserted into the roof first.

Foglight

17 Remove the lower screw and withdraw the insert.
18 Disconnect the bulb wiring, then release the spring clip and remove the bulb.
19 When fitting the new bulb make sure that the locating lug is correctly positioned.

Instrument panel light

20 Remove the instrument panel as described in Section 23.
21 Twist the bulbholder through 90° to remove it then pull out the bulb (photo).

27.8 Removing the front indicator lamp bulb

27.9 Removing the front indicator lamp

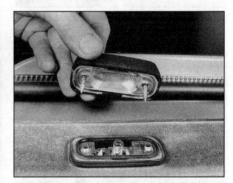

27.11 Removing the number plate light lens and cover

9

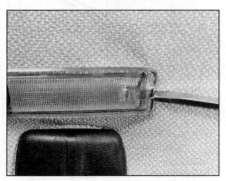

27.14A Depress the spring clip . . .

27.14B . . . and withdraw the interior light

27.21 Removing an instrument panel light bulb

27.23A Removing the bulb from the hazard warning switch

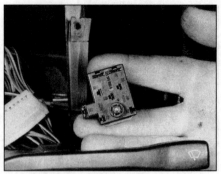

27.23B Showing the lighting switch connector and illumination bulb

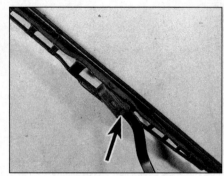

28.1A Depress the clip . . .

Facia switch lights

22 Remove the relevant facia switch as described in Section 19.
23 Remove the bulb from the switch or connector as applicable (photos).

28.1B . . . and slide the wiper blade from the arm

29.2 Location of wiper arm retaining nut

30.3 Windscreen wiper motor and pull rods

28 Wiper blades - renewal

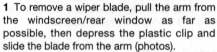

1 To remove a wiper blade, pull the arm from the windscreen/rear window as far as possible, then depress the plastic clip and slide the blade from the arm (photos).
2 If necessary the wiper rubber may be renewed separately. To do this use pliers to compress the rubber so that it can be removed from the blade.
3 Refitting is a reversal of removal.

29 Wiper arms - removal and refitting

1 Make sure that the wiper arms are in their parked position then remove the wiper blade as described in Section 28.
2 Lift the hinged cover and unscrew the nut (photo).
3 Ease the wiper arm from the spindle taking care not to damage the paintwork.
4 Refitting is a reversal of removal. In the parked position, the end of the wiper arm (ie middle of the blade), should be 43 mm (1.69 in) from the bottom of the windscreen for the passenger side wiper or 37 mm (1.46 in) for the driver's side wiper. On the rear window the dimension is 25 mm (1 in).

30 Windscreen wiper motor - removal and refitting

1 Open the bonnet and disconnect the battery negative lead.
2 Pull the weatherstrip from the front of the plenum chamber and remove the plastic cover.
3 Unscrew the nut and remove the crank from the motor spindle (photo).
4 Disconnect the wiring multi-plug.
5 Unscrew the bolts and withdraw the wiper motor from the frame.
6 Refitting is a reversal of removal, but when

fitting the crank to the spindle (motor in parked position) make sure that the marks are aligned.

31 Rear window wiper motor - removal and refitting

1 Disconnect the battery negative lead.
2 Open the tailgate and prise off the inner trim panel.
3 Remove the wiper arm as described in Section 29, and unscrew the outer nut. Remove the spacers.
4 Remove the mounting bracket cross-head screws and withdraw the motor sufficient to disconnect the wiring plug (photo). Note the location of any spacers.
5 Refitting is a reversal of removal.

32 Windscreen wiper linkage - removal and refitting

1 Disconnect the battery negative lead.

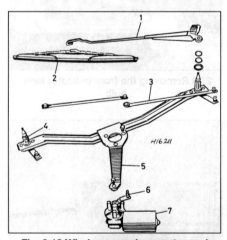

Fig. 9.10 Windscreen wiper motor and linkage (Secs 30 and 32)

1 Wiper arm	5 Windscreen wiper
2 Wiper blade	frame
3 Pull rods	6 Parking position
4 Wiper bearing	7 Wiper motor

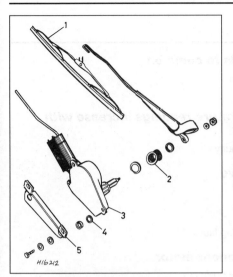

Fig. 9.11 Exploded view of the rear window wiper motor (Sec 31)

1 *Wiper blade*   4 *Spacer washer*
2 *Outer spacer*   5 *Securing plate*
3 *Rear wiper motor*

2 Remove the wiper arms as described in Section 29, then unscrew the bearing nuts and remove the spacers.
3 Pull the weatherstrips from the front of the plenum chamber and remove the plastic cover.
4 Disconnect the wiring multi-plug.
5 Unscrew the frame mounting bolt, then

33.4A Front view of the horn and mounting bolt

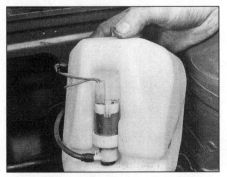

34.1 Showing windscreen washer fluid reservoir and pump

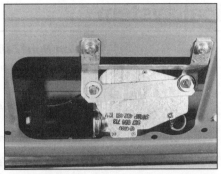

31.4 Rear window wiper motor location in the tailgate

withdraw the assembly from the bulkhead.
6 Prise the pull rods from the motor crank and bearing levers.
7 Unbolt the wiper motor from the frame.
8 Refitting is a reversal of removal, but lubricate the bearing units and pull rod joints with molybdenum disulphide grease.

33 Horn - removal and refitting

1 The horn is located behind the radiator grille.
2 To remove the horn, first disconnect the battery negative lead.
3 Remove the radiator grille as described in Chapter 11.

33.4B Rear view of the horn

35.4A Fuel consumption gauge sender unit

4 Unscrew the mounting bolt, disconnect the wires, and withdraw the horn (photos).
5 If the horn emits an unsatisfactory sound it may be possible to adjust it by removing the sealant from the adjusting screw and turning it one way or the other.
6 Refitting is a reversal of removal.

34 Windscreen washer system - general

1 The windscreen washer fluid reservoir is located on the left-hand side of the engine compartment, and the pump and motor is fitted to the side of the reservoir (photo).
2 The reservoir should be regularly topped up with the recommended washer fluid.
3 To adjust the jets for the windscreen washer, use a needle to direct the spray into the centre of the wiped area. A special tool (VW tool 3019 A) is necessary to direct the headlight washer spray to the centre of the headlights although a needle may be used as an alternative.

35 Gearchange and consumption gauge - general

1 On Formel E models a gearchange and consumption gauge is fitted in the instrument panel in place of the coolant temperature gauge.
2 The gearchange indicator lights up in all gears except top gear, when better economy without loss of power can be obtained by changing up to a higher gear. The indicator does not operate during acceleration or deceleration, or with the choke knob pulled out.
3 The consumption gauge operates only in top gear and it indicates the actual fuel consumption in mpg.
4 The gearchange and consumption gauge is operated by a switch on the gearbox and a sender in the vacuum line to the distributor (photos).

9

35.4B Disconnecting the wiring from the fuel consumption gauge sender unit

Fault finding - electrical system

Starter fails to turn engine

- ☐ Battery discharged or defective
- ☐ Battery terminal and/or earth leads loose
- ☐ Starter motor connections loose
- ☐ Starter solenoid faulty
- ☐ Starter brushes worn or sticking
- ☐ Starter commutator dirty or worn
- ☐ Starter field coils earthed

Starter turns engine very slowly

- ☐ Battery discharged
- ☐ Starter motor connections loose
- ☐ Starter brushes worn or sticking

Starter noisy

- ☐ Pinion or flywheel ring gear badly worn
- ☐ Mounting bolts loose

Battery will not hold charge

- ☐ Battery defective
- ☐ Electrolyte level too low
- ☐ Battery terminals loose
- ☐ Alternator drivebelt slipping
- ☐ Alternator or regulator faulty
- ☐ Short circuit in wiring

Ignition light stays on

- ☐ Alternator faulty
- ☐ Alternator drivebelt faulty

Ignition light fails to come on

- ☐ Warning bulb blown
- ☐ Alternator faulty

Fuel and temperature readings increase with engine speed

- ☐ Voltage stabiliser faulty

Lights inoperative

- ☐ Fuse blown
- ☐ Bulb blown
- ☐ Switch faulty
- ☐ Connections or wiring faulty

Failure of component motor

- ☐ Commutator dirty or burnt
- ☐ Armature faulty
- ☐ Brushes sticking or worn
- ☐ Armature bearings seized
- ☐ Fuse blown

Failure of individual component

- ☐ Wiring loose or broken
- ☐ Fuse blown
- ☐ Switch faulty
- ☐ Component faulty

Chapter 10 Suspension and steering

For modifications, and information applicable to later models, see Supplement at end of manual

Contents

Degrees of difficulty

| **Easy,** suitable for novice with little experience | 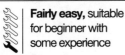 | **Fairly easy,** suitable for beginner with some experience | 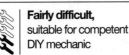 | **Fairly difficult,** suitable for competent DIY mechanic | | **Difficult,** suitable for experienced DIY mechanic | | **Very difficult,** suitable for expert DIY or professional | |

Specifications

Front suspension
Type .... Independent with spring struts, lower track control arms, and anti-roll bar. Telescopic shock absorbers incorporated in struts

Rear suspension
Type .... Semi-independent incorporating torsion axle beam, trailing arms, and spring struts/shock absorbers

Steering
Type .... Rack and pinion with safety column coupling
Steering roll radius .... Negative 4.17 mm (0.164 in)
Steering wheel turns lock to lock 3.66
Steering ratio .... 17.6 to 1
Steering gear lubricant type/specification .... VW grease AOF 063 000 04

Front wheel alignment
Total toe .... 0° ± 10' (0 ± 1 mm/0.04in)
Camber .... +20' ± 30'
  Maximum difference side to side .... 30'
Castor .... 2° 20' ± 30'
  Maximum difference side to side .... 1°

Rear wheel alignment

	To chassis number 86-CW 028 390	From chassis number 86-CW 028 391
Total toe	+20' ± 40'	+25' ± 15'
Camber	-30' ± 35'	-1° 40' ± 20'
Maximum difference side to side	30'	30'

Wheels
Type .... Pressed steel disc or alloy
Size:
  Polo, Polo Classic .... 4 1/2 J x 13
  Polo Coupé .... 5 1/2 J x 13

10

Tyres

Size	Standard	Optional
Polo, Polo Classic		
29 kW engine	135 SR 13	155/70 SR 13
37 and 44kW engine	145 SR 13	155/70SR 13
Polo Coupé	165/65 SR 13	

Pressures - bar (lbf/in²)	Front	Rear
135 SR 13 - half load	1.7 (25)	1.7 (25)
135 SR 13 - full load	1.9 (28)	2.2 (32)
All other sizes - half load	1.6 (23)	1.6 (23)
All other sizes - full load	1.7 (25)	2.1 (30)

Torque wrench settings

	lbf ft	Nm
Front suspension		
Strut to body	44	60
Shock absorber rod to top mounting	37	50
Strut cap	110	150
Steering knuckle	37	50
Track control arm to body	41	55
Anti-roll bar to control arm	55	75
Anti-roll bar to body	22	30
Anti-roll bar mounting	89	120
Rear suspension		
Trailing arm to trunnion	30	40
Trunnion to body	89	120
Stub axle	44	60
Shock absorber to trailing arm	33	45
Shock absorber to body	15	20
Steering		
Tie-rod (outer)	26	35
Flange tube	18	25
Column tube	15	20
Steering wheel	30	40
Steering gear	18	25
Tie-rod inner	22	30
Tie-rod carrier	30	40
Tie-rod locknut	30	40
Wheel bolts	81	110

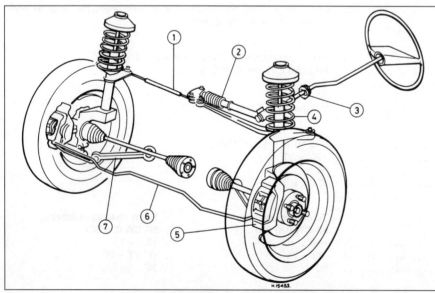

Fig. 10.1 Diagram of front suspension (Sec 1)

1 Tie-rod
2 Rack and pinion steering
3 Steering column
4 Suspension strut
5 Brake caliper
6 Anti-roll bar
7 Track control arm

1 General description

The front suspension is of independent type with spring struts, lower track control arms and an anti-roll bar. Each strut incorporates a telescopic shock absorber which can be renewed separately in the event of failure. The track control arms are attached to the wheel bearing housings by balljoints. The pivot points of the struts are positioned to give a negative roll in the interests of steering stability. The anti-roll bar which stabilises the car when cornering, also acts as a radius arm for each track control arm. The front wheel hubs are mounted in twin track ball bearings in the front bearing housings.

The rear suspension is of semi-independent type with trailing arms located at each end of the torsion axle beam. The shock absorbers are an integral part of the spring struts. The axle beam is attached to the trailing arms behind the pivot points.

The steering is of rack and pinion type mounted on the front of the bulkhead, and the

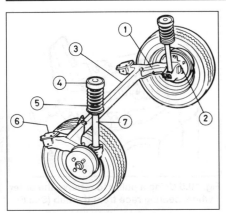

Fig. 10.2 Diagram of rear suspension (Sec 1)

1 Trailing arm
2 Stub axle
3 Axle beam
4 Suspension strut mounting
5 Suspension strut
6 Trunnion with bonded rubber bush
7 Shock absorber

column coupling consists of two pins which automatically disengage in the event of a severe front end impact.

2 Routine maintenance

1 Every 10 000 miles (15 000 km) check the tie-rod end balljoints for wear and the dust caps for condition (photo). Renew the balljoints if any play is evident.
2 At the same time check the suspension balljoints for wear and condition of the dust caps. Also check the steering gear bellows.
3 Check the tyres for condition and tread depth.

3 Front suspension strut - removal and refitting

1 Remove the wheel trim from the relevant wheel.
2 With the handbrake applied loosen the driveshaft nut (photo). The nut is tightened to a high torque and a socket extension may be required.
3 Jack up the front of the car and support it on axle stands. Remove the roadwheel.
4 Remove the brake disc and splash plate with reference to Chapter 8.
5 Unscrew the nut securing the tie-rod end to the strut, then use a balljoint separator to release the tie-rod.
6 Remove the anti-roll bar as described in Section 8.
7 Unscrew and remove the bolt securing the track control arm to the wheel bearing housing noting that the bolt head faces forward.

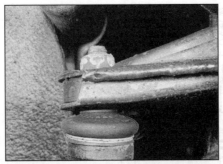

2.1 Check the tie-rod and balljoint dust caps regularly

3.10A Removing the front suspension strut top cap

8 Push the control arm down to disconnect the balljoint then move the strut sideways.
9 Pull the strut out and at the same time tap the driveshaft through the hub with a mallet.
10 Working in the engine compartment prise

3.2 Showing the driveshaft nut

3.10B View of the front suspension strut upper mounting from below

the cap from the top of the strut then unscrew the self-locking nut while supporting the strut from below (photos). If necessary hold the shock absorber rod stationary with a spanner.
11 Lower the strut from under the car.

1 Self-locking nut
2 Self-locking nut
3 Self-locking nut
4 Tie-rod
5 Suspension strut
6 Driveshaft
7 Brake caliper
8 Self-locking nut
9 Self-locking nut
10 Hexagon bolt
11 Inner wishbone bush
12 Wishbone
13 Self locking nut
14 Self locking nut
15 Outer wishbone bush
16 Anti-roll bar
17 Hexagon bolt
18 Hexagon bolt
19 Anti-roll bar locating bracket

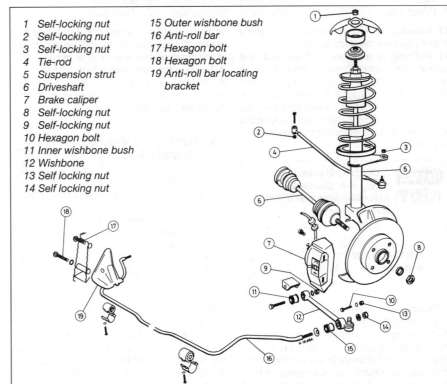

Fig, 10.3 Exploded view of front suspension components (Sec 3)

10

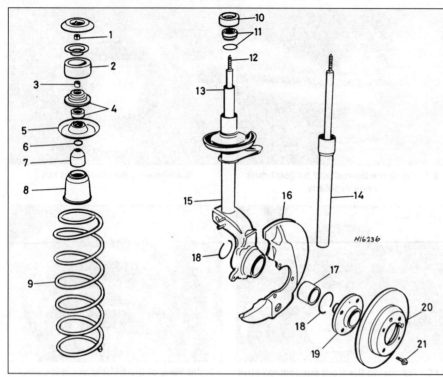

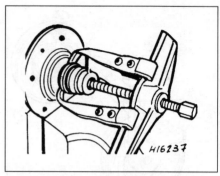

Fig. 10.5 Using a puller to remove the outer wheel bearing race from the hub (Sec 6)

Fig. 10.4 Exploded view of front suspension strut (Sec 4)

1 Self-locking nut	8 Boot	15 Wheel bearing housing
2 Damping ring	9 Coil spring	16 Splash plate
3 Slotted nut	10 Screw cap	17 Wheel bearing
4 Suspension strut bearing	11 Piston rod guide seal	18 Circlip
5 Spring retainer	12 Shock absorber	19 Wheel hub
6 Washer	13 Wet type shock absorber	20 Brake disc
7 Bump stop	14 Shock absorber cartridge	21 Wheel bolt

12 If necessary remove the cups and rubber mountings from the body panel.

13 Refitting is a reversal of removal, but renew the upper rubber mountings if necessary. Refer to Section 8 when refitting the anti-roll bar, Chapter 8 when refitting the brake disc and Chapter 7 when tightening the driveshaft nut. Finally check and if necessary adjust the front wheel tracking as described in Section 21.

 If difficulty is experienced fitting the upper rubber mounting first dust it with talcum powder.

4 Front coil spring - removal and refitting

1 Remove the front suspension strut as described in Section 3.

2 Using a spring compression tool compress the coil spring until it is clear of the upper retainer. *Do not attempt to use anything other than a purpose made spring compressor tool.*

3 Unscrew the slotted nut from the shock absorber rod and withdraw the spring retainer, washer, bump stop, boot, and coil spring. If a special tool to engage the slotted nut is not available, use a pair of grips.

4 Remove the compressor tool.

5 Refitting is a reversal of removal with reference to Section 3. Tighten the slotted nut to the specified torque.

5 Front shock absorber - removal and refitting

1 A faulty shock absorber will normally make a knocking noise as the car is driven over rough surfaces. Note that it is normal for a small amount of fluid to be present on the exterior of the shock absorber.

2 To remove the shock absorber first remove the front coil spring as described in Section 4.

3 Using VW tool 40-201 A unscrew the screw cap from the top of the strut and remove the piston rod guide and seal. If necessary first mount the strut in a vice.

4 Pull the shock absorber out of the strut then pour the remaining fluid out and discard it. Clean the inside of the strut with paraffin and wipe dry.

5 Replacement shock absorbers are supplied as dry type cartridges, the wet type are only fitted by the factory when new.

6 With the new shock absorber upright, operate it fully several times and check that the resistance is even without any tight spots.

7 Insert the shock absorber in the strut and fit the guide together with a new seal.

8 Fit the screw cap and tighten it to the specified torque.

9 Refit the coil spring as described in Section 4.

6 Front wheel bearings - testing and renewal

1 Jack up the front of the car and support on axle stands. With neutral selected, spin the wheel. A rumbling noise will be evident if the bearings are worn and excessive play will be apparent when the wheel is rocked, however check that the lower balljoint is not responsible for the play.

2 To renew the wheel bearings first remove the suspension strut as described in Section 3.

3 Support the outside of the strut, then using a suitable metal tube, drive the hub from the wheel bearing. The outer bearing race will be forced from the bearing during this procedure and therefore it is not possible to re-use the bearing.

4 Mount the hub in a vice and use a suitable puller to remove the race.

5 Extract the circlips then support the strut again and use a suitable metal tube to drive out the wheel bearing.

6 Clean the inside of the bearing housing in the strut.

7 Fit the outer circlip to the strut.

8 Support the strut then smear a little grease on the bearing contact surfaces and drive in the bearing using a metal tube on the outer race only. Fit the inner circlip.

9 Place the hub upright on the bench and smear a little grease on the bearing contact area.

10 Locate the strut horizontally on the hub, then using a metal tube on the bearing inner race drive the bearing fully onto the hub.

11 Refit the suspension strut as described in Section 3.

7 Front track control arm and balljoint - removal and refitting

1 Jack up the front of the car and support on axle stands. Apply the handbrake and remove the roadwheel.

2 Unscrew the nut and remove the bolt securing the control arm balljoint to the strut. Press the control arm down from the strut. Note that the bolt head faces forward.

3 Unscrew the nut and remove the bolt from the inner end of the control arm. Note that the bolt head faces forward, and also mark its position on the bracket.

4 Press the control arm down from the bracket, then unscrew the nut from the end of the anti-roll bar and pull off the control arm.

5 If the balljoint is worn excessively, renew the complete control arm. Check the condition of the bushes and if necessary press them out using a metal tube, nut and bolt, and washers. Fit the new bushes using the same method, but first dip them in soapy water.

6 Refitting is a reversal of removal, but delay fully tightening the inner pivot bolt and the anti-roll bar nut until the full weight of the car is on the roadwheels. Note that where camber angle adjustment has been made, the bolt hole in the bracket may have been elongated and in this case it is imperative that the bolt is refitted in its original position otherwise the adjustment must be repeated.

8 Front anti-roll bar - removal and refitting

1 Jack up the front of the car and support with axle stands. Remove both wheels and apply the handbrake.

2 Note that with the anti-roll bar correctly fitted, the bend in the front of the bar faces upwards.

3 Unscrew the bolts and remove the mounting clamps securing the front of the bar to the underbody (photo).

4 Unscrew and remove the nuts and washers from the ends of the anti-roll bar.

5 Pull the anti-roll bar from the control arms and withdraw it from under the car. If difficulty is experienced, temporarily jack up the control arms to give a little extra width for the removal of the bar.

6 Check the bar and rubber bushes for wear and deterioration and renew as necessary. If the bush in the control arm is worn, renew it with reference to Section 7.

7 Refitting is a reversal of removal, but delay fully tightening the nuts and bolts until the full weight of the car is on the roadwheels. Note that the castor angle is determined by the position of the control arms on the anti-roll bar, therefore any adjustment washers should be refitted in their original locations.

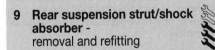

8.3 View of an anti-roll bar front mounting from above (engine removed from car)

9 Rear suspension strut/shock absorber - removal and refitting

1 Check the front wheels then jack up the rear of the car and support on axle stands. Remove the rear wheel.

2 Working inside the rear of the car, remove the parcel tray then remove the cap from the

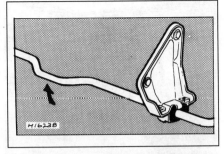

Fig. 10.6 Correct fitting of the anti-roll bar (Sec 8)

Arrow shows bend facing upwards

top of the strut by twirling it anti-clockwise (photo).

3 Support the trailing arm with a trolley jack.

4 Unscrew the nut from the top of the shock absorber rod, if necessary holding the rod stationary with a spanner. Remove the cup and upper buffer.

5 Working beneath the car remove the lower mounting bolt, then lower the trailing arm as far as possible and withdraw the strut/shock absorber. Keep the coil spring, seat and bump

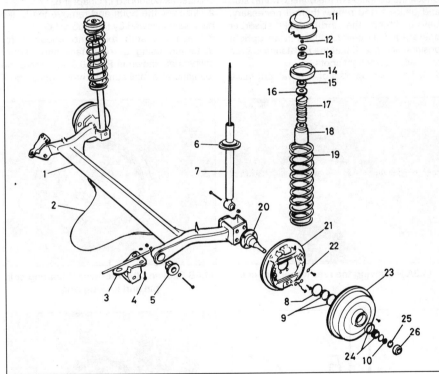

Fig. 10.7 Exploded view of the rear suspension components (Sec 9)

1 Axle beam	10 Hexagon nut	19 Coil spring
2 Handbrake cable	11 Cover for strut mounting	20 Stub axle
3 Bracket	12 Hexagon nut	21 Backplate complete
4 Collar screw	13 Upper buffer	22 Lock ring
5 Bonded rubber bush	14 Spring seat	23 Brake drum
6 Spring retainer	15 Lower buffer	24 Outer wheel bearing
7 Shock absorber	16 Washer	25 Slotted ring
8 Seal	17 Bump stop	26 Brake drum cap
9 Inner wheel bearing	18 Bellows	

10

9.2 Removing the cap from the top of the rear suspension strut

9.5A Rear suspension strut lower mounting bolt

9.5B View of the rear suspension strut upper mounting from below

stop components in their fitted positions on the strut (photos).

6 Remove the upper spring seat, coil spring, lower buffer, washer, bump stop and bellows and, if the unit is to be renewed, the lower spring retainer.

7 If the shock absorber is faulty it will normally make a knocking noise as the car is driven over rough surfaces, however with the unit removed uneven resistance tight spots will be evident as the central rod is operated. Check the condition of the buffers, bump stop and bellows and renew them if necessary. Before fitting the strut/shock absorber operate it fully several times in an upright position and check that the resistance is even and without any tight spots.

8 Refitting is a reversal of removal, but make

sure that the coil spring is correctly located in the seats. Delay tightening the lower mounting bolt until the full weight of the car is on the roadwheels.

10 Rear stub axle - removal and refitting

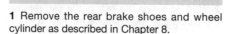

1 Remove the rear brake shoes and wheel cylinder as described in Chapter 8.
2 Unscrew the bolts and remove the brake backplate followed by the stub axle.
3 Clean the stub axle and check it for distortion using a try-square and vernier calipers as shown in Fig. 10.8. Compare the readings at a minimum of three points and if

the difference between the maximum and minimum readings exceeds 0.01 in (0.25 mm), renew the stub axle.

4 Refitting is a reversal of removal, but make sure that all mating faces are clean and tighten the bolts to the specified torque. Refer to Chapter 8 as necessary and adjust the wheel bearings as described in Section 11.

11 Rear wheel bearings - testing, renewal and adjustment

1 Chock the front wheels, then jack up the rear of the car and support on axle stands. Release the handbrake.
2 Spin the wheel. A rumbling noise will be evident if the bearings are worn in which case they must be renewed.
3 Remove the wheel then prise off the hub cap and extract the split pin. Remove the locking ring (photos).
4 Unscrew the hub nut and remove the thrust washer and outer wheel bearing (photos).
5 Withdraw the brake drum. If difficulty is experienced, the brake shoes must be backed away from the drum first. To do this, insert a screwdriver through one of the bolt holes and push the automatic adjuster wedge upwards against the spring tension. This will release the shoes from the drum.
6 Prise the seal from the inside of the drum with a screwdriver.

11.3A Removing the rear wheel hub cap

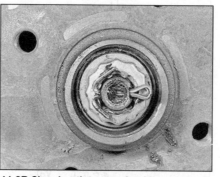

11.3B Showing the rear wheel bearing split pin and locking ring

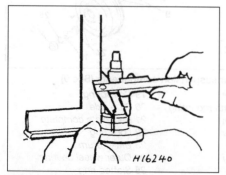

Fig. 10.8 Checking the rear wheel stub axle for distortion (Sec 10)

11.4A Showing the rear wheel bearing thrust washer

11.4B Removing the rear wheel outer bearing

11.16 Checking the rear wheel bearing adjustment with a screwdriver

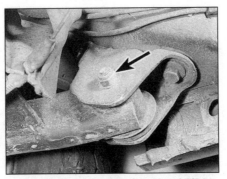

12.7 Showing a rear axle pivot bolt

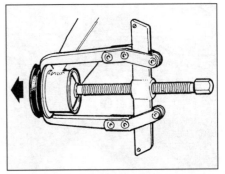

Fig. 10.9 Using a puller to remove the rear axle beam pivot bushes (Sec 13)

7 Remove the inner bearing, then using a soft metal drift, drive out the bearing outer races.

8 Clean the components in paraffin, wipe them dry, then examine them for wear and deterioration. Check the rollers and races for signs of pitting. Renew the bearings as necessary and obtain a new oil seal. Wipe clean the stub axle.

9 Using a suitable metal tube, drive the outer races into the drum/hub.

10 Lubricate the bearings with lithium based grease then locate the inner bearing in its race.

11 Smear the lips of the new seal with a little grease. Using a block of wood drive the seal squarely into the drum/hub with the lips facing inwards.

12 Refit the drum and locate the outer bearing on the stub axle.

13 Fit the thrust washer and hub nut, and tighten the nut hand tight.

14 Refit the wheel.

15 With the hub cap, split pin, and locking ring removed, tighten the hub nut firmly while turning the wheel in order to settle the bearings.

16 Back off the nut then tighten it until it is just possible to move the thrust washer laterally with a screwdriver under finger pressure. Do not twist the screwdriver or lever it (photo).

17 Fit the locking ring together with a new split pin, then tap the hub cap into the drum with a mallet.

18 Lower the car to the ground.

12 Rear axle beam - removal and refitting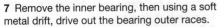

Note: If the axle beam is suspected of being distorted it should be checked in position by a VW garage using an optical alignment instrument

1 Remove the rear stub axles as described in Section 10.

2 Support the weight of the trailing arms with axle stands then disconnect the struts/shock absorbers by removing the lower mounting bolts.

3 Remove the tail section of the exhaust system with reference to Chapter 3.

4 Disconnect the handbrake cables from the axle beam and from the left-hand side underbody bracket with reference to Chapter 8.

5 Remove the brake fluid reservoir filler cap and tighten it down onto a piece of polythene sheet in order to reduce the loss of hydraulic fluid.

6 Lower the axle beam and disconnect the brake hydraulic hoses with reference to Chapter 8.

7 Support the weight of the axle beam with axle stands then unscrew and remove the pivot bolts and lower the axle beam to the ground. Note that the pivot bolt heads face outwards (photo).

8 If the bushes are worn renew them as described in Section 13. If necessary the

trunnion brackets can be removed by unscrewing the bolts. Discard the bolts.

9 Refit the trunnion brackets if necessary, but coat the new bolt threads with locking compound before tightening them to the specified torque.

10 Refitting is a reversal of removal, but delay tightening the strut/shock absorber lower mounting bolts and the axle beam pivot bolts to the specified torques until the full weight of the car is on the roadwheels. Bleed the brake hydraulic system as described in Chapter 8.

13 Rear axle beam pivot bushes - renewal

1 Check the front wheels then jack up the rear of the car and support on axle stands. Release the handbrake and remove the rear wheels.

2 Remove the tail section of the exhaust system with reference to Chapter 3.

3 Disconnect the handbrake cables from the underbody brackets with reference to Chapter 8.

4 Unscrew and remove the pivot bolts and lower the axle beam onto axle stands making sure that the flexible brake hoses are not strained.

5 Using a two-arm puller, force the bushes from the axle beam. Dip the new bushes in soapy water before pressing them in from the outside with the puller.

6 Refit the pivot bolts, handbrake cables, exhaust and rear wheels using a reversal of the removal procedure, but delay tightening the pivot bolt nuts to the specified torque until the full weight of the car is on the roadwheels.

14 Steering wheel - removal and refitting

1 Set the front wheels in the straight-ahead position.

2 Prise the cover from the centre of the steering wheel, note the location of the wires and disconnect them from the terminals on the cover (photos).

14.2A Prise the cover from the steering wheel . . .

14.2B . . . and disconnect the wires

10

14.3 Removing the steering wheel nut and washer

3 Mark the steering wheel and inner column in relation to each other, then unscrew the nut and withdraw the steering wheel. Remove the washer (photo).

4 Refitting in a reversal of removal, but make sure that the turn signal lever is in its neutral position, otherwise damage may occour to the cancelling arm. Tighten the nut to the specified torque.

15 Steering column - removal and refitting

1 Disconnect the battery negative lead.
2 Remove the steering wheel as described in Section 14.
3 Remove the screws and withdraw the steering column lower shroud (photo).
4 Remove the three screws and withdraw the combination switch. Disconnect the wiring plug.
5 Remove the screws and withdraw the lower facia trim panel.
6 Remove the column mounting bolts. An

15.3 Removing the steering column lower shroud

Allen key is required to unscrew one bolt, but the remaining bolt is a shear bolt and therefore its head must be drilled out using an 8.5 mm (0.335 in) diameter drill.

7 Lower the steering column and push it downwards to release the two pins from the flange tube, then withdraw the column from the car. Disconnect the ignition switch wiring plug.

8 Check the condition of the flange tube bushes and if necessary renew them. Lever the old bushes out with a screwdriver, then press in the new bushes after dipping them in soapy water. Unscrew the old shear bolt and obtain a new one.

9 Refitting is a reversal of removal, but make sure that the column is correctly positioned before tightening the shear bolt until its head is broken off.

16 Steering lock - removal and refitting

1 Disconnect the battery negative lead.

2 Remove the steering wheel as described in Section 14.
3 Remove the screws and withdraw the steering column lower shroud.
4 Remove the three screws and withdraw the combination switch. Disconnect the wiring plug.
5 Using an Allen key unscrew the clamp bolt securing the steering lock.
6 Prise the lockwasher from the inner column and remove the spring and contact ring.
7 Disconnect the wiring plug and withdraw the steering lock from the top of the column together with the upper shroud. Note that the ignition key must be inserted to ensure that the lock is in its released position.
8 Remove the screw and withdraw the switch from the lock housing.
9 To remove the lock cylinder, drill a 3.0 mm (0.118in) diameter hole in the location shown in Fig. 10.11, depress the spring pin, and extract the cylinder.
10 Refitting is a reversal of removal, but renew the inner column lockwasher and press it fully onto the stop while supporting the lower end of the column.

17 Steering column - dismantling and reassembly

1 With the steering column removed as described in Section 15, prise the lockwasher from the inner column and remove the spring and contact ring.
2 Using an Allen key unscrew the clamp bolt securing the steering lock and withdraw the lock. Note that the ignition key must be inserted and the lock released.
3 Withdraw the inner column from the outer columns and remove the support ring.
4 Clean the components and examine them for wear. Renew them as necessary.
5 Reassembly is a reversal of dismantling, but lubricate bearing surfaces with multi-purpose grease and renew the inner column lockwasher.

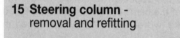

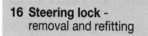

1 Horn plate
2 Steering wheel
3 Slip ring
4 Trim
5 Steering column switch
6 Lock washer
7 Spring
8 Contact ring
9 Steering lock housing
10 Support ring
11 Trim
12 Cheese head screw

13 Column tube
14 Shear bolt
15 Steering column
16 Bush
17 Flange tube
18 Clamp

Fig. 10.10 Exploded view of the steering column (Sec 15)

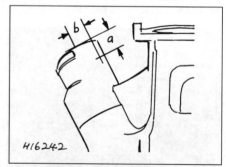

Fig. 10.11 Showing drilling position when removing steering lock cylinder (Sec 16)

a = 12 mm (0.472 in)
b = 10 mm (0.394 in)

18.2 Steering tie-rod centre bolts

18.4A Unscrew the nut . . .

18.4B . . . and then use a balljoint separator tool . . .

18 Tie-rods and balljoints - removal and refitting

1 If the steering tie-rod and balljoints are worn, play will be evident as the roadwheel is rocked from side to side, and the balljoint must then be renewed. On RHD models the left-hand tie-rod is adjustable and the balljoint on this tie-rod can be renewed separately, however the right-hand tie-rod must be renewed complete. On LHD models the tie-rods are vice versa.

2 If the complete tie-rod is to be removed unscrew the centre bolt with the weight of the car on the wheels otherwise the rubber bush may be damaged (photo).

3 Jack up the front of the car and support on axle stands. Apply the handbrake and remove the front wheel(s).

4 Unscrew the balljoint nut then use a balljoint separator tool to release the joint from the strut (photos).

5 Withdraw the tie-rod or if applicable loosen the locknut and unscrew the tie-rod end.

6 Refitting is a reversal of removal, but tighten the nuts to the specified torque and check the front wheel alignment as described in Section 21.

18.4C . . . and release the tie-rod

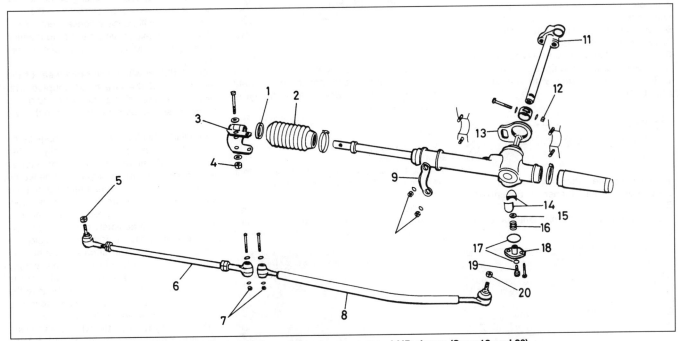

Fig, 10.12 Exploded view of the steering gear – LHD shown (Secs 19 and 20)

1 Retaining ring
2 Bellows
3 Bracket
4 Self-locking hexagon nut
5 Self-locking hexagon nut
6 Right tie-rod
7 Self-locking hexagon nut

8 Left tie-rod
9 Clamp
10 Self-locking hexagon nut
11 Flange tube
12 Self-locking hexagon nut
13 Seal
14 Thrust piece

15 Thrust washer
16 Spring
17 Sealing ring
18 Cover
19 Adjusting screw
20 Self-locking hexagon nut

10

20.5 Showing the clutch cable hole in the steering gear housing

19 Steering gear bellows - renewal

1 Remove the air cleaner as described in Chapter 3.
2 Unscrew and remove the clamp bolt from the end of the steering gear rack. Note that the bolt engages a groove on the side of the rack. Separate the bracket from the rack.
3 Loosen the clip and withdraw the bellows from the steering gear together with the retaining ring.
4 Smear a little steering gear grease on the rack then fit the new bellows together with the inner clip. Locate the bellows on the housing and tighten the clip.
5 Push on the retaining ring and locate the bellows in the outer groove.
6 Fit the bracket then insert the bolt so that it engages the groove and tighten the nut.
7 Refit the air cleaner with reference to Chapter 3.

20 Steering gear - removal, refitting and adjustment

1 Disconnect the battery negative lead.
2 Remove the air cleaner as described in Chapter 3.
3 Lift out the windscreen washer bottle and place it to one side.

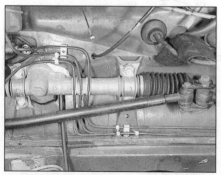

20.10A Steering gear location (engine removed from car)

4 Remove the screws and withdraw the lower facia panel shelf from around the steering column.
5 Where applicable remove the clutch cable with reference to Chapter 5 (photo).
6 Set the front wheels in the straight-ahead position then unscrew the clamp bolt securing the flange tube to the steering gear pinion.
7 Prise the flange tube up from the pinion. Do not bend the clamp open.
8 Unscrew and remove the tie-rod centre bolts and move the tie-rods to one side.
9 Jack up the front of the car and support on axle stands. Apply the handbrake and remove the front wheels.
10 Unscrew the nuts and remove the mounting clamps (photos).
11 Withdraw the steering gear upwards from the car. Remove the sealing gasket.
12 Refitting is a reversal of removal, but do not fully tighten the mounting clamp nuts until the steering gear is correctly aligned.
13 With the front of the car supported on axle stands turn the steering from lock to lock and check that there are no tight spots or excessive play. If necessary turn the self-locking adjusting screw on the bottom of the steering gear in to reduce play or out to reduce tight spots. Turn the screw in 20° stages and initially make the adjustment with the front wheels in the straight ahead position.

21 Wheel alignment - checking and adjusting

1 Accurate wheel alignment is essential for good steering and slow tyre wear. Before checking it, make sure that the car is only loaded to kerbside weight and the tyres correctly inflated.
2 Place the car on level ground with the wheels in the straight-ahead position, then roll the car backwards 12ft (4m) and forwards again.
3 Using a wheel alignment gauge, check that the front wheel toe-in dimension is as given in the Specifications.
4 If adjustment is necessary, loosen the locknuts on the adjustable tierod, turn the tie-rod as necessary, then tighten the locknuts.

20.10B Showing right-hand side mounting clamp on the steering gear

5 After making an adjustment give the car a test run and check that the steering wheel spokes are horizontal when travelling straight ahead. If necessary remove the steering wheel and reposition it on the inner column splines.
6 Camber and castor angles can be checked by a garage having a special optical alignment gauge.

22 Roadwheels and tyres - general

Wheels and tyres should give no real problems in use provided that a close eye is kept on them with regard to excessive wear or damage. To this end, the following points should be noted.

Ensure that tyre pressures are checked regularly and maintained correctly. Checking should be carried out with the tyres cold and not immediately after the vehicle has been in use. If the pressures are checked with the tyres hot, an apparently high reading will be obtained owing to heat expansion. Under no circumstances should an attempt be made to reduce the pressures to the quoted cold reading in this instance, or effective underinflation will result.

Underinflation will cause overheating of the tyre owing to excessive flexing of the casing, and the tread will not sit correctly on the road surface. This will cause a consequent loss of adhesion and excessive wear, not to mention the danger of sudden tyre failure due to heat build-up.

Overinflation will cause rapid wear of the centre part of the tyre tread coupled with reduced adhesion, harsher ride, and the danger of shock damage occurring in the tyre casing.

Regularly check the tyres for damage in the form of cuts or bulges, especially in the sidewalls. Remove any nails or stones embedded in the tread before they penetrate the tyre to cause deflation. If removal of a nail *does* reveal that the tyre has been punctured, refit the nail so that its point of penetration is marked. Then immediately change the wheel and have the tyre repaired by a tyre dealer. Do not drive on a tyre in such a condition. In many cases a puncture can be simply repaired by the use of an inner tube of the correct size and type. If in any doubt as to the possible consequences of any damage found, consult your local tyre dealer for advice.

Periodically remove the wheels and clean any dirt or mud from the inside and outside surfaces. Examine the wheel rims for signs of rusting, corrosion or other damage. Light alloy wheels are easily damaged by 'kerbing' whilst parking, and similarly steel wheels may become dented or buckled. Renewal of the wheel is very often the only course of remedial action possible.

The balance of each wheel and tyre

assembly should be maintained to avoid excessive wear, not only to the tyres but also to the steering and suspension components. Wheel imbalance is normally signified by vibration through the vehicle's bodyshell, although in many cases it is particularly noticeable through the steering wheel. Conversely, it should be noted that wear or damage in suspension or steering components may cause excessive tyre wear. Out-of-round or out-of-true tyres, damaged wheels and wheel bearing wear/ maladjustment also fall into this category. Balancing will not usually cure vibration caused by such wear.

Wheel balancing may be carried out with the wheel either on or off the vehicle. If balanced on the vehicle, ensure that the wheel-to-hub relationship is marked in some way prior to subsequent wheel removal so that it may be refitted in its original position.

General tyre wear is influenced to a large degree by driving style harsh braking and acceleration or fast cornering will all produce more rapid tyre wear. Interchanging of tyres may result in more even wear, but this should only be carried out where there is no mix of tyre types on the vehicle. However, it is worth bearing in mind that if this is completely effective, the added expense of replacing a complete set of tyres simultaneously is incurred, which may prove financially restrictive for many owners.

Front tyres may wear unevenly as a result of wheel misalignment. The front wheels should always be correctly aligned according to the settings specified by the vehicle manufacturer.

Legal restrictions apply to the mixing of tyre types on a vehicle. Basically this means that a vehicle must not have tyres of differing construction on the same axle. Although it is not recommended to mix tyre types between front axle and rear axle, the only legally permissible combination is crossply at the front and radial at the rear. When mixing radial ply tyres, textile braced radials must always go on the front axle, with steel braced radials at the rear. An obvious disadvantage of such mixing is the necessity to carry two spare tyres to avoid contravening the law in the event of a puncture.

In the UK, the Motor Vehicles Construction and Use Regulations apply to many aspects of tyre fitting and usage. It is suggested that a copy of these regulations is obtained from your local police if in doubt as to the current legal requirements with regard to tyre condition, minimum tread depth, etc.

Fault finding - suspension and steering

Excessive play in steering
☐ Worn steering gear or tie-rod balljoints and bushes
☐ Worn lower control arm balljoints

Wanders or pulls to one side
☐ Incorrect wheel alignment
☐ Worn tie-rod balljoints and bushes
☐ Worn lower control arm balljoints
☐ Uneven tyre pressures
☐ Faulty shock absorber

Heavy or stiff steering
☐ Seized balljoint
☐ Incorrect wheel alignment
☐ Low tyre pressures
☐ Lack of lubricant in steering gear

Wheel wobble and vibration
☐ Roadwheels out of balance
☐ Roadwheels damaged
☐ Worn shock absorbers
☐ Worn wheel bearings

Excessive tyre wear
☐ Incorrect wheel alignment
☐ Worn shock absorbers
☐ Incorrect tyre pressures
☐ Roadwheels out of balance

Notes

Chapter 11 Bodywork and fittings

For modifications, and information applicable to later models, see Supplement at end of manual

Contents

Degrees of difficulty

Easy, suitable for novice with little experience	**Fairly easy,** suitable for beginner with some experience	**Fairly difficult,** suitable for competent DIY mechanic	**Difficult,** suitable for experienced DIY mechanic	**Very difficult,** suitable for expert DIY or professional

1 General description

The body is of all-steel unit construction with impact-absorbing front and rear crumple zones which take the brunt of any accident, leaving the passenger compartment with minimum distortion. The front wings are bolted in position and are easily removed should renewal be necessary after a front end collision.

2 Maintenance - bodywork and underframe

The general condition of a vehicle's bodywork is the one thing that significantly affects its value. Maintenance is easy, but needs to be regular. Neglect, particularly after minor damage, can lead quickly to further deterioration and costly repair bills. It is important also to keep watch on those parts of the vehicle not immediately visible, for instance the underside, inside all the wheel arches, and the lower part of the engine compartment.

The basic maintenance routine for the bodywork is washing - preferably with a lot of water, from a hose. This will remove all the loose solids which may have stuck to the vehicle. It is important to flush these off in such a way as to prevent grit from scratching the finish. The wheel arches and underframe need washing in the same way, to remove any accumulated mud, which will retain moisture and tend to encourage rust. Paradoxically enough, the best time to clean the underframe and wheel arches is in wet weather, when the mud is thoroughly wet and soft. In very wet weather, the underframe is usually cleaned of large accumulations automatically, and this is a good time for inspection.

Periodically, except on vehicles with a wax-based underbody protective coating, it is a good idea to have the whole of the underframe of the vehicle steam-cleaned, engine compartment included, so that a thorough inspection can be carried out to see what minor repairs and renovations are necessary. Steam-cleaning is available at many garages, and is necessary for the removal of the accumulation of oily grime, which sometimes is allowed to become thick in certain areas. If steam-cleaning facilities are not available, there are some excellent grease solvents available which can be brush-applied; the dirt can then be simply hosed off. Note that these methods should not be used on vehicles with wax-based underbody protective coating, or the coating will be removed. Such vehicles should be inspected annually, preferably just prior to Winter, when the underbody should be washed down, and any damage to the wax coating repaired. Ideally, a completely fresh coat should be applied. It would also be worth considering the use of such wax-based protection for injection into door panels, sills, box sections, etc, as an additional safeguard against rust damage, where such protection is not provided by the vehicle manufacturer.

After washing paintwork, wipe off with a chamois leather to give an unspotted clear finish. A coat of clear protective wax polish will give added protection against chemical pollutants in the air. If the paintwork sheen has dulled or oxidised, use a cleaner/polisher combination to restore the brilliance of the shine. This requires a little effort, but such dulling is usually caused because regular washing has been neglected. Care needs to be taken with metallic paintwork, as special non-abrasive cleaner/polisher is required to avoid damage to the finish. Always check that the door and ventilator opening drain holes and pipes are completely clear, so that water can be drained out (photos). Brightwork should be treated in the same way as paintwork. Windscreens and windows can be kept clear of the smeary film which often appears, by the use of proprietary glass cleaner. Never use any form of wax or other body or chromium polish on glass.

11

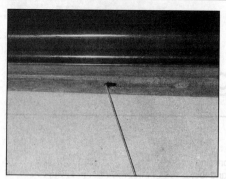

2.4A Clearing a door drain hole

2.4B Clearing a sill drain hole

3 Maintenance - upholstery and carpets

Mats and carpets should be brushed or vacuum-cleaned regularly, to keep them free of grit. If they are badly stained, remove them from the vehicle for scrubbing or sponging, and make quite sure they are dry before refitting. Seats and interior trim panels can be kept clean by wiping with a damp cloth. If they do become stained (which can be more apparent on light-coloured upholstery), use a little liquid detergent and a soft nail brush to scour the grime out of the grain of the material. Do not forget to keep the headlining clean in the same way as the upholstery. When using liquid cleaners inside the vehicle, do not over-wet the surfaces being cleaned. Excessive damp could get into the seams and padded interior, causing stains, offensive odours or even rot.

HAYNES HiNT *If the inside of the vehicle gets wet accidentally, it is worthwhile taking some trouble to dry it out properly, particularly where carpets are involved. Do not leave oil or electric heaters inside the vehicle for this purpose.*

4 Minor body damage - repair

Note: *For more detailed information about bodywork repair, Haynes Publishing produce a book by Lindsay Porter called "The Car Bodywork Repair Manual". This incorporates information on such aspects as rust treatment, painting and glass-fibre repairs, as well as details on more ambitious repairs involving welding and panel beating.*

Repairs of minor scratches in bodywork

If the scratch is very superficial, and does not penetrate to the metal of the bodywork, repair is very simple. Lightly rub the area of the scratch with a paintwork renovator, or a very fine cutting paste, to remove loose paint from the scratch, and to clear the surrounding bodywork of wax polish. Rinse the area with clean water.

Apply touch-up paint to the scratch using a fine paint brush; continue to apply fine layers of paint until the surface of the paint in the scratch is level with the surrounding paintwork. Allow the new paint at least two weeks to harden, then blend it into the surrounding paintwork by rubbing the scratch area with a paintwork renovator or a very fine cutting paste. Finally, apply wax polish.

Where the scratch has penetrated right through to the metal of the bodywork, causing the metal to rust, a different repair technique is required. Remove any loose rust from the bottom of the scratch with a penknife, then apply rust-inhibiting paint to prevent the formation of rust in the future. Using a rubber or nylon applicator, fill the scratch with bodystopper paste. If required, this paste can be mixed with cellulose thinners to provide a very thin paste which is ideal for filling narrow scratches. Before the stopper-paste in the scratch hardens, wrap a piece of smooth cotton rag around the top of a finger. Dip the finger in cellulose thinners, and quickly sweep it across the surface of the stopper-paste in the scratch; this will ensure that the surface of the stopper-paste is slightly hollowed. The scratch can now be painted over as described earlier in this Section.

Repairs of dents in bodywork

When deep denting of the vehicle's bodywork has taken place, the first task is to pull the dent out, until the affected bodywork almost attains its original shape. There is little point in trying to restore the original shape completely, as the metal in the damaged area will have stretched on impact, and cannot be reshaped fully to its original contour. It is better to bring the level of the dent up to a point which is about 3 mm below the level of the surrounding bodywork. In cases where the dent is very shallow anyway, it is not worth trying to pull it out at all. If the underside of the dent is accessible, it can be hammered out gently from behind, using a mallet with a wooden or plastic head. Whilst doing this, hold a suitable block of wood firmly against the outside of the panel, to absorb the impact from the hammer blows and thus prevent a large area of the bodywork from being "belled-out".

Should the dent be in a section of the bodywork which has a double skin, or some other factor making it inaccessible from behind, a different technique is called for. Drill several small holes through the metal inside the area - particularly in the deeper section. Then screw long self-tapping screws into the holes, just sufficiently for them to gain a good purchase in the metal. Now the dent can be pulled out by pulling on the protruding heads of the screws with a pair of pliers.

The next stage of the repair is the removal of the paint from the damaged area, and from an inch or so of the surrounding "sound" bodywork. This is accomplished most easily by using a wire brush or abrasive pad on a power drill, although it can be done just as effectively by hand, using sheets of abrasive paper. To complete the preparation for filling, score the surface of the bare metal with a screwdriver or the tang of a file, or alternatively, drill small holes in the affected area. This will provide a really good "key" for the filler paste.

To complete the repair, see the Section on filling and respraying.

Repairs of rust holes or gashes in bodywork

Remove all paint from the affected area, and from an inch or so of the surrounding "sound" bodywork, using an abrasive pad or a wire brush on a power drill. If these are not available, a few sheets of abrasive paper will do the job most effectively. With the paint removed, you will be able to judge the severity of the corrosion, and therefore decide whether to renew the whole panel (if this is possible) or to repair the affected area. New body panels are not as expensive as most people think, and it is often quicker and more satisfactory to fit a new panel than to attempt to repair large areas of corrosion.

Remove all fittings from the affected area, except those which will act as a guide to the original shape of the damaged bodywork (eg headlight shells etc). Then, using tin snips or a hacksaw blade, remove all loose metal and any other metal badly affected by corrosion. Hammer the edges of the hole inwards, in order to create a slight depression for the filler paste.

Wire-brush the affected area to remove the powdery rust from the surface of the remaining metal. Paint the affected area with rust-inhibiting paint, if the back of the rusted area is accessible, treat this also.

Before filling can take place, it will be necessary to block the hole in some way. This can be achieved by the use of aluminium or plastic mesh, or aluminium tape.

Aluminium or plastic mesh, or glass-fibre matting, is probably the best material to use for a large hole. Cut a piece to the approximate size and shape of the hole to be filled, then position it in the hole so that its edges are below the level of the surrounding bodywork. It can be retained in position by several blobs of filler paste around its periphery.

Aluminium tape should be used for small or very narrow holes. Pull a piece off the roll, trim it to the approximate size and shape required, then pull off the backing paper (if used) and stick the tape over the hole; it can be overlapped if the thickness of one piece is insufficient. Burnish down the edges of the tape with the handle of a screwdriver or similar, to ensure that the tape is securely attached to the metal underneath.

Bodywork repairs - filling and respraying

Before using this Section, see the Sections on dent, deep scratch, rust holes and gash repairs.

Many types of bodyfiller are available, but generally speaking, those proprietary kits which contain a tin of filler paste and a tube of resin hardener are best for this type of repair. A wide, flexible plastic or nylon applicator will be found invaluable for imparting a smooth and well-contoured finish to the surface of the filler.

Mix up a little filler on a clean piece of card or board - measure the hardener carefully (follow the maker's instructions on the pack), otherwise the filler will set too rapidly or too slowly. Using the applicator, apply the filler paste to the prepared area; draw the applicator across the surface of the filler to achieve the correct contour and to level the surface. As soon as a contour that approximates to the correct one is achieved, stop working the paste - if you carry on too long, the paste will become sticky and begin to "pick-up" on the applicator. Continue to add thin layers of filler paste at 20-minute intervals, until the level of the filler is just proud of the surrounding bodywork.

Once the filler has hardened, the excess can be removed using a metal plane or file. From then on, progressively-finer grades of abrasive paper should be used, starting with a 40-grade production paper, and finishing with a 400-grade wet-and-dry paper. Always wrap the abrasive paper around a flat rubber, cork, or wooden block - otherwise the surface of the filler will not be completely flat. During the smoothing of the filler surface, the wet-and-dry paper should be periodically rinsed in water. This will ensure that a very smooth finish is imparted to the filler at the final stage.

At this stage, the "dent" should be surrounded by a ring of bare metal, which in turn should be encircled by the finely "feathered" edge of the good paintwork. Rinse the repair area with clean water, until all

of the dust produced by the rubbing-down operation has gone.

Spray the whole area with a light coat of primer - this will show up any imperfections in the surface of the filler. Repair these imperfections with fresh filler paste or bodystopper, and once more smooth the surface with abrasive paper. Repeat this spray-and-repair procedure until you are satisfied that the surface of the filler, and the feathered edge of the paintwork, are perfect. Clean the repair area with clean water, and allow to dry fully.

> **HAYNES HINT**
>
> *If bodystopper is used, it can be mixed with cellulose thinners to form a really thin paste which is ideal for filling small holes.*

The repair area is now ready for final spraying. Paint spraying must be carried out in a warm, dry, windless and dust-free atmosphere. This condition can be created artificially if you have access to a large indoor working area, but if you are forced to work in the open, you will have to pick your day very carefully. If you are working indoors, dousing the floor in the work area with water will help to settle the dust which would otherwise be in the atmosphere. If the repair area is confined to one body panel, mask off the surrounding panels; this will help to minimise the effects of a slight mis-match in paint colours. Bodywork fittings (eg chrome strips, door handles etc) will also need to be masked off. Use genuine masking tape, and several thicknesses of newspaper, for the masking operations.

Before commencing to spray, agitate the aerosol can thoroughly, then spray a test area (an old tin, or similar) until the technique is mastered. Cover the repair area with a thick coat of primer; the thickness should be built up using several thin layers of paint, rather than one thick one. Using 400-grade wet-and-dry paper, rub down the surface of the primer until it is really smooth. While doing this, the work area should be thoroughly doused with water, and the wet-and-dry paper periodically rinsed in water. Allow to dry before spraying on more paint.

Spray on the top coat, again building up the thickness by using several thin layers of paint. Start spraying at one edge of the repair area, and then, using a side-to-side motion, work until the whole repair area and about 2 inches of the surrounding original paintwork is covered. Remove all masking material 10 to 15 minutes after spraying on the final coat of paint.

Allow the new paint at least two weeks to harden, then, using a paintwork renovator, or a very fine cutting paste, blend the edges of the paint into the existing paintwork. Finally, apply wax polish.

5 Major body damage - repair

Where serious damage has occurred or large areas need renewal due to neglect, it means certainly that completely new sections or panels will need welding in and this is best left to professionals. If the damage is due to impact, it will also be necessary to completely check the alignment of the bodyshell structure. Due to the principle of construction, the strength and shape of the whole car can be affected by damage to one part. In such instances the services of a VW agent with specialist checking jigs are essential. If a body is left misaligned, it is first of all dangerous as the car will not handle properly, and secondly uneven stresses will be imposed on the steering, engine and transmission, causing abnormal wear or complete failure. Tyre wear may also be excessive.

6 Maintenance - hinges and locks

1 Every 10 000 miles (15 000 km) lubricate the door, bonnet and tailgate/boot lid hinges with a little oil. Similarly lubricate the bonnet release mechanism and door, bonnet and tailgate/boot lid locks.
2 At the same time lubricate the door check straps with a little multi-purpose grease.
3 Do not attempt to lubricate the steering lock.

7 Door rattles - tracing and rectification

1 Check first that the door is not loose at the hinges, and that the latch is holding the door firmly in position. Check also that the door lines up with the aperture in the body. If the door is out of alignment, adjust it as described in Section 15.
2 If the latch is holding the door in the correct position but the latch still rattles, the lock mechanism is worn and should be renewed.
3 Other rattles from the door could be caused by wear in the window operating mechanism, interior lock mechanism, or loose glass channels.

11

8 Bonnet - removal, refitting and adjustment

1 Support the bonnet in its open position, and place some cardboard or rags beneath the corners by the hinges.

8.2 Bonnet hinge

8.3 Disconnecting the windscreen washer tubes from the bonnet

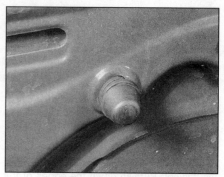

8.5 Bonnet rubber buffer

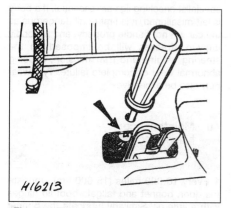

Fig. 11.1 Tightening the bonnet lock inner cable securing screw (Sec 9)

2 Mark the location of the hinges with a pencil then loosen the four retaining bolts (photo).
3 Disconnect the windscreen washer tubes from the jets on the bonnet (photo).
4 With the help of an assistant, release the stay, remove the bolts, and withdraw the bonnet from the car.
5 Refitting is a reversal of removal, but adjust the hinges to their original positions and check that the bonnet is level with the surrounding bodywork. If necessary adjust the height of the bonnet front edge by screwing the rubber buffers in or out (photo), and also adjust the bonnet lock if necessary with reference to Section 9.

9 Bonnet cable and lock - removal, refitting and adjustment

1 Inside the car, remove the trim on the left under the dash. The cable is accessible on the inside end. Before it can be removed it must be released from the lock which is bolted to the centre support of the grille.
2 Open the bonnet, remove the radiator grille and disconnect the cable.
3 Now back inside the car, remove the bonnet catch release handle bracket and lift the bracket away from the trim. In the centre of the upper end of the operating handle is a small clamping plate. Bend this outwards and the handle may be released from the bracket.

The cable may now be pulled out of the handle and out of the car.

> **HAYNES HiNT** *Tie a piece of thin wire or cord to the inside end and pull that into the place the cable occupied to make fitting a new cable more simple.*

4 Refitting is a reversal of removal, but make sure that the cable is positioned without any sharp bends. With the handle fully released, bend the end of the inner cable to attach it to the lock, but make sure it is free of tension. With the outer cable free of tension tighten the crosshead screw on the lock.
5 To remove the lock, remove the radiator grille and disconnect the cable.
6 Using an Allen key remove the retaining bolts and withdraw the lock (photo).
7 Refitting is a reversal of removal, but if necessary adjust the height of the bonnet front edge by loosening the retaining bolts and repositioning the lock within the elongated holes. The safety catch and anti-rattle spring should be checked for condition at the same time (photo).

10 Radiator grille - removal and refitting

1 Support the bonnet in its open position.
2 Release the clips from the top of the grille (photos).

9.6 Bonnet lock and retaining bolts

10.2A Depress the plastic tab with a screwdriver . . .

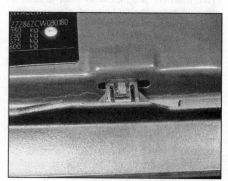

10.2B . . . and pull out the radiator grille

9.7 Bonnet safety catch and anti-rattle spring

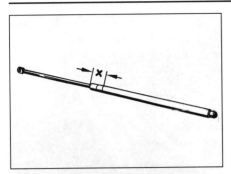

Fig. 11.2 Showing vice mounting area when depressurising the tailgate support strut (Sec 11)

11.2 Body mounting of the tailgate strut

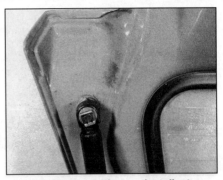

11.3 Strut mounting on the tailgate

3 Withdraw the grille upwards from the front valance.
4 Refitting is a reversal of removal.

11 Tailgate support strut - removal and refitting

1 Open and support the tailgate.
2 Unhook the spring clip from the end of the strut attached to the body, pull up the ball head, and disconnect the strut from the ball-pin (photo).
3 Lever the spring clip from the other end of the strut, remove the washer, and withdraw the strut from the pivot pin (photo).
4 If the strut is to be renewed, the old unit can be depressurised by clamping it in a vice within the area shown in Fig. 11.2, then using a hacksaw to cut into the cylinder within the first third of the cylinder measured from the piston rod end. *Protective glasses and clothing must be worn and in addition rag should be wrapped around the area to be cut.*
5 Refitting is a reversal of removal.

12 Tailgate - removal and refitting

1 Open and support the tailgate.
2 Remove the trim panel using a wide blade

screwdriver, and disconnect the wiring from the heated rear window and wiper motor. Disconnect the washer tube and pull the wiring and tube from the tailgate.
3 Pull the weatherseal from the body aperture by the hinge positions (photo).
4 Carefully pull the headlining down to reveal the hinge bolts.
5 Lever the spring clips from the struts, remove the washers, and disconnect the struts from the tailgate.
6 Unscrew the hinge bolts and withdraw the tailgate from the car.
7 Refitting is a reversal of removal, but before tightening the hinge bolts make sure that the tailgate closes centrally within the body aperture. If necessary adjust the lock as described in Section 13.

13 Tailgate lock - removal, refitting and adjustment

1 Open the tailgate and using an Allen key unscrew the two lock retaining screws. Withdraw the lock (photo).
2 If necessary remove the cross-head screw and withdraw the lock cylinder and seal. Unscrew the striker from the body and remove the washer (photo).
3 Refitting is a reversal of removal, but before fully tightening the striker, close and open the tailgate two or three times to centralise it.

12.3 Tailgate hinge

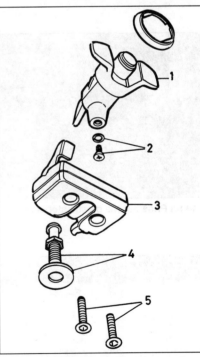

Fig. 11.3 Tailgate lock components (Sec 13)

1 Lock cylinder with housing
2 Fillister head screw with washer
3 Tailgate latch
4 Locking pin with washer
5 Socket head screws

13.1 Tailgate lock

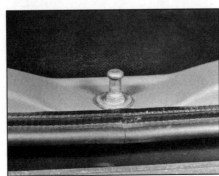

13.2 Tailgate striker

11

14.2 Removing the door inner handle surround

14.3A Prise off the covers . . .

14.3B . . . and remove the door pull screws

14.4A Remove the screw . . .

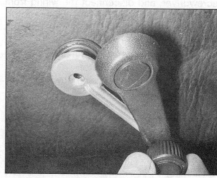

14.4B . . . and withdraw the window regulator handle

14 Door trim panel -
removal and refitting

1 Unscrew and remove the locking knob.
2 Remove the inner handle surround by sliding it to the rear (photo).
3 Prise the covers from the door pull with a small screwdriver, remove the cross-head screws, and withdraw the door pull (photos).
4 Note the position of the window regulator handle with the window shut then prise off the cover, remove the cross-head screw and withdraw the handle and washer (photos).
5 Remove the self-tapping screws and withdraw the storage compartment panel (where applicable).
6 Prise out the stoppers and remove the cross-head screws from the trim panel (photos).
7 Using a wide blade screwdriver prise the trim panel clips from the door taking care not to damage the panel. Remove the panel (photos).
8 Remove the window regulator handle packing.
9 If necessary peel the protective sheet from the door.
10 Refitting is a reversal of removal, however it is recommended that the window regulator handle retaining screw is locked by coating its threads with a liquid locking agent.

14.6A Prise out the plastic stoppers . . .

14.6B . . . and remove the door trim panel screws

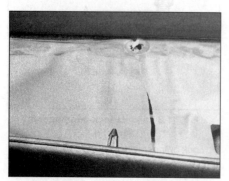

14.7A Door trim panel upper clips

14.7B Door trim panel lower clips

15.1 Door check strap

15.3 Door hinge and bolt

15.4 Door striker

16.4 View of exterior door handle from inside the door

15 Door - removal and refitting

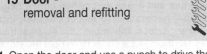

1 Open the door and use a punch to drive the pivot pin up from the check strap (photo).
2 Mark the position of the door on the hinges.
3 Support the door then unscrew and remove the lower hinge bolt followed by the upper hinge bolt, and withdraw the door from the car (photo).
4 Refitting is a reversal of removal, but if necessary adjust the position of the door on the hinges so that, when closed, it is level with the surrounding bodywork and central within the body aperture. Lubricate the hinges with a little oil and the check strap with grease. If necessary adjust the position of the door striker (photo).

16 Door handle (exterior) - removal and refitting

1 Remove the trim panel as described in Section 14.
2 Using a small screwdriver lever the plastic strip from the exterior door handle.
3 Remove the cross-head screws from the handle grip and the end of the door.
4 Withdraw the handle and release it from the lock (photo). Remove the gaskets.
5 Refitting is a reversal of removal, but fit new gaskets if necessary.

17 Door handle (interior) - removal and refitting

1 Remove the trim panel as described in Section 14.
2 Pull the foam seal away then prise the retainer from the bottom of the handle (photo).
3 Press the fingerplate forwards out of the door and unhook it from the rod (photo). Remove the foam seal.
4 Refitting is a reversal of removal.

1 Window channel
2 Glass
3 Door handle
4 Outer window slot seal
5 Inner window slot seal
6 Locking rod with sleeve
7 Door lock
8 Door lock remote control
9 Remote control seal
10 Fixed corner window with seal
11 Mirror
12 Front guide rail with window channel

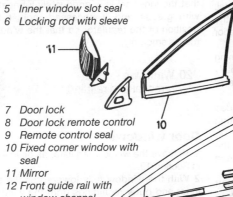
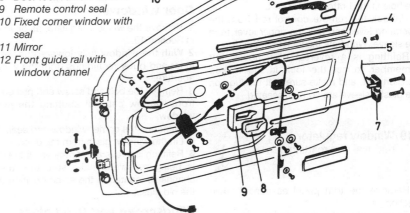

Fig. 11.4 Exploded view of door components (Secs 16 to 20)

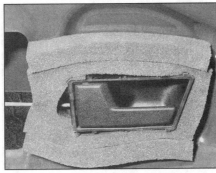
17.2 Interior door handle and foam seal

17.3 Removing the interior door handle and fingerplate

11

18.2 Door lock

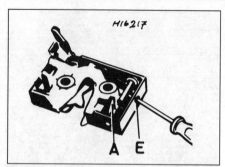

Fig. 11.5 Using a screwdriver through the door lock hole (E) to retain the operating lever (A) in the extended position (Sec 18)

18 Door lock - removal and refitting

1 It is not necessary to remove the trim panel. First open the door and set the lock in the locked position either by moving the interior knob or by turning the exterior key.
2 Using an Allen key, unscrew the retaining screws and withdraw the lock approximately 12 mm (0.5 in) to expose the operating lever (photo).
3 Retain the operating lever in the extended position by inserting a screwdriver through the hole in the bottom of the lock.
4 Unhook the remote control rod from the operating lever and pull the upper lever from the sleeve. Withdraw the lock from the door.
5 Refitting is a reversal of removal, but remember to set the lock in the locked position first, and make sure that the lugs on the plastic sleeve are correctly seated.

19 Window regulator - removal and refitting

1 Remove the trim panel as described in Section 14.
2 Temporarily refit the window regulator handle and lower the window until the lifting plate is visible.
3 Remove the bolts securing the regulator to

19.3A Window regulator control mounting bolts

the door and the bolts securing the lifting plate to the window channel (photos).
4 Release the regulator from the door and remove it through the aperture.
5 Refitting is a reversal of removal, but ensure that the inner cable is adequately lubricated with grease and if necessary adjust the position of the regulator so that the window moves smoothly.

20 Windows - removal and refitting

Door windows

1 Remove the window regulator as described in Section 19.
2 With the window fully lowered unclip the inner and outer mouldings from the window aperture.
3 Remove the bolt and screw and pull out the front window channel abutting the corner window.
4 Withdraw the corner window and seal.
5 Lift the window glass from the door.
6 Refitting is a reversal of removal. If the glass is being renewed, make sure that the lift channel is located in the same position as in the old glass.

Windscreen and fixed glass

7 Removal and refitting of the windscreen and fixed glass windows is best left to a VW garage or windscreen specialist who will have

19.3B Window regulator tube mounting bolts

the necessary equipment and expertise to complete the work properly.

21 Boot lid and lock (Classic models) - removal and refitting

1 Open the boot lid and mark the position of the hinges with a pencil.
2 With the help of an assistant unscrew the bolts and withdraw the boot lid.
3 The boot lock and striker are each secured by two cross-head screws, but when removing the lock it will be necessary to unhook the connecting rod.
4 Refitting is a reversal of removal, but make sure that the boot lid is central within the aperture and adjust its position on the hinge bolts if necessary. To adjust the boot lock striker, loosen the mounting screws then tighten them just sufficiently to hold the striker in position. Fully close the boot lid then open it again and fully tighten the screws. Adjust the stop rubbers if necessary.

22 Front wing - removal and refitting

1 A damaged front wing may be renewed complete. First remove the front bumper as described in Section 23.
2 Remove the screws and withdraw the splash guard from inside the wing (in Coupé models also drill out the rivets).
3 Remove all the screws and lever the wing from the guides. If necessary warm the sealing joints with a blowlamp to melt the adhesive underseal, *but be sure to take the necessary fire precautions*.
4 Clean the mating faces and treat with rust inhibitor if necessary.
5 Apply sealer along the line of the screws before fitting the wing. Once in place, apply underseal as necessary. Paint the wing then fit the splash guard and front bumper.

23 Bumpers - removal and refitting

Front bumper

1 Working inside the engine compartment first disconnect the battery negative lead, then disconnect the wiring to the direction indicator lights.
2 Unscrew the bumper nuts on each side then pull the bumper forwards out of the side guides and at the same time feed the direction indicator wiring through the body channels.
3 Refitting is a reversal of removal.

Rear bumper

4 Disconnect the battery negative lead.

5 Working in the luggage compartment remove the screw and detach the earth cable from the body.
6 Disconnect the number plate wiring at the connector then pull the wires out from the rear of the body together with the grommet.
7 Unscrew the bumper nuts on each side then pull the bumper rearwards out of the side guides.
8 Refitting is a reversal of removal.

24 Exterior mirror - removal and refitting

Non-remote control type

1 Prise the plastic cover from inside the door (photo).
2 Unscrew the cross-head screws and remove the clips.
3 Withdraw the outer cover and mirror.
4 Refitting is a reversal of removal.

Remote control type

5 Pull off the adjusting knob and bellows from the inside of the door.
6 Remove the door trim panel as described in Section 14.
7 Unscrew the locknut and remove the adjusting knob from the bracket.
8 Prise off the plastic cover then unscrew the cross-head screws and remove the clips.
9 Withdraw the mirror together with the adjusting knob and gasket.
10 Refitting is a reversal of removal, but fit a new gasket if necessary.

25 Sunroof - removal, refitting and adjustment

1 Half open the sunroof then prise off the trim clips.
2 Close the sunroof and push the trim to the rear.
3 Unscrew the guide screws from the front of the sunroof and remove the guides.
4 Disengage the leaf springs from the rear guides by pulling them inwards.
5 Remove the screws and withdraw the rear support plates.
6 Lift the sunroof from the car.
7 To refit the sunroof locate it in the aperture and fit the front guides.
8 With the sunroof closed and correctly aligned, fit the rear guides and leaf springs.
9 The correct adjustment of the sunroof is shown in Fig. 11.8 - the front edge must be level with or a maximum of 1.0 mm (0.040 in) below the roof panel, and the rear edge must be level with or a maximum of 1.0 mm (0.040 in) above the roof panel.
10 To adjust the front edge of the sunroof loosen the front guide screws and turn the adjustment screws as necessary, then tighten the guide screws.

24.1 Removing the inner plastic cover when removing the exterior mirror

11 To adjust the rear edge, detach the leaf springs, loosen the slotted screws and move the sunroof as necessary in the serrations. Tighten the screws and refit the leaf springs after making the adjustment.
12 Refit the trim with the clips.

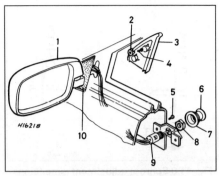
Fig. 11.6 Exploded diagram of remote control exterior mirror (Sec 24)

1 Outer mirror
2 Retainer
3 Cover
4 Fillister head screw
5 Phillips screws
6 Adjusting knob
7 Bellows
8 Lock nut
9 Retainer
10 Mirror mounting

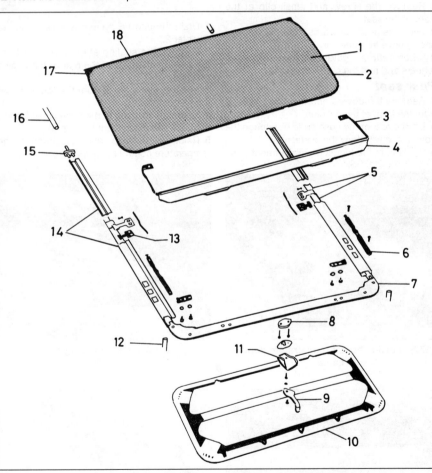
Fig. 11.7 Exploded view of the sunroof (Sec 25)

1 Sliding roof panel
2 Moulded seal
3 Deflector arm
4 Wind deflector
5 Rear guide with cable (one part)
6 Cover moulding
7 Cable guide
8 Cable drive mechanism
9 Crank
10 Panel headlining
11 Finger plate
12 Front water drain hose
13 Support plate
14 Guide rail
15 Guide rails end section
16 Rear water drain hose
17 Water trap plate
18 Panel seat

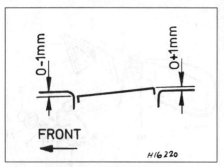
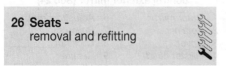

Fig. 11.8 Sunroof adjustment dimensions (Sec 25)

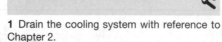

27.3 Removing the heater wiring block

27.4 Disconnecting the heater hoses

26 Seats -
removal and refitting

Front seats

1 Remove the screw and small clip at the front of the seat.
2 Slide the seat rearwards from the runners and remove from the car.
3 When refitting guide the seat onto the runners and refit the clip.

Rear seat

4 Remove the covers and mounting screws from the front of the cushion.
5 Lift the rear of the cushion to disengage the hooks then withdraw the cushion.
6 Working in the luggage compartment prise

the backrest upper hooks from the panel, then withdraw the backrest from the car.
7 Refitting is a reversal of removal.

27 Heater unit and matrix -
removal and refitting

1 Drain the cooling system with reference to Chapter 2.
2 Remove the sealing strip and cover from the plenum chamber at the rear of the engine compartment.
3 Pull the wiring block from the terminals on the heater (photo).
4 Note the locations of the hoses then loosen the clips and disconnect them (photo).
5 Release the clip and disconnect the temperature control cable (photo).

6 Prise out the clips, ease the heater from the fresh air box, and withdraw it from the bulkhead. Remove all traces of gasket and sealing compound (photos).
7 Remove the cross-head screws and slide the matrix from the housing (photos).
8 Clean all the components. The motor can be removed by separating the housing halves but the motor is not obtainable as a separate item (photo).
9 Refitting is a reversal of removal, but fit a new gasket if necessary. Make sure that the hoses are correctly fitted (photo). To fit the temperature control cable turn the lever fully clockwise to the closed position, pull the inner cable out of the outer cable, then locate the inner cable on the lever and secure the outer cable with the clip. Bleed the cooling system as described in Chapter 2.

27.5 Showing heater temperature control cable

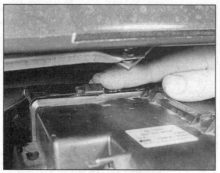

27.6A Prise off the clips . . .

27.6B . . . and withdraw the heater

27.6C Showing the heater air box on the bulkhead

27.7A Matrix retaining screw locations in the heater body

27.7B Removing the heater matrix

27.7C Heater matrix and temperature control valve

27.8 Heater motor connections

27.9 Showing flow direction arrow on the upper heater outlet – beneath the outlet with temperature valve fitted

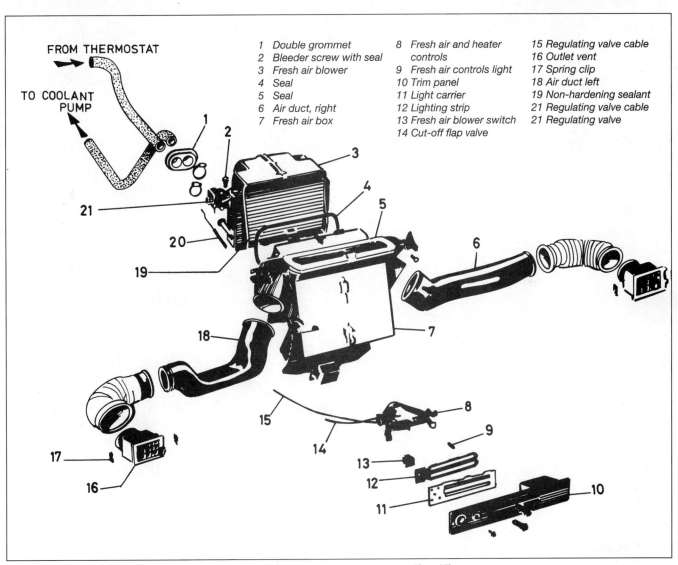

1 Double grommet	8 Fresh air and heater controls
2 Bleeder screw with seal	9 Fresh air controls light
3 Fresh air blower	10 Trim panel
4 Seal	11 Light carrier
5 Seal	12 Lighting strip
6 Air duct, right	13 Fresh air blower switch
7 Fresh air box	14 Cut-off flap valve
15 Regulating valve cable	
16 Outlet vent	
17 Spring clip	
18 Air duct left	
19 Non-hardening sealant	
21 Regulating valve cable	
21 Regulating valve	

FROM THERMOSTAT

TO COOLANT PUMP

Fig. 11.9 Exploded view of the heater (Sec 27)

11

Notes

Chapter 12 Supplement
Revisions and information on later models

Contents

Degrees of difficulty

Easy, suitable for novice with little experience	**Fairly easy,** suitable for beginner with some experience	**Fairly difficult,** suitable for competent DIY mechanic	**Difficult,** suitable for experienced DIY mechanic	**Very difficult,** suitable for expert DIY or professional

1 Introduction

This supplement contains details of modifications made to the Polo range of vehicles since 1982 and additional information which has become available since the original publication of this manual. The Sections in this Supplement follow the same order as the Chapters to which they relate. The Specifications are all grouped together for convenience, but follow Chapter order.

It is recommended that before any particular operation is undertaken, reference be made to the appropriate Section(s) of the Supplement. In this way any changes to procedure or components can be noted before referring to the main Chapters.

2 Specifications

The following specifications are revisions of, or supplementary to, the main specifications given at the beginning of Chapters 1 to 11

Engine - 1983 to September 1985

General

Code letters .... HK
Cubic capacity .... 1272 cc
Bore .... 75 mm (2.95 in)
Stroke .... 72 mm (2.84 in)
Compression ratio 9.5:1
Output .... 40 kW (54 bhp) at 5400 rpm
Torque (max) .... 96 Nm at 3300 rpm
Compression pressures:
  New .... 10 to 15 bar (145 to 218 lbf/in²)
  Wear limit .... 7 bar (102 lbf/in²)
  Maximum difference between cylinders .... 3 bar (44 lbf/in²)

Valves

Valve length .... 110.5 mm (4.350 in)

Valve timing (at 1 mm/0.04 in valve lift with zero valve clearance)

Inlet opens .... 3° BTDC
Inlet closes .... 38° ABDC
Exhaust opens .... 41° BBDC
Exhaust closes .... 3° BTDC

Engine - August 1985 onwards

General

	HZ	MH and 2G
Code letters	HZ	MH and 2G
Cubic capacity	1043 cc	1272 cc
Bore	75 mm (2.95 in)	75 mm (2.95 in)
Stroke	59 mm (2.33 in)	72 mm (2.84 in)
Compression ratio	9.5:1	9.5:1
Output	33 kW (45 bhp) at 5600 rpm	40 kW (55 bhp) at 5200 rpm
Torque (max)	74 Nm at 3600 rpm	96 Nm at 3400 rpm
Compression pressures	As for HK engine	As for HK engine

Lubrication data

Capacity:
  Without filter change .... 3.0 litres (5.3 pints)
  With filter change .... 3.5 litres (6.2 pints)
Dipstick MIN to MAX .... 1.0 litre (1.8 pints)
Oil pump:
  Gear teeth backlash:
    New .... 0.05 mm (0.002 in)
    Wear limit .... 0.20 mm (0.008 in)
  Gear teeth axial play (wear limit) .... 0.15 mm (0.006 in)
  Chain drive deflection .... 1.5 to 2.5 mm (0.06 to 0.10 in)

Cylinder head

Minimum dimension after machining (skimming) .... 135.6 mm (5.34 in)

Camshaft

Run-out (max) .... 0.01 mm (0.0004 in)

Valves

Head diameter:
  Inlet .... 36.0 mm (1.42 in)
  Exhaust .... 29.0 mm (1.14 in)
Valve length:
  Inlet .... 98.9 mm (3.897 in)
  Exhaust .... 99.1 mm (3.905 in)
Seat width .... 2.2 mm (0.087 in)

Hydraulic tappets

Free travel (max) .... 0.1 mm (0.004 in)

Valve timing (at 1 mm/0.04 in valve lift with zero valve clearance)

	HZ	MH and 2G
Inlet opens	12° ATDC	5° ATDC
Inlet closes	28° ABDC	29° ABDC
Exhaust opens	25° BBDC	33° BBDC
Exhaust closes	9° BTDC	9° BTDC

Torque wrench setting

	lbf ft	Nm
Valve cover bolts	7	10
Camshaft sprocket bolt	59	80
Crankshaft sprocket bolt	59	80
Timing bolt backplate (dust cover):		
Upper bolt	7	10
Lower bolts	15	20
Camshaft bearing cap nuts:		
Stage 1	4	6
Stage 2	Tighten by further 90°	Tighten by further 90°
Camshaft No. 5 bearing cap screws	7	10
Cylinder head bolts:		
Stage 1	30	40
Stage 2	44	60
Stage 3	Tighten by further 180° (or 2 turns of 90°)	Tighten by further 180° (or 2 turns of 90°)
Crankshaft pulley-to-sprocket bolts	15	20
Sump to block (except two screws at flywheel end)	15	20
Sump to block (two socket-headed screws at flywheel end)	6	8
Oil pump bolts	15	20
Oil pump strainer and bracket bolts	7	10
Crankshaft front oil seal carrier bolts	7	10
Main bearing cap bolts	48	65
Connecting rod cap nuts:		
Stage 1	22	30
Stage 2	Tighten by further 90°	Tighten by further 90°
Flywheel bolts (use new bolts)	74	100
Sump drain plug	22	30

Fuel system - later models

Pierburg 1B3 carburettor

Application	1.05 litre, HZ engine (before approximately 6.89)
Idling speed	800 ± 50 rpm
CO content	2.0 ± 0.5%
Accelerator pump capacity	1.0 ± 0.15 cm³/stroke
Choke valve gap	1.8 ± 0.2 mm
Fast idle speed	2000 ± 100 rpm
Venturi diameter	22 mm
Main jet	105
Air correction jet	57.5
Idle fuel/air jet	50/130
Pump injection tube	32.5/150

Pierburg 1B3 carburettor

Application	1.05 litre, HZ engine (after approximately 6.89)
Idling speed	800 ± 50 rpm
CO content	2.0 ± 0.5%
Venturi diameter	23 mm
Main jet	X 102.5
Air correction jet	100
Idle fuel/air jet	50/132.5
Auxiliary fuel/air jet	32.5/155
Pump injection tube	0.4/0.4
Needle valve	1.5
Choke cover identification	343

12

Pierburg 2E3 carburettor

Application .... 1.3 litre, MH and 2G engine
Idling speed .... 800 ± 50 rpm
CO content .... 2.0 ± 0.5%
Accelerator pump capacity .... 1.0 ± 0.15 cm³/stroke
Choke valve gap:
   Single stage pull-down .... 2.0 ± 0.1 mm
   Two stage pull-down - stage 1 .... 1.6 ± 0.1 mm
   Two stage pull-down - stage 2 .... 2.8 ± 0.15 mm
Fast idle speed .... 2000 ± 100 rpm
Venturi diameter .... 19/23 mm
Main jet .... X 102.5/X 110
Air correction jet 110/130
Idle fuel/air jet 47.5/130
Full throttle enrichment jet 80
Pump injection tube .... 0.3 mm

Pierburg 2E3 carburettor

Application .... 1.3 litre, HK engine
Idling speed .... 800 ± 50 rpm
CO content .... 2.0 ± 0.5%
Accelerator pump capacity .... 1.0 ± 0.15 cm³/stroke
Choke valve gap .... 2.4 ± 0.2 mm
Fast idle speed .... 2000 ± 100 rpm
Venturi diameter .... 19/23 mm
Main jet .... X 95/X 110
Air correction jet 120/130
Full throttle enrichment jet 95
Pump injection tube .... 0.35 mm

Weber 32 TLA carburettor

Application .... 1.05 litre, HZ engine
Idling speed .... 800 ± 50 rpm
CO content .... 2.0 ± 0.5%
Accelerator pump capacity .... 1.0 ± 0.15 cm³/stroke
Choke valve gap:
   Pull-down .... 2.5 ± 0.2 mm
   Wide open kick .... 2.3 ± 0.5 mm
Fast idle speed .... 2000 ± 100 rpm
Venturi diameter .... 22 mm
Main jet 102
Air correction jet 100
Emulsion tube F96
Idle fuel jet 47
Idle air jet 145
Auxiliary fuel jet 30
Auxiliary air jet 170
Pump injection tube .... 0.35 mm
Float needle valve diameter .... 1.75 mm
Float needle washer thickness .... 0.75 mm
Float setting .... 28 ± 1.0 mm

CO content on engines fitted with a catalytic converter

Engine code GL .... 0 to 1.5%
Engine code HB .... 0 to 1.5%
Engine code HH .... 0 to 1.5%
Engine code HK .... 0 to 3.5%

Fuel tank capacity (1985 on) .... 9.2 gallons (42 litres) approx

Ignition system - August 1985 onwards

General

Type .... TCI-H breakerless electronic ignition

Ignition timing

GL engine - vacuum hoses connected .... 5° ± 1° BTDC @ 2000 to 2500 rpm
HZ, MH and 2G engines - vacuum hoses disconnected
and plugged .... 5° ± 1° BTDC @ 800 ± 50 rpm

Spark plugs

	Copper core	Double copper core
Type:		
All models up to 7.85:		
Except 1.3 Coupé	Champion N7YC	Champion N7YCC
1.3 Coupé	Champion N6YC	Champion N6YCC
All models from 8.85:		
1.0	Champion N7BYC	Champion N7YCC
1.3	Champion N7BYC	Champion N7YCC
Electrode gap:		
All models up to 7.85	0.7 mm (0.028 in)	0.8 mm (0.032 in)
All models from 8.85	0.8 mm (0.032 in)	0.8 mm (0.032 in)

Clutch

Clutch disc diameter (later models) .... 190 mm (7.48 in)

Manual gearbox and final drive

Four-speed (code 084)

Code letters:

1.3 litre engine (standard) .... GX (from 10.82 to 12.86)

1.3 litre engine (Formel E) .... 3F (3.84 to 8.85)

1.05 litre 33 kW engine .... AKV (from 1.87)

1.3 litre 40 kW engines .... AKY (from 1.87)

Ratios (teeth):	GX	3F	AKV	AKY
1st	3.45:1 (38:11)	3.45:1 (38:11)	3.46:1 (38:11)	3.46:1 (38:11)
2nd	1.95:1 (41:21)	1.77:1 (39:22)	1.96:1 (47:24)	1.96:1 (47:24)
3rd	1.25:1 (60:48)	1.08:1 (56:52)	1.25:1 (45:36)	1.25:1 (45:36)
4th	0.89:1 (51:57)	0.80:1 (48:60)	0.89:1 (41:46)	0.89:1 (41:46)
Reverse	3.38:1 (44:13)	3.38:1 (44:13)	3.38:1 (44:13)	3.38:1 (44:13)
Final drive	4.06:1 (65:16)	3.875:1 (62:16)	4.27:1 (64:15)	4.06:1 (65:16)

Five-speed (code 085)

Code letters:

1.05 litre engine .... AFA or AHZ

1.3 litre engine .... 8P or AEB

Ratios (teeth) - AFA, 8P and AEB:	AFA		8P and AEB
1st	3.455:1 (38:11)		3.455:1 (38:11)
2nd	2.087:1 (48:23)		1.958:1 (47:24)
3rd	1.469:1 (47:32)		1.250:1 (45:36)
4th	1.122:1 (46:41)		0.891:1 (41:46)
5th	0.891:1 (41:46)		0 740:1 (37:50)
Reverse	3.384:1 (44:13)		3.384:1 (44:13)
Final drive	4.267:1 (64:15)		4.063:1 (65:18)

Ratios (teeth) - AHZ:

1st	3.455:1 (38:11)
2nd	2.087:1 (48:23)
3rd	1.469:1 (47:32)
4th	1.098:1 (45:41)
5th	0.851:1 (40:47)
Reverse	3.384:1 (44.13)
Final drive	4.267:1 (64:15)

Oil capacity .... 5.5 pints (3.1 litres)

Torque wrench settings (five-speed gearbox)

	lbf ft	Nm
Gearbox to engine	41	55
Gearbox mountings and brackets	44	60
Clutch housing to gearbox housing	18	25
End cover	6	8
Gear lever bracket bolt	11	15
Release bearing guide sleeve bolts	15	20
Filler and drain plugs	18	25
Reversing light switch	22	30

Braking system

Torque wrench settings

	lbf ft	Nm
VW 'Mk I' and 'Mk II' caliper frame to wheel bearing housing	52	70
VW 'Mk I' and 'Mk II' calipers to caliper frames	18	25

12

Suspension and steering

Front wheel camber - August 1984 onwards .... 0° ± 30°

Tyre pressures - August 1985 onwards - bar (lbf/in²)	Front	Rear
135 SR 13:		
Half load	1.7 (25)	1.7 (25)
Full load	2.1 (30)	2.4 (34)
145 SR 13:		
Half load	1.6 (23)	1.6 (23)
Full load	1.9 (28)	2.3 (33)
155/70 SR 13:		
Half load	1.6 (23)	1.6 (23)
Full load	1.9 (28)	2.3 (33)
165/65 SR 13:		
Half load	1.6 (23)	1.6 (23)
Full load	1.9 (28)	2.3 (33)

Dimensions, weights and capacities (1985 on)

Dimensions

As for earlier models except:

Overall length - Saloon .... 156.5 in (3975 mm) (157.1 in/3990 mm with headlight washer)
Overall width - Coupé .... 62.6 in (1590 mm)
Overall width - Saloon .... 63.0 in (1600 mm)
Ground clearance - Coupé .... 4.7 in (118 mm)
Ground clearance - Saloon .... 4.6 in (117 mm)
Track - Saloon and some Coupé models:
    Front .... 52.0 in (1320 mm)
    Rear .... 53.0 in (1346 mm)

Weights

Gross vehicle weight:
    Hatchback and Coupé .... 2580 lb (1170 kg)
    Saloon .... 2624 lb (1190 kg)
Kerb weight .... 1610 to 1698 lb (730 to 770 kg) according to model
Maximum trailer weight:
    Unbraked (1.05 litre models) .... 882 lb (400 kg)
    Unbraked (1.3 litre models) .... 904 lb (410 kg)
    Braked (all models) .... 1433 lb (650 kg)

Capacities

Engine oil (hydraulic tappet engines):
    With filter change .... 6.2 pints (3.5 litres)
    Without filter change .... 5.3 pints (3.0 litres)
Cooling system .... 12.4 pints (5.6 litres) approx
Fuel tank .... 9.2 gallons (42 litres) approx

---

3 Engine

Engines - general

1 During 1983 an additional 1.3 litre engine was added to the range shown in the Specifications at the beginning of Chapter 1. This engine, code HK, is identical in design and construction to the previous 1.3 litre unit, code HH, apart from minor changes to the specification. All repair and overhaul operations described in Chapter 1 apply equally to the new engine, and the changes to Specification are given at the beginning of this Supplement.

2 In August 1985 a major design change occurred and two new engines of 1.05 litre (code HZ) and 1.3 litre (code MH) were introduced. The 1.1 litre engine was deleted from the range at the end of 1983, and the 1.3 MH engine was superseded by the 1.3 2G in January 1989. All the new engines have a redesigned cylinder head incorporating hydraulically-operated bucket tappets in place of the previous rocker finger type, and a revised engine oil pump driven by a chain from the crankshaft. Additionally, different ancillary components such as carburettor and distributor are fitted.

3 Where changes to the specification of the new engines occur, these will be found at the beginning of this Supplement. Changes to repair and overhaul procedures are covered in

the following sub-sections. All other information is the same as for earlier engines and reference should be made to Chapter 1.

Cylinder head - removal

4 The procedure for removal of the cylinder head on engines with hydraulic tappets is basically the same as described in Chapter 1, but note the following points.

5 The valve cover is different, being held in place by three bolts (photo)

6 There is a plastic oil shield over the camshaft at the distributor end of the cylinder head (photo).

7 The fuel and coolant pipes differ according to model.

8 Spring type re-usable hose clips may be fitted. These are removed by pinching their

3.5 Later type valve cover with three bolt fixing

3.6 Plastic oil shield location over camshaft

3.11 Method of preventing camshaft rotation while undoing the sprocket retaining bolt

ends together to expand the clip and then sliding it down the hose.

9 The clips on the fuel hoses are designed to be used only once, so obtain new ones or replace them with screw type clips when refitting the hoses.

Camshaft - removal, inspection and refitting

10 Refer to Chapter 1, Section 10, all paragraphs up to number 4 (inclusive) .

11 Devise a method to prevent the camshaft turning, and remove the sprocket bolt (photo). Remove the camshaft sprocket. Remove the oil shield from the distributor end of the camshaft.

12 The camshaft bearing caps must be refitted in the same places from which they were removed, and the same way round. They are usually numbered, but centre-punch marks on them, if necessary, to ensure correct refitting.

13 Remove bearing caps 5, 1 and 3 in that order. Now undo the nuts holding 2 and 4 in a diagonal pattern and the camshaft will lift them up as the pressure of the valve springs is exerted. When they are free, lift the caps off.

14 If the caps are stuck, give them a sharp tap with a hide-faced mallet to loosen them. Do not try to lever them off with a screwdriver.

15 Lift out the camshaft; the oil seal will come with it.

16 Clean the camshaft, then inspect the journals and cam peaks for pitting, scoring, cracking and wear.

17 The camshaft bearings are machined directly into the cylinder head and the bearing caps.

18 The camshaft bearing radial play can only be checked accurately using Plastigage and if wear is suspected in this area it is advisable to consult your VAG dealer.

19 To refit the camshaft, lubricate all the bucket tappets, the camshaft journals and the camshaft liberally with clean engine oil.

20 Place the camshaft in position on the cylinder head (photo).

21 Fit a new camshaft oil seal (photo).

22 Refit the bearing caps, ensuring they are the right way round and in their correct position (they are numbered 1 to 5 and these numbers should be readable from the exhaust manifold side of the head).

23 Thread on the cap retaining nuts loosely, then tighten the nuts on number 2 and 4 caps in a diagonal sequence to the Stage 1 torque figure given in the Specifications (photo).

24 Tighten the nuts on caps 1, 3 and 5 to the Stage 1 torque.

25 Once all nuts have been tightened to the Stage 1 torque, tighten all nuts a further 90° (Stage 2). Fit and tighten No 5 cap screws to the correct torque.

26 Refit the camshaft sprocket. The lug on

the sprocket must engage with the slot in the camshaft. Fit the sprocket bolt and tighten it to the specified torque (photo).

27 If the cylinder head is in the car, follow the procedure given in Chapter 1, Section 38, paragraphs 9 to 18.

28 Ignore any reference to the oil spray tube, and be sure to refit the oil shield at the distributor end of the camshaft before the valve cover is refitted.

Hydraulic bucket tappets - removal, inspection and refitting

29 Remove the camshaft, as previously described.

3.20 Fitting the camshaft

3.21 Camshaft oil seal in position

3.23 Tightening the camshaft bearing cap nuts

3.26 Fitting the camshaft sprocket bolt

12

3.30 Removing the bucket tappets

3.45 Lift out the valve spring upper seat

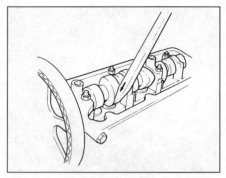

Fig. 12.1 Checking the hydraulic tappet free travel (Sec 3)

30 Lift out the tappets one by one (photo), ensuring they are kept in their correct order and so are replaced in their original positions.
31 Place them, face down (cam contact surface), on a clean sheet of paper as they are removed.
32 Inspect the tappets for wear, indicated by ridging on the clean surface, pitting and cracks.
33 Tappets cannot be repaired, and if found worn must be renewed.
34 Before fitting the tappets, oil all parts liberally and slip the tappets back into their original bore. Refit the camshaft.
Caution: If new tappets are fitted, the engine must not be started after fitting for approximately 30 minutes, or the valves will strike the pistons.

3.46A Remove the outer . . .

Hydraulic bucket tappets - checking free travel

35 Start the engine and run it until the radiator cooling fan has switched on once.
36 Increase engine speed to about 2500 rpm for about 2 minutes.
37 Irregular noises are normal when starting, but should become quiet after a few minutes running.
38 If the valves are still noisy carry out the following check to identify worn tappets.
39 Stop the engine and remove the valve cover from the cylinder head.
40 Turn the crankshaft clockwise, using a wrench on the crankshaft pulley securing bolt, until the cam of the tappet to be checked is facing upward, and is not exerting any pressure on the tappet.
41 Press the tappet down using a wooden or plastic wedge.
42 If free travel of the tappet exceeds that given in the Specifications the tappet must be renewed.

Inlet and exhaust valves - removal, inspection and refitting

43 Remove the cylinder head, camshaft and tappets, as described previously.
44 Using a valve spring compressor with a deep reach, compress the valve springs, remove the two cotters and release the compressor and springs.
45 Lift out the upper spring seat (photo).

46 Remove the outer and inner valve springs (photos).
47 Lift out the valve (photo).
48 The valves should be inspected as described in Chapter 1, Section 30. Refer to the Specifications for dimensions.
49 Valves cannot be reworked, but must be renewed if they are worn. They should be ground in in the normal manner.
50 If possible, check the valve spring lengths against new ones. Renew the whole set if any are too short.
51 Fit the valves in their correct locations in the cylinder head.
52 Remove the valve stem oil seals and fit new seals as follows.
53 Locate the special plastic sleeve provided with the seals over the valve stem in order to prevent damage to the seal.
54 Slide the new seal over the valve stem and sleeve and press it firmly onto the guide using a metal tube or deep socket bit. Remove the plastic sleeve.
55 Refit the valve springs, upper spring seats and cotters using the reverse of the removal procedure.
56 Refit the camshaft, tappets and cylinder head as described elsewhere in this Section.

Cylinder head - refitting

57 Clean all traces of old gasket from the cylinder block and cylinder head faces.
58 Using a new gasket, fit the inlet manifold (photos).

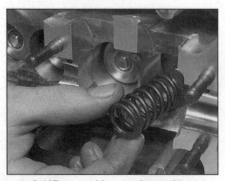

3.46B . . . and inner valve springs

3.47 Lift out the valve

3.58A Fitting a new inlet manifold gasket

3.58B Fitting the inlet manifold and carburettor

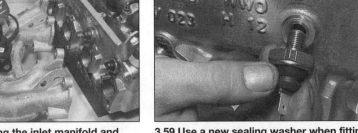

3.59 Use a new sealing washer when fitting the oil pressure switch

3.60 Thermostat housing with new O-ring seal (arrowed) in place

59 If they have been removed, refit the oil pressure switches, using new copper sealing washers (photo).
60 Refit the thermostat housing using a new O-ring seal (photo).
61 Refit the coolant hoses, ensuring they are connected up in their correct positions (photo).
62 Lubricate the fuel pump driveshaft with clean engine oil and slip it into its housing in the cylinder head (photo).
63 Refit the fuel pump (photo) and fit and tighten the bolts, not forgetting the lifting eye (photo).
64 Slide the distributor into position and ensure that it goes fully home (photo) .
65 Fit the distributor rotor arm (photo).
66 Fit the distributor cap and connect up the earth lead (photo).

3.61 Coolant hoses in position

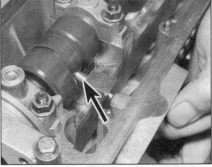

3.62 Fitting the fuel pump driveshaft (arrowed)

67 Check the timing marks on the cylinder head and camshaft sprocket are lined up.
68 The pistons in the cylinder block must not

be at TDC when refitting the cylinder head.
69 Position a new cylinder head gasket on the cylinder block (photo).

3.63A Fitting the fuel pump . . .

3.63B . . . together with the lifting eye

3.64 Fit the distributor . . .

3.65 . . . rotor arm . . .

3.66 . . . cap and earth lead

3.69 Place a new cylinder head gasket on the block

12

3.73 Refit the plastic oil shield

3.74 Locating dowel for valve cover gasket

3.75 Fitting a new exhaust manifold gasket

70 Lower the cylinder head gently into position. Special guides are used by Volkswagen both to line up the gasket and guide the cylinder head into position, but this can be done using suitable sized rods inserted in two cylinder head bolt holes.

71 Refer to Chapter 1 and refit the cylinder head bolts in the sequence given in Fig. 1.4, but use the torque figures and stages given in the Specifications section of this Supplement.

72 It is not necessary to retighten the bolts after a period of service, as is normally the case.

73 Refit the plastic oil shield (photo).

74 Using a new rubber sealing gasket, properly located over the dowels, refit the valve cover (photo).

75 Fit a new gasket to the exhaust manifold (photo).

76 Fit the exhaust manifold, do up the nuts (photo), and fit the hot air shroud (photo).

77 Connect up the exhaust downpipe and any other exhaust brackets loosened during removal.

78 Refit all remaining hoses of the cooling system and fuel system, referring to the relevant Chapter where necessary.

79 Refit all electrical connections disturbed during dismantling (distributor, carburettor, oil pressure transmitter, coolant temperature, inlet manifold preheater, etc). Do not forget the earth lead under the inlet manifold nut (photos).

80 Refit the distributor vacuum hose.

81 With reference to Chapter 1, Section 40, refit the timing belt and covers.

82 Refer to Chapter 3 and refit the throttle cable.

83 Refit the spark plugs, air cleaner and associated pipework and electrical leads.

84 Check oil and coolant levels, refilling as necessary.

85 Adjust the ignition timing by the stroboscopic method as described in Chapter 4, Section 6.

Oil pump - description

86 The oil pump fitted to engines produced since August 1985 has been changed from the crescent type to a gear type pump, driven by chain from the engine crankshaft.

87 Only the oil pump has been changed, the rest of the lubrication system remains as before.

3.76A Exhaust manifold bolted into position

3.76B Fitting the hot air shroud

3.79A Distributor multi-plug connection

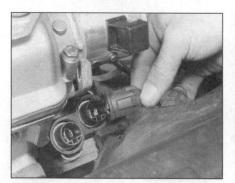

3.79B Coolant temperature sender multi-plug connection

3.79C Oil pressure switch and lead

3.79D Earth lead under the inlet manifold nut

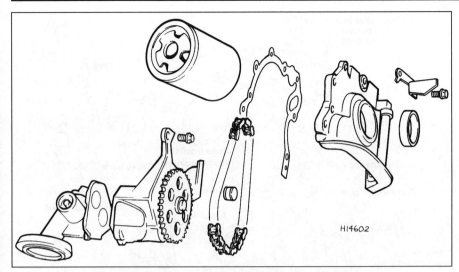

Fig. 12.2 Exploded view of the gear type oil pump (Sec 3)

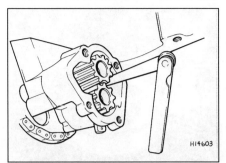

Fig. 12.3 Checking the oil pump gear
backlash (Sec 3)

Oil pump - removal, inspection and refitting

88 The oil pump can be removed with the engine still in the vehicle.
89 Drain the oil from the sump.
90 Refer to the relevant Chapters and disconnect the exhaust downpipe and right-hand driveshaft to give room to remove the sump.
91 Remove the sump.
92 If it is only desired to check backlash in the gears, this can be done by removing the oil pump cover and strainer assembly from the back of the pump.
93 Refer to Figs. 12.3 and 12.4 and check backlash and axial play against the tolerances in the Specifications.
94 If the tolerances are exceeded then the oil pump should be renewed as follows.
95 Refer to the relevant Chapters and remove:
(a) Camshaft drivebelt (timing belt)
(b) Alternator drivebelt
(c) Crankshaft pulley
(d) Timing belt backplate
(e) Front cover and TDC setting bracket
96 If they are still in position remove the bolts holding the rear stay bracket.

97 Remove the two bolts holding the oil pump to the cylinder block.
98 This will release the tension on the chain and allow the pump to be removed.
99 If sufficient slack in the chain cannot be achieved by this method, then slide the pump, chain and crankshaft drive sprocket forward together.
100 Check the chain and teeth of the drive sprockets and renew any parts which are worn.
101 If a new pump is being fitted, it would be as well to renew all other parts at the same time.
102 Refitting is a reversal of removal, but bear in mind the following points.
103 Use new gaskets on all components.
104 Oil all new parts liberally.
105 If the small plug in the front cover is at all damaged, replace it.
106 Similarly, fit a new crankshaft oil seal to the cover. The old seal can be prised out and a new one pressed fully home.
107 The chain is tensioned by moving the pump housing against its mounting bolts.
108 With light thumb pressure exerted on the chain, deflection should be as given in the Specifications.
109 Whenever the sump is removed with the

engine *in situ*, the two hexagon screws in the sealing flange at the flywheel end should be replaced by socket-headed screws and spring washers, and tightened to the figure given in the Specifications.

Crankshaft sprocket - modification

110 As from August 1986, a different method is used to secure the crankshaft sprocket to the front of the crankshaft. A slot is now provided in the crankshaft with a corresponding lug on the sprocket, instead of the previous method of using a Woodruff key. The securing bolt and tightening procedure has been changed and, on rocker finger engines, the oil pump is different.
111 The securing bolt must always be renewed after removal.
112 Before fitting the bolt apply a little oil to its threads. Tightening of the bolt should be carried out in two stages: first tighten the bolt to 90 Nm then angle-tighten the bolt by 180°.
113 If an old type crankshaft is being replaced, the new version will be supplied by the VW dealer. It will therefore also be necessary to renew the sprocket, securing bolt and, in the case of the rocker finger type engine, the oil pump.

4 Fuel system

Pierburg 2E3 carburettor - general

1 The 1.3 litre engine, code HK, introduced during 1983, is fitted with the Pierburg 2E3 carburettor. This carburettor is similar to the unit fitted to later engines from August 1985 onwards and information will be found later in this Section.

Carburettors (August 1985 onwards) general

2 In conjunction with the introduction of the revised engines in August 1985, different carburettors were also fitted according to engine size.

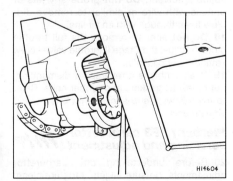

Fig. 12.4 Checking the oil pump gear axial
play (Sec 3)

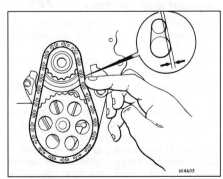

Fig. 12.5 Checking the oil pump drive chain
tension (Sec 3)

12

4.20A Top cover securing screws (arrowed) – 2E3 carburettor

4.20B Underside view of the 2E3 carburettor top cover

1 Stage I main jet
2 Stage II main jet
3 Full throttle enrichment lift pipe
4 Stage II progression lift pipe

4.20C Outer view of the 2E3 carburettor

1 Fast idle cam
2 Fast idle adjustment screw
3 Stage II vacuum unit

4.20D Choke housing and cover alignment – 2E3 carburettor

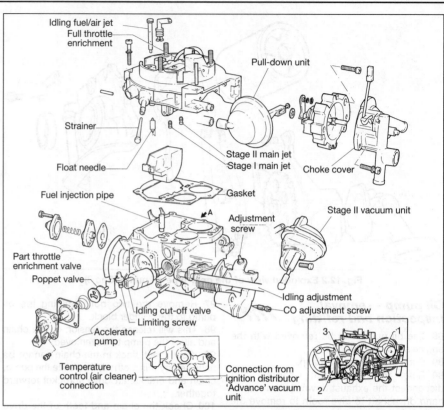

Fig. 12.6 Exploded view of the Pierburg 2E3 carburettor. Inset shows two-stage pull-down unit fitted to later models (Sec 4)

1 Pull-down unit   2 Thermotime valve   3 Vent cap

3 They are either the Weber 32 TLA or Pierburg 1B3, fitted to engines code lettered HZ, or the Pierburg 2E3 fitted to engines code lettered MH.

4 The following sub-sections deal only with those operations not fully covered, or different from those described in Chapter 3; where these are the same, cross-reference to Chapter 3 will be made.

5 The Specifications Section of this Supplement should also be referred to before carrying out any servicing or adjustment, to ensure all relevant information is taken into account.

Carburettors (August 1985 onwards) – removal and refitting

6 Disconnect the battery negative lead.
7 Remove the air cleaner as described in Chapter 3.
8 Drain half of the coolant from the cooling system, with reference to Chapter 2.
9 Disconnect the coolant hoses from the automatic choke.
10 As applicable, disconnect the wiring from the automatic choke and fuel cut-off solenoid.
11 Disconnect the accelerator cable.
12 Disconnect the fuel and vacuum hoses.
13 Unscrew the through-bolts or nuts, and lift the carburettor from the inlet manifold. Remove the insulating flange gasket.
14 Refitting is a reversal of removal, but

clean the mating faces of the carburettor and inlet manifold and always fit a new gasket. Tighten the mounting bolts evenly.

Carburettors (August 1985 onwards) - dismantling, servicing and reassembly (general)

15 Wash the exterior of the carburettor with a suitable solvent and allow to dry.
16 Dismantle the carburettor with reference to the relevant Figs. and photos. Before dismantling, obtain a set of gaskets. Be sure to mark the relationship of the automatic choke to the carburettor body before separating them.
17 Clean the internal components with a suitable solvent. **Do not** probe any jets or orifices with wire or similar to remove dirt; blow them through with an air line.
18 **Do not** alter or remove the full throttle stop, or adjust the Stage II throttle valve screw settings (if applicable).
19 Reassembly is a reversal of dismantling, but renew all gaskets and rubber rings. Refer to the following sub-sections for checks and adjustments.

Pierburg 2E3 carburettor - servicing and adjustment

20 Before undertaking any carburettor adjustments, be sure all jets, etc., are clean. Dismantling and reassembly are described in the previous subsections (photos).

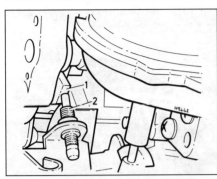

Fig. 12.7 Fast idle cam (1) and choke valve gap adjusting screw (2) – 2E3 carburettor (Sec 4)

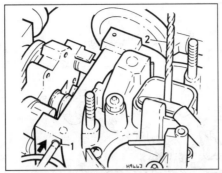

Fig. 12.8 Checking the choke valve gap – 2E3 carburettor (Sec 4)

1 *Choke valve operating rod (push in direction of arrow)*
2 *Twist drill*

Fig. 12.9 Accelerator pump adjustment – 2E3 carburettor (Sec 4)

1 *Fast idle cam locking screw*
2 *Fast idle cam*
A *Increases injection capacity*
B *Decreases injection capacity*

21 If the part throttle enrichment valve is removed, it must be renewed.

Cut-off valve

22 To check the cut-off valve, apply battery voltage. The valve must be heard to click when voltage is applied.

Choke valve gap

23 To check the choke valve gap the choke cover must be removed. Move the throttle valve and the fast idle cam so that the adjustment screw is against the highest cam stop. Now push the choke valve operating rod fully towards the adjustment screw (and pull-down unit), then check the choke valve-to-barrel clearance using a twist drill as a gauge. If necessary turn the adjuster screw as required to provide the specified choke valve gap (Fig. 12.7 and 12.8).

Accelerator pump capacity

24 The accelerator pump injection capacity can be checked in the same manner as that described in Chapter 3, Section 12. Allow 1 second per stroke, and 3 seconds between strokes. If necessary, refer to Fig. 12.9 and make suitable adjustments. Ensure the injection pipe is correctly positioned (photo).

Automatic choke and pull-down unit

25 Ensure that the automatic choke cover and the choke housing alignment marks correspond. To check the choke, connect up

a test lamp between the battery positive terminal and the choke lead. The test lamp should illuminate; if it doesn't then the choke unit is defective and must be renewed.

26 The choke pull-down unit can be checked whilst it is removed but, as this requires the use of a vacuum pump and gauge, it is a check best entrusted to your VAG dealer. The pull-down unit can also be tested when the carburettor is in position in the car. The air cleaner unit must be removed. Run the engine at idle speed then close the choke valve by hand and check that a resistance is felt over the final 3 mm (0.12 in) of travel. If no resistance is felt, there may be a leak in the vacuum connections, or the pull-down unit diaphragm broken, in which case the unit must be renewed. For later models with the two-stage pull-down unit, refer to the end of this Section.

Stage II throttle valve

27 The basic Stage II throttle valve adjustment is made during manufacture and cannot be further adjusted.

Idle speed and mixture

28 Refer to Chapter 3, Section 13, paragraphs 1 to 7 (photo).

Fast idle speed

29 To check and adjust the fast idle, first check that the engine is still at normal

operating temperature. The air cleaner must be removed and the other provisional conditions must apply as for the idle adjustment. Plug the air cleaner temperature control hose.

30 Restart the engine and open the throttle to give an engine speed of 2500 rpm (approximately). Press down the fast idle cam to its stop then move the throttle valve back so that the adjuster screw is on the second highest step on the fast idle cam. In this position the fast idle speed should be as specified. If the setting is incorrect, turn the adjustment screw in the required direction until it is correct - Fig. 12.10 (Note that the screw may have a tamperproof cap fitted.)

31 On completion unplug the temperature control connector and refit the air cleaner.

Pierburg 1B3 carburettor - servicing and adjustment

32 Before undertaking any carburettor adjustments, be sure all jets, etc, are clean. Dismantling and reassembly are described previously in this Section.

33 When inserting the accelerator pump piston seal, press it towards the opposite side of the vent drilling. The piston retaining ring must be pressed flush into the carburettor body.

Fig. 12.10 Fast idle adjustment screw (2) – 2E3 carburettor (Sec 4)

4.24 Injection pipe must align with recess (arrowed) – 2E3 carburettor

4.28 2E3 carburettor adjustment points

1 *Idle speed and guide sleeve*
2 *Mixture screw*

12

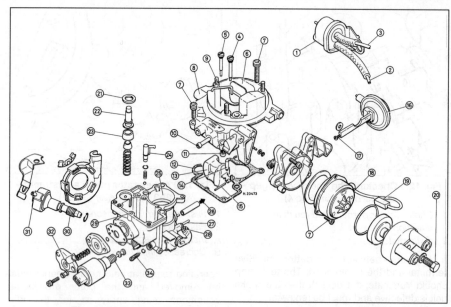

Fig. 12.11 Exploded view of the Pierburg 1B3 carburettor (Sec 4)

1 Two-way valve (idle speed boost control)	13 Float
2 To idle speed adjustment screw	14 Needle valve
	15 Float pivot pin
3 To vacuum source	16 Pull-down unit
4 Idle fuel/air jet	17 Pull-down adjustment screw
5 Auxiliary fuel/air jet	
6 Choke valve	18 Choke cover
7 Cover screws	19 Connector
8 Top cover	20 Centre bolt
9 Enrichment tube	21 Bearing ring
10 Fuel connection	22 Pump piston
11 Main jet	23 Seal
12 Gasket	24 Injection tube
	25 Main body

26 To pull-down unit
27 Air cleaner connection
28 Fast idle adjusting screw
29 Part throttle enrichment screw
30 Idle speed adjustment screw
31 To two-way valve
32 Part throttle enrichment valve
33 Bypass air cut-off valve
34 Idle mixture (CO) adjustment screw

General

34 All checks and adjustments are as described for the Pierburg 2E3 carburettor, with the following additions.

Enrichment tube

35 With the choke valve closed, the bottom of the enrichment tube should be level with the upper surface of the valve, as shown in Fig. 12.12.

Idle speed and mixture

36 Before making any adjustment, make sure that the automatic choke is fully open, otherwise the throttle valve linkage may still be on the fast idle cam. Disconnect and plug the vacuum hose from the idle speed adjustment screw before making adjustments, and reconnect it on completion (photo).

Fast idle speed

37 With the engine at normal operating temperature and switched off, connect a tachometer and remove the air cleaner.
38 Fully open the throttle valve, then turn the fast idle cam and release the throttle valve so that the adjustment screw is positioned on the highest part of the cam.
39 Without touching the accelerator pedal,

start the engine and check that the fast idling speed is as given in the Specifications. If not, turn the adjustment screw on the linkage as necessary.

Choke valve gap

40 Fully open the throttle valve, then turn the fast idle cam and release the throttle valve so that the adjustment screw is positioned on the highest part of the cam.
41 Press the choke operating rod as far as possible towards the pull-down unit.

Fig. 12.12 Correct position of the enrichment tube – 1B3 carburettor (Sec 4)

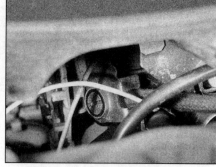

4.36 Idle speed adjustment screw – 1B3 carburettor (arrowed)

42 Using the shank of a twist drill, check that the distance from the choke valve to the carburettor wall is as given in the Specifications. If not, adjust the screw behind the automatic choke.

Idle speed boost control

43 Special equipment is needed to check the two-way valve and its control unit. Problems in this area should be referred to a VW dealer or other specialist.
44 The idle speed adjustment screw may be checked by applying vacuum to its connector with the engine idling. Idle speed must increase when vacuum is applied; renew the screw if not.

Accelerator pump capacity

45 Hold the carburettor over a funnel and measuring glass.
46 Turn the fast idle cam so that the adjusting screw is off the cam. Hold the cam in this position during the following procedure.
47 Fully open the throttle ten times, allowing at least three seconds per stroke. Divide the total quantity by ten and check that the resultant injection capacity is as given in the Specifications. If not, refer to Fig. 12.13 and loosen the cross-head screw, turn the cam plate as required and tighten the screw.
48 If difficulty is experienced in making the adjustment, check the pump seal and make sure that the return check valve and injection tube are clear.

Fig. 12.13 Accelerator pump adjustment – 1B3 carburettor (Sec 4)

a Cam locking screw
b Cam plate

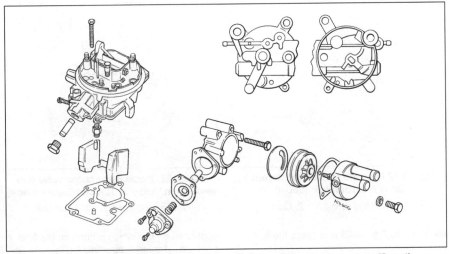

Fig. 12.14 Exploded view of the Weber 32 TLA carburettor top cover (Sec 4)

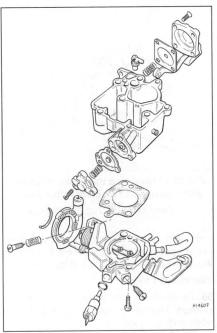

Fig. 12.15 Exploded view of the Weber 32 TLA carburettor main body (Sec 4)

Weber 32 TLA carburettor - servicing and adjustment

49 Before undertaking any carburettor adjustments, be sure all jets, etc, are clean. Dismantling and reassembly are described previously in this Section.
50 Note: Before loosening the throttle lever, the accelerator pump cam must be held in place with an M4 screw (Fig. 12.16).

Float level

51 With the upper part of the carburettor inverted and held at an angle of approximately 45°, the measurement 'a' in Fig. 12.17 should be as shown in the Specifications.

52 The ball of the float needle should not be pressed in against the spring when making the measurement.

Idle speed and mixture

53 The procedure for checking and adjusting the idling speed and CO content are basically the same as given previously for the Pierburg carburettors.
54 However, refer to Figs. 12.18 and 12.19 for the location of adjustment screws and to the Specifications in this Supplement for settings.

Choke valve gap (pulldown)

55 Remove the choke cover.
56 Place the fast idling speed adjusting screw on the highest step of the cam (Fig. 12.20). Apply vacuum to the pull-down unit using a hand vacuum pump or a modified bicycle pump.
57 Measure the choke valve gap using a drill

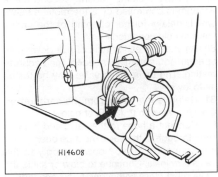

Fig. 12.16 Secure the accelerator pump cam with an M4 screw (arrowed) before loosening the throttle lever – 32 TLA carburettor (Sec 4)

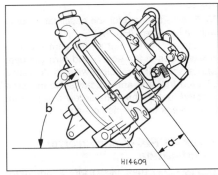

Fig. 12.17 Checking the float level – 32 TLA carburettor (Sec 4)

$a = 28 \pm 1.0\ mm$ $b = 45°$

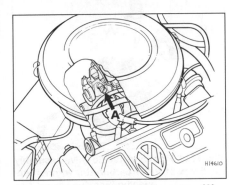

Fig. 12.18 Idle speed adjusting screw (A) – 32 TLA carburettor (Sec 4)

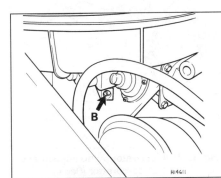

Fig. 12.19 Mixture adjusting screw (B) – 32 TLA carburettor (Sec 4)

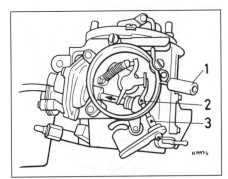

Fig. 12.20 Cam setting prior to checking choke valve gap (pull-down) – 32 TLA carburettor (Sec 4)

1 Apply vacuum 2 Cam 3 Adjusting screw

12

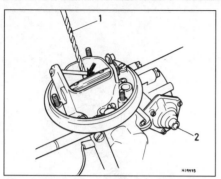

Fig. 12.21 Checking the choke valve gap (pull-down) – 32 TLA carburettor (Sec 4)

1 Twist drill   2 Adjusting screw

shank (Fig. 12.21). The gap should be as given in the Specifications. Adjustment is made on the screw at the end of the pulldown device.

Idle cut-off valve

58 To check the cut-off valve, apply battery voltage. The valve must be heard to click when voltage is applied.

Fast idle speed

59 Before carrying out this check, ensure that ignition timing and idling adjustments are correct. The engine should be at normal operating temperature.
60 Remove the air cleaner.
61 Plug the temperature regulator connection.
62 Connect up a tachometer.
63 Remove the choke cover and set the fast idle speed adjusting screw on the second highest step on the cam (Fig. 12.22).
64 Tension the operating lever with a rubber band so that the choke flap is fully open.
65 Without touching the accelerator pedal, start the engine, which should run at fast idle speed given in the Specifications.
66 Adjust on the screw as necessary.

Choke valve gap (wide open kick)

67 Remove the air cleaner.
68 Fully open the throttle and hold it in this position.

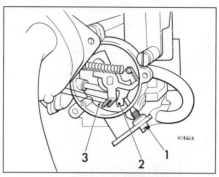

Fig. 12.22 Fast idle speed adjustment – 32 TLA carburettor (Sec 4)

1 Adjusting screw   2 Cam

69 Refer to Fig. 12.23 and press the lever (1) upwards.
70 Check the gap with a twist drill, which should be as given in the Specifications. Adjust by bending the lever (Fig. 12.24).

Accelerator pump capacity

71 This can be checked by following the procedure in Chapter 3, Section 12 with the following differences.
72 Open the throttle valve quickly when operating the pump (ie 1 second per stroke, with pauses of 3 seconds between strokes).
73 The amount of fuel injected can be altered, but only very slightly, as follows.
74 Take the accelerator cable cam off the throttle valve lever.
75 Secure the cam for the accelerator pump with an M4 screw (Fig. 12.25).
76 Loosen the locknut on the cam securing screw. Loosen the screw and turn the cam with a screwdriver - clockwise to decrease injected fuel and anti-clockwise to increase injected fuel. Tighten the screw and locknut and recheck the injection capacity.

Solex 31 PIC-7 carburettor - modification

77 From May 1983, the 31 PIC-7 carburettor on 1.05 litre models has been fitted with a

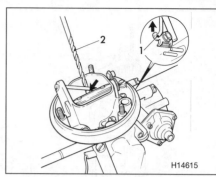

Fig. 12.23 Checking the choke valve gap (wide open kick) – 32 TLA carburettor (Sec 4)

1 Press upwards   2 Twist drill

float needle valve which is hung on the float to give a forced opening (Fig. 12.26). Carburettors with this modification have the numbers 146-3 in their code number.
78 When refitting the float and needle, ensure the needle valve is located correctly in the slot in the float suspension arm.

Pierburg 2E3 carburettor - modifications (1987 on)

79 From February 1987 this carburettor is fitted with a two-stage choke pull-down unit. Vacuum is applied to the first stage all the time that the engine is running, so opening the choke valve a small amount. Second stage vacuum is controlled by a thermotime valve, which delays further opening of the choke valve in cold conditions
80 As with the earlier type of pull-down unit, special equipment is needed for accurate testing. The thermotime valve may be tested as follows.
81 Remove the valve from the carburettor. Cool the valve to 0° (32°F) or below.
82 Connect a hose to the valve and blow or suck through it: the valve must be open.
83 Connect a 12 volt power supply to the valve terminals. Continue to blow or suck: the valve must close within one to six seconds. If not, renew it.

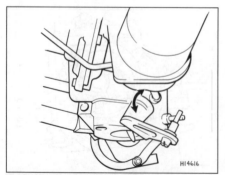

Fig. 12.24 Adjusting the choke valve gap (wide open kick) – 32 TLA carburettor (Sec 4)

Bend the lever to make adjustments

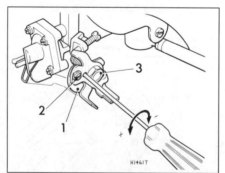

Fig. 12.25 Accelerator pump adjustment – 32 TLA carburettor (Sec 4)

1 Cam   3 Cam locking nut
2 M4 screw securing cam

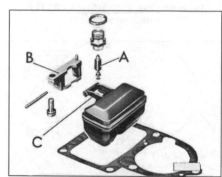

Fig. 12.26 Float and needle valve assembly on Solex 31 PIC-7 carburettor with forced opening (Sec 4)

A Needle valve   B Bracket   C Float arm

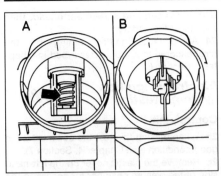

Fig. 12.27 Air cleaner intake control (Sec 4)

A *Thermostatic control*
B *Vacuum control*

Air cleaner with vacuum-operated control

84 Since January 1 1984 some air cleaners have been modified by having the thermostatic control of the air intake changed to purely vacuum control (Fig. 12.27).
85 Both types of air cleaner are interchangeable.

Unleaded fuel - general

86 With the exception of Formel E models with the engine code HB8 (9.7:1 compression ratio), all models covered by this manual may be run on 91 or 95 RON unleaded petrol. No modifications are necessary. (91 RON unleaded petrol is not at present available in the UK, but may be found elsewhere in Europe.)
87 Formel E models with the engine code HB8 (9.7:1 compression ratio) require 98 RON unleaded petrol or premium grade leaded petrol. They must not use 95 RON unleaded petrol, as this could cause engine damage as a result of pre-ignition.

Catalytic converters - general

88 A catalytic converter may be fitted as an option to certain new models from September 1989. although VW can provide kits to fit catalytic converters to all models from Autumn 1979. The kits include stainless steel exhaust components, a modified (restricted) fuel filler and the catalytic converter itself. The 1.05 litre engine is fitted with an unregulated micro-catalyst unit, whereas the larger engines are fitted with a three-way unregulated exhaust catalyst unit.
89 It is only permissible to use lead-free (unleaded) fuel on models fitted with a catalytic converter.

Engines fitted with catalytic converter - slow running adjustments

90 The catalytic converter is designed to function correctly when the incoming exhaust gas has a specific composition and minimum temperature. It is therefore important to adjust the slow running speed and mixture within fine limits, and it follows that the use of an exhaust gas analyser is imperative. The following paragraphs describe the procedure for the slow running adjustments. Where tamperproof caps are fitted over the adjustment screws, make sure that the local by-laws permit their removal and, if necessary, fit new ones after completing the adjustments.
91 Check the condition and security of all vacuum pipes and crankcase ventilation hoses, also check that the air cleaner is serviceable and that the catalytic converter and exhaust system is secure and in good condition.
92 Run the engine to normal operating temperature.
93 Check and if necessary adjust the ignition timing.
94 With the engine stopped, connect the CO meter to the measuring pipe (where applicable) near the exhaust manifold on the engine, making sure that the hose is fitted tightly. Also connect a tachometer to the engine.
95 Disconnect the crankcase ventilation hose from the air cleaner body and plug the air cleaner outlet.
96 Start the engine and run it at idling speed.
97 Adjust the idling speed and CO content to the values given in the Specifications. Make note of the final CO content for comparison in paragraph 99.
98 Disconnect the CO meter from the measuring pipe, then run the engine for approximately 1 minute at 3000 rpm.

99 Connect the CO meter to the exhaust tailpipe and measure the CO content with the engine idling. The catalytic converter is functioning correctly if the CO content in the exhaust tailpipe is lower than that recorded in the measuring pipe. Note that the CO on engines fitted with the micro-catalyst unit may drop to zero even though the mixture has been set correctly.
100 Stop the engine and disconnect the tachometer. Reconnect the crankcase ventilation hose.
101 Run the engine again at idling speed. If the CO content now increases, this does not mean that the slow running adjustments are incorrect but that the engine oil is diluted with fuel due to frequent stop/start driving. A long fast drive will reduce the amount of fuel in the oil and the CO content will return to normal.
102 Stop the engine and disconnect the CO meter from the exhaust tailpipe.

5 Ignition system

Electronic ignition system - description

1 A transistorised coil ignition system (TCI-H) working on the Hall effect principle is fitted to

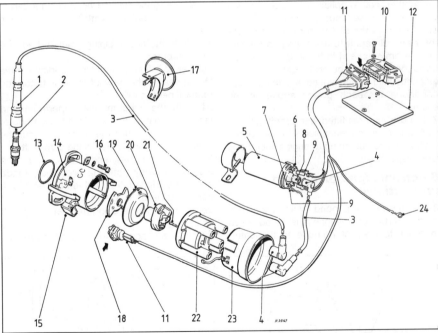

Fig. 12.28 Exploded view of the TCI-H electronic ignition system components (Sec 5)

1 *Spark plug connector*	9 *Main loom LT wiring*
2 *Spark plug*	10 *TCI-H control unit*
3 *HT lead*	11 *Control unit multi-plug*
4 *H T lead connectors*	12 *Heat sink*
5 *Ignition coil*	13 *Distributor O-ring*
6 *Coil terminal 1 (–)*	14 *Distributor*
7 *Coil terminal 4 (HT)*	15 *Hall sender*
8 *Coil terminal 15 (+)*	16 *Retaining bolt*

17 *Vacuum unit*
18 *Bearing plate*
19 *Plastic shield*
20 *Rotor arm*
21 *Carbon brush*
22 *Distributor cap*
23 *Screen*
24 *Earth lead*

12

later models and comprises the battery, coil, distributor, ignition control unit, spark plugs and associated leads and wiring.

2 The system is divided into two circuits, low tension and high tension. The high tension (HT) circuit is similar to that of a conventional ignition system and consists of the high tension coil windings, distributor, rotor arm, spark plugs and HT leads. The low tension (LT) circuit consists of the battery, ignition switch, low tension or primary coil windings, and a rotor and pick-up unit operating in conjunction with the control unit. The rotor and pick-up unit are located in the distributor, and perform the same function as the contact breaker points used in conventional systems.

3 The rotor is a four-toothed wheel (one for each cylinder) which is fitted to, and rotates with, the distributor shaft.

4 The pick-up unit is fitted to the distributor baseplate and basically consists of a coil and permanent magnet.

5 The control unit is located at the rear of the engine compartment and is an amplifier module which is used to boost the voltage induced by the pick-up coil.

6 When the ignition switch is on, the ignition primary circuit is energised. When the distributor rotor teeth approach the pick-up coil assembly, a voltage is induced which signals the amplifier to switch off the coil primary circuit, causing the magnetic field in the ignition coil to collapse, inducing a high voltage in the secondary windings. This is conducted to the distributor cap where the rotor arm directs it to the appropriate spark plug. A timing circuit in the amplifier module turns on the coil current again after the magnetic field has collapsed, and the process continues for each power stroke of the engine.

7 The distributor is fitted with centrifugal and vacuum advance mechanisms to control the ignition timing according to engine speed and load respectively.

Electronic ignition system - precautions

8 On models equipped with electronic ignition certain precautions must be observed in order to prevent damage to the semi-conductor components and in order to prevent personal injury.

9 Before disconnecting wires from the system make sure that the ignition is switched off.

10 When turning the engine at starter speed without starting, the HT lead must be pulled from the centre of the distributor cap and kept earthed to a suitable part of the engine or bodywork.

11 Disconnect the battery leads before carrying out electric welding on any part of the car.

12 If the system develops a fault and it is necessary to tow the car with the ignition key switched on, the wiring must be disconnected from the TCI-H control unit.

13 Do not under any circumstances connect a condenser to the coil terminals.

14 Take care to avoid receiving electric shocks from the HT system.

Electronic ignition distributor - removal and refitting

15 Disconnect the battery negative lead.

16 Disconnect the interference screen earth lead, release the two distributor cap spring clips and remove the cap and screen.

17 Disconnect the distributor wiring multi-plug and the vacuum advance hose.

18 Mark the position of the distributor flange in relation to the cylinder head using a dab of quick drying paint or with two small punch marks.

19 Undo the two retaining bolts and remove the distributor.

20 Before refitting, check the condition of the O-ring seal at the base of the distributor and renew if necessary.

21 With the vacuum unit uppermost and facing the rear of the car, place the distributor in position and turn the rotor arm until the drive dog coupling engages the camshaft.

22 Insert the retaining bolts, turn the distributor body until the previously made marks are aligned, then tighten the bolts. If a new distributor is being fitted, position it centrally within its elongated retaining bolt holes.

23 Refit the vacuum hose, wiring multi-plug, distributor cap and screen earth lead, then reconnect the battery.

24 Adjust the ignition timing by the stroboscopic method as described in Chapter 4, Section 6.

Electronic ignition system - testing

Control unit

25 When making this test the coil must be in good condition (see Chapter 4, Section 7).

26 Remove the plastic cover on the left-hand side of the plenum chamber for access to the control unit.

27 Disconnect the multi-plug from the control unit and connect a voltmeter between terminals 4 and 2, as shown in Fig. 12.29.

28 Switch on the ignition and check that battery voltage, or slightly less, is available. If not, there is an open-circuit in the supply wires.

29 Switch off the ignition and reconnect the multi-plug to the control unit.

30 Pull the multi-plug from the Hall sender on the side of the distributor, then connect a voltmeter across the low tension terminals on the coil (Fig. 12.30).

31 Switch on the ignition and check that there is initially 2 volts, dropping to zero after 1 to 2 seconds. If this is not the case, renew the control unit and coil.

32 Using a length of wire, earth the centre terminal of the distributor multi-plug briefly; the voltage should rise to at least 2 volts. If not, there is an open-circuit or the control unit is faulty.

Hall sender

33 Check that the ignition system wiring and plugs are fitted correctly.

34 The coil must be known to be in good condition (see Chapter 4, Section 7), also the control unit as previously described.

35 Pull the HT lead from the centre of the distributor cap, and earth the lead to a suitable part of the engine or bodywork.

36 Pull back the rubber boot from the control unit and connect a voltmeter between terminals 6 and 3, as shown in Fig. 12.31.

37 Switch on the ignition and turn the engine by hand in its normal direction of rotation. The

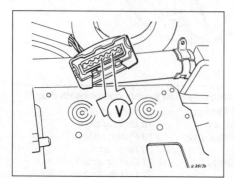

Fig. 12.29 Voltmeter connections at control unit multi-plug (Sec 5)

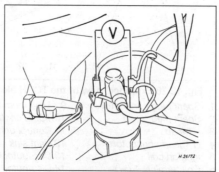

Fig. 12.30 Voltmeter connected across coil LT terminals (Sec 5)

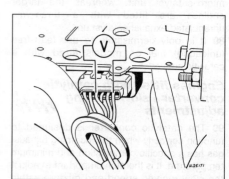

Fig. 12.31 Voltmeter connected to terminals 6 and 3 of control unit multi-plug (Sec 5)

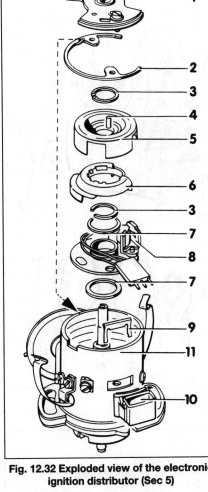

Fig. 12.32 Exploded view of the electronic ignition distributor (Sec 5)

1 Bearing plate
2 Bearing plate
  retaining ring
3 Circlip
4 Locating pin
5 Rotor
6 Wiring cover
7 Shim
8 Hall sender
9 Clip
10 Wiring connector
11 Main body

voltage should alternate from between 0 and a minimum of 2 volts. If not, the Hall sender is faulty and must be renewed.

Electronic ignition distributor - overhaul

38 With the distributor removed from the engine, remove the rotor arm and, where fitted, the plastic shield.
39 Undo the two screws and withdraw the bearing plate.
40 Mark the position of the lug on the bearing plate retaining ring in relation to the distributor body, then remove the retaining ring. This can be done by compressing the ring slightly using circlip pliers engaged with the two screw holes.
41 Extract the rotor retaining circlip, then carefully prise up the rotor using two screwdrivers at opposite points as levers.

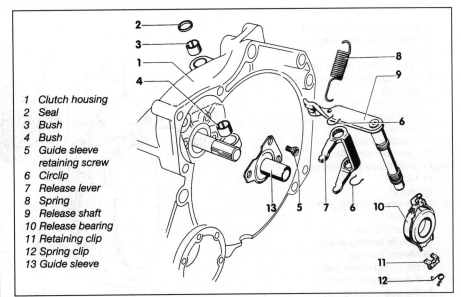

1 Clutch housing
2 Seal
3 Bush
4 Bush
5 Guide sleeve
  retaining screw
6 Circlip
7 Release lever
8 Spring
9 Release shaft
10 Release bearing
11 Retaining clip
12 Spring clip
13 Guide sleeve

Fig. 12.33 Exploded view of the clutch release mechanism – five-speed gearbox
(Sec 6)

Recover the small locating pin as the rotor is released.
42 Lift out the wiring cover, then extract the Hall sender retaining circlip and shim.
43 Remove the wiring connector, disengage the Hall sender from the vacuum unit rod and remove the sender.
44 Undo the two screws and remove the vacuum unit.
45 Renew any components as necessary which are available in the form of a distributor repair kit.
46 Reassembly is a reversal of dismantling. Lightly grease the Hall sender contact surfaces and ensure that the bearing plate retaining ring is refitted in its original position, as noted during removal.

6 Clutch

Self-adjusting clutch - general

1 Later models are fitted with a self-adjusting clutch mechanism. This is located in the cable and automatically adjusts the free play to cater for wear of the clutch friction linings.
2 To remove the cable, first fully depress the clutch pedal several times.
3 Pull the release arm on the gearbox away from the cable in order to compress the adjustment mechanism, then hold the end fitting and disconnect it from the release lever.
4 Prise the rubber grommet from the bracket on the gearbox, then disconnect the cable from the pedal inside the car and withdraw it from the steering gear housing.
5 Refitting is a reversal of removal, but make

sure that the flats on the cable are located correctly on the steering gear housing. Grease the cable attachment point on the pedal. Do not grease the cable before fitting it to the steering gear housing, as there is a danger of grease blocking the breather vent with possible danger to the steering gear. Check that the clutch operates correctly by depressing the pedal several times. Also pull the release lever approximately 10 mm away from the cable to check that it is free. Self-adjusting clutch cables may be fitted to earlier models, but it is important to remove the return spring. If the spring is left in position, the self-adjusting mechanism will not operate correctly and the clutch will not fully disengage.

Release bearing and shaft (five-speed gearbox) - removal, checking and refitting

6 Removal and checking procedures for the release bearing are the same as for the four-speed gearbox as described in Chapter 5, Section 7, paragraphs 1 to 4 inclusive. To remove the release shaft, proceed as follows.
7 Extract the circlips securing the release lever to the release shaft, then withdraw the shaft from its bushes and the release lever. Note that there is a master spline on the shaft and lever allowing fitment in only one position.
8 Check the bushes and bearing surfaces of the shaft for wear, and also check the release bearing guide sleeve for scoring. The bushes may be removed using a drift, and new bushes fitted in a similar fashion. Fit the bushes so that the oil seal will be flush with the housing when in position.
9 Refitting is a reversal of removal, but lubricate all bearing surfaces with a high melting point grease.

12

1 Drive flange retaining bolt
2 Right-hand drive flange
3 Bolt
4 Speedometer driven gear
5 Speedometer driven gear guide bushing
6 Clutch housing
7 Differential
8 Dowel
9 Gearbox housing
10 Left-hand drive flange
11 Drive flange retaining bolt
12 Magnet
13 Dowel
14 5th speed driving gear
15 Circlip
16 Thrust washer
17 Needle bearing sleeve
18 Needle bearing
19 5th speed driven gear
20 5th gear synchro ring
21 5th gear synchro hub
22 Locking clip
23 5th gear selector fork
24 5th gear synchro sleeve
25 Gasket seal
26 End cover
27 Bolt

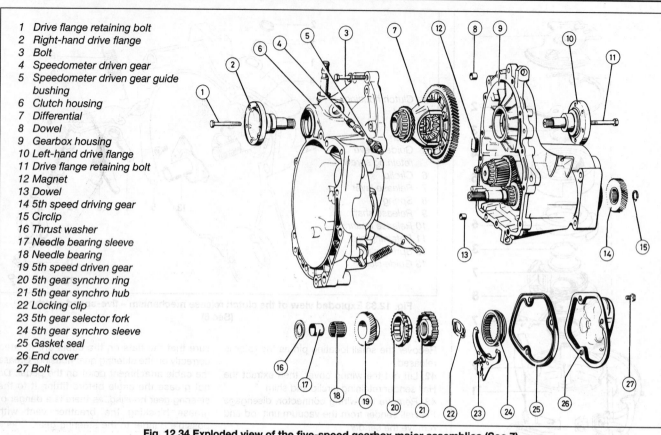

Fig. 12.34 Exploded view of the five-speed gearbox major assemblies (Sec 7)

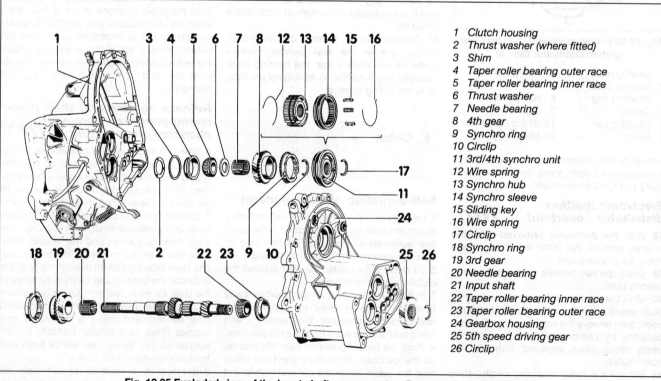

1 Clutch housing
2 Thrust washer (where fitted)
3 Shim
4 Taper roller bearing outer race
5 Taper roller bearing inner race
6 Thrust washer
7 Needle bearing
8 4th gear
9 Synchro ring
10 Circlip
11 3rd/4th synchro unit
12 Wire spring
13 Synchro hub
14 Synchro sleeve
15 Sliding key
16 Wire spring
17 Circlip
18 Synchro ring
19 3rd gear
20 Needle bearing
21 Input shaft
22 Taper roller bearing inner race
23 Taper roller bearing outer race
24 Gearbox housing
25 5th speed driving gear
26 Circlip

Fig. 12.35 Exploded view of the input shaft components – five-speed gearbox (Sec 7)

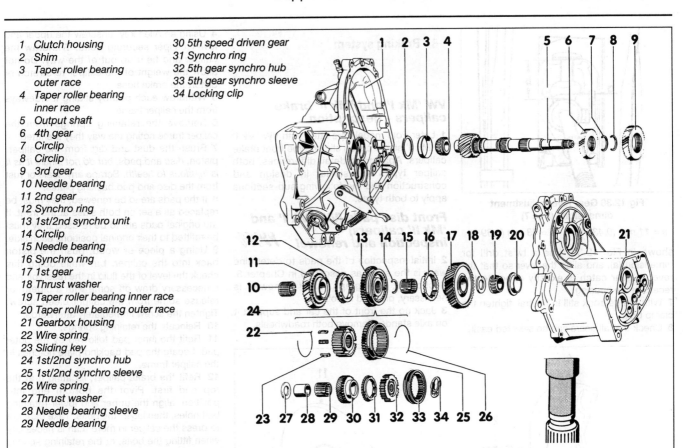

1 Clutch housing	30 5th speed driven gear
2 Shim	31 Synchro ring
3 Taper roller bearing	32 5th gear synchro hub
outer race	33 5th gear synchro sleeve
4 Taper roller bearing	34 Locking clip
inner race	
5 Output shaft	
6 4th gear	
7 Circlip	
8 Circlip	
9 3rd gear	
10 Needle bearing	
11 2nd gear	
12 Synchro ring	
13 1st/2nd synchro unit	
14 Circlip	
15 Needle bearing	
16 Synchro ring	
17 1st gear	
18 Thrust washer	
19 Taper roller bearing inner race	
20 Taper roller bearing outer race	
21 Gearbox housing	
22 Wire spring	
23 Sliding key	
24 1st/2nd synchro hub	
25 1st/2nd synchro sleeve	
26 Wire spring	
27 Thrust washer	
28 Needle bearing sleeve	
29 Needle bearing	

Fig. 12.36 Exploded view of the output shaft components – five-speed gearbox (Sec 7)

7 Manual gearbox

Five-speed gearbox - general

1 Certain later Polo models are available with a five-speed manual gearbox, code number 085.

2 Removal and refitting of the five-speed gearbox is the same as described in Chapter 6 for the four-speed unit.

Gearchange mechanism - modifications

3 The gearchange mechanism components on all five-speed models, and four-speed models from April 1989, vary slightly to those shown in Chapter 6. The bush (item 15 in Fig. 6.4) is now in two parts, and both parts are destroyed when removing the mechanism. When fitting the new parts, ensure that the two plastic cups are not pushed apart.

4 The VW tools for adjusting the modified mechanism are numbered 3234 for 4-speed models, and 3153 for 5-speed models, but the following method may be used. First select neutral.

5 With the car raised and supported on axle stands, loosen the shift rod clamp bolt.

6 Have an assistant position the gear lever as

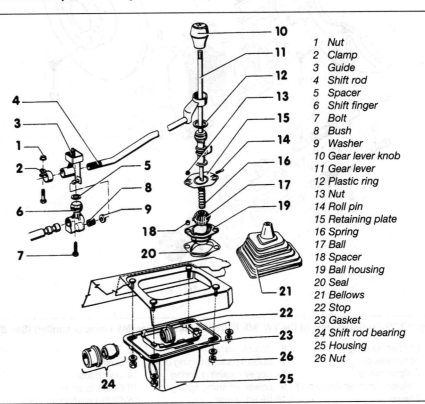

1 Nut
2 Clamp
3 Guide
4 Shift rod
5 Spacer
6 Shift finger
7 Bolt
8 Bush
9 Washer
10 Gear lever knob
11 Gear lever
12 Plastic ring
13 Nut
14 Roll pin
15 Retaining plate
16 Spring
17 Ball
18 Spacer
19 Ball housing
20 Seal
21 Bellows
22 Stop
23 Gasket
24 Shift rod bearing
25 Housing
26 Nut

Fig 12.37 Gearchange mechanism components on later models (Sec 7)

12

Fig 12.38 Gear lever adjustment dimensions (Sec 7)

a = 11 mm (0.433 in)   b = 43 mm (1.69 in)

shown in Fig. 12.38. Use a twist drill for dimension (a), and align the lever so that the reverse gear catch is exactly opposite the recess in the housing.

7 With the gearbox still in neutral, tighten the clamp bolt.

8 Check that all gears can be selected easily.

8 Braking system

VW 'Mk I' and 'Mk II' brake calipers - description

1 Later Polo models are fitted with VW 'Mk I' or 'Mk II' single piston sliding type front brake calipers. Apart from detail differences, both caliper types are similar in design and construction and the following sub-sections apply to both types.

Front disc pads (VW 'Mk I' and 'Mk II' calipers) - inspection and renewal

2 Initial inspection of the pads to determine wear is the same as described in Chapter 8, Section 3, paragraph 1. If renewal is necessary, proceed as follows.

3 Jack up the front of the car and support it on axle stands. Remove both roadwheels.

4 Using an Allen key, unscrew the upper and lower caliper securing bolts. Withdraw the caliper and tie it up out of the way. Do not allow the weight of the caliper to stretch or distort the brake hose.

5 Withdraw each pad by sliding it sideways from the caliper frame.

6 Remove the retaining springs from the caliper frame noting the way they are fitted.

7 Brush the dust and dirt from the caliper, piston, disc and pads, *but do not inhale it as it is injurious to health*. Scrape any scale or rust from the disc and pad backing plates.

8 If the pads are to be renewed, they must be replaced as a set on both sides at the front. If the original pads are to be re-used they must be refitted to their original positions each side.

9 Using a piece of wood, push the piston back into the caliper, but while doing this check the level of the fluid in the reservoir and if necessary draw off some with a pipette or release some from the caliper bleed screw. Tighten the screw immediately afterwards.

10 Relocate the retaining springs.

11 Refit the inner pad followed by the outer pad. Locate the pad backing plate notches in the caliper frame.

12 Refit the brake caliper, locating it at the top end first. Pivot the bottom end into position, align the upper and lower retaining bolt holes, then insert the bolts. Take care not to press the caliper in more than is necessary when fitting the bolts, or the retaining springs may be distorted which, in turn, will give noisy braking. Tighten the bolts to the specified torque.

13 On completion, the brake pedal should be depressed firmly several times with the car stationary so that the brake pads take up their normal running positions. Also check the brake hydraulic fluid level in the master cylinder reservoir and top up if necessary.

Front brake caliper (VW 'Mk I' and 'Mk II' calipers) removal, overhaul and refitting

14 Unbolt and remove the caliper from the caliper frame as described in the previous sub-section.

15 Clamp the flexible brake hose using a brake hose clamp or self-locking wrench with suitably protected jaws.

16 Slacken the brake hose union at the caliper, then hold the union and unscrew the caliper from it. Plug the hose union to prevent dirt ingress.

17 Clean the external surfaces of the caliper with paraffin and wipe dry; plug the fluid inlet during this operation.

18 Prise free and remove the dust seal from the piston.

19 Using air pressure from a foot pump in the fluid inlet, blow the piston from the cylinder, but take care not to drop the piston. Prise the sealing ring from the cylinder bore. Take care not to scratch the cylinder bore.

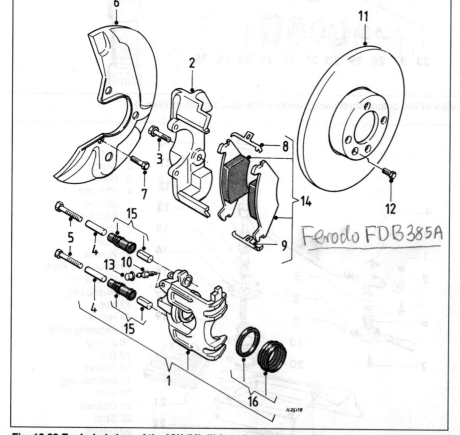

Ferodo FDB385A

Fig. 12.39 Exploded view of the VW 'Mk II' front brake caliper (Mk I caliper similar) (Sec 8)

1 Caliper housing components	6 Splash plate	12 Screw
2 Caliper frame	7 Splash plate retaining bolt	13 Dust cap
3 Caliper frame retaining bolt	8 Upper retaining spring	14 Disc pads
4 Sleeve	9 Lower retaining spring	15 Guide bushes
5 Caliper securing bolts	10 Bleed screw	16 Piston sealing ring and
	11 Brake disc	dust seal

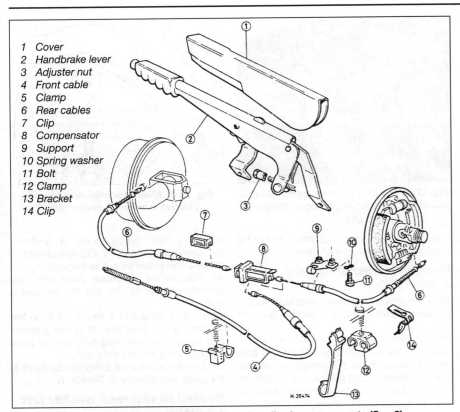

1 Cover
2 Handbrake lever
3 Adjuster nut
4 Front cable
5 Clamp
6 Rear cables
7 Clip
8 Compensator
9 Support
10 Spring washer
11 Bolt
12 Clamp
13 Bracket
14 Clip

Fig. 12.40 Exploded view of later type handbrake components (Sec 8)

20 Clean the components with methylated spirit and allow to dry. Inspect the surfaces of the piston, cylinder and frames for wear, damage and corrosion. If evident renew the caliper but, if the components are in good condition obtain a repair kit of seals.
21 Dip the new sealing ring in brake fluid and locate it in the cylinder bore groove using the fingers only to manipulate it.
22 Manipulate the new dust cap into position on the piston, the inner seal lip engaging in the piston groove. Use a suitable screwdriver to ease it into position, but take care not to damage the seal or scratch the piston.
23 Smear the piston with brake fluid and press it into position in the caliper bore.
24 Check that the brake hose union is clean,

then unplug it and refit it to the caliper, but do not fully tighten it at this stage.
25 Refit the caliper as described in the previous sub-section.
26 Tighten the brake hose union so that the hose is not twisted or in a position where it will chafe against surrounding components.
27 Remove the hose clamp, top up the brake fluid reservoir and bleed the brakes, described in Chapter 8.

Front brake hydraulic hose - modification

28 With the introduction of the VW 'Mk I' and 'Mk II' brake calipers, the wheel bearing housing has also been modified in the area of the clip used to secure the latest type brake hose.

Fig. 12.41 Stop-start system automatic control unit retaining screws – arrowed (Sec 9)

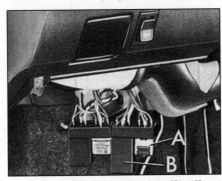

Fig. 12.42 Double relay plate (Sec 9)

A Heated rear window and oil pressure warning cut-off relay
B Gearshift indicator control unit

29 Should it be necessary to renew a wheel bearing housing, the modified brake hose must also be obtained.

Handbrake components (later models) - general

30 The handbrake lever, cables and associated components have been modified on later models - see Fig. 12.40.
31 A minor alteration to the basic handbrake adjusting procedure has been introduced in that this is made with the lever at the fourth notch.

9 Electrical system

Automatic stop-start system - description

1 From March 1984, Formel E models are equipped with an automatic stop-start (SSA) system, in addition to the gearshift/consumption indicator (GCI).
2 The system requires specialist test equipment to check its operation and diagnose faults, and if it fails to operate satisfactorily it is recommended that the vehicle is taken to your local VAG dealer.

Description of operation

3 The SSA system is switched on or off, as required, by a switch on the facia panel.
4 For the system to become operative, the coolant temperature must be above 55°C (131°F) and the vehicle road-speed in excess of 5 km/hour (3 mph).
5 The engine is automatically switched off when road-speed drops below this point and 1st, 2nd or reverse gears are not engaged.
6 When the SSA system is in operation, the heated rear window and oil pressure warning light are switched off.
7 The engine will be started automatically when the gear lever is moved from neutral toward 1st, 2nd or reverse, and the clutch pedal depressed .
8 Should the engine stall when moving off, the engine may be restarted by moving the gear lever back to neutral and then into 1st, 2nd or reverse gear within 6 seconds of stalling.
9 Wiring diagrams for the SSA system appear at the end of this Section; the following paragraphs and figures show component location and removal/refitting procedures for individual components.

SSA components - removal and refitting

10 The stop-start automatic control unit is located under the facia panel .
11 Remove the two screws (Fig. 12.41) and pull the control unit off the relay plate.
12 The heated rear window and oil pressure warning cut-off relay is located on the double relay plate by the steering column. behind the shelf (Fig. 12.42).

12

Fig. 12.43 Speed sensor retaining screws – arrowed (Sec 9)

Fig. 12.44 The SSA gearbox switch (A) and gearshift/consumption indicator switch (B) (Sec 9)

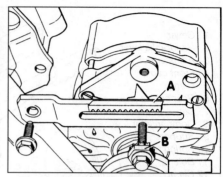

Fig. 12.45 Alternator adjusting link with positive tensioning device (Sec 9)

13 To remove the relay, first remove the shelf and then pull the relay off the relay plate.

14 The gearshift indicator control unit is on the same relay plate.

15 The speed sensor is located in the instrument panel (Fig. 12.43).

16 Remove the instrument panel, undo the screws (arrowed) and remove the speed sensor unit.

17 The SSA master switch is located on the facia panel.

18 To remove it, carefully lever the switch out and pull off the connector.

19 The SSA gearbox switch is located on the underside of the gearbox (Fig. 12.44).

20 To remove the switch, disconnect the wiring connector and unscrew the switch. Retain the shim.

21 When refitting the switch, use a shim of the same thickness as that removed.

22 The gearbox switch for gearshift/consumption indicator can also be seen in Fig. 12.44.

23 Refitting for all items is a reversal of the removal procedure.

24 Check gearbox oil level and top up as necessary.

Oil pressure warning system (1983 on) - description

25 All models from 1983 on are equipped with an optical and acoustic oil pressure warning system.

26 The oil pressure switches for these warning systems are mounted on the cylinder head.

27 The switches are 1.8 bar (white insulation) and 0.3 bar (brown insulation).

28 On starting the engine, as soon as the oil pressure rises about 0.3 bar, the oil pressure warning light will go out.

29 At engine speeds above 2000 rpm the high pressure switch comes Into operation, and should the oil pressure drop below 1.8 bar, the oil warning light will come on and the buzzer will sound.

30 On some earlier models, the buzzer will also sound in the low pressure mode on start-up.

31 Apart from changing the oil pressure switches, little can be done by way of

maintenance, and your VAG dealer should be consulted if the system malfunctions.

Headlamp washer system description

32 Later Polo models are available with a headlamp washer system as an optional extra.

33 The system comprises a fluid reservoir, located in the engine compartment and also serving the windscreen washers, an electric pump attached to the reservoir, a washer jet for each headlamp located in the bumper overriders, two check valves and associated hoses.

Headlamp washer system jets - adjustment, removal and refitting

34 The jets should be adjusted so that the flow of water strikes the headlamp 10 mm (0.4 in) above the centre of the lamp glass.

35 Should it be necessary to remove the jets for cleaning, prise the ballhead out using a screwdriver and clean using compressed air. Before fitting, operate the washers briefly to clear the hoses and check valve, then push the ball-head back into place.

36 Access to the check valves and hoses can be gained after removing the bumper as described in Chapter 11.

Dim-dip lighting system

37 Recent legislation requires that all vehicles registered in the UK after the 1st April 1987 should be equipped with a dim-dip lighting system.

38 The system provides the headlamps with a brightness between that of the sidelamps and the headlamps on normal dipped beam. The purpose of the system is to prevent vehicles being driven on sidelamps only.

39 Full information will be given in the vehicle handbook, but basically, the dim-dip lamps are in operation whenever the light switch is in the 'ON' position and the ignition is switched on.

Alternator drivebelt (later models) - adjustment

40 On some later models the alternator

adjusting link incorporates a positive tensioning device (Fig. 12.45). Adjustment of the drivebelt is carried out as follows.

41 Slacken the alternator pivot bolt, the adjusting link pivot bolt and the tensioning bolt.

42 Apply a torque of 4 Nm (3 lbf ft) to the tensioning nut. Hold the nut in this position and tighten the tensioning bolt, the link pivot bolt and the alternator pivot bolt.

43 Check the drivebelt deflection by hand in the usual way (Chapter 9, Section 7).

Heated windscreen washer jets - general

44 Some later models are equipped with heated windscreen washer jets. The jets are switched on automatically with the ignition.

10 Suspension and steering

Steering column (later models) - general

1 From October 1986 a one-piece telescopic steering column has been introduced to replace the two-piece version used previously (Fig. 12.46). The relevant procedures contained in Chapter 10 are still applicable to the new version.

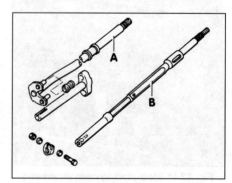

Fig. 12.46 Telescopic steering column details (Sec 10)

A Two-piece type   B One-piece type

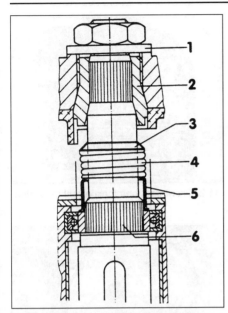

Fig. 12.47 Cross section of the steering wheel adaptor fitted from August 1988 onwards (Sec 10)

1 Washer (3 mm thick)
2 Adaptor sleeve
3 Clamping disc
4 Spring
5 Contact ring
6 Support ring

Front wheel bearing housing - renewal

2 With the introduction of the VW 'Mk I' and 'Mk II' front brake calipers, a revised pattern brake hose was also introduced using a different method of securing it to the wheel bearing housing. Consequently the wheel bearing housing was also modified and only this modified version will in future be available from VAG parts stockists. It the later wheel bearing housing is being fitted to an earlier car the modified brake hose must also be obtained.

Steering wheel - modifications

3 As from August 1988 a steering wheel adaptor was fitted in order to improve the fine

11.9 Centre pivot bracket spring clip (arrowed)

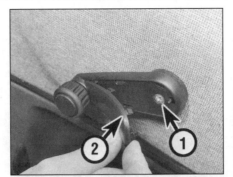

11.1 Later type window regulator handle

1 Retaining screw   2 Plastic cover

adjustment of the steering wheel. The adaptor is located over the existing splines and therefore the steering column remains the same as original.

4 The adaptor and new steering wheel may be fitted to earlier models.

5 A puller is required to remove the adaptor from the top of the steering column. When refitting the adaptor it must be pressed fully onto the column with the steering wheel nut before refitting the steering wheel.

11 Bodywork and fittings

Window regulator handles - later models

1 Access to the window regulator handle retaining screw is gained by prising off the plastic cover (photo).
2 Undo the screw, and the handle may be removed.
3 Reverse the operation to replace the handle.

Split rear seats - removal and refitting

4 To remove the seat squab, pull the seats upwards using the plastic pull handles provided.

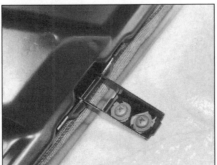

11.10 Backrest securing screws

11.5 Seat squab retaining screws (arrowed)

5 Tilt the seats right forward, which will allow access to the retaining screws (photo).
6 There are two screws for each seat squab.
7 Remove the screws and lift out the seat squabs.
8 The seat backrests may be removed by operating the seat back release mechanism and tilting the backrest forward.
9 Remove the spring clip from the centre pivot bracket by pulling it vertically (photo).
10 Now undo the two screws securing each backrest to the luggage compartment floor (photo).
11 Remove the centre pivot pin, and the seat backs may be lifted out.
12 Refitting is a reversal of this procedure.

Seat back release mechanism - removal and refitting

13 With the seat backs released, the release mechanism can be removed by prising off the retaining clip, unhooking the return spring, and sliding the mechanism off the spigot (photo).
14 Refit in the reverse order to removal.

Front seat belts - removal and refitting

Lower outboard mounting

15 Push the front seat right forward.

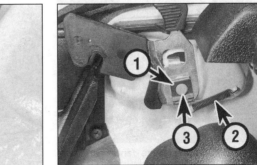

11.13 Seat back release mechanism

1 Spring clip   2 Return spring   3 Spigot

12

11.16 Front seat belt lower mounting

11.21 Front seat belt top mounting

11.23 Front seat belt inertia reel mounting bolt (arrowed)

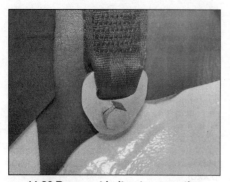

11.26 Rear seat belt outer mounting

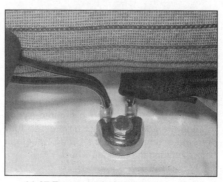

11.27 Rear seat belt inner mounting

11.28 Rear seat belt inertia reel mounting nuts (arrowed)

16 Pull back the plastic cover from the lower seat belt mounting (photo) .
17 Count the number of coils in the spring.
18 Unhook the spring and gently allow the tension to be released by allowing the spring to unwind.
19 Remove the spring from the retaining bolt head.
20 Undo the bolt.

Top mounting

21 Prise off the plastic cover and undo the retaining bolt (photo).

Inertia reel mounting

22 Remove the trim panel from the side of the passenger rear seat.

Fig. 12.48 Removing the centre console (Sec 11)

1 Retaining screws   2 Retainers
Lift out in direction of arrows

23 Undo the retaining bolt holding the inertia reel in place (photo).

All mountings

24 Refitting of all three mountings is a reversal of removal.

Rear seat belts - removal and refitting

25 The rear seat belts are removed in much the same way as the front belts.
26 The outer mountings are held by one bolt (photo).
27 The inboard mounting is undone after lifting the seat squabs (photo).
28 The inertia reel mechanism is held in place in the double skin of the luggage compartment by two bolts (photo).
29 Refit in the reverse order of removal.

Fig. 12.49 Front apron trim rivet locations – arrowed (Sec 11)

Centre console - removal and refitting

30 A centre console may be fitted to models which do not have one as standard; the screw retainers on the gear lever housing and air ducting under the facia are provided.
31 Remove the gear lever knob.
32 Unclip and remove the rubber boot.
33 Remove the screws from the front end of console (Fig. 12.48).
34 Pull the console rearward, and lift it from the retainers.
35 Lift out the console in the direction of the arrows.
36 Refitting is a reversal of removal.

Front apron trim - removal and refitting

37 Drill out the rivet heads (arrowed in Fig. 12.49).
38 Lift the trim forward and clear of the towing eye.
39 Knock out the rest of the rivets inwards with a punch.
40 When refitting a new trim, start riveting from the centre and work outwards.

Wheel arch mouldings - removal and refitting

41 The wheel arch mouldings are removed and refitted in the same way as the front apron trim.

Fig. 12.50 Wheel arch moulding rivet locations – arrowed (Sec 11)

Roof railing (roof rack) - description

42 A roof railing is available as an extra for 'square back' Polo models from 1986.

43 The railing can also be installed on 'square back' models from March 1985.

44 Fitting of the roof railing is best left to your VAG dealer.

Glass sunroof - removal and refitting

45 Unlatch the glass panel and remove it.

46 Pull the seal from the flange.

47 Unclip the tilt mechanism cover by driving the spreader pins inwards.

48 Unscrew the screws and remove the tilt mechanism, then remove the rear spacers located by the rear drain hoses.

49 Prise away the headlining and noise insulating strips which are secured by double-sided tape.

50 Remove the moulded frame by extracting the screws, disconnecting the drain hoses, and pulling off the clamping frame.

51 Refitting is a reversal of removal, but note the following additional points:

(a) *The tilt element must always be screwed into position, together with the glass panel*

(b) *Remove all traces of old sealant from the metal flange*

(c) *Apply a little sealant between the short flange of the inner seal and the moulding*

Heated seats - general

52 1990 Coupé S models may be fitted with seat heating as an optional extra. Both the seat cushion and the backrest are supplied with heating elements and the system is controlled by a knurled disc located on the instrument panel.

Plastic components - repair

With the use of more and more plastic body components by the vehicle manufacturers (eg bumpers. spoilers, and in some cases major body panels), rectification of more serious damage to such items has become a matter of either entrusting repair work to a specialist in this field, or renewing complete components. Repair of such damage by the DIY owner is not really feasible, owing to the cost of the equipment and materials required for effecting such repairs. The basic technique involves making a groove along the line of the crack in the plastic, using a rotary burr in a power drill. The damaged part is then welded back together, using a hot-air gun to heat up and fuse a plastic filler rod into the groove. Any excess plastic is then removed, and the area rubbed down to a smooth finish. It is important that a filler rod of the correct plastic is used, as body components can be made of a variety of different types (eg polycarbonate, ABS, polypropylene).

Damage of a less serious nature (abrasions, minor cracks etc) can be repaired by the DIY owner using a two-part epoxy filler repair material. Once mixed in equal proportions, this is used in similar fashion to the bodywork filler used on metal panels. The filler is usually cured in twenty to thirty minutes, ready for sanding and painting.

If the owner is renewing a complete component himself, or if he has repaired it with epoxy filler, he will be left with the problem of finding a suitable paint for finishing which is compatible with the type of plastic used. At one time, the use of a universal paint was not possible, owing to the complex range of plastics encountered in body component applications. Standard paints, generally speaking, will not bond to plastic or rubber satisfactorily. However, it is now possible to obtain a plastic body parts finishing kit which consists of a pre-primer treatment, a primer and coloured top coat. Full instructions are normally supplied with a kit, but basically, the method of use is to first apply the pre-primer to the component concerned, and allow it to dry for up to 30 minutes. Then the primer is applied, and left to dry for about an hour before finally applying the special-coloured top coat. The result is a correctly-coloured component, where the paint will flex with the plastic or rubber, a property that standard paint does not normally possess.

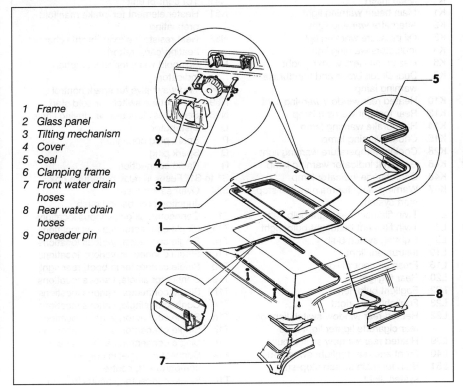

1 Frame
2 Glass panel
3 Tilting mechanism
4 Cover
5 Seal
6 Clamping frame
7 Front water drain hoses
8 Rear water drain hoses
9 Spreader pin

Fig. 12.51 Glass sunroof components (Sec 11)

12

Key to all wiring diagrams

Designation	
A	Battery
B	Starter
C	Alternator
C1	Voltage regulator
D	Ignition/starter switch
E1	Lighting switch
E2	Turn signal switch
E3	Hazard warning light switch
E4	Headlight dimmer/flasher switch
E9	Fresh air blower switch
E15	Heated rear window switch
E19	Parking light switch
E20	Instrument panel lighting control
E22	Intermittent wiper switch
E23	Foglight and rear foglight switch
E101	Main switch for stop-start system
F	Brake light switch
F1	Oil pressure switch
F2	Door contact switch, front left
F3	Door contact switch, front right
F4	Reversing light switch
F9	Handbrake warning switch
F12	Choke warning system contact
F18	Radiator fan thermo switch
F22	Oil pressure switch
F25	Throttle valve switch
F34	Brake fluid level warning contact
F35	Thermoswitch for automatic choke or for intake manifold preheating
F62	Gearshift indicator vacuum switch
F68	Gear switch for gearshift/consumption indicator
F90	Gearbox switch for stop-start system
G	Fuel gauge sender
G1	Fuel gauge
G2	Coolant temperature gauge sender or gearchange/consumption sensors
G3	Coolant temperature gauge or gearchange/consumption gauge
G5	Rev. counter
G40	Hall sender
G51	Consumption indicator
G54	Speed sensor for stop-start system
H	Horn control
H1	Horn
J2	Hazard warning flasher relay
J4	Dual tone horn relay

Designation	
J5	Fog light relay
J6	Voltage stabiliser
J30	Rear wash/wipe relay
J31	Intermittent wash/wipe relay
J39	Headlight washer system relay
J59	Relief relay for x contact
J81	Intake manifold preheating relay
J98	Control unit for gearchange indicator
J107	Control unit-stop-start system
J112	Switch off relay for heated rear window, driving lights and oil pressure control
J113	Speed switch for spark control
J114	Oil pressure warning control unit
K	Dash insert
K1	Main beam warning light
K2	Alternator warning light
K3	Oil pressure warning light
K5	Indicators warning light
K6	Hazard flashers warning light
K7	Dual circuit brake and handbrake warning lamp
K10	Heated rear window warning light
K13	Rear foglight warning lamp
K14	Handbrake warning lamp
K15	Choke warning lamp
K28	Coolant temperature warning light
K48	Gearshift indicator warning lamp
K48	Gearchange indicator lamp
K67	Warning lamp for main switch stop-start system
L1	Twin filament headlight bulb, left
L2	Twin filament headlight bulb, right
L9	Lighting switch bulb
L10	Instrument light
L16	Fresh air control light
L20	Rear foglight
L22	Foglight bulb, left
L23	Foglight bulb, right
L32	Heated rear window switch light or rear cigarette lighter light bulb
L39	Heated rear window switch bulb
L40	Front and rear foglight switch bulb
L51	Bulb for main switch stop-start system light
M1	Sidelight bulb, left
M2	Tail light bulb, right

Designation	
M3	Side light bulb, right
M4	Tail light bulb, left
M5	Indicator bulb, front left
M6	Indicator bulb, rear left
M7	Indicator bulb, front right
M8	Indicator bulb, rear right
M9	Brake light bulb, left
M10	Brake light bulb, right
M17	Reversing light bulb, right
N	Ignition coil
N3	By-pass air cut-off valve
N1	Automatic choke
N6	Resistance wire
N23	Resistance for fresh air blower
N41	TCI control unit
N51	Heater element for intake manifold preheating
N52	Heat resistance (part throttle channel heating/carburettor)
N60	Solenoid valve for consumption indicator
N64	Two way valve for spark control
N69	Thermotime switch for cold start
N98	Series resistance-town driving lights
O	Distributor
P	Spark plug connector
Q	Spark plug
R	Radio connection
S1 to S16	Fuses in relay plate/fuse box
S24	Overheating fuse
T	Junction box, behind dash
T1	Connector, single, various locations
T1a	Single connector, various locations
T1b	Single connector, various locations
T1c	Single connector, various locations
T1d	Single connector in boot, rear right
T1e	Connector single, various locations
T1f	Single connector, various locations
T1g	Connector single, various locations
T1h	Single connector, various locations
T1i	Single connector, various locations
T1j	Single connector, near carburettor
T1k	Connector single, in engine compartment, centre
T1l	Single connector, various locations
T1m	Single connector, various locations
T2	Connector 2 pin, various locations

Key to all wiring diagrams (continued)

T2a	Connector, 2 pin, various locations	T2l	Connector, 2 pin, in engine compartment, front left	T6/	Connector 6 pin on dash insert
T2b	Connector, 2 pin, various locations	T3	Connector 3 pin, various locations	T8	Connector, 8 pin, various locations
T2c	Connector 2 pin, various locations	T3a	Connector, 3 pin, behind dash panel	U1	Cigarette lighter
T2d	Connector 2 pin, various locations	T12	Connector, 12 pin, various locations	V	Windscreen wiper motor
T2e	Connector, 2 pin, various locations	T14/	Connector, 14 pin, on dash panel insert	V2	Fresh air blower
T2e	Connector, 2 pin, in engine compartment, front left	T20/	Connector, 20 pin, on relay plate/fuse box	V5	Windscreen washer pump
T2f	Connector, two pin, various locations			V7	Radiator fan
T2g	Connector 2 pin, various locations	T20a/	Connector, 20 pin, on relay plate/fuse box	V13	Rear washer pump motor
T2h	Connector 2 pin, in engine compartment, various locations	T29	Connector 29 pin, behind dash panel	V11	Headlight washer pump
				V12	Rear wiper motor
T2i	Connector 2 pin, various locations	T32	Connector, 32 pin, on relay plate/fuse box	V13	Rear washer pump motor
T2j	Connector 2 pin, right of engine compartment			V59	Windscreen washer pump
		T4	Connector 4 pin, various locations	W	Interior light, front
T2k	Connector 2 pin, in engine compartment, right	T4a	Connector 4 pin	X	Number plate light
				Y	Clock
				Z1	Heated rear window

Earth points

A4	Positive (+) connection (58b), in dash panel wiring loom	16	Earthing point, in wiring loom insulating hose, engine compartment, right	84	Earth connection, engine block, in front right wiring loom
1	Battery earth strap	17	Earthing point, bound with insulating tape, in instrument panel loom	85	Earth connection, in engine compartment wiring loom
2	Earthing strap, from engine to body				
3	Engine earth strap	18	Earthing point, bound with insulating tape, in instrument panel loom		
8	Earthing point, bound with insulating tape, in instrument panel loom	22	58b in wiring loom for instruments		
10	Earthing point, on taillight, left or on steering gear	23	Earth wire, above steering gear		
		40	Earth point, under seat, right		**Colour code**
11	Earthing point, under rear seat or on thermostat housing	52	Earth point, in tailgate, left	bl	Blue
		53	Earth point, in tailgate, right	br	Brown
12	Earth point, on rear cross panel left or in engine compartment, left	54	Earth point, on rear cross panel	ge	Yellow
		80	Earth connection -1-, in wiring loom for instruments	gn	Green
13	Earthing point, on fuel pump			gr	Grey
14	Earthing point, on tailgate lock carrier or left hand tail light	81	Earth connection, in dash panel wiring loom	li	Lilac
		82	Earth connection, in front left wiring loom (wiring via 2 pin connector)	ro	Red
15	Earthing point, in wiring loom insulating hose, engine compartment, left			sw	Black
				ws	White

13

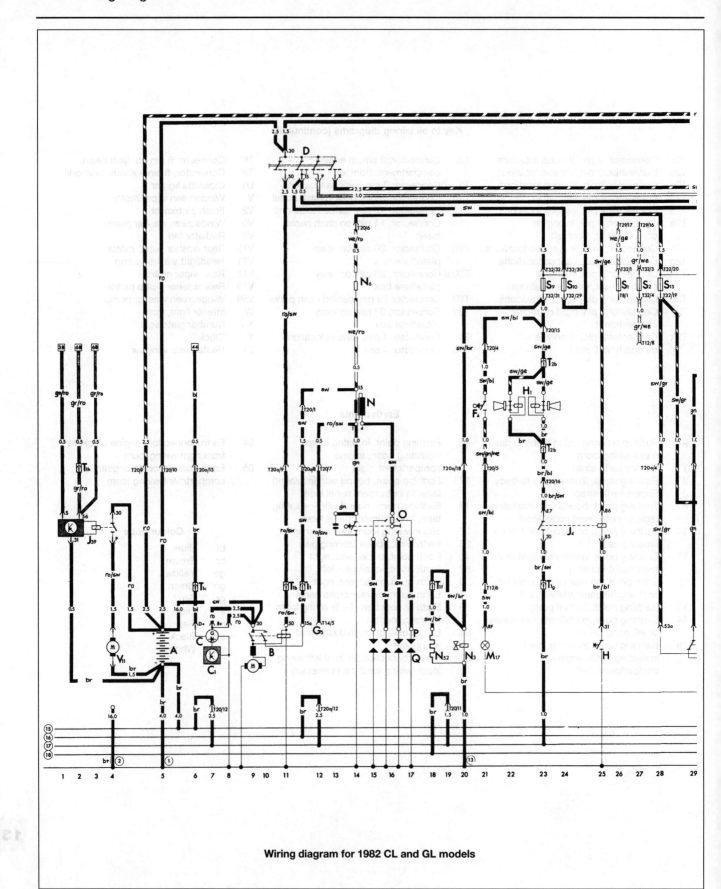

Wiring diagram for 1982 CL and GL models

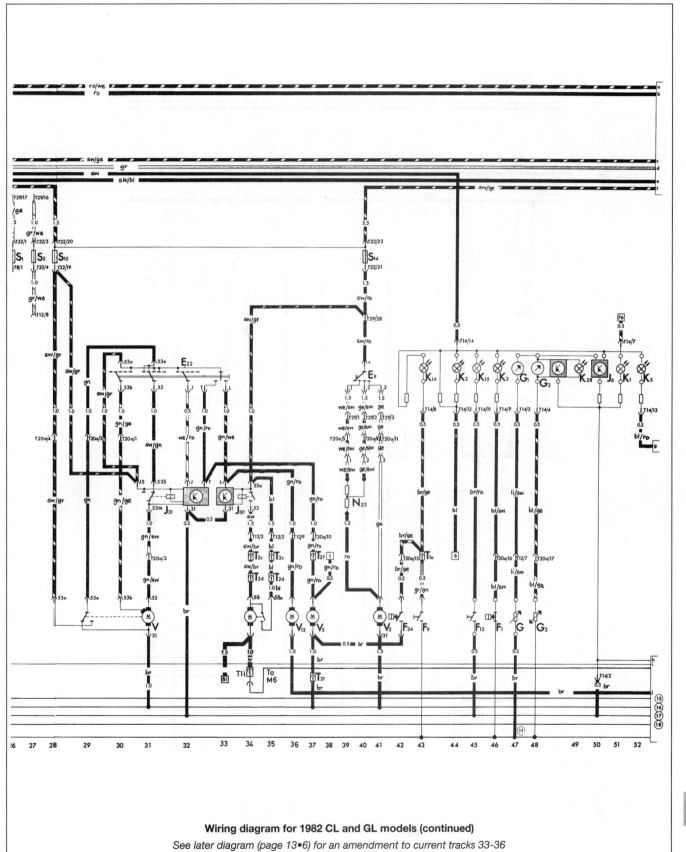

Wiring diagram for 1982 CL and GL models (continued)

See later diagram (page 13•6) for an amendment to current tracks 33-36

13

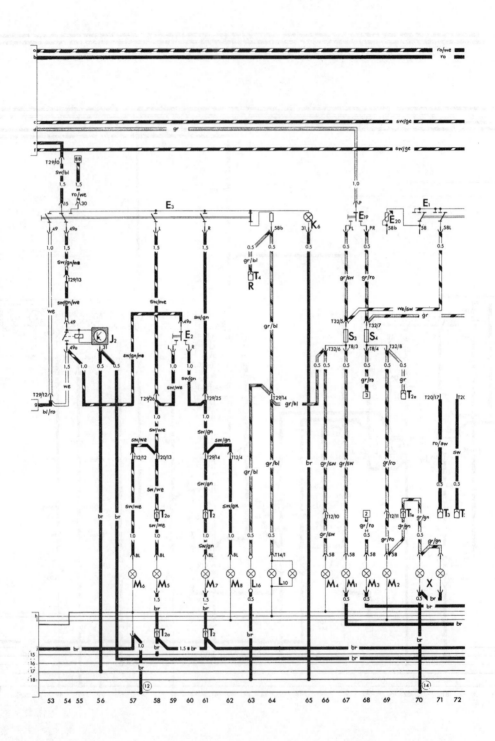

Wiring diagram for 1982 CL and GL models (continued)

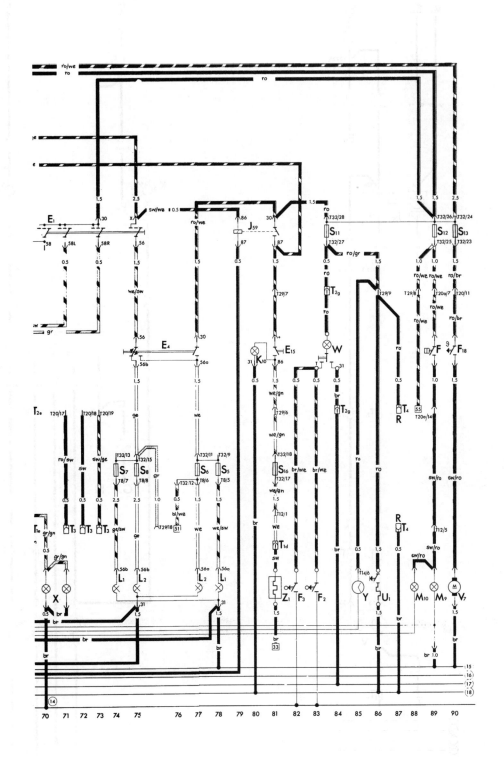

Wiring diagram for 1982 CL and GL models (continued)

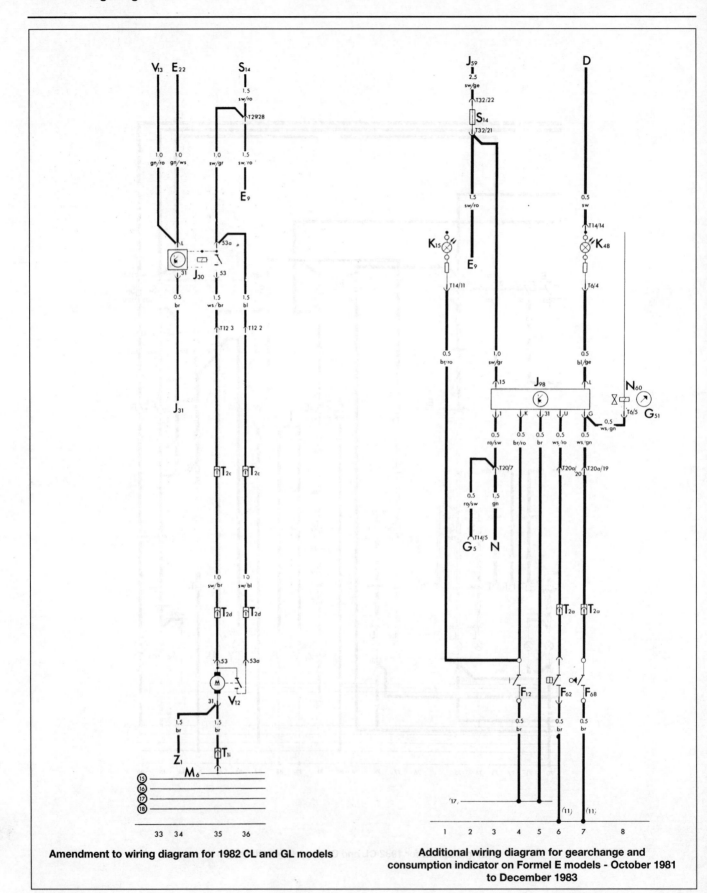

Amendment to wiring diagram for 1982 CL and GL models

Additional wiring diagram for gearchange and consumption indicator on Formel E models - October 1981 to December 1983

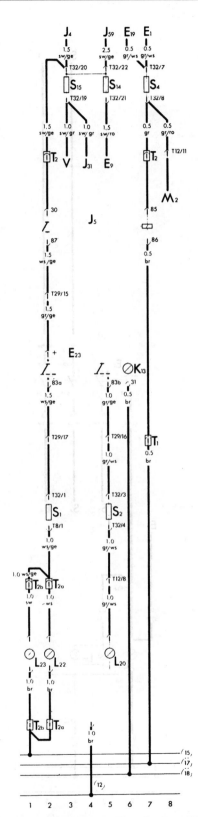

Additional wiring diagram for fog lights - October 1981 to July 1983

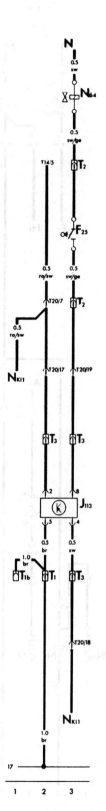

Additional wiring diagram for spark control on the 1.05 litre engine

13

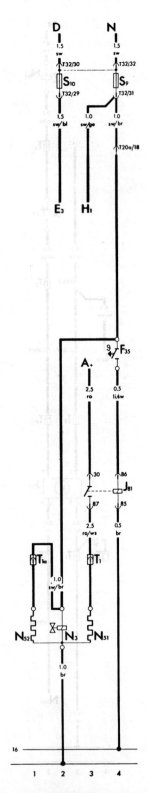

Additional wiring diagram for inlet manifold preheating on the 1.05 litre engine

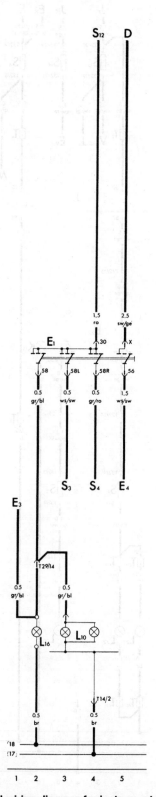

Additional wiring diagram for instrument lighting

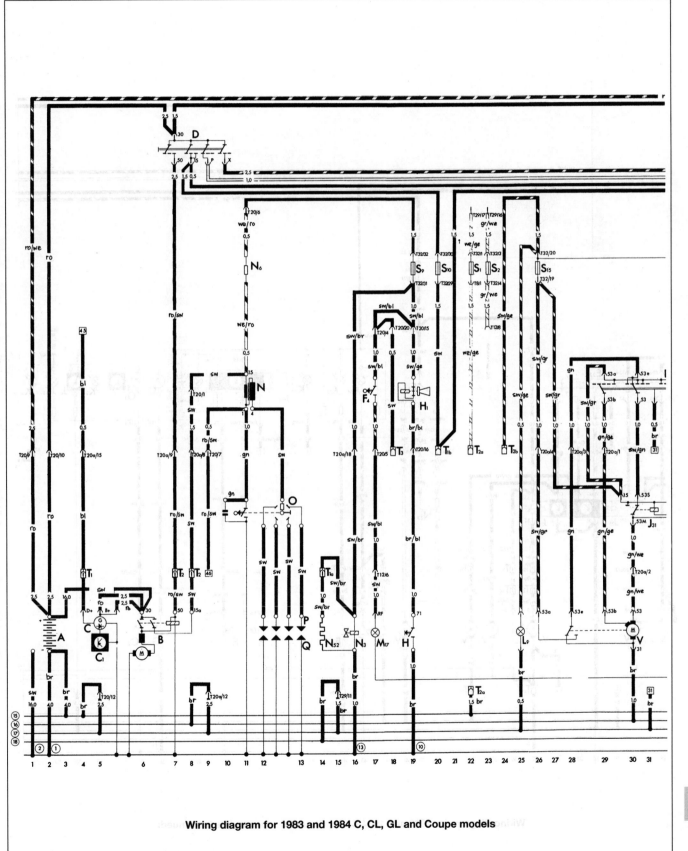

Wiring diagram for 1983 and 1984 C, CL, GL and Coupe models

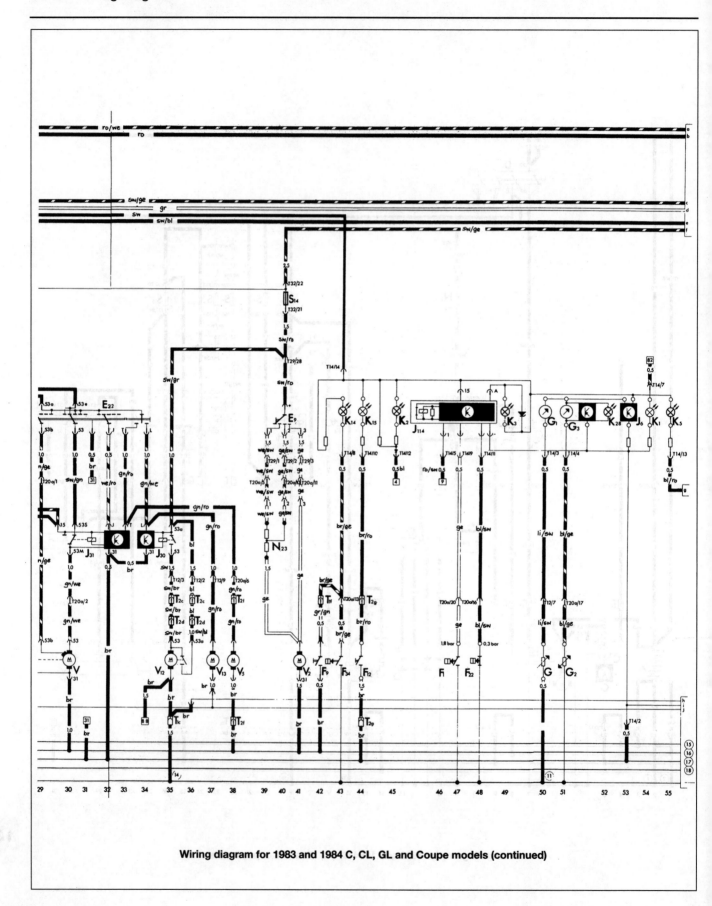

Wiring diagram for 1983 and 1984 C, CL, GL and Coupe models (continued)

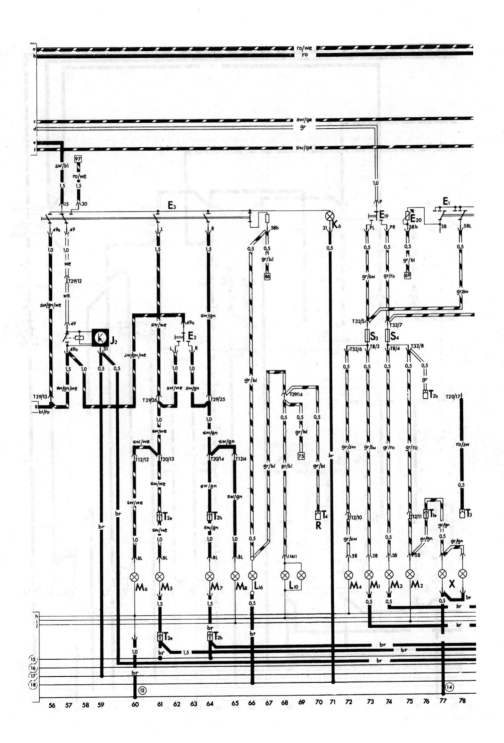

Wiring diagram for 1983 and 1984 C, CL, GL and Coupe models (continued)

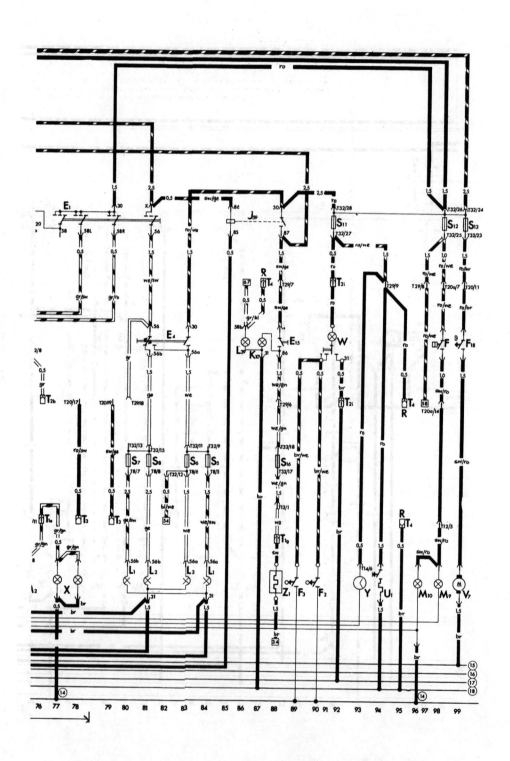

Wiring diagram for 1983 and 1984 C, CL, GL and Coupe models (continued)

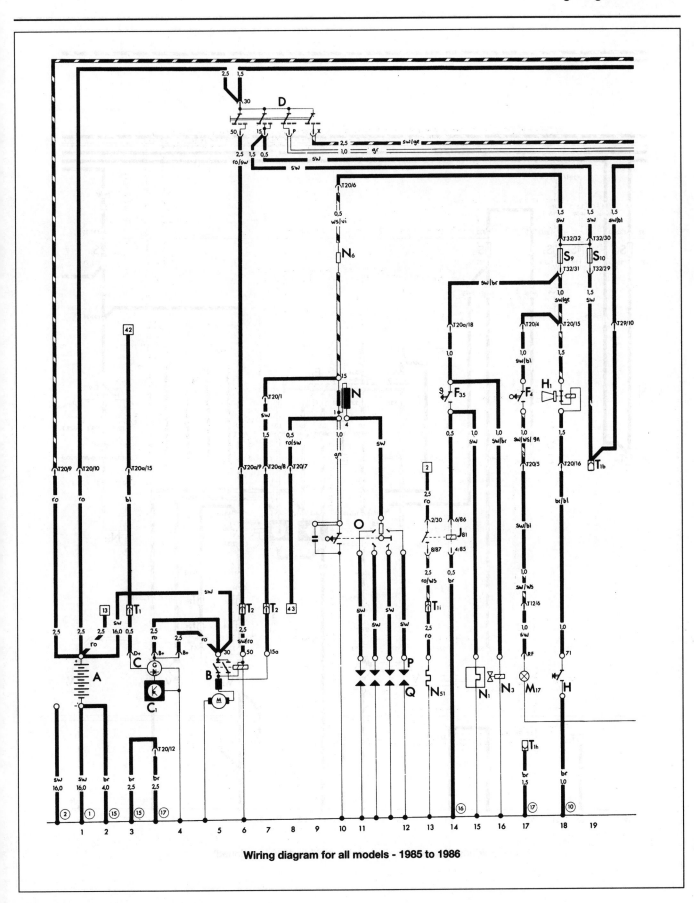

Wiring diagram for all models - 1985 to 1986

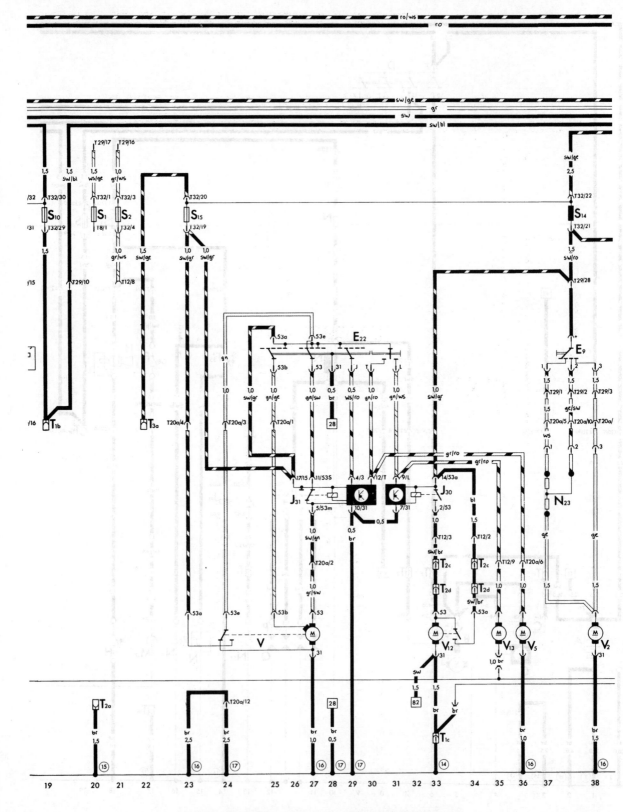

Wiring diagram for all models - 1985 to 1986 (continued)

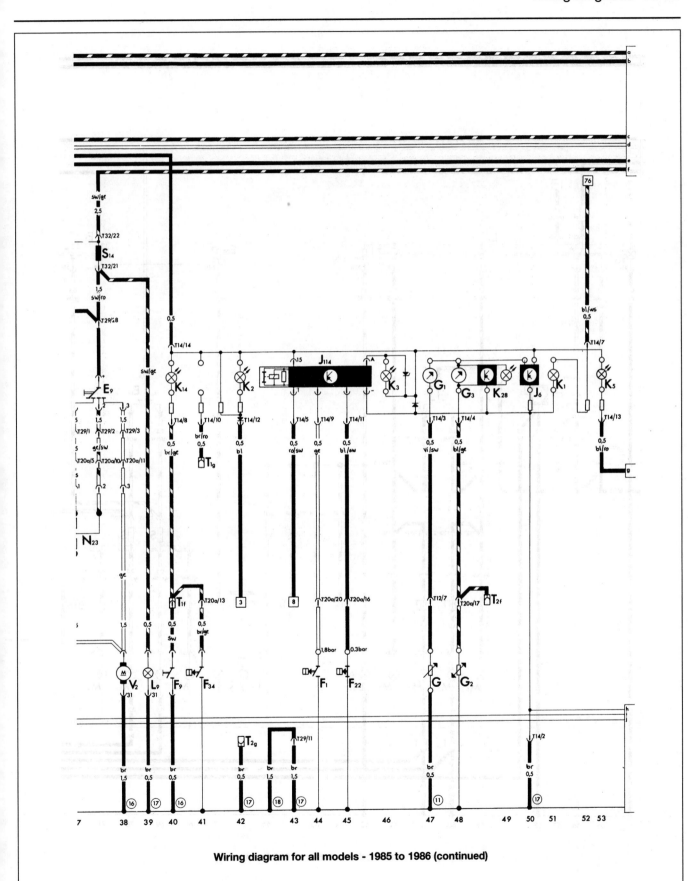

Wiring diagram for all models - 1985 to 1986 (continued)

13

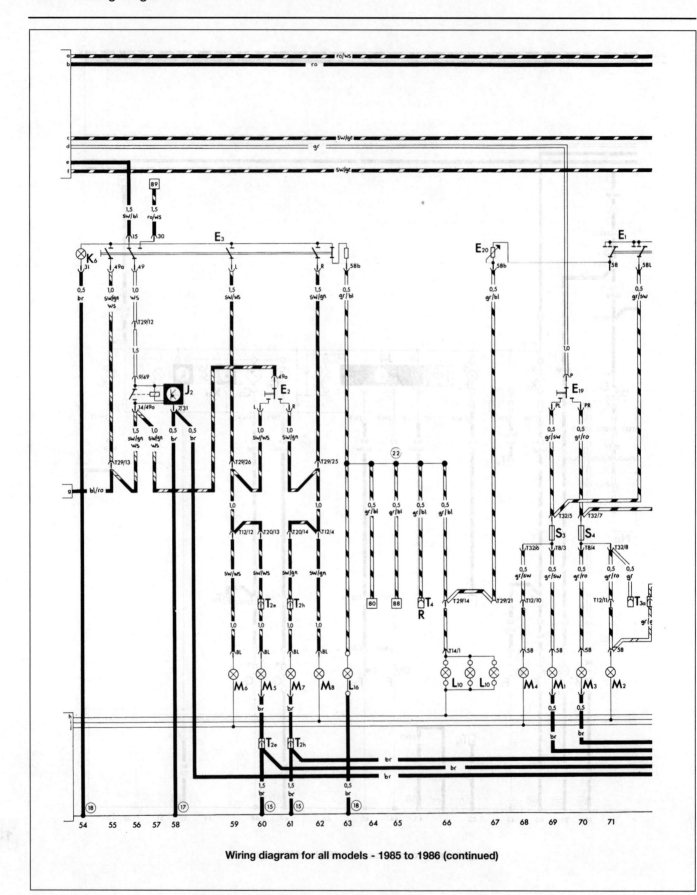

Wiring diagram for all models - 1985 to 1986 (continued)

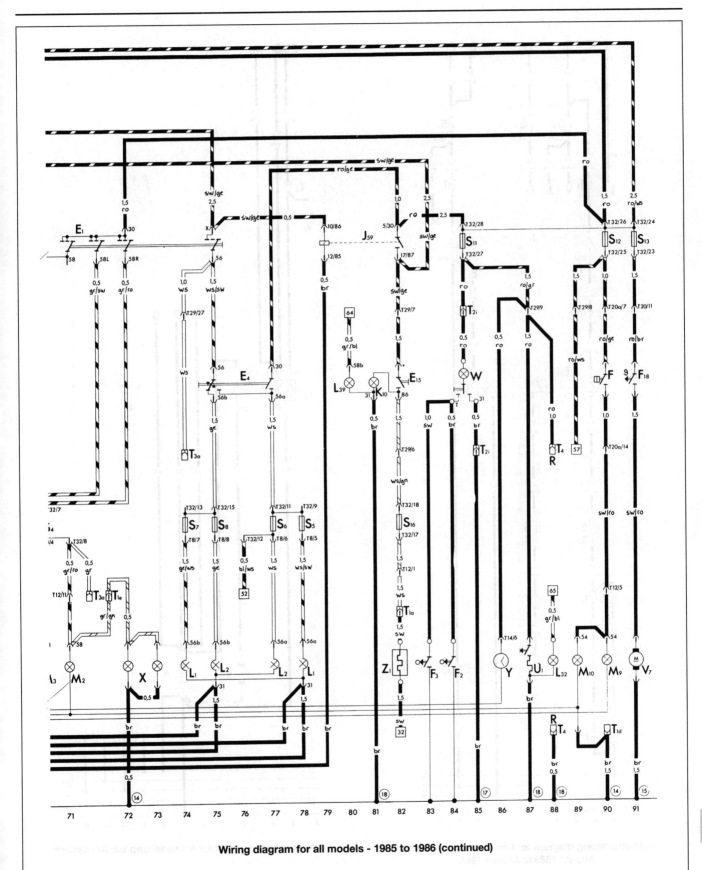

Wiring diagram for all models - 1985 to 1986 (continued)

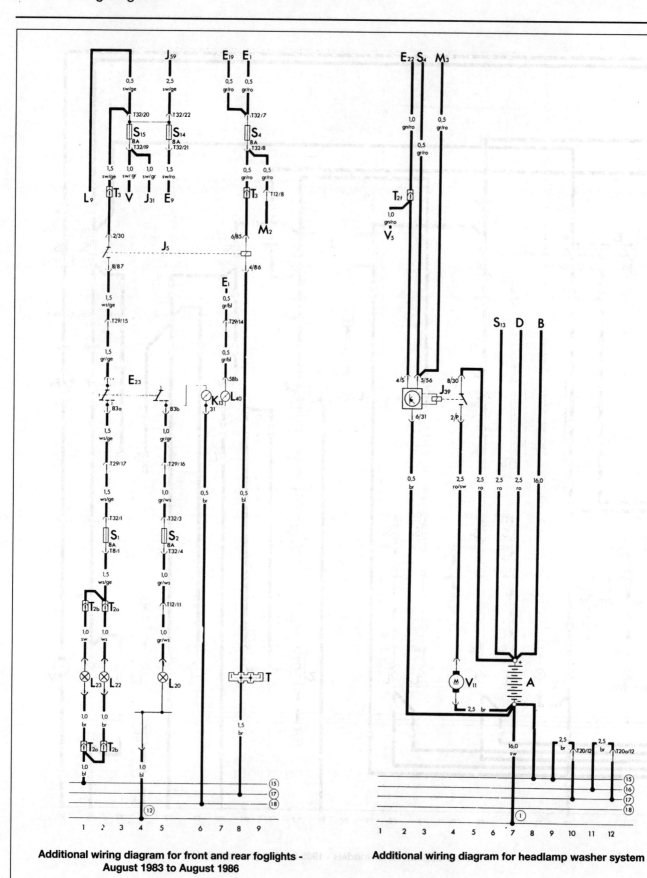

Additional wiring diagram for front and rear foglights - August 1983 to August 1986

Additional wiring diagram for headlamp washer system

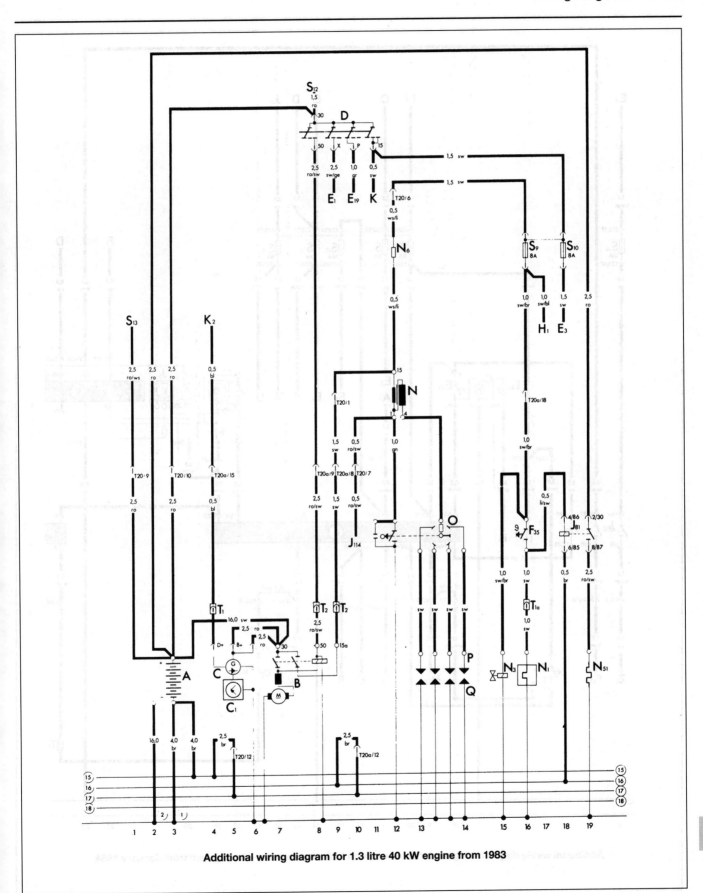

Additional wiring diagram for 1.3 litre 40 kW engine from 1983

13

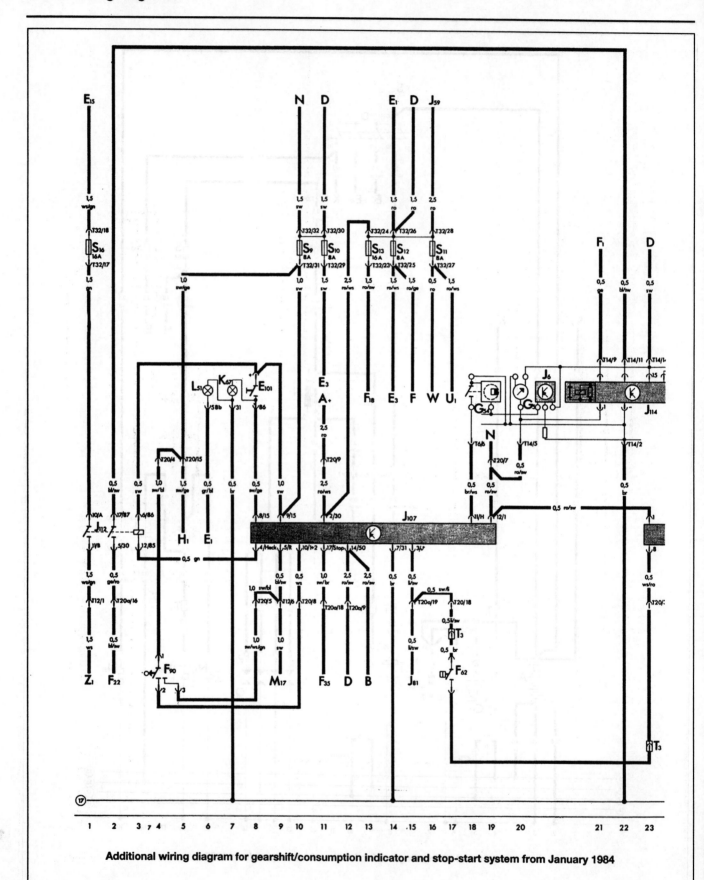

Additional wiring diagram for gearshift/consumption indicator and stop-start system from January 1984

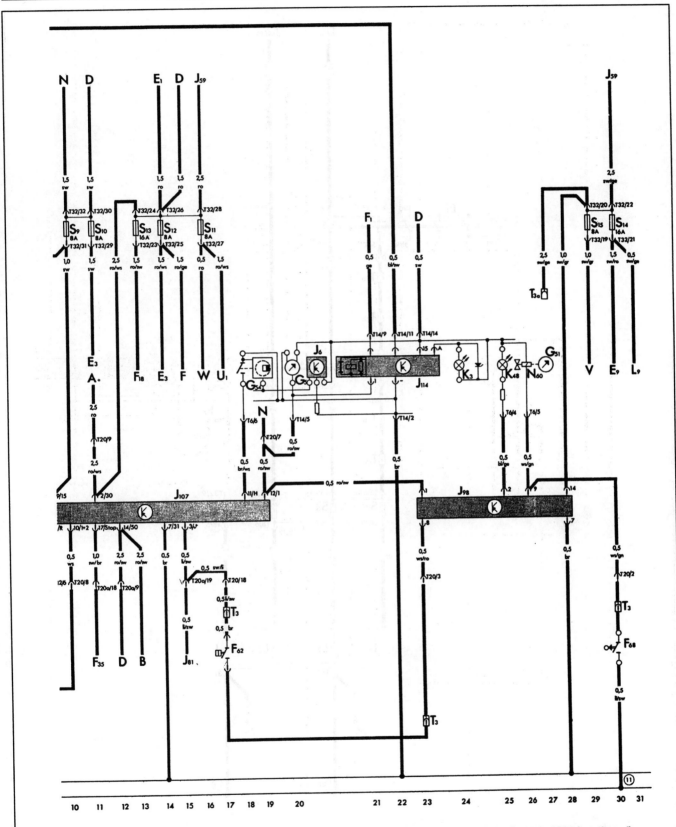

Additional wiring diagram for gearshift/consumption indicator and stop-start system from January 1984 (continued)

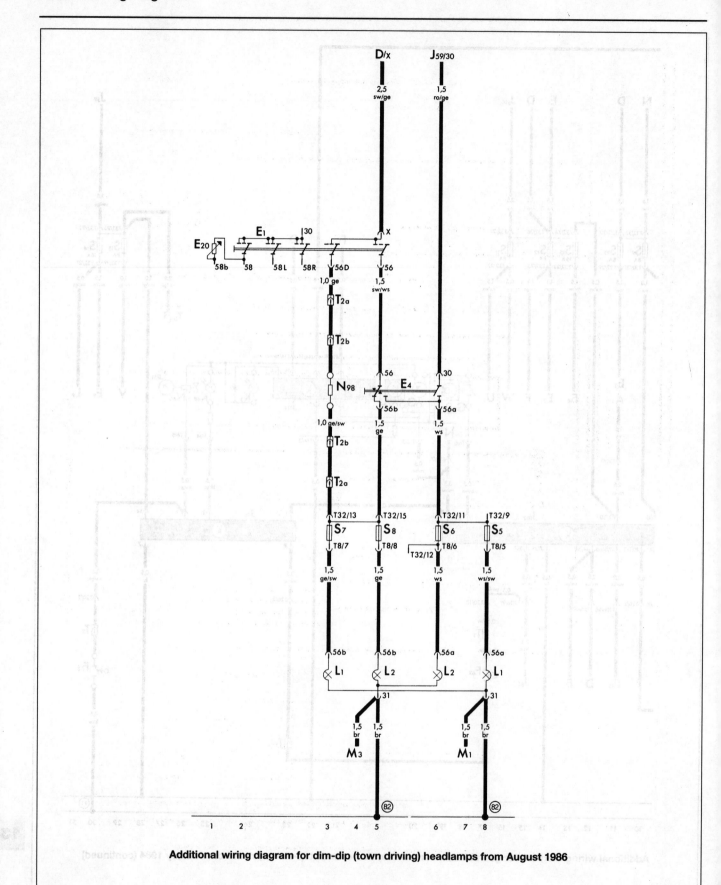

Additional wiring diagram for dim-dip (town driving) headlamps from August 1986

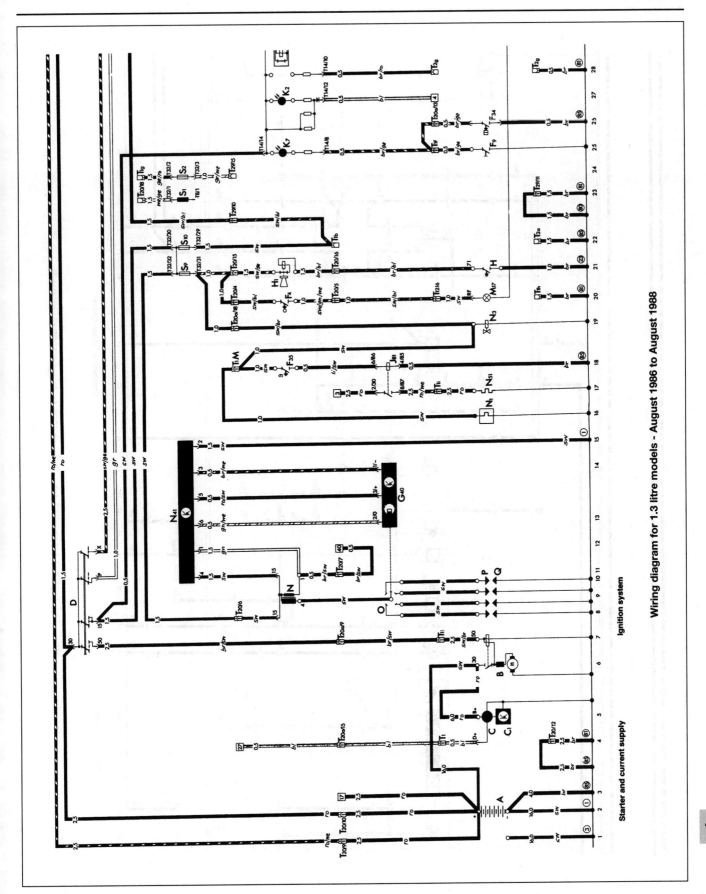

Wiring diagram for 1.3 litre models – August 1986 to August 1988

Ignition system

Starter and current supply

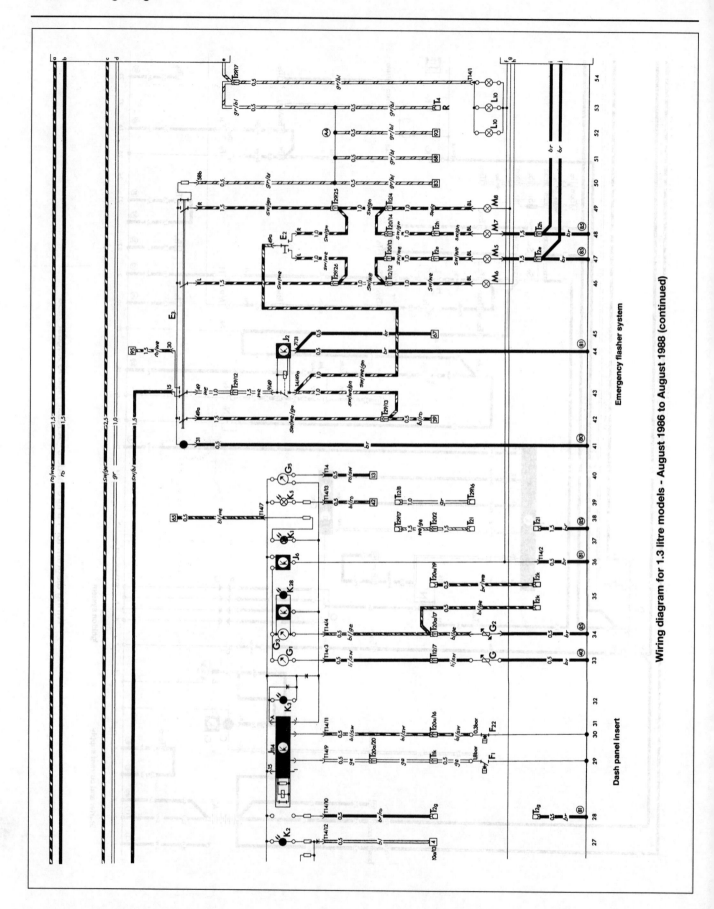

Wiring diagram for 1.3 litre models - August 1986 to August 1988 (continued)

Emergency flasher system

Dash panel insert

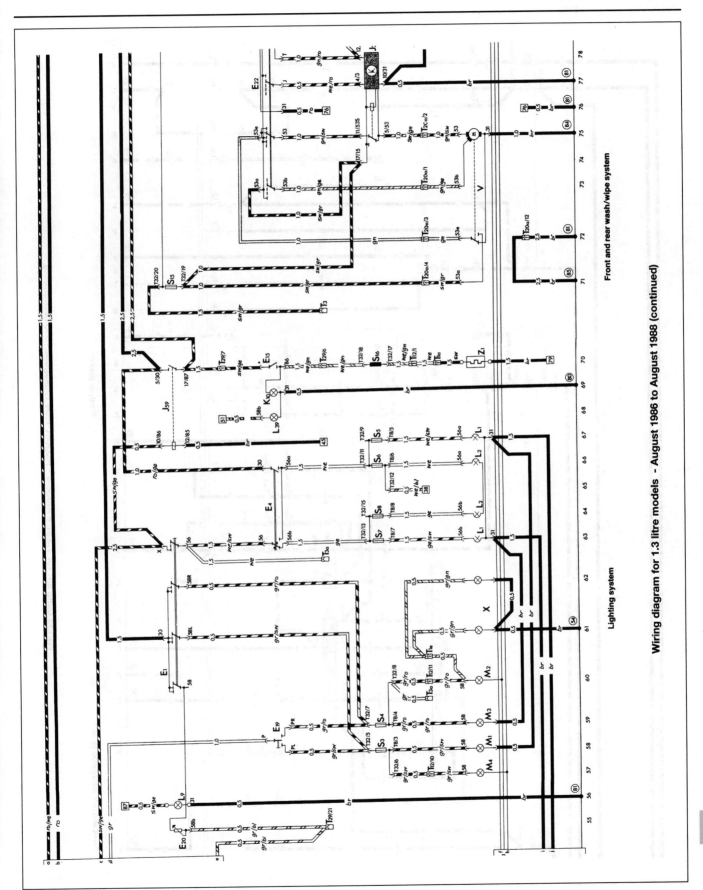

Front and rear wash/wipe system

Lighting system

Wiring diagram for 1.3 litre models – August 1986 to August 1988 (continued)

13

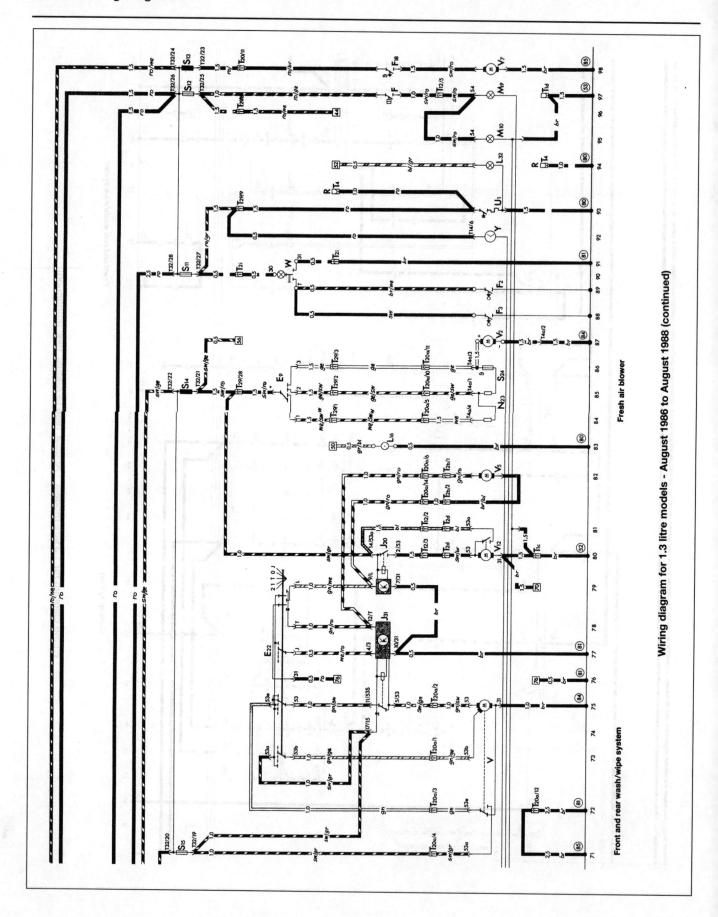

Wiring diagram for 1.3 litre models – August 1986 to August 1988 (continued)

Fresh air blower

Front and rear wash/wipe system

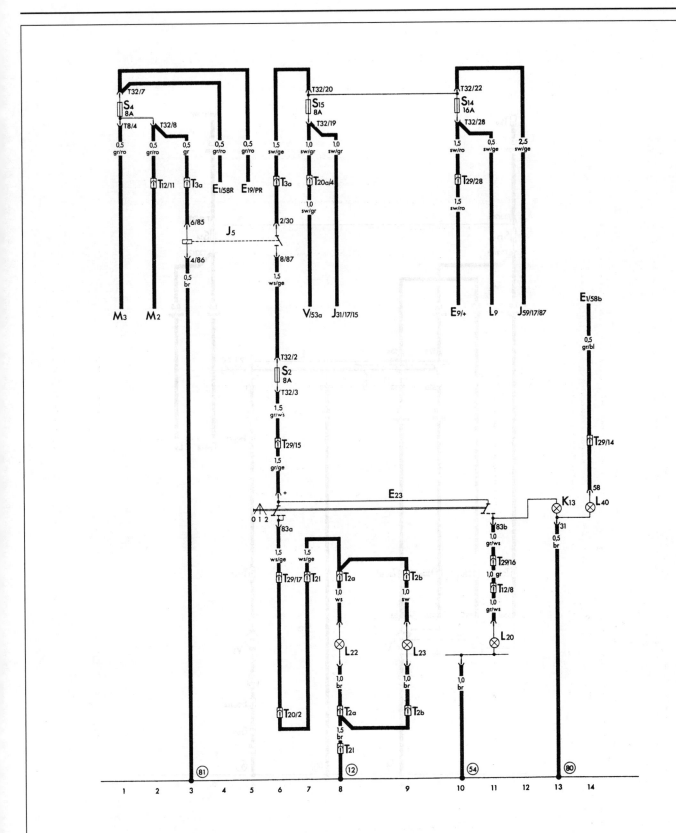

Additional wiring diagram for front and rear foglights from August 1986

13

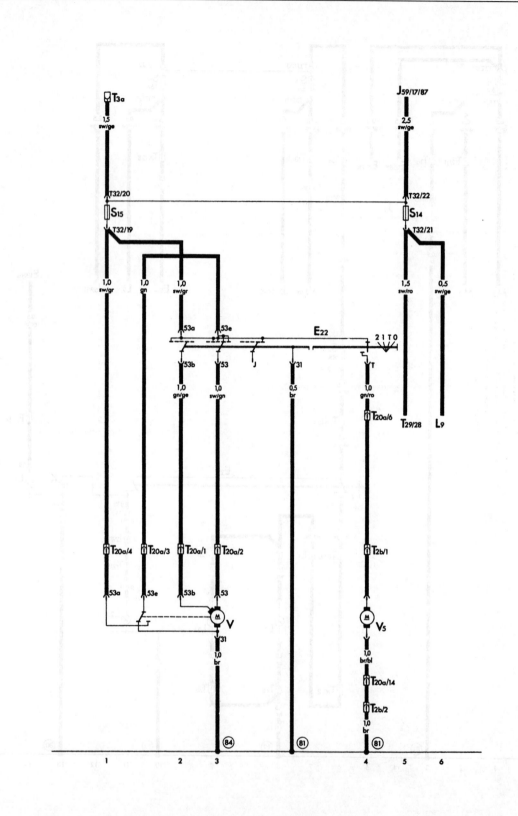

Additional wiring diagram for windscreen wipers without intermittent facility from August 1986

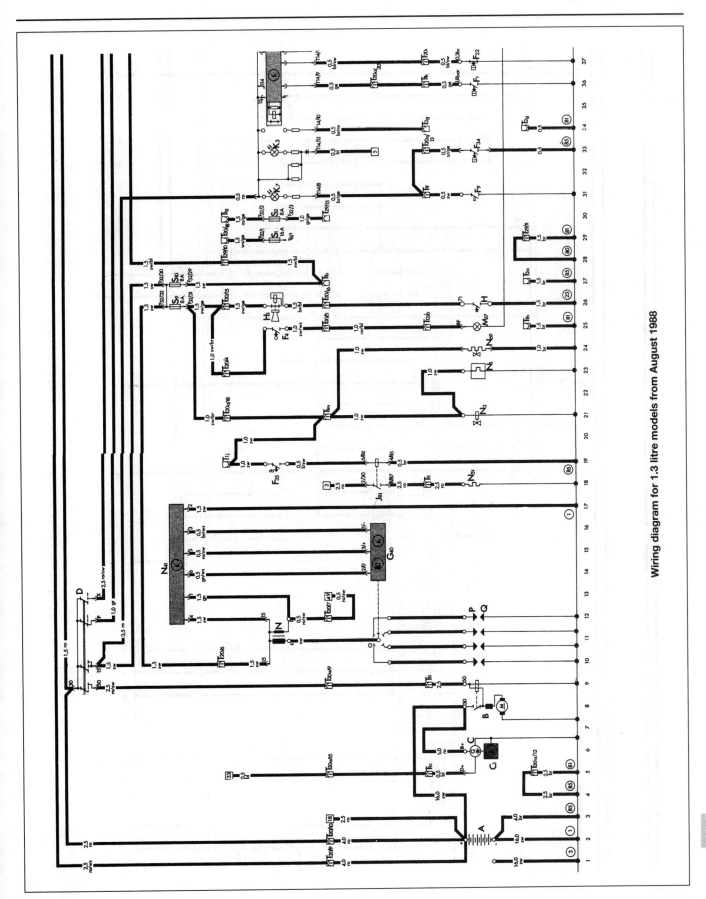

Wiring diagram for 1.3 litre models from August 1988

13

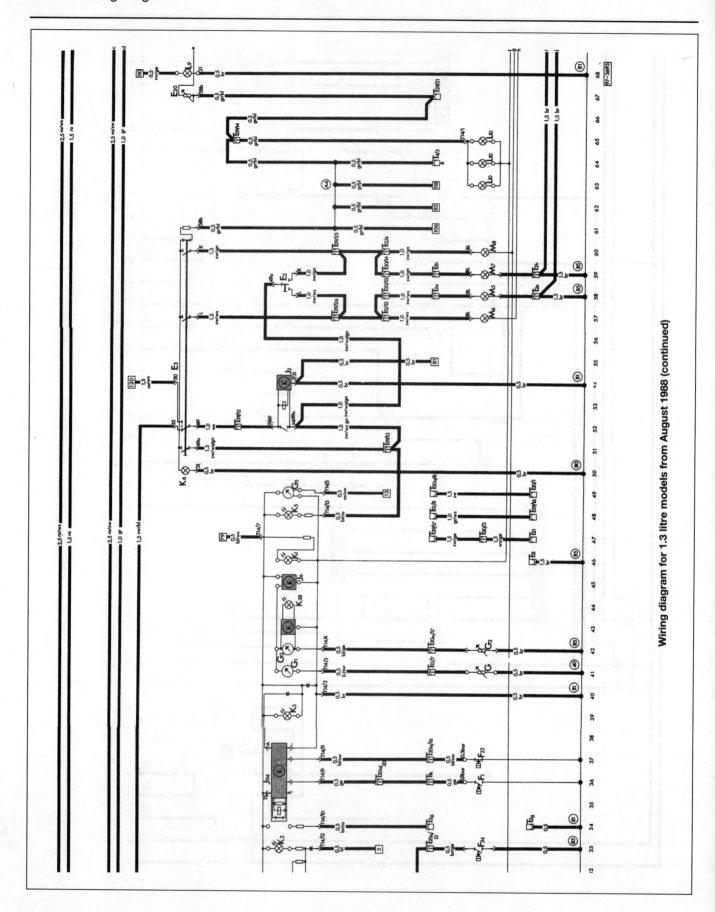

Wiring diagram for 1.3 litre models from August 1988 (continued)

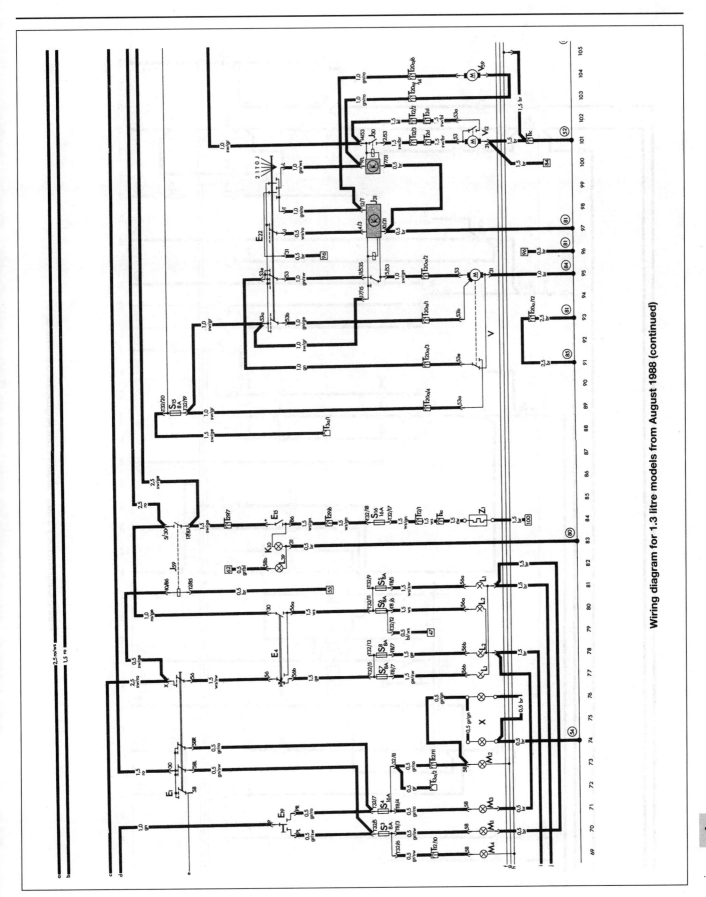

Wiring diagram for 1.3 litre models from August 1988 (continued)

13

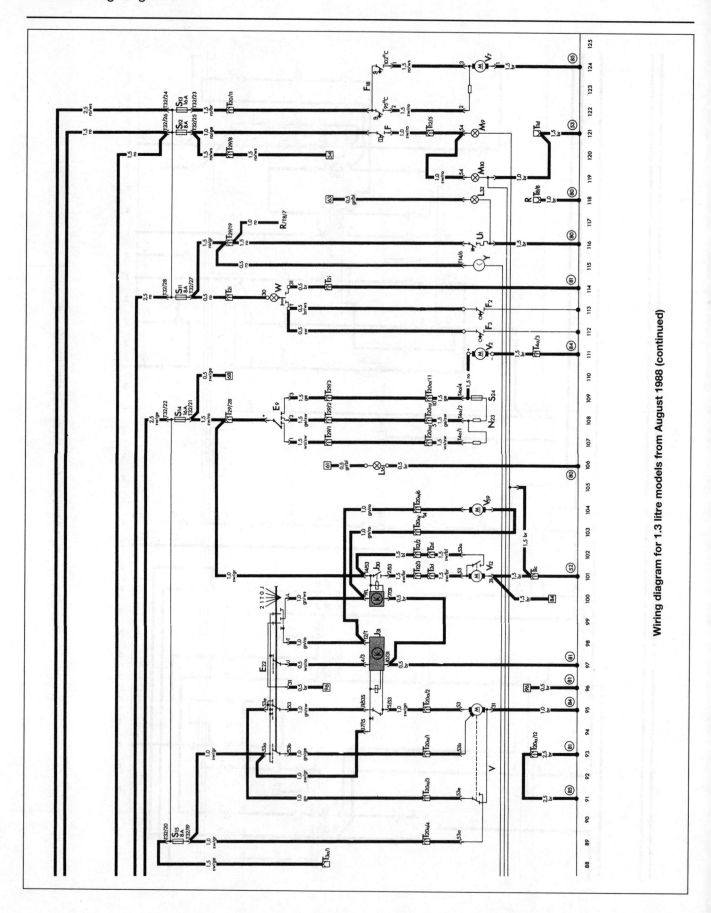

Wiring diagram for 1.3 litre models from August 1988 (continued)

This is a guide to getting your vehicle through the MOT test. Obviously it will not be possible to examine the vehicle to the same standard as the professional MOT tester. However, working through the following checks will enable you to identify any problem areas before submitting the vehicle for the test.

Where a testable component is in borderline condition, the tester has discretion in deciding whether to pass or fail it. The basis of such discretion is whether the tester would be happy for a close relative or friend to use the vehicle with the component in that condition. If the vehicle presented is clean and evidently well cared for, the tester may be more inclined to pass a borderline component than if the vehicle is scruffy and apparently neglected.

It has only been possible to summarise the test requirements here, based on the regulations in force at the time of printing. Test standards are becoming increasingly stringent, although there are some exemptions for older vehicles. For full details obtain a copy of the Haynes publication Pass the MOT! (available from stockists of Haynes manuals).

An assistant will be needed to help carry out some of these checks.

The checks have been sub-divided into four categories, as follows:

1 Checks carried out **FROM THE DRIVER'S SEAT**

2 Checks carried out **WITH THE VEHICLE ON THE GROUND**

3 Checks carried out **WITH THE VEHICLE RAISED AND THE WHEELS FREE TO TURN**

4 Checks carried out on **YOUR VEHICLE'S EXHAUST EMISSION SYSTEM**

---

1 Checks carried out **FROM THE DRIVER'S SEAT**

Handbrake

☐ Test the operation of the handbrake. Excessive travel (too many clicks) indicates incorrect brake or cable adjustment.

☐ Check that the handbrake cannot be released by tapping the lever sideways. Check the security of the lever mountings.

Footbrake

☐ Depress the brake pedal and check that it does not creep down to the floor, indicating a master cylinder fault. Release the pedal, wait a few seconds, then depress it again. If the pedal travels nearly to the floor before firm resistance is felt, brake adjustment or repair is necessary. If the pedal feels spongy, there is air in the hydraulic system which must be removed by bleeding.

☐ Check that the brake pedal is secure and in good condition. Check also for signs of fluid leaks on the pedal, floor or carpets, which would indicate failed seals in the brake master cylinder.

☐ Check the servo unit (when applicable) by operating the brake pedal several times, then keeping the pedal depressed and starting the engine. As the engine starts, the pedal will move down slightly. If not, the vacuum hose or the servo itself may be faulty.

Steering wheel and column

☐ Examine the steering wheel for fractures or looseness of the hub, spokes or rim.

☐ Move the steering wheel from side to side and then up and down. Check that the steering wheel is not loose on the column, indicating wear or a loose retaining nut. Continue moving the steering wheel as before, but also turn it slightly from left to right.

☐ Check that the steering wheel is not loose on the column, and that there is no abnormal

movement of the steering wheel, indicating wear in the column support bearings or couplings.

Windscreen and mirrors

☐ The windscreen must be free of cracks or other significant damage within the driver's field of view. (Small stone chips are acceptable.) Rear view mirrors must be secure, intact, and capable of being adjusted.

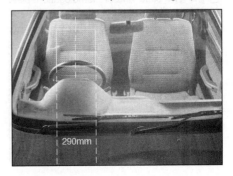

Seat belts and seats

Note: *The following checks are applicable to all seat belts, front and rear.*

☐ Examine the webbing of all the belts (including rear belts if fitted) for cuts, serious fraying or deterioration. Fasten and unfasten each belt to check the buckles. If applicable, check the retracting mechanism. Check the security of all seat belt mountings accessible from inside the vehicle.

☐ The front seats themselves must be securely attached and the backrests must lock in the upright position.

Doors

☐ Both front doors must be able to be opened and closed from outside and inside, and must latch securely when closed.

2 Checks carried out WITH THE VEHICLE ON THE GROUND

Vehicle identification

☐ Number plates must be in good condition, secure and legible, with letters and numbers correctly spaced – spacing at (A) should be twice that at (B).

☐ The VIN plate and/or homologation plate must be legible.

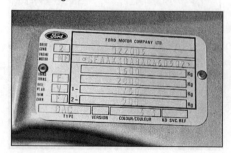

Electrical equipment

☐ Switch on the ignition and check the operation of the horn.

☐ Check the windscreen washers and wipers, examining the wiper blades; renew damaged or perished blades. Also check the operation of the stop-lights.

☐ Check the operation of the sidelights and number plate lights. The lenses and reflectors must be secure, clean and undamaged.

☐ Check the operation and alignment of the headlights. The headlight reflectors must not be tarnished and the lenses must be undamaged.

☐ Switch on the ignition and check the operation of the direction indicators (including the instrument panel tell-tale) and the hazard warning lights. Operation of the sidelights and stop-lights must not affect the indicators - if it does, the cause is usually a bad earth at the rear light cluster.

☐ Check the operation of the rear foglight(s), including the warning light on the instrument panel or in the switch.

Footbrake

☐ Examine the master cylinder, brake pipes and servo unit for leaks, loose mountings, corrosion or other damage.

☐ The fluid reservoir must be secure and the fluid level must be between the upper (A) and lower (B) markings.

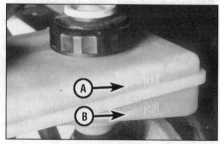

☐ Inspect both front brake flexible hoses for cracks or deterioration of the rubber. Turn the steering from lock to lock, and ensure that the hoses do not contact the wheel, tyre, or any part of the steering or suspension mechanism. With the brake pedal firmly depressed, check the hoses for bulges or leaks under pressure.

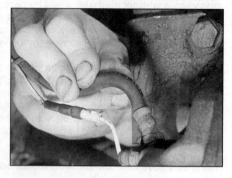

Steering and suspension

☐ Have your assistant turn the steering wheel from side to side slightly, up to the point where the steering gear just begins to transmit this movement to the roadwheels. Check for excessive free play between the steering wheel and the steering gear, indicating wear or insecurity of the steering column joints, the column-to-steering gear coupling, or the steering gear itself.

☐ Have your assistant turn the steering wheel more vigorously in each direction, so that the roadwheels just begin to turn. As this is done, examine all the steering joints, linkages, fittings and attachments. Renew any component that shows signs of wear or damage. On vehicles with power steering, check the security and condition of the steering pump, drivebelt and hoses.

☐ Check that the vehicle is standing level, and at approximately the correct ride height.

Shock absorbers

☐ Depress each corner of the vehicle in turn, then release it. The vehicle should rise and then settle in its normal position. If the vehicle continues to rise and fall, the shock absorber is defective. A shock absorber which has seized will also cause the vehicle to fail.

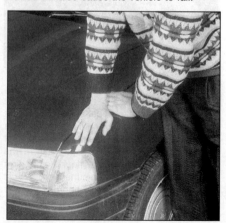

Exhaust system

☐ Start the engine. With your assistant holding a rag over the tailpipe, check the entire system for leaks. Repair or renew leaking sections.

3 Checks carried out **WITH THE VEHICLE RAISED AND THE WHEELS FREE TO TURN**

Jack up the front and rear of the vehicle, and securely support it on axle stands. Position the stands clear of the suspension assemblies. Ensure that the wheels are clear of the ground and that the steering can be turned from lock to lock.

Steering mechanism

☐ Have your assistant turn the steering from lock to lock. Check that the steering turns smoothly, and that no part of the steering mechanism, including a wheel or tyre, fouls any brake hose or pipe or any part of the body structure.
☐ Examine the steering rack rubber gaiters for damage or insecurity of the retaining clips. If power steering is fitted, check for signs of damage or leakage of the fluid hoses, pipes or connections. Also check for excessive stiffness or binding of the steering, a missing split pin or locking device, or severe corrosion of the body structure within 30 cm of any steering component attachment point.

Front and rear suspension and wheel bearings

☐ Starting at the front right-hand side, grasp the roadwheel at the 3 o'clock and 9 o'clock positions and shake it vigorously. Check for free play or insecurity at the wheel bearings, suspension balljoints, or suspension mountings, pivots and attachments.
☐ Now grasp the wheel at the 12 o'clock and 6 o'clock positions and repeat the previous inspection. Spin the wheel, and check for roughness or tightness of the front wheel bearing.

☐ If excess free play is suspected at a component pivot point, this can be confirmed by using a large screwdriver or similar tool and levering between the mounting and the component attachment. This will confirm whether the wear is in the pivot bush, its retaining bolt, or in the mounting itself (the bolt holes can often become elongated).

☐ Carry out all the above checks at the other front wheel, and then at both rear wheels.

Springs and shock absorbers

☐ Examine the suspension struts (when applicable) for serious fluid leakage, corrosion, or damage to the casing. Also check the security of the mounting points.
☐ If coil springs are fitted, check that the spring ends locate in their seats, and that the spring is not corroded, cracked or broken.
☐ If leaf springs are fitted, check that all leaves are intact, that the axle is securely attached to each spring, and that there is no deterioration of the spring eye mountings, bushes, and shackles.

☐ The same general checks apply to vehicles fitted with other suspension types, such as torsion bars, hydraulic displacer units, etc. Ensure that all mountings and attachments are secure, that there are no signs of excessive wear, corrosion or damage, and (on hydraulic types) that there are no fluid leaks or damaged pipes.
☐ Inspect the shock absorbers for signs of serious fluid leakage. Check for wear of the mounting bushes or attachments, or damage to the body of the unit.

Driveshafts (fwd vehicles only)

☐ Rotate each front wheel in turn and inspect the constant velocity joint gaiters for splits or damage. Also check that each driveshaft is straight and undamaged.

Braking system

☐ If possible without dismantling, check brake pad wear and disc condition. Ensure that the friction lining material has not worn excessively, (A) and that the discs are not fractured, pitted, scored or badly worn (B).

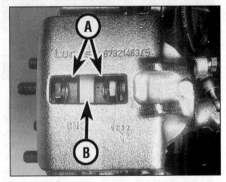

☐ Examine all the rigid brake pipes underneath the vehicle, and the flexible hose(s) at the rear. Look for corrosion, chafing or insecurity of the pipes, and for signs of bulging under pressure, chafing, splits or deterioration of the flexible hoses.
☐ Look for signs of fluid leaks at the brake calipers or on the brake backplates. Repair or renew leaking components.
☐ Slowly spin each wheel, while your assistant depresses and releases the footbrake. Ensure that each brake is operating and does not bind when the pedal is released.

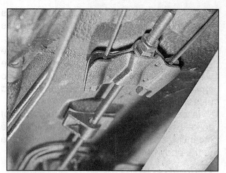

□ Examine the handbrake mechanism, checking for frayed or broken cables, excessive corrosion, or wear or insecurity of the linkage. Check that the mechanism works on each relevant wheel, and releases fully, without binding.

□ It is not possible to test brake efficiency without special equipment, but a road test can be carried out later to check that the vehicle pulls up in a straight line.

Fuel and exhaust systems

□ Inspect the fuel tank (including the filler cap), fuel pipes, hoses and unions. All components must be secure and free from leaks.

□ Examine the exhaust system over its entire length, checking for any damaged, broken or missing mountings, security of the retaining clamps and rust or corrosion.

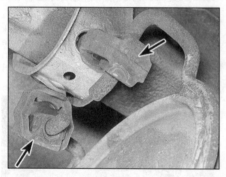

Wheels and tyres

□ Examine the sidewalls and tread area of each tyre in turn. Check for cuts, tears, lumps, bulges, separation of the tread, and exposure of the ply or cord due to wear or damage. Check that the tyre bead is correctly seated on the wheel rim, that the valve is sound and

properly seated, and that the wheel is not distorted or damaged.

□ Check that the tyres are of the correct size for the vehicle, that they are of the same size and type on each axle, and that the pressures are correct.

□ Check the tyre tread depth. The legal minimum at the time of writing is 1.6 mm over at least three-quarters of the tread width. Abnormal tread wear may indicate incorrect front wheel alignment.

Body corrosion

□ Check the condition of the entire vehicle structure for signs of corrosion in load-bearing areas. (These include chassis box sections, side sills, cross-members, pillars, and all suspension, steering, braking system and seat belt mountings and anchorages.) Any corrosion which has seriously reduced the thickness of a load-bearing area is likely to cause the vehicle to fail. In this case professional repairs are likely to be needed.

□ Damage or corrosion which causes sharp or otherwise dangerous edges to be exposed will also cause the vehicle to fail.

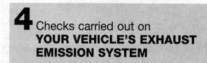

4 Checks carried out on
YOUR VEHICLE'S EXHAUST EMISSION SYSTEM

Petrol models

□ Have the engine at normal operating temperature, and make sure that it is in good tune (ignition system in good order, air filter element clean, etc).

□ Before any measurements are carried out, raise the engine speed to around 2500 rpm, and hold it at this speed for 20 seconds. Allow

the engine speed to return to idle, and watch for smoke emissions from the exhaust tailpipe. If the idle speed is obviously much too high, or if dense blue or clearly-visible black smoke comes from the tailpipe for more than 5 seconds, the vehicle will fail. As a rule of thumb, blue smoke signifies oil being burnt (engine wear) while black smoke signifies unburnt fuel (dirty air cleaner element, or other carburettor or fuel system fault).

□ An exhaust gas analyser capable of measuring carbon monoxide (CO) and hydrocarbons (HC) is now needed. If such an instrument cannot be hired or borrowed, a local garage may agree to perform the check for a small fee.

CO emissions (mixture)

□ At the time of writing, the maximum CO level at idle is 3.5% for vehicles first used after August 1986 and 4.5% for older vehicles. From January 1996 a much tighter limit (around 0.5%) applies to catalyst-equipped vehicles first used from August 1992. If the CO level cannot be reduced far enough to pass the test (and the fuel and ignition systems are otherwise in good condition) then the carburettor is badly worn, or there is some problem in the fuel injection system or catalytic converter (as applicable).

HC emissions

□ With the CO emissions within limits, HC emissions must be no more than 1200 ppm (parts per million). If the vehicle fails this test at idle, it can be re-tested at around 2000 rpm; if the HC level is then 1200 ppm or less, this counts as a pass.

□ Excessive HC emissions can be caused by oil being burnt, but they are more likely to be due to unburnt fuel.

Diesel models

□ The only emission test applicable to Diesel engines is the measuring of exhaust smoke density. The test involves accelerating the engine several times to its maximum unloaded speed.

Note: *It is of the utmost importance that the engine timing belt is in good condition before the test is carried out.*

□ Excessive smoke can be caused by a dirty air cleaner element. Otherwise, professional advice may be needed to find the cause.

Introduction

A selection of good tools is a fundamental requirement for anyone contemplating the maintenance and repair of a motor vehicle. For the owner who does not possess any, their purchase will prove a considerable expense, offsetting some of the savings made by doing-it-yourself. However, provided that the tools purchased meet the relevant national safety standards and are of good quality, they will last for many years and prove an extremely worthwhile investment.

To help the average owner to decide which tools are needed to carry out the various tasks detailed in this manual, we have compiled three lists of tools under the following headings: *Maintenance and minor repair, Repair and overhaul*, and *Special*. Newcomers to practical mechanics should start off with the *Maintenance and minor repair* tool kit, and confine themselves to the simpler jobs around the vehicle. Then, as confidence and experience grow, more difficult tasks can be undertaken, with extra tools being purchased as, and when, they are needed. In this way, a *Maintenance and minor repair* tool kit can be built up into a *Repair and overhaul* tool kit over a considerable period of time, without any major cash outlays. The experienced do-it-yourselfer will have a tool kit good enough for most repair and overhaul procedures, and will add tools from the *Special* category when it is felt that the expense is justified by the amount of use to which these tools will be put.

Maintenance and minor repair tool kit

The tools given in this list should be considered as a minimum requirement if routine maintenance, servicing and minor repair operations are to be undertaken. We recommend the purchase of combination spanners (ring one end, open-ended the other); although more expensive than open-ended ones, they do give the advantages of both types of spanner.

☐ *Combination spanners: 10, 11, 12, 13, 14 and 17 mm*
☐ *Adjustable spanner - 35 mm jaw (approx)*
☐ *Gearbox drain plug key*
☐ *Set of feeler gauges*
☐ *Spark plug spanner (with rubber insert)*
☐ *Spark plug gap adjustment tool*
☐ *Brake bleed nipple spanner*

☐ *Screwdrivers: Flat blade and cross blade – approx 100 mm long x 6 mm dia*
☐ *Combination pliers*
☐ *Hacksaw (junior)*
☐ *Tyre pump*
☐ *Tyre pressure gauge*
☐ *Oil can*
☐ *Oil filter removal tool*
☐ *Fine emery cloth*
☐ *Wire brush (small)*
☐ *Funnel (medium size)*

Repair and overhaul tool kit

These tools are virtually essential for anyone undertaking any major repairs to a motor vehicle, and are additional to those given in the *Maintenance and minor repair* list. Included in this list is a comprehensive set of sockets. Although these are expensive, they will be found invaluable as they are so versatile - particularly if various drives are included in the set. We recommend the half-inch square-drive type, as this can be used with most proprietary torque wrenches. If you cannot afford a socket set, even bought piecemeal, then inexpensive tubular box spanners are a useful alternative.

The tools in this list will occasionally need to be supplemented by tools from the *Special* list:

☐ *Sockets (or box spanners) to cover range in previous list*
☐ *Reversible ratchet drive (for use with sockets) (see illustration)*
☐ *Extension piece, 250 mm (for use with sockets)*
☐ *Universal joint (for use with sockets)*
☐ *Torque wrench (for use with sockets)*
☐ *Self-locking grips*
☐ *Ball pein hammer*
☐ *Soft-faced mallet (plastic/aluminium or rubber)*
☐ *Screwdrivers:*
  Flat blade - long & sturdy, short (chubby), and narrow (electrician's) types
  Cross blade - Long & sturdy, and short (chubby) types
☐ *Pliers:*
  Long-nosed
  Side cutters (electrician's)
  Circlip (internal and external)
☐ *Cold chisel - 25 mm*
☐ *Scriber*
☐ *Scraper*
☐ *Centre-punch*

☐ *Pin punch*
☐ *Hacksaw*
☐ *Brake hose clamp*
☐ *Brake bleeding kit*
☐ *Selection of twist drills*
☐ *Steel rule/straight-edge*
☐ *Allen keys (inc. splined/Torx type if necessary*
☐ *Selection of files*
☐ *Wire brush*
☐ *Axle stands*
☐ *Jack (strong trolley or hydraulic type)*
☐ *Light with extension lead*
☐ *Torx bits*

Special tools

The tools in this list are those which are not used regularly, are expensive to buy, or which need to be used in accordance with their manufacturers' instructions. Unless relatively difficult mechanical jobs are undertaken frequently, it will not be economic to buy many of these tools. Where this is the case, you could consider clubbing together with friends (or joining a motorists' club) to make a joint purchase, or borrowing the tools against a deposit from a local garage or tool hire specialist. It is worth noting that many of the larger DIY superstores now carry a large range of special tools for hire at modest rates.

The following list contains only those tools and instruments freely available to the public, and not those special tools produced by the vehicle manufacturer specifically for its dealer network. You will find occasional references to these manufacturers' special tools in the text of this manual. Generally, an alternative method of doing the job without the vehicle manufacturers' special tool is given. However, sometimes there is no alternative to using them. Where this is the case and the relevant tool cannot be bought or borrowed, you will have to entrust the work to a franchised garage.

☐ *Valve spring compressor (see illustration)*
☐ *Valve grinding tool*
☐ *Piston ring compressor (see illustration)*
☐ *Piston ring removal/installation tool (see illustration)*
☐ *Cylinder bore hone (see illustration)*
☐ *Balljoint separator*
☐ *Coil spring compressors (where applicable)*
☐ *Two/three-legged hub and bearing puller (see illustration)*

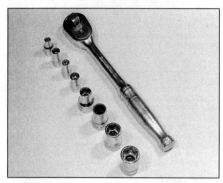

Sockets and reversible ratchet drive

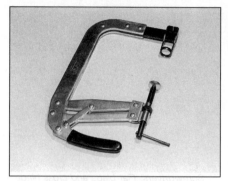

Valve spring compressor

Piston ring compressor

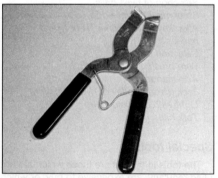

Piston ring removal/installation tool

Cylinder bore hone

Three-legged hub and bearing puller

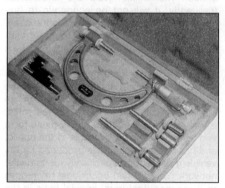

Micrometer set

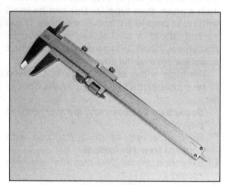

Vernier calipers

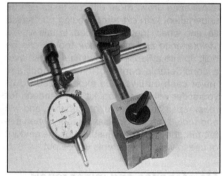

Dial test indicator and magnetic stand

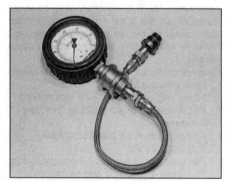

Compression testing gauge

Clutch plate alignment set

Brake shoe steady spring cup removal tool

☐ Impact screwdriver
☐ Micrometer and/or vernier calipers **(see illustrations)**
☐ Dial gauge **(see illustration)**
☐ Universal electrical multi-meter
☐ Cylinder compression gauge **(see illustration)**
☐ Clutch plate alignment set **(see illustration)**
☐ Brake shoe steady spring cup removal tool **(see illustration)**
☐ Bush and bearing removal/installation set **(see illustration)**
☐ Stud extractors **(see illustration)**
☐ Tap and die set **(see illustration)**
☐ Lifting tackle
☐ Trolley jack

Buying tools

For practically all tools, a tool factor is the best source, since he will have a very comprehensive range compared with the average garage or accessory shop. Having said that, accessory shops often offer excellent quality tools at discount prices, so it pays to shop around.

Remember, you don't have to buy the most expensive items on the shelf, but it is always advisable to steer clear of the very cheap tools. There are plenty of good tools around at reasonable prices, but always aim to purchase items which meet the relevant national safety standards. If in doubt, ask the proprietor or manager of the shop for advice before making a purchase.

Care and maintenance of tools

Having purchased a reasonable tool kit, it is necessary to keep the tools in a clean and serviceable condition. After use, always wipe off any dirt, grease and metal particles using a clean, dry cloth, before putting the tools away. Never leave them lying around after they have been used. A simple tool rack on the garage or workshop wall for items such as screwdrivers and pliers is a good idea. Store all normal spanners and sockets in a metal box. Any measuring instruments, gauges, meters, etc, must be carefully stored where they cannot be damaged or become rusty.

Take a little care when tools are used. Hammer heads inevitably become marked, and screwdrivers lose the keen edge on their blades from time to time. A little timely attention with emery cloth or a file will soon restore items like this to a good serviceable finish.

Working facilities

Not to be forgotten when discussing tools is the workshop itself. If anything more than routine maintenance is to be carried out, some form of suitable working area becomes essential.

It is appreciated that many an owner-mechanic is forced by circumstances to remove an engine or similar item without the benefit of a garage or workshop. Having done this, any repairs should always be done under the cover of a roof.

Wherever possible, any dismantling should be done on a clean, flat workbench or table at a suitable working height.

Any workbench needs a vice; one with a jaw opening of 100 mm is suitable for most jobs. As mentioned previously, some clean dry storage space is also required for tools, as well as for any lubricants, cleaning fluids, touch-up paints and so on, which become necessary.

Another item which may be required, and which has a much more general usage, is an electric drill with a chuck capacity of at least 8 mm. This, together with a good range of twist drills, is virtually essential for fitting accessories.

Last, but not least, always keep a supply of old newspapers and clean, lint-free rags available, and try to keep any working area as clean as possible.

Bush and bearing removal/installation set

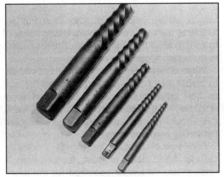

Stud extractor set

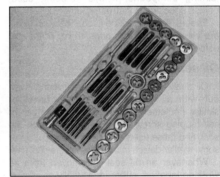

Tap and die set

Whenever servicing, repair or overhaul work is carried out on the car or its components, observe the following procedures and instructions. This will assist in carrying out the operation efficiently and to a professional standard of workmanship.

Joint mating faces and gaskets

When separating components at their mating faces, never insert screwdrivers or similar implements into the joint between the faces in order to prise them apart. This can cause severe damage which results in oil leaks, coolant leaks, etc upon reassembly. Separation is usually achieved by tapping along the joint with a soft-faced hammer in order to break the seal. However, note that this method may not be suitable where dowels are used for component location.

Where a gasket is used between the mating faces of two components, a new one must be fitted on reassembly; fit it dry unless otherwise stated in the repair procedure. Make sure that the mating faces are clean and dry, with all traces of old gasket removed. When cleaning a joint face, use a tool which is unlikely to score or damage the face, and remove any burrs or nicks with an oilstone or fine file.

Make sure that tapped holes are cleaned with a pipe cleaner, and keep them free of jointing compound, if this is being used, unless specifically instructed otherwise.

Ensure that all orifices, channels or pipes are clear, and blow through them, preferably using compressed air.

Oil seals

Oil seals can be removed by levering them out with a wide flat-bladed screwdriver or similar implement. Alternatively, a number of self-tapping screws may be screwed into the seal, and these used as a purchase for pliers or some similar device in order to pull the seal free.

Whenever an oil seal is removed from its working location, either individually or as part of an assembly, it should be renewed.

The very fine sealing lip of the seal is easily damaged, and will not seal if the surface it contacts is not completely clean and free from scratches, nicks or grooves. If the original sealing surface of the component cannot be restored, and the manufacturer has not made provision for slight relocation of the seal relative to the sealing surface, the component should be renewed.

Protect the lips of the seal from any surface which may damage them in the course of fitting. Use tape or a conical sleeve where possible. Lubricate the seal lips with oil before fitting and, on dual-lipped seals, fill the space between the lips with grease.

Unless otherwise stated, oil seals must be fitted with their sealing lips toward the lubricant to be sealed.

Use a tubular drift or block of wood of the appropriate size to install the seal and, if the seal housing is shouldered, drive the seal down to the shoulder. If the seal housing is unshouldered, the seal should be fitted with its face flush with the housing top face (unless otherwise instructed).

Screw threads and fastenings

Seized nuts, bolts and screws are quite a common occurrence where corrosion has set in, and the use of penetrating oil or releasing fluid will often overcome this problem if the offending item is soaked for a while before attempting to release it. The use of an impact driver may also provide a means of releasing such stubborn fastening devices, when used in conjunction with the appropriate screwdriver bit or socket. If none of these methods works, it may be necessary to resort to the careful application of heat, or the use of a hacksaw or nut splitter device.

Studs are usually removed by locking two nuts together on the threaded part, and then using a spanner on the lower nut to unscrew the stud. Studs or bolts which have broken off below the surface of the component in which they are mounted can sometimes be removed using a stud extractor. Always ensure that a blind tapped hole is completely free from oil, grease, water or other fluid before installing the bolt or stud. Failure to do this could cause the housing to crack due to the hydraulic action of the bolt or stud as it is screwed in.

When tightening a castellated nut to accept a split pin, tighten the nut to the specified torque, where applicable, and then tighten further to the next split pin hole. Never slacken the nut to align the split pin hole, unless stated in the repair procedure.

When checking or retightening a nut or bolt to a specified torque setting, slacken the nut or bolt by a quarter of a turn, and then retighten to the specified setting. However, this should not be attempted where angular tightening has been used.

For some screw fastenings, notably cylinder head bolts or nuts, torque wrench settings are no longer specified for the latter stages of tightening, "angle-tightening" being called up instead. Typically, a fairly low torque wrench setting will be applied to the bolts/nuts in the correct sequence, followed by one or more stages of tightening through specified angles.

Locknuts, locktabs and washers

Any fastening which will rotate against a component or housing during tightening should always have a washer between it and the relevant component or housing.

Spring or split washers should always be renewed when they are used to lock a critical component such as a big-end bearing retaining bolt or nut. Locktabs which are folded over to retain a nut or bolt should always be renewed.

Self-locking nuts can be re-used in non-critical areas, providing resistance can be felt when the locking portion passes over the bolt or stud thread. However, it should be noted that self-locking stiffnuts tend to lose their effectiveness after long periods of use, and should then be renewed as a matter of course.

Split pins must always be replaced with new ones of the correct size for the hole.

When thread-locking compound is found on the threads of a fastener which is to be re-used, it should be cleaned off with a wire brush and solvent, and fresh compound applied on reassembly.

Special tools

Some repair procedures in this manual entail the use of special tools such as a press, two or three-legged pullers, spring compressors, etc. Wherever possible, suitable readily-available alternatives to the manufacturer's special tools are described, and are shown in use. In some instances, where no alternative is possible, it has been necessary to resort to the use of a manufacturer's tool, and this has been done for reasons of safety as well as the efficient completion of the repair operation. Unless you are highly-skilled and have a thorough understanding of the procedures described, never attempt to bypass the use of any special tool when the procedure described specifies its use. Not only is there a very great risk of personal injury, but expensive damage could be caused to the components involved.

Environmental considerations

When disposing of used engine oil, brake fluid, antifreeze, etc, give due consideration to any detrimental environmental effects. Do not, for instance, pour any of the above liquids down drains into the general sewage system, or onto the ground to soak away. Many local council refuse tips provide a facility for waste oil disposal, as do some garages. If none of these facilities are available, consult your local Environmental Health Department, or the National Rivers Authority, for further advice.

With the universal tightening-up of legislation regarding the emission of environmentally-harmful substances from motor vehicles, most vehicles have tamperproof devices fitted to the main adjustment points of the fuel system. These devices are primarily designed to prevent unqualified persons from adjusting the fuel/air mixture, with the chance of a consequent increase in toxic emissions. If such devices are found during servicing or overhaul, they should, wherever possible, be renewed or refitted in accordance with the manufacturer's requirements or current legislation.

Note: It is antisocial and illegal to dump oil down the drain. To find the location of your local oil recycling bank, call this number free.

Buying spare parts

Spare parts are available from many sources, for example: VW garages, other garages and accessory shops, and motor factors. Our advice regarding spare part sources is as follows:

Officially appointed VW garages - This is the best source of parts which are peculiar to your vehicle and are otherwise not generally available (eg; complete cylinder heads, internal gearbox components, badges, interior trim, etc). It is also the only place at which you should buy parts if your car is still under warranty - non-VW components may invalidate the warranty. To be sure of obtaining the correct parts it will always be necessary to give the storeman your car's engine and chassis number and, if possible, to take the 'old' part along for positive identification. Remember that many parts are

available on a factory exchange scheme - any parts returned should always be clean! It obviously makes good sense to go straight to the specialists on your car for this type of part, for they are best equipped to supply you.

Other garages and accessory shops - These are often very good places to buy materials and components needed for the maintenance of your car (eg; oil filters, spark plugs, bulbs, fanbelts, oils and greases, touch-up paint, filler paste, etc). They also sell general accessories, usually have convenient opening hours, may charge lower prices and can often be found not far from home.

Motor factors - Good factors will stock all of the more important components which wear out relatively quickly (eg; clutch components, pistons, valves, exhaust system, brake cylinders/pipes/hoses/seals/ shoes and pads, etc). Motor factors will often provide new or reconditioned components on a part

exchange basis - this can save a considerable amount of money.

Vehicle identification numbers

Modifications are a continuing and unpublicised process in vehicle manufacture quite apart from major model changes. It is therefore essential to give as much information as possible when ordering spare parts. Quote the car model and year of manufacture, and also if necessary the body and engine numbers.

The vehicle identification plate is located on the front engine compartment panel, next to the bonnet lock.

The chassis number is located on the bulkhead panel behind the air cleaner.

The engine number is located on the front face of the cylinder head at the timing belt end (photo).

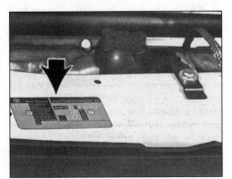

Vehicle identification plate location

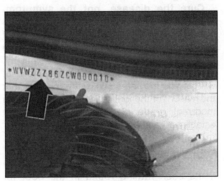

Chassis number location

Engine number location

Introduction

The vehicle owner who does his or her own maintenance according to the recommended schedules should not have to use this section of the manual very often. Modern component reliability is such that, provided those items subject to wear or deterioration are inspected or renewed at the specified intervals, sudden failure is comparatively rare. Faults do not usually just happen as a result of sudden failure, but develop over a period of time. Major mechanical failures in particular are usually preceded by characteristic symptoms over hundreds or even thousands of miles. Those components which do occasionally fail without warning are often small and easily carried in the vehicle.

With any fault finding, the first step is to decide where to begin investigations. Sometimes this is obvious, but on other occasions a little detective work will be necessary. The owner who makes half a dozen haphazard adjustments or replacements may be successful in curing a fault (or its symptoms), but he will be none the wiser if the fault recurs and he may well have spent more time and money than was necessary. A calm and logical approach will be found to be more satisfactory in the long run. Always take into account any warning signs or abnormalities that may have been noticed in the period preceding the fault – power loss, high or low gauge readings, unusual noises or smells, etc – and remember that failure of components such as fuses or spark plugs may only be pointers to some underlying fault.

The pages which follow here are intended to help in cases of failure to start or breakdown on the road. There is also a Fault Diagnosis Section at the end of each Chapter which should be consulted if the preliminary checks prove unfruitful. Whatever the fault, certain basic principles apply. These are as follows:

Verify the fault. This is simply a matter of being sure that you know what the symptoms are before starting work. This is particularly important if you are investigating a fault for someone else who may not have described it very accurately.

Don't overlook the obvious. For example, if the vehicle won't start, is there petrol in the tank? (Don't take anyone else's word on this particular point, and don't trust the fuel gauge either!) If an electrical fault is indicated, look for loose or broken wires before digging out the test gear.

Cure the disease, not the symptom. Substituting a flat battery with a fully charged one will get you off the hard shoulder, but if the underlying cause is not attended to, the new battery will go the same way. Similarly, changing oil-fouled spark plugs for a new set will get you moving again, but remember that the reason for the fouling (if it wasn't simply an incorrect grade of plug) will have to be established and corrected.

Don't take anything for granted. Particularly, don't forget that a 'new' component may itself be defective (especially if it's been rattling round in the boot for months), and don't leave components out of a fault diagnosis sequence just because they are new or recently fitted. When you do finally diagnose a difficult fault, you'll probably realise that all the evidence was there from the start.

Electrical faults

Electrical faults can be more puzzling than straightforward mechanical failures, but they are no less susceptible to logical analysis if the basic principles of operation are understood. Vehicle electrical wiring exists in extremely unfavourable conditions – heat, vibration and chemical attack and the first things to look for are loose or corroded connections and broken or chafed wires, especially where the wires pass through holes in the bodywork or are subject to vibration.

All metal-bodied vehicles in current production have one pole of the battery 'earthed', ie connected to the vehicle bodywork, and in nearly all modern vehicles it is the negative (–) terminal. The various electrical components – motors, bulb holders, etc – are also connected to earth, either by means of a lead or directly by their mountings. Electric current flows through the component and then back to the battery via the bodywork. If the component mounting is loose or corroded, or if a good path back to the battery is not available, the circuit will be incomplete and malfunction will result. The engine and/or gearbox are also earthed by means of flexible metal straps to the body or subframe; if these straps are loose or missing, starter motor, generator and ignition trouble may result.

Assuming the earth return to be satisfactory, electrical faults will be due either to component malfunction or to defects in the current supply. Individual components are dealt with in Chapter 9. If supply wires are broken or cracked internally this results in an open-circuit, and the easiest way to check for this is to bypass the suspect wire temporarily with a length of wire having a crocodile clip or suitable connector at each end. Alternatively, a 12V test lamp can be used to verify the presence of supply voltage at various points along the wire and the break can be thus isolated.

If a bare portion of a live wire touches the bodywork or other earthed metal part, the electricity will take the low-resistance path thus formed back to the battery: this is known as a short-circuit. Hopefully a short-circuit will blow a fuse, but otherwise it may cause burning of the insulation (and possibly further short-circuits) or even a fire. This is why it is inadvisable to bypass persistently blowing fuses with silver foil or wire.

Spares and tool kit

Most vehicles are supplied only with sufficient tools for wheel changing; the *Maintenance and minor repair* tool kit detailed in *Tools and working facilities,* with the addition of a hammer, is probably sufficient for those repairs that most motorists would consider attempting at the roadside. In addition a few items which can be fitted without too much trouble in the event of a breakdown should be carried. Experience and available space will modify the list below, but the following may save having to call on professional assistance:

- [ ] *Spark plugs, clean and correctly gapped*
- [ ] *HT lead and plug cap – long enough to reach the plug furthest from the distributor*
- [ ] *Distributor rotor, condenser and contact breaker*
- [ ] *Drivebelt(s) — emergency type may suffice*
- [ ] *Spare fuses*
- [ ] *Set of principal light bulbs*
- [ ] *Tin of radiator sealer and hose bandage*
- [ ] *Exhaust bandage*
- [ ] *Roll of insulating tape*
- [ ] *Length of soft iron wire*
- [ ] *Length of electrical flex*
- [ ] *Torch or inspection lamp (can double as test lamp)*
- [ ] *Battery jump leads*

- [ ] *Tow-rope*
- [ ] *Ignition waterproofing aerosol*
- [ ] *Litre of engine oil*
- [ ] *Sealed can of hydraulic fluid*
- [ ] *Emergency windscreen*
- [ ] *Wormdrive clips*
- [ ] *Tube of filler paste*

If spare fuel is carried, a can designed for the purpose should be used to minimise risks of leakage and collision damage. A first aid kit and a warning triangle, whilst not at present compulsory in the UK, are obviously sensible items to carry in addition to the above. When touring abroad it may be advisable to carry additional spares which, even if you cannot fit them yourself, could save having to wait while parts are obtained. The items below may be worth considering:

- [ ] *Clutch, choke and throttle cables*
- [ ] *Cylinder head gasket*
- [ ] *Alternator brushes*
- [ ] *Tyre valve core*

One of the motoring organisations will be able to advise on availability of fuel, etc, in foreign countries.

Engine will not start

Engine fails to turn when starter operated

- [ ] Flat battery (recharge use jump leads or push start)
- [ ] Battery terminals loose or corroded
- [ ] Battery earth to body defective
- [ ] Engine earth strap loose or broken
- [ ] Starter motor (or solenoid) wiring loose or broken
- [ ] Ignition/starter switch faulty
- [ ] Major mechanical failure (seizure)
- [ ] Starter or solenoid internal fault (see Chapter 9)

Starter motor turns engine slowly

- [ ] Partially discharged battery (recharge, use jump leads, or push start)
- [ ] Battery terminals loose or corroded

- [ ] Battery earth to body defective
- [ ] Engine earth strap loose
- [ ] Starter motor (or solenoid) wiring loose
- [ ] Starter motor internal fault (see Chapter 9)

Starter motor spins without turning engine

- [ ] Flywheel gear teeth damaged or worn
- [ ] Starter motor mounting bolts loose

Engine turns normally but fails to start

- [ ] Damp or dirty HT leads and distributor cap (crank engine and check for spark)
- [ ] No fuel in tank (check for delivery)
- [ ] Fouled or incorrectly gapped spark plugs (remove, clean and regap)
- [ ] Other ignition system fault (see Chapter 4)
- [ ] Other fuel system fault (see Chapter 3)

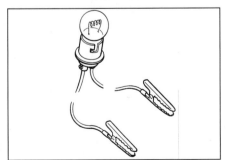

A simple test lamp is useful for checking electrical faults

Carrying a few spares may save you a long walk!

☐ Poor compression (see Chapter 1)
☐ Major mechanical failure (eg camshaft drive)

Engine fires but will not run

☐ Air leaks at carburettor or inlet manifold
☐ Fuel starvation (see Chapter 3)
☐ Ignition fault (see Chapter 4)

Engine cuts out and will not restart

Engine cuts out suddenly – ignition fault

☐ Loose or disconnected LT wires
☐ Wet HT leads or distributor cap (after traversing water splash)
☐ Coil failure (check for spark)
☐ Other ignition fault (see Chapter 4)

Engine misfires before cutting out – fuel fault

☐ Fuel tank empty
☐ Fuel pump defective or filter blocked (check for delivery)

Crank engine and check for spark. Note use of insulated tool

☐ Fuel tank filler vent blocked (suction will be evident on releasing cap)
☐ Carburettor needle valve sticking
☐ Carburettor jets blocked (fuel contaminated)
☐ Other fuel system fault (see Chapter 3)

Engine cuts out – other causes

☐ Serious overheating
☐ Major mechanical failure (eg camshaft drive)

Engine overheats

Temperature gauge reads high

☐ Coolant loss due to internal or external leakage (see Chapter 2)
☐ Thermostat defective
☐ Low oil level
☐ Brakes binding
☐ Radiator clogged externally or internally
☐ Engine waterways clogged
☐ Ignition timing incorrect or automatic advance malfunctioning
☐ Mixture too weak
Note: *Do not add cold water to an overheated engine or damage may result*

Low engine oil pressure

Note: *Low oil pressure in a high-mileage engine at tickover is not necessarily a cause for concern. Sudden pressure loss at speed is far more significant. In any event check the gauge or warning light sender before condemning the engine.*

Gauge reads low or warning light illuminated with engine running

☐ Oil level low or incorrect grade
☐ Defective gauge or sender unit

☐ Wire to sender unit earthed
☐ Engine overheating
☐ Oil filter clogged or bypass valve defective
☐ Oil pressure relief valve defective
☐ Oil pick-up strainer clogged
☐ Oil pump worn or mountings loose
☐ Worn main or big-end bearings

Engine noises

Pre-ignition (pinking) on acceleration

☐ Incorrect grade of fuel
☐ Ignition timing incorrect
☐ Distributor faulty or worn
☐ Worn or maladjusted carburettor
☐ Excessive carbon build-up in engine

Whistling or wheezing noises

☐ Leaking vacuum hose
☐ Leaking carburettor or manifold gasket
☐ Blowing head gasket

Tapping or rattling

☐ Worn valve gear
☐ Worn timing chain or belt
☐ Broken piston ring (ticking noise)

Knocking or thumping

☐ Unintentional mechanical contact (eg fan blades)
☐ Worn drivebelt
☐ Peripheral component fault (generator, water pump, etc)
☐ Worn big-end bearings (regular heavy knocking, perhaps less under load)
☐ Worn main bearings (rumbling and knocking, perhaps worsening under load)
☐ Piston slap (most noticeable when cold)

Length (distance)

Inches (in)	x 25.4	= Millimetres (mm)	x 0.0394	= Inches (in)	
Feet (ft)	x 0.305	= Metres (m)	x 3.281	= Feet (ft)	
Miles	x 1.609	= Kilometres (km)	x 0.621	= Miles	

Volume (capacity)

Cubic inches (cu in; in³)	x 16.387	= Cubic centimetres (cc; cm³)	x 0.061	= Cubic inches (cu in; in³)	
Imperial pints (Imp pt)	x 0.568	= Litres (l)	x 1.76	= Imperial pints (Imp pt)	
Imperial quarts (Imp qt)	x 1.137	= Litres (l)	x 0.88	= Imperial quarts (Imp qt)	
Imperial quarts (Imp qt)	x 1.201	= US quarts (US qt)	x 0.833	= Imperial quarts (Imp qt)	
US quarts (US qt)	x 0.946	= Litres (l)	x 1.057	= US quarts (US qt)	
Imperial gallons (Imp gal)	x 4.546	= Litres (l)	x 0.22	= Imperial gallons (Imp gal)	
Imperial gallons (Imp gal)	x 1.201	= US gallons (US gal)	x 0.833	= Imperial gallons (Imp gal)	
US gallons (US gal)	x 3.785	= Litres (l)	x 0.264	= US gallons (US gal)	

Mass (weight)

Ounces (oz)	x 28.35	= Grams (g)	x 0.035	= Ounces (oz)	
Pounds (lb)	x 0.454	= Kilograms (kg)	x 2.205	= Pounds (lb)	

Force

Ounces-force (ozf; oz)	x 0.278	= Newtons (N)	x 3.6	= Ounces-force (ozf; oz)	
Pounds-force (lbf; lb)	x 4.448	= Newtons (N)	x 0.225	= Pounds-force (lbf; lb)	
Newtons (N)	x 0.1	= Kilograms-force (kgf; kg)	x 9.81	= Newtons (N)	

Pressure

Pounds-force per square inch (psi; lbf/in²; lb/in²)	x 0.070	= Kilograms-force per square centimetre (kgf/cm²; kg/cm²)	x 14.223	= Pounds-force per square inch (psi; lbf/in²; lb/in²)	
Pounds-force per square inch (psi; lbf/in²; lb/in²)	x 0.068	= Atmospheres (atm)	x 14.696	= Pounds-force per square inch (psi; lbf/in²; lb/in²)	
Pounds-force per square inch (psi; lbf/in²; lb/in²)	x 0.069	= Bars	x 14.5	= Pounds-force per square inch (psi; lbf/in²; lb/in²)	
Pounds-force per square inch (psi; lbf/in²; lb/in²)	x 6.895	= Kilopascals (kPa)	x 0.145	= Pounds-force per square inch (psi; lbf/in²; lb/in²)	
Kilopascals (kPa)	x 0.01	= Kilograms-force per square centimetre (kgf/cm²; kg/cm²)	x 98.1	= Kilopascals (kPa)	
Millibar (mbar)	x 100	= Pascals (Pa)	x 0.01	= Millibar (mbar)	
Millibar (mbar)	x 0.0145	= Pounds-force per square inch (psi; lbf/in²; lb/in²)	x 68.947	= Millibar (mbar)	
Millibar (mbar)	x 0.75	= Millimetres of mercury (mmHg)	x 1.333	= Millibar (mbar)	
Millibar (mbar)	x 0.401	= Inches of water (inH₂O)	x 2.491	= Millibar (mbar)	
Millimetres of mercury (mmHg)	x 0.535	= Inches of water (inH₂O)	x 1.868	= Millimetres of mercury (mmHg)	
Inches of water (inH₂O)	x 0.036	= Pounds-force per square inch (psi; lbf/in²; lb/in²)	x 27.68	= Inches of water (inH₂O)	

Torque (moment of force)

Pounds-force inches (lbf in; lb in)	x 1.152	= Kilograms-force centimetre (kgf cm; kg cm)	x 0.868	= Pounds-force inches (lbf in; lb in)	
Pounds-force inches (lbf in; lb in)	x 0.113	= Newton metres (Nm)	x 8.85	= Pounds-force inches (lbf in; lb in)	
Pounds-force inches (lbf in; lb in)	x 0.083	= Pounds-force feet (lbf ft; lb ft)	x 12	= Pounds-force inches (lbf in; lb in)	
Pounds-force feet (lbf ft; lb ft)	x 0.138	= Kilograms-force metres (kgf m; kg m)	x 7.233	= Pounds-force feet (lbf ft; lb ft)	
Pounds-force feet (lbf ft; lb ft)	x 1.356	= Newton metres (Nm)	x 0.738	= Pounds-force feet (lbf ft; lb ft)	
Newton metres (Nm)	x 0.102	= Kilograms-force metres (kgf m; kg m)	x 9.804	= Newton metres (Nm)	

Power

Horsepower (hp)	x 745.7	= Watts (W)	x 0.0013	= Horsepower (hp)	

Velocity (speed)

Miles per hour (miles/hr; mph)	x 1.609	= Kilometres per hour (km/hr; kph)	x 0.621	= Miles per hour (miles/hr; mph)	

Fuel consumption*

Miles per gallon (mpg)	x 0.354	= Kilometres per litre (km/l)	x 2.825	= Miles per gallon (mpg)	

Temperature

Degrees Fahrenheit = (°C x 1.8) + 32   Degrees Celsius (Degrees Centigrade; °C) = (°F - 32) x 0.56

* It is common practice to convert from miles per gallon (mpg) to litres/100 kilometres (l/100km), where mpg x l/100 km = 282

A

ABS (Anti-lock brake system) A system, usually electronically controlled, that senses incipient wheel lockup during braking and relieves hydraulic pressure at wheels that are about to skid.

Air bag An inflatable bag hidden in the steering wheel (driver's side) or the dash or glovebox (passenger side). In a head-on collision, the bags inflate, preventing the driver and front passenger from being thrown forward into the steering wheel or windscreen.

Air cleaner A metal or plastic housing, containing a filter element, which removes dust and dirt from the air being drawn into the engine.

Air filter element The actual filter in an air cleaner system, usually manufactured from pleated paper and requiring renewal at regular intervals.

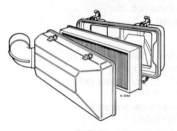

Air filter

Allen key A hexagonal wrench which fits into a recessed hexagonal hole.

Alligator clip A long-nosed spring-loaded metal clip with meshing teeth. Used to make temporary electrical connections.

Alternator A component in the electrical system which converts mechanical energy from a drivebelt into electrical energy to charge the battery and to operate the starting system, ignition system and electrical accessories.

Alternator (exploded view)

Ampere (amp) A unit of measurement for the flow of electric current. One amp is the amount of current produced by one volt acting through a resistance of one ohm.

Anaerobic sealer A substance used to prevent bolts and screws from loosening. Anaerobic means that it does not require oxygen for activation. The Loctite brand is widely used.

Antifreeze A substance (usually ethylene glycol) mixed with water, and added to a vehicle's cooling system, to prevent freezing of the coolant in winter. Antifreeze also contains chemicals to inhibit corrosion and the formation of rust and other deposits that

would tend to clog the radiator and coolant passages and reduce cooling efficiency.

Anti-seize compound A coating that reduces the risk of seizing on fasteners that are subjected to high temperatures, such as exhaust manifold bolts and nuts.

Anti-seize compound

Asbestos A natural fibrous mineral with great heat resistance, commonly used in the composition of brake friction materials. Asbestos is a health hazard and the dust created by brake systems should never be inhaled or ingested.

Axle A shaft on which a wheel revolves, or which revolves with a wheel. Also, a solid beam that connects the two wheels at one end of the vehicle. An axle which also transmits power to the wheels is known as a live axle.

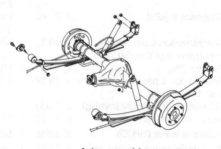

Axle assembly

Axleshaft A single rotating shaft, on either side of the differential, which delivers power from the final drive assembly to the drive wheels. Also called a driveshaft or a halfshaft.

B

Ball bearing An anti-friction bearing consisting of a hardened inner and outer race with hardened steel balls between two races.

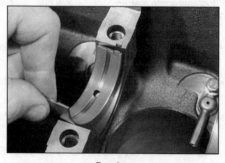

Bearing

Bearing The curved surface on a shaft or in a bore, or the part assembled into either, that permits relative motion between them with minimum wear and friction.

Big-end bearing The bearing in the end of the connecting rod that's attached to the crankshaft.

Bleed nipple A valve on a brake wheel cylinder, caliper or other hydraulic component that is opened to purge the hydraulic system of air. Also called a bleed screw.

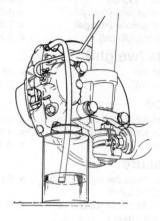

Brake bleeding

Brake bleeding Procedure for removing air from lines of a hydraulic brake system.

Brake disc The component of a disc brake that rotates with the wheels.

Brake drum The component of a drum brake that rotates with the wheels.

Brake linings The friction material which contacts the brake disc or drum to retard the vehicle's speed. The linings are bonded or riveted to the brake pads or shoes.

Brake pads The replaceable friction pads that pinch the brake disc when the brakes are applied. Brake pads consist of a friction material bonded or riveted to a rigid backing plate.

Brake shoe The crescent-shaped carrier to which the brake linings are mounted and which forces the lining against the rotating drum during braking.

Braking systems For more information on braking systems, consult the *Haynes Automotive Brake Manual*.

Breaker bar A long socket wrench handle providing greater leverage.

Bulkhead The insulated partition between the engine and the passenger compartment.

C

Caliper The non-rotating part of a disc-brake assembly that straddles the disc and carries the brake pads. The caliper also contains the hydraulic components that cause the pads to pinch the disc when the brakes are applied. A caliper is also a measuring tool that can be set to measure inside or outside dimensions of an object.

Camshaft A rotating shaft on which a series of cam lobes operate the valve mechanisms. The camshaft may be driven by gears, by sprockets and chain or by sprockets and a belt.

Canister A container in an evaporative emission control system; contains activated charcoal granules to trap vapours from the fuel system.

Canister

Carburettor A device which mixes fuel with air in the proper proportions to provide a desired power output from a spark ignition internal combustion engine.

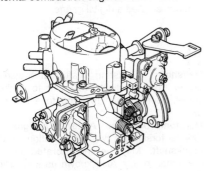

Carburettor

Castellated Resembling the parapets along the top of a castle wall. For example, a castellated balljoint stud nut.

Castellated nut

Castor In wheel alignment, the backward or forward tilt of the steering axis. Castor is positive when the steering axis is inclined rearward at the top.

Catalytic converter A silencer-like device in the exhaust system which converts certain pollutants in the exhaust gases into less harmful substances.

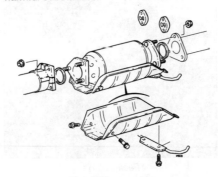

Catalytic converter

Circlip A ring-shaped clip used to prevent endwise movement of cylindrical parts and shafts. An internal circlip is installed in a groove in a housing; an external circlip fits into a groove on the outside of a cylindrical piece such as a shaft.

Clearance The amount of space between two parts. For example, between a piston and a cylinder, between a bearing and a journal, etc.

Coil spring A spiral of elastic steel found in various sizes throughout a vehicle, for example as a springing medium in the suspension and in the valve train.

Compression Reduction in volume, and increase in pressure and temperature, of a gas, caused by squeezing it into a smaller space.

Compression ratio The relationship between cylinder volume when the piston is at top dead centre and cylinder volume when the piston is at bottom dead centre.

Constant velocity (CV) joint A type of universal joint that cancels out vibrations caused by driving power being transmitted through an angle.

Core plug A disc or cup-shaped metal device inserted in a hole in a casting through which core was removed when the casting was formed. Also known as a freeze plug or expansion plug.

Crankcase The lower part of the engine block in which the crankshaft rotates.

Crankshaft The main rotating member, or shaft, running the length of the crankcase, with offset "throws" to which the connecting rods are attached.

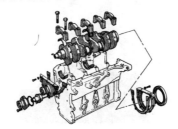

Crankshaft assembly

Crocodile clip See Alligator clip

D

Diagnostic code Code numbers obtained by accessing the diagnostic mode of an engine management computer. This code can be used to determine the area in the system where a malfunction may be located.

Disc brake A brake design incorporating a rotating disc onto which brake pads are squeezed. The resulting friction converts the energy of a moving vehicle into heat.

Double-overhead cam (DOHC) An engine that uses two overhead camshafts, usually one for the intake valves and one for the exhaust valves.

Drivebelt(s) The belt(s) used to drive accessories such as the alternator, water pump, power steering pump, air conditioning compressor, etc. off the crankshaft pulley.

Accessory drivebelts

Driveshaft Any shaft used to transmit motion. Commonly used when referring to the axleshafts on a front wheel drive vehicle.

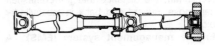

Driveshaft

Drum brake A type of brake using a drum-shaped metal cylinder attached to the inner surface of the wheel. When the brake pedal is pressed, curved brake shoes with friction linings press against the inside of the drum to slow or stop the vehicle.

Drum brake assembly

E

EGR valve A valve used to introduce exhaust gases into the intake air stream.

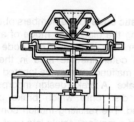

EGR valve

Electronic control unit (ECU) A computer which controls (for instance) ignition and fuel injection systems, or an anti-lock braking system. For more information refer to the *Haynes Automotive Electrical and Electronic Systems Manual.*

Electronic Fuel Injection (EFI) A computer controlled fuel system that distributes fuel through an injector located in each intake port of the engine.

Emergency brake A braking system, independent of the main hydraulic system, that can be used to slow or stop the vehicle if the primary brakes fail, or to hold the vehicle stationary even though the brake pedal isn't depressed. It usually consists of a hand lever that actuates either front or rear brakes mechanically through a series of cables and linkages. Also known as a handbrake or parking brake.

Endfloat The amount of lengthwise movement between two parts. As applied to a crankshaft, the distance that the crankshaft can move forward and back in the cylinder block.

Engine management system (EMS) A computer controlled system which manages the fuel injection and the ignition systems in an integrated fashion.

Exhaust manifold A part with several passages through which exhaust gases leave the engine combustion chambers and enter the exhaust pipe.

Exhaust manifold

F

Fan clutch A viscous (fluid) drive coupling device which permits variable engine fan speeds in relation to engine speeds.

Feeler blade A thin strip or blade of hardened steel, ground to an exact thickness, used to check or measure clearances between parts.

Feeler blade

Firing order The order in which the engine cylinders fire, or deliver their power strokes, beginning with the number one cylinder.

Flywheel A heavy spinning wheel in which energy is absorbed and stored by means of momentum. On cars, the flywheel is attached to the crankshaft to smooth out firing impulses.

Free play The amount of travel before any action takes place. The "looseness" in a linkage, or an assembly of parts, between the initial application of force and actual movement. For example, the distance the brake pedal moves before the pistons in the master cylinder are actuated.

Fuse An electrical device which protects a circuit against accidental overload. The typical fuse contains a soft piece of metal which is calibrated to melt at a predetermined current flow (expressed as amps) and break the circuit.

Fusible link A circuit protection device consisting of a conductor surrounded by heat-resistant insulation. The conductor is smaller than the wire it protects, so it acts as the weakest link in the circuit. Unlike a blown fuse, a failed fusible link must frequently be cut from the wire for replacement.

G

Gap The distance the spark must travel in jumping from the centre electrode to the side

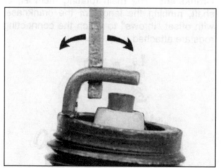

Adjusting spark plug gap

electrode in a spark plug. Also refers to the spacing between the points in a contact breaker assembly in a conventional points-type ignition, or to the distance between the reluctor or rotor and the pickup coil in an electronic ignition.

Gasket Any thin, soft material - usually cork, cardboard, asbestos or soft metal - installed between two metal surfaces to ensure a good seal. For instance, the cylinder head gasket seals the joint between the block and the cylinder head.

Gasket

Gauge An instrument panel display used to monitor engine conditions. A gauge with a movable pointer on a dial or a fixed scale is an analogue gauge. A gauge with a numerical readout is called a digital gauge.

H

Halfshaft A rotating shaft that transmits power from the final drive unit to a drive wheel, usually when referring to a live rear axle.

Harmonic balancer A device designed to reduce torsion or twisting vibration in the crankshaft. May be incorporated in the crankshaft pulley. Also known as a vibration damper.

Hone An abrasive tool for correcting small irregularities or differences in diameter in an engine cylinder, brake cylinder, etc.

Hydraulic tappet A tappet that utilises hydraulic pressure from the engine's lubrication system to maintain zero clearance (constant contact with both camshaft and valve stem). Automatically adjusts to variation in valve stem length. Hydraulic tappets also reduce valve noise.

I

Ignition timing The moment at which the spark plug fires, usually expressed in the number of crankshaft degrees before the piston reaches the top of its stroke.

Inlet manifold A tube or housing with passages through which flows the air-fuel mixture (carburettor vehicles and vehicles with throttle body injection) or air only (port fuel-injected vehicles) to the port openings in the cylinder head.

J

Jump start Starting the engine of a vehicle with a discharged or weak battery by attaching jump leads from the weak battery to a charged or helper battery.

L

Load Sensing Proportioning Valve (LSPV) A brake hydraulic system control valve that works like a proportioning valve, but also takes into consideration the amount of weight carried by the rear axle.

Locknut A nut used to lock an adjustment nut, or other threaded component, in place. For example, a locknut is employed to keep the adjusting nut on the rocker arm in position.

Lockwasher A form of washer designed to prevent an attaching nut from working loose.

M

MacPherson strut A type of front suspension system devised by Earle MacPherson at Ford of England. In its original form, a simple lateral link with the anti-roll bar creates the lower control arm. A long strut - an integral coil spring and shock absorber - is mounted between the body and the steering knuckle. Many modern so-called MacPherson strut systems use a conventional lower A-arm and don't rely on the anti-roll bar for location.

Multimeter An electrical test instrument with the capability to measure voltage, current and resistance.

N

NOx Oxides of Nitrogen. A common toxic pollutant emitted by petrol and diesel engines at higher temperatures.

O

Ohm The unit of electrical resistance. One volt applied to a resistance of one ohm will produce a current of one amp.

Ohmmeter An instrument for measuring electrical resistance.

O-ring A type of sealing ring made of a special rubber-like material; in use, the O-ring is compressed into a groove to provide the sealing action.

O-ring

Overhead cam (ohc) engine An engine with the camshaft(s) located on top of the cylinder head(s).

Overhead valve (ohv) engine An engine with the valves located in the cylinder head, but with the camshaft located in the engine block.

Oxygen sensor A device installed in the engine exhaust manifold, which senses the oxygen content in the exhaust and converts this information into an electric current. Also called a Lambda sensor.

P

Phillips screw A type of screw head having a cross instead of a slot for a corresponding type of screwdriver.

Plastigage A thin strip of plastic thread, available in different sizes, used for measuring clearances. For example, a strip of Plastigage is laid across a bearing journal. The parts are assembled and dismantled; the width of the crushed strip indicates the clearance between journal and bearing.

Plastigage

Propeller shaft The long hollow tube with universal joints at both ends that carries power from the transmission to the differential on front-engined rear wheel drive vehicles.

Proportioning valve A hydraulic control valve which limits the amount of pressure to the rear brakes during panic stops to prevent wheel lock-up.

R

Rack-and-pinion steering A steering system with a pinion gear on the end of the steering shaft that mates with a rack (think of a geared wheel opened up and laid flat). When the steering wheel is turned, the pinion turns, moving the rack to the left or right. This movement is transmitted through the track rods to the steering arms at the wheels.

Radiator A liquid-to-air heat transfer device designed to reduce the temperature of the coolant in an internal combustion engine cooling system.

Refrigerant Any substance used as a heat transfer agent in an air-conditioning system. R-12 has been the principle refrigerant for many years; recently, however, manufacturers have begun using R-134a, a non-CFC substance that is considered less harmful to

the ozone in the upper atmosphere.

Rocker arm A lever arm that rocks on a shaft or pivots on a stud. In an overhead valve engine, the rocker arm converts the upward movement of the pushrod into a downward movement to open a valve.

Rotor In a distributor, the rotating device inside the cap that connects the centre electrode and the outer terminals as it turns, distributing the high voltage from the coil secondary winding to the proper spark plug. Also, that part of an alternator which rotates inside the stator. Also, the rotating assembly of a turbocharger, including the compressor wheel, shaft and turbine wheel.

Runout The amount of wobble (in-and-out movement) of a gear or wheel as it's rotated. The amount a shaft rotates "out-of-true." The out-of-round condition of a rotating part.

S

Sealant A liquid or paste used to prevent leakage at a joint. Sometimes used in conjunction with a gasket.

Sealed beam lamp An older headlight design which integrates the reflector, lens and filaments into a hermetically-sealed one-piece unit. When a filament burns out or the lens cracks, the entire unit is simply replaced.

Serpentine drivebelt A single, long, wide accessory drivebelt that's used on some newer vehicles to drive all the accessories, instead of a series of smaller, shorter belts. Serpentine drivebelts are usually tensioned by an automatic tensioner.

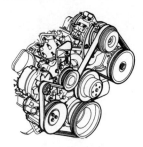

Serpentine drivebelt

Shim Thin spacer, commonly used to adjust the clearance or relative positions between two parts. For example, shims inserted into or under bucket tappets control valve clearances. Clearance is adjusted by changing the thickness of the shim.

Slide hammer A special puller that screws into or hooks onto a component such as a shaft or bearing; a heavy sliding handle on the shaft bottoms against the end of the shaft to knock the component free.

Sprocket A tooth or projection on the periphery of a wheel, shaped to engage with a chain or drivebelt. Commonly used to refer to the sprocket wheel itself.

Starter inhibitor switch On vehicles with an

automatic transmission, a switch that prevents starting if the vehicle is not in Neutral or Park.

Strut See MacPherson strut.

T

Tappet A cylindrical component which transmits motion from the cam to the valve stem, either directly or via a pushrod and rocker arm. Also called a cam follower.

Thermostat A heat-controlled valve that regulates the flow of coolant between the cylinder block and the radiator, so maintaining optimum engine operating temperature. A thermostat is also used in some air cleaners in which the temperature is regulated.

Thrust bearing The bearing in the clutch assembly that is moved in to the release levers by clutch pedal action to disengage the clutch. Also referred to as a release bearing.

Timing belt A toothed belt which drives the camshaft. Serious engine damage may result if it breaks in service.

Timing chain A chain which drives the camshaft.

Toe-in The amount the front wheels are closer together at the front than at the rear. On rear wheel drive vehicles, a slight amount of toe-in is usually specified to keep the front wheels running parallel on the road by offsetting other forces that tend to spread the wheels apart.

Toe-out The amount the front wheels are closer together at the rear than at the front. On front wheel drive vehicles, a slight amount of toe-out is usually specified.

Tools For full information on choosing and using tools, refer to the *Haynes Automotive Tools Manual.*

Tracer A stripe of a second colour applied to a wire insulator to distinguish that wire from another one with the same colour insulator.

Tune-up A process of accurate and careful adjustments and parts replacement to obtain the best possible engine performance.

Turbocharger A centrifugal device, driven by exhaust gases, that pressurises the intake air. Normally used to increase the power output from a given engine displacement, but can also be used primarily to reduce exhaust emissions (as on VW's "Umwelt" Diesel engine).

U

Universal joint or U-joint A double-pivoted connection for transmitting power from a driving to a driven shaft through an angle. A U-joint consists of two Y-shaped yokes and a cross-shaped member called the spider.

V

Valve A device through which the flow of liquid, gas, vacuum, or loose material in bulk may be started, stopped, or regulated by a movable part that opens, shuts, or partially obstructs one or more ports or passageways. A valve is also the movable part of such a device.

Valve clearance The clearance between the valve tip (the end of the valve stem) and the rocker arm or tappet. The valve clearance is measured when the valve is closed.

Vernier caliper A precision measuring instrument that measures inside and outside dimensions. Not quite as accurate as a micrometer, but more convenient.

Viscosity The thickness of a liquid or its resistance to flow.

Volt A unit for expressing electrical "pressure" in a circuit. One volt that will produce a current of one ampere through a resistance of one ohm.

W

Welding Various processes used to join metal items by heating the areas to be joined to a molten state and fusing them together. For more information refer to the *Haynes Automotive Welding Manual.*

Wiring diagram A drawing portraying the components and wires in a vehicle's electrical system, using standardised symbols. For more information refer to the *Haynes Automotive Electrical and Electronic Systems Manual.*

Index REF•19

Accelerator cable - 3•5
Accelerator pedal - 3•6
Accelerator pump - 12•13, 12•14, 12•16
Acknowledgements - 0•4
Air bags - 0•5
Air cleaner - 3•2, 3•3, 12•17
Air temperature control - 3•3
Alternator - 9•3, 9•4, 9•5, 12•24
Anti-roll bar - 10•5
Antifreeze - 0•6, 0•16, 2•1, 2•3, 12•6
Asbestos - 0•5
Automatic stop-start system - 12•23
Axle beam - 10•7

B

Backfire - 1•20
Balljoints - 10•5, 10•9
Battery - 0•5, 9•2, 9•3
Battery fault - 9•14
Bellows - 10•10
Bleeding brakes - 8•7
Bodywork and fittings - 0•12, 11•1 *et seq*, 12•25 *et seq*, REF•4
Bonnet - 11•3, 11•4
Boot lid - 11•8
Brake fluid - 0•16, 8•1

Braking system - 0•12, 8•1 *et seq*, 12•22 *et seq*, REF•1, REF•2, REF•3
Braking system fault finding - 8•9
Bulbs - 9•10
Bumpers - 11•8
Burning - 0•5

C

Cables - 3•5, 5•1, 5•2, 8•8, 9•8, 11•4
Calipers - 8•4, 12•22
Camshaft - 1•7, 1•14, 1•17, 12•7
Capacities - 0•6, 12•6
Carburettors - 3•6, 3•7, 3•8, 12•11, 12•12, 12•13, 12•15, 12•16
Carpets - 11•2
Catalytic converters - 12•17
Centre console - 12•26
Charging battery - 9•3
Choke - 3•5, 12•13, 12•14, 12•15, 12•16
Cigarette lighter - 9•8
Clutch - 0•11, 5•1 *et seq*, 12•19 *et seq*
Clutch fault finding - 5•4
CO emissions (mixture) - REF•4
Coil - 4•6
Coil spring - 10•4
Condenser - 4•4
Connecting rods - 1•11, 1•14, 1•15
Console - 12•26
Consumption gauge - 9•13

Contact breaker points - 4•2, 4•3
Contents - 0•2
Control unit - 12•18
Conversion factors - REF•13
Coolant - 0•6, 0•16, 2•1, 2•3, 12•6
Cooling system - 0•11, 2•1 *et seq*
Cooling system fault finding - 2•5
Courtesy light - 9•8
Crankcase ventilation system - 1•12
Crankshaft - 1•9, 1•11, 1•13, 1•15, 12•11
Crushing - 0•5
Cut-off valve - 12•13
Cylinder block - 1•13
Cylinder head - 1•6, 1•8, 1•14, 1•17, 1•18, 12•6, 12•8

D

Decarbonising - 1•14
Dents in bodywork - 11•2
Dim-dip lighting - 12•24
Dimensions - 0•6, 12•6
Direction indicators - 9•7, 9•11
Discs - 8•5
Distributor - 4•4, 12•18, 12•19
Doors - 11•3, 11•6, 11•7, 11•8, REF•2
Drivebelt - 9•3, 12•24
Driveshafts - 0•12, 7•1 *et seq*, REF•3
Driveshafts fault finding - 7•3
Drums - 8•6

Haynes Manuals – The Complete List

Title	Book No.
ALFA ROMEO	
Alfa Romeo Alfasud/Sprint (74 - 88)	0292
Alfa Romeo Alfetta (73 - 87)	0531
AUDI	
Audi 80 (72 - Feb 79)	0207
Audi 80, 90 (79 - Oct 86) & Coupe (81 - Nov 88)	0605
Audi 80, 90 (Oct 86 - 90) & Coupe (Nov 88 - 90)	1491
Audi 100 (Oct 76 - Oct 82)	0428
Audi 100 (Oct 82 - 90) & 200 (Feb 84 - Oct 89)	0907
AUSTIN	
Austin Ambassador (82 - 84)	0871
Austin/MG Maestro 1.3 & 1.6 (83 - 95)	0922
Austin Maxi (69 - 81)	0052
Austin/MG Metro (80 - May 90)	0718
Austin Montego 1.3 & 1.6 (84 - 94)	1066
Austin/MG Montego 2.0 (84 - 95)	1067
Mini (59 - 69)	0527
Mini (69 - Oct 96)	0646
Austin/Rover 2.0 litre Diesel Engine (86 - 93)	1857
BEDFORD	
Bedford CF (69 - 87)	0163
Bedford Rascal (86 - 93)	3015
BL	
BL Princess & BLMC 18-22 (75 - 82)	0286
BMW	
BMW 316, 320 & 320i (4-cyl) (75 - Feb 83)	0276
BMW 320, 320i, 323i & 325i (6-cyl) (Oct 77 - Sept 87)	0815
BMW 3-Series (Apr 91 - 96)	3210
BMW 3-Series (sohc) (83 - 91)	1948
BMW 520i & 525e (Oct 81 - June 88)	1560
BMW 525, 528 & 528i (73 - Sept 81)	0632
BMW 5-Series (sohc) (81 - 91)	1948
BMW 1500, 1502, 1600, 1602, 2000 & 2002 (59 - 77)	0240
CITROEN	
Citroen 2CV, Ami & Dyane (67 - 90)	0196
Citroen AX Petrol & Diesel (87 - 94)	3014
Citroen BX (83 - 94)	0908
Citroen CX (75 - 88)	0528
Citroen Visa (79 - 88)	0620
Citroen Xantia Petrol & Diesel (93 - Oct 95)	3082
Citroen XM Petrol & Diesel (89 - 97)	3451
Citroen ZX Diesel (91 - 93)	1922
Citroen ZX Petrol (91 - 94)	1881
Citroen 1.7 & 1.9 litre Diesel Engine (84 - 96)	1379
COLT	
Colt 1200, 1250 & 1400 (79 - May 84)	0600
DAIMLER	
Daimler Sovereign (68 - Oct 86)	0242
Daimler Double Six (72 - 88)	0478
DATSUN (see also **Nissan**)	
Datsun 120Y (73 - Aug 78)	0228
Datsun 1300, 1400 & 1600 (69 - Aug 72)	0123
Datsun Cherry (71 - 76)	0195
Datsun Pick-up (75 - 78)	0277
Datsun Sunny (Aug 78 - May 82)	0525
Datsun Violet (78 - 82)	0430

Title	Book No.
FIAT	
Fiat 126 (73 - 87)	0305
Fiat 127 (71 - 83)	0193
Fiat 500 (57 - 73)	0090
Fiat 850 (64 - 81)	0038
Fiat Panda (81 - 95)	0793
Fiat Punto (94 - 96)	3251
Fiat Regata (84 - 88)	1167
Fiat Strada (79 - 88)	0479
Fiat Tipo (88 - 91)	1625
Fiat Uno (83 - 95)	0923
Fiat X1/9 (74 - 89)	0273
FORD	
Ford Capri II (& III) 1.6 & 2.0 (74 - 87)	0283
Ford Capri II (& III) 2.8 & 3.0 (74 - 87)	1309
Ford Cortina Mk IV (& V) 1.6 & 2.0 (76 - 83)	0343
Ford Cortina Mk IV (& V) 2.3 V6 (77 - 83)	0426
Ford Escort (75 - Aug 80)	0280
Ford Escort (Sept 80 - Sept 90)	0686
Ford Escort (Sept 90 - 97)	1737
Ford Escort Mk II Mexico, RS 1600 & RS 2000 (75 - 80)	0735
Ford Fiesta (inc. XR2) (76 - Aug 83)	0334
Ford Fiesta (inc. XR2) (Aug 83 - Feb 89)	1030
Ford Fiesta (Feb 89 - Oct 95)	1595
Ford Fiesta Petrol & Diesel (Oct 95 - 97)	3397
Ford Granada (Sept 77 - Feb 85)	0481
Ford Granada (Mar 85 - 94)	1245
Ford Mondeo 4-cyl (93 - 96)	1923
Ford Orion (83 - Sept 90)	1009
Ford Orion (Sept 90 - 93)	1737
Ford Sierra 1.3, 1.6, 1.8 & 2.0 (82 - 93)	0903
Ford Sierra 2.3, 2.8 & 2.9 (82 - 91)	0904
Ford Scorpio (Mar 85 - 94)	1245
Ford Transit Petrol (Mk 1) (65 - Feb 78)	0377
Ford Transit Petrol (Mk 2) (78 - Jan 86)	0719
Ford Transit Petrol (Mk 3) (Feb 86 - 89)	1468
Ford Transit Diesel (Feb 86 - 95)	3019
Ford 1.6 & 1.8 litre Diesel Engine (84 - 96)	1172
Ford 2.1, 2.3 & 2.5 litre Diesel Engine (77 - 90)	1606
FREIGHT ROVER	
Freight Rover Sherpa (74 - 87)	0463
HILLMAN	
Hillman Avenger (70 - 82)	0037
HONDA	
Honda Accord (76 - Feb 84)	0351
Honda Accord (Feb 84 - Oct 85)	1177
Honda Civic (Feb 84 - Oct 87)	1226
Honda Civic (Nov 91 - 96)	3199
HYUNDAI	
Hyundai Pony (85 - 94)	3398
JAGUAR	
Jaguar E Type (61 - 72)	0140
Jaguar MkI & II, 240 & 340 (55 - 69)	0098
Jaguar XJ6, XJ & Sovereign (68 - Oct 86)	0242
Jaguar XJ6 & Sovereign (Oct 86 - Sept 94)	3261
Jaguar XJ12, XJS & Sovereign (72 - 88)	0478

Title	Book No.
JEEP	
Jeep Cherokee Petrol (93 - 96)	1943
LADA	
Lada 1200, 1300, 1500 & 1600 (74 - 91)	0413
Lada Samara (87 - 91)	1610
LAND ROVER	
Land Rover 90, 110 & Defender Diesel (83 - 95)	3017
Land Rover Discovery Diesel (89 - 95)	3016
Land Rover Series IIA & III Diesel (58 - 85)	0529
Land Rover Series II, IIA & III Petrol (58 - 85)	0314
MAZDA	
Mazda 323 fwd (Mar 81 - Oct 89)	1608
Mazda 626 fwd (May 83 - Sept 87)	0929
Mazda B-1600, B-1800 & B-2000 Pick-up (72 - 88)	0267
MERCEDES-BENZ	
Mercedes-Benz 190, 190E & 190D Petrol & Diesel (83 - 93)	3450
Mercedes-Benz 200, 240, 300 Diesel (Oct 76 - 85)	1114
Mercedes-Benz 250 & 280 (68 - 72)	0346
Mercedes-Benz 250 & 280 (123 Series) (Oct 76 - 84)	0677
Mercedes-Benz 124 Series (85 - Aug 93)	3253
MG	
MGB (62 - 80)	0111
MG Maestro 1.3 & 1.6 (83 - 95)	0922
MG Metro (80 - May 90)	0718
MG Midget & AH Sprite (58 - 80)	0265
MG Montego 2.0 (84 - 95)	1067
MITSUBISHI	
Mitsubishi 1200, 1250 & 1400 (79 - May 84)	0600
Mitsubishi Shogun & L200 Pick-Ups (83 - 94)	1944
MORRIS	
Morris Ital 1.3 (80 - 84)	0705
Morris Marina 1700 (78 - 80)	0526
Morris Marina 1.8 (71 - 78)	0074
Morris Minor 1000 (56 - 71)	0024
NISSAN (See also Datsun)	
Nissan Bluebird 160B & 180B rwd (May 80 - May 84)	0957
Nissan Bluebird fwd (May 84 - Mar 86)	1223
Nissan Bluebird (T12 & T72) (Mar 86 - 90)	1473
Nissan Cherry (N12) (Sept 82 - 86)	1031
Nissan Micra (K10) (83 - Jan 93)	0931
Nissan Micra (93 - 96)	3254
Nissan Primera (90 - Oct 96)	1851
Nissan Stanza (82 - 86)	0824
Nissan Sunny (B11) (May 82 - Oct 86)	0895
Nissan Sunny (Oct 86 - Mar 91)	1378
Nissan Sunny (Apr 91 - 95)	3219
OPEL	
Opel Ascona & Manta (B Series) (Sept 75 - 88)	0316
Opel Ascona (81 - 88)	3215
Opel Astra (Oct 91 - 96)	3156
Opel Corsa (83 - Mar 93)	3160
Opel Corsa (Mar 93 - 94)	3159
Opel Kadett (Nov 79 - Oct 84)	0634

Title	Book No.
Opel Kadett (Oct 84 - Oct 91)	3196
Opel Omega & Senator (86 - 94)	3157
Opel Rekord (Feb 78 - Oct 86)	0543
Opel Vectra (88 - Oct 95)	3158
PEUGEOT	
Peugeot 106 Petrol & Diesel (91 - June 96)	1882
Peugeot 205 (83 - 95)	0932
Peugeot 305 (78 - 89)	0538
Peugeot 306 Petrol & Diesel (93 - 95)	3073
Peugeot 309 (86 - 93)	1266
Peugeot 405 Petrol (88 - 96)	1559
Peugeot 405 Diesel (88 - 96)	3198
Peugeot 406 Petrol & Diesel (96 - 97)	3394
Peugeot 505 (79 - 89)	0762
Peugeot 1.7 & 1.9 litre Diesel Engines (82 - 96)	0950
Peugeot 2.0, 2.1, 2.3 & 2.5 litre Diesel Engines (74 - 90)	1607
PORSCHE	
Porsche 911 (65 - 85)	0264
Porsche 924 & 924 Turbo (76 - 85)	0397
PROTON	
Proton (89 - 97)	3255
RANGE ROVER	
Range Rover V8 (70 - Oct 92)	0606
RELIANT	
Reliant Robin & Kitten (73 - 83)	0436
RENAULT	
Renault 5 (72 - Feb 85)	0141
Renault 5 (Feb 85 - 96)	1219
Renault 9 & 11 (82 - 89)	0822
Renault 12 (70 - 80)	0097
Renault 15 & 17 (72 - 79)	0763
Renault 18 (79 - 86)	0598
Renault 19 Petrol (89 - 94)	1646
Renault 19 Diesel (89 - 95)	1946
Renault 21 (86 - 94)	1397
Renault 25 (84 - 92)	1228
Renault Clio Petrol (91 - 93)	1853
Renault Clio Diesel (91 - June 96)	3031
Renault Espace (85 - 96)	3197
Renault Fuego (80 - 86)	0764
Renault Laguna (94 - 96)	3252
Renault Mégane Petrol & Diesel (96 - 97)	3395
ROVER	
Rover 111 & 114 (95 - 96)	1711
Rover 213 & 216 (84 - 89)	1116
Rover 214 & 414 (89 - 96)	1689
Rover 216 & 416 (89 - 96)	1830
Rover 618, 620 & 623 (93 - 97)	3257
Rover 820, 825 & 827 (86 - 95)	1380
Rover 2000, 2300 & 2600 (77 - 87)	0468
Rover 3500 (76 - 87)	0365
Rover Metro (May 90 - 94)	1711
SAAB	
Saab 90, 99 & 900 (79 - Oct 93)	0765
Saab 9000 (4-cyl) (85 - 95)	1686

Title	Book No.
SEAT	
Seat Ibiza & Malaga (85 - 92)	1609
SIMCA	
Simca 1100 & 1204 (67 - 79)	0088
Simca 1301 & 1501 (63 - 76)	0199
SKODA	
Skoda Estelle 105, 120, 130 & 136 (77 - 89)	0604
Skoda Favorit (89 - 92)	1801
SUBARU	
Subaru 1600 & 1800 (Nov 79 - 90)	0995
SUZUKI	
Suzuki SJ Series, Samurai & Vitara (82 - 97)	1942
Suzuki Supercarry (86 - Oct 94)	3015
TALBOT	
Talbot Alpine, Solara, Minx & Rapier (75 - 86)	0337
Talbot Horizon (78 - 86)	0473
Talbot Samba (82 - 86)	0823
TOYOTA	
Toyota Carina E (May 92 - 97)	3256
Toyota Celica (Feb 82 - Sept 85)	1135
Toyota Corolla (fwd) (Sept 83 - Sept 87)	1024
Toyota Corolla (rwd) (80 - 85)	0683
Toyota Corolla (Sept 87 - 92)	1683
Toyota Corolla (Aug 92 - 97)	3259
Toyota Hi-Ace & Hi-Lux (69 - Oct 83)	0304
Toyota Starlet (78 - Jan 85)	0462
TRIUMPH	
Triumph Acclaim (81 - 84)	0792
Triumph Herald (59 - 71)	0010
Triumph Spitfire (62 - 81)	0113
Triumph Stag (70 - 78)	0441
Triumph TR7 (75 - 82)	0322
VAUXHALL	
Vauxhall Astra (80 - Oct 84)	0635
Vauxhall Astra & Belmont (Oct 84 - Oct 91)	1136
Vauxhall Astra (Oct 91 - 96)	1832
Vauxhall Carlton (Oct 78 - Oct 86)	0480
Vauxhall Carlton (Nov 86 - 94)	1469
Vauxhall Cavalier 1300 (77 - July 81)	0461
Vauxhall Cavalier 1600, 1900 & 2000 (75 - July 81)	0315
Vauxhall Cavalier (81 - Oct 88)	0812
Vauxhall Cavalier (Oct 88 - Oct 95)	1570
Vauxhall Chevette (75 - 84)	0285
Vauxhall Corsa (93 - 97)	1985
Vauxhall Nova (83 - 93)	0909
Vauxhall Rascal (86 - 93)	3015
Vauxhall Senator (Sept 87 - 94)	1469
Vauxhall Vectra Petrol & Diesel (95 - 98)	3396
Vauxhall Viva HB Series (ohv) (66 - 70)	0026
Vauxhall Viva & Firenza (ohc) (68 - 73)	0093
Vauxhall/Opel 1.5, 1.6 & 1.7 litre Diesel Engines (82 - 96)	1222
VOLKSWAGEN	
VW Beetle 1200 (54 - 77)	0036
VW Beetle 1300 & 1500 (65 - 75)	0039
VW Beetle 1302 & 1302S (70 - 72)	0110

Title	Book No.
VW Beetle 1303, 1303S & GT (72 - 75)	0159
VW Golf Mk 1 1.1 & 1.3 (74 - Feb 84)	0716
VW Golf Mk 1 1.5, 1.6 & 1.8 (74 - 85)	0726
VW Golf Mk 1 Diesel (78 - Feb 84)	0451
VW Golf Mk 2 (Mar 84 - Feb 92)	1081
VW Golf Mk 3 Petrol & Diesel (Feb 92 - 96)	3097
VW Jetta Mk 1 1.1 & 1.3 (80 - June 84)	0716
VW Jetta Mk 1 1.5, 1.6 & 1.8 (80 - June 84)	0726
VW Jetta Mk 1 Diesel (81 - June 84)	0451
VW Jetta Mk 2 (July 84 - 92)	1081
VW LT vans & light trucks (76 - 87)	0637
VW Passat (Sept 81 - May 88)	0814
VW Passat (May 88 - 91)	1647
VW Polo & Derby (76 - Jan 82)	0335
VW Polo (82 - Oct 90)	0813
VW Polo (Nov 90 - Aug 94)	3245
VW Santana (Sept 82 - 85)	0814
VW Scirocco Mk 1 1.5, 1.6 & 1.8 (74 - 82)	0726
VW Scirocco (82 - 90)	1224
VW Transporter 1600 (68 - 79)	0082
VW Transporter 1700, 1800 & 2000 (72 - 79)	0226
VW Transporter with air-cooled engine (79 - 82)	0638
VW Transporter (82 - 90)	3452
VW Vento Petrol & Diesel (Feb 92 - 96)	3097
VOLVO	
Volvo 66 & 343, Daf 55 & 66 (68 - 79)	0293
Volvo 142, 144 & 145 (66 - 74)	0129
Volvo 240 Series (74 - 93)	0270
Volvo 262, 264 & 260/265 (75 - 85)	0400
Volvo 340, 343, 345 & 360 (76 - 91)	0715
Volvo 440, 460 & 480 (87 - 92)	1691
Volvo 740 & 760 (82 - 91)	1258
Volvo 850 (92 - 96)	3260
Volvo 940 (90 - 96)	3249
YUGO/ZASTAVA	
Yugo/Zastava (81 - 90)	1453
TECH BOOKS	
Automotive Brake Manual	3050
Automotive Carburettor Manual	3288
Automotive Diesel Engine Service Guide	3286
Automotive Electrical & Electronic Systems	3049
Automotive Engine Management and Fuel Injection Systems Manual	3344
Automotive Tools Manual	3052
Automotive Welding Manual	3053
In-Car Entertainment Manual (3rd Edition)	3363
CAR BOOKS	
Automotive Fuel Injection Systems	9755
Car Bodywork Repair Manual	9864
Caravan Manual (2nd Edition)	9894
Haynes Technical Data Book (89 - 98)	1998
How to Keep Your Car Alive	9868
Japanese Vehicle Carburettors	1786
Small Engine Repair Manual	1755
SU Carburettors	0299
Weber Carburettors (to 79)	0393

CL05.01/98

Preserving Our Motoring Heritage

< *The Model J Duesenberg Derham Tourster. Only eight of these magnificent cars were ever built – this is the only example to be found outside the United States of America*

Almost every car you've ever loved, loathed or desired is gathered under one roof at the Haynes Motor Museum. Over 300 immaculately presented cars and motorbikes represent every aspect of our motoring heritage, from elegant reminders of bygone days, such as the superb Model J Duesenberg to curiosities like the bug-eyed BMW Isetta. There are also many old friends and flames. Perhaps you remember the 1959 Ford Popular that you did your courting in? The magnificent 'Red Collection' is a spectacle of classic sports cars including AC, Alfa Romeo, Austin Healey, Ferrari, Lamborghini, Maserati, MG, Riley, Porsche and Triumph.

A Perfect Day Out

Each and every vehicle at the Haynes Motor Museum has played its part in the history and culture of Motoring. Today, they make a wonderful spectacle and a great day out for all the family. Bring the kids, bring Mum and Dad, but above all bring your camera to capture those golden memories for ever. You will also find an impressive array of motoring memorabilia, a comfortable 70 seat video cinema and one of the most extensive transport book shops in Britain. The Pit Stop Cafe serves everything from a cup of tea to wholesome, home-made meals or, if you prefer, you can enjoy the large picnic area nestled in the beautiful rural surroundings of Somerset.

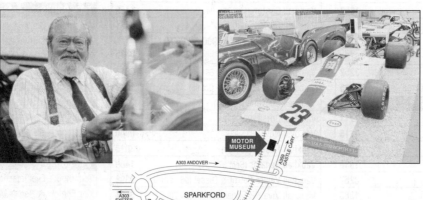

> *John Haynes O.B.E., Founder and Chairman of the museum at the wheel of a Haynes Light 12.*

< *Graham Hill's Lola Cosworth Formula 1 car next to a 1934 Riley Sports.*

The Museum is situated on the A359 Yeovil to Frome road at Sparkford, just off the A303 in Somerset. It is about 40 miles south of Bristol, and 25 minutes drive from the M5 intersection at Taunton.
Open 9.30am - 5.30pm (10.00am - 4.00pm Winter) 7 days a week, *except Christmas Day, Boxing Day and New Years Day*
Special rates available for schools, coach parties and outings Charitable Trust No. 292048